DIVINE POETRY

Church History Prefigured by the Old
Testament in Chronological Order

D1528308

First Printing 3/19/24

Second Printing 04/13/24 – Minor corrections in grammar and spelling, but no substantial changes were made

I dedicate this work to Our Lady of Lourdes with devotion and gratitude. Without her, we would be lost. My wife and I visited Lourdes in 2004 and she forever changed our lives. She lifted us out of mortal sin as God raised the dry bones to life. She gave us a new heart and placed us in the land of the living. She revealed to us a path when we were trapped. She continues to fill our hearts with joy and comforts us in our crosses. She is our Mother, the Star of the Sea and the Gate of Heaven. Ave Maria!

Acknowledgments

Thank you to…

Our Lord and Our Lady for everything

All the clergy for dedicating your lives to the Church. Thank you for feeding us with the Sacraments and sound doctrine

All other religious for giving edifying examples of prayer and mortification

His Excellency, Bishop McGuire and Fr. McKenna for taking the time to listen

Dan, for proposing that I write this book

Fran, Vincent, Victor, Bill, Jeremiah and Anthony for editing

My family and friends, for listening to me talk about parallels for years and years

All those who have contacted me with encouragement, questions, ideas and advice

All those who have donated to my work, especially Paul. Your generosity is truly appreciated

Lauren, for working so hard over the years to educate our children, cook, clean, earn money, encourage and believe in this work

Foreword

"Contemplare et contemplata aliis trader"

The above quote is one of the unofficial mottos of the Dominican Order, which translates to "Contemplate and share with others the fruits of your contemplation". This book is a perfect example of just this good work, as Dominic Caggeso has spent years reading Holy Scriptures and contemplating all he has read. Such a good and holy practice could never be a fruitless exercise.

In his fifth proof of the existence of God, St. Thomas points out that we are able to reason to the existence of God by realizing that all of nature operates according to a design (Summa I, 2, iii). Moreover, His providence directs all things, especially man on a pathway toward salvation as "an arrow is directed by the archer towards a mark". (Summa I, 23, i). It follows that God orders certain events in time to help guide and lead man to eternal Truths and the One True Catholic Faith, which is necessary for salvation, the ultimate end of man. In the Old Testament, many prophecies are given to ensure that man recognizes the Messias when He comes. Likewise, many figures prefigure Christ, events that parallel later moments in the life of the Savior of man, and historical connections that ensure that the chosen people would best be able to recognize when the time of redemption was at hand and who that Redeemer is. It is no surprise, therefore, that the Sacred Scriptures should continue to also foreshadow important events and figures in the life of the Church. This ensures that the faithful, the new chosen people of God, continue to realize that we, indeed, possess the True Faith and that God's Divine Providence continues to guide us…to not only convince us of this reality, but aid the Faith being more firmly rooted in our hearts so that we may best be able to love, serve, and defend God and His Eternal Truths well. As Christ is the "way, the truth, and the life" (John 14:6), it is no surprise that His Truth, as contained in the Sacred Scriptures, continues to point out, for us, the *way* of our salvation, and be applicable to events tied to the *life* of His Church and His faithful.

In this book, Dominic points out many connections he has found between events contained in the Old Testament and Church history. They are not meant to be treated as authoritative, as such an authority of interpretation is possessed by the Church alone, the Divinely protected and infallible Bride of Christ and Ark of Salvation. Instead, they are meant to be, for the reader, exactly what they have been for the author...interesting fruits of study and reflection that show God's continual hand of Providence in the life of His Church. Such reflections are meant to strengthen the reader's Faith and inspire him to engage in the important and improving practice of reading and meditating on the Word of God. A practice, which is so important that just fifteen minutes of reading of Scripture has a 300 day indulgence attached to it by the Church and a plenary indulgence for those who do this every day for a month. It is meant to inspire the reader to find the Scriptures to be, as St. Athanasius says, "fountains of salvation, so that he who thirsts may be satisfied by the oracles contained in them." May the fruits of the author's contemplation be the means of planting seeds of study in your own hearts and may these seeds blossom into your own abundantly fruitful trees of increased faith and love of God and His Church.

-Fr. Stephen McKenna
St. Gertrude the Great Church
March 9, 2024

Table Of Contents

Table of Contents

Table of Contents

Preface

Let us begin by saying one Hail Mary to honor our Blessed Mother. "Hail Mary, full of grace, the Lord is with thee. Blessed art thou among women, and blessed is the fruit of thy womb, Jesus. Holy Mary, Mother of God, pray for us sinners now and at the hour of our death. Amen."

The Plight of Those Who Love the Church

Dear reader, St. Francis de Sales addressed his masterpiece, *Introduction to the Devout Life,* to an anonymous reader, *Philothea,* which means *lover of God.* Because the Catholic Church is under such an insidious attack today, I would like to address this work to those who still love the Catholic Church. In the same way that St. Francis de Sales addressed his work to Philothea, I would like to address this to you, *Philoecclesia,* meaning *lover of the Church.* Our Lord gave us the Catholic Church for our salvation. The Church is His Mystical Body, and we cling to the Church as a drowning person clings to a life raft. Philoecclesia, you are the intended audience of this book.

As a lover of the Catholic Church, you are undoubtedly aware of the damage and confusion that has resulted from the Second Vatican Council. These events have dispersed Catholics in various theological directions, causing some to lose the Faith entirely and others to hold on to it more firmly. If you are a lover of the Church, you have suffered through the confusion and the mental anguish that God has mysteriously permitted. As the prophecy says, "Strike the shepherd, and the sheep will be scattered." (Zech 13:7)

In the aftermath of the council, black clouds have swirled over Israel's camp. Contradiction and confusion have descended like a heavy fog. Our response to this darkness has been to cling to what is sure, to hold fast to Tradition. We have diligently studied the deposit of Faith and, in so doing, have built our house on the rock.

I

Keeping the Catholic Faith in the face of so many errors and so much confusion is complex and requires a sober mind, diligence and perseverance. We have become accustomed to studying and contemplating a vast body of Church teaching from the past. This has been all together good and necessary.

However, in this book, I want to present another perspective, departing from the technical and veering toward the poetic. This less trodden avenue is more revealing than one would initially expect, shedding new light on our current ecclesial condition. It is not a novelty, but a rediscovery of something ancient and timeless. It is both old and new[a]. It is something beautiful and dazzling and truly demonstrates God's breathtaking power! The dark clouds give way to heavenly light when we see the history of the Church prefigured by the history of Israel in the Old Testament.

Wonder and a Burning Heart

It is prudent to temper our emotions and wise to speak cautiously. But I cannot help but to proclaim the glory of God and be amazed at His works! I say to you, Philoecclesia, that great wonders await you in the pages of this book. These wonders and marvels are, no doubt, dimmed by my poor attempt to explain them. To the extent that my shortcomings do not obstruct, you will see things that have been hidden in plain sight for centuries. Perhaps the best way to express the greatness of these prefigurements of Church history is to compare them to the Gospel story of the disciples on the road to Emmaus.

At the end of the Gospels, after Our Lord's resurrection, two disciples were discussing His crucifixion as they walked. They were sad and confused because the One they believed was the Messias had been tortured and killed. At that moment, Our Lord found them, walked with them and opened up the Scriptures to them. He showed them that the entire Old Testament was a prophecy of His life. Their later response was, "Was not our

---

a   "Therefore every scribe instructed in the kingdom of heaven, is like to a man that is a householder, who bringeth forth out of his treasure **new** things and old." - Matthew 13:52

II

heart burning within us, whilst He spoke in this way, and opened to us the scriptures?" (Luke 24:32)

Philoecclesia, we know the maxim, "As Christ goes, so goes His Church". After all, the Church is His Mystical Body. Thus, just as Our Lord was tortured and crucified, so too did the Church experience Her passion during the Second Vatican Council and its aftermath. Using this analogy, it appears that we, the faithful, are sad and confused as we discuss what has happened to the Mystical Body of Christ, the Catholic Church. Then, like those disciples, we see that the entire history of the Catholic Church was prefigured by the Old Testament, and the Scriptures are opened for us. The crucifixion of the Church is over and the veil is lifted. This book comes bearing good news for devout Catholics! To quote a Catholic hymn:

> The strife is o'er, the battle done; the victory of life is
> won; the song of triumph has begun. Alleluia.

Many times I have said, "My heart burns within me when I see the Scriptures opened up to prefigure the Church". I hope you will experience and express the same, dear Philoecclesia.

Implications and Consequences

Before we start, I would like to share a conversation I had with AI (artificial intelligence) about this concept. I recognize in AI a detached calculus on most subjects, although it is slanted and biased toward particular politically charged agendas. However, the topic of this book most likely flies below the radar of those agendas. As you will see, AI responded in a logical and clear way when I asked about the possibility of this prefigurement of Church history.

> **Me:** Can you comment on the significance to us if the Old Testament prefigures Church history in the same chronological order?

Artificial Intelligence: If the entire history of the Church were prefigured by the entire Old Testament in the same chronological order, it could have significant implications for the interpretation of both the Old and New Testaments. It could suggest that the events and teachings of the Old Testament were not only relevant to their historical context but also had a prophetic dimension, foreshadowing the development of the Church. This could provide a new perspective on the relationship between the two Testaments and their respective histories.

Such a correspondence could also have implications for the understanding of biblical prophecy and its fulfillment. It could suggest that the events of Church history were not only foretold but also followed a predetermined pattern, providing further evidence for the divine inspiration of the Bible.

In addition, this correspondence could have practical implications for the interpretation of current events and the future direction of the Church. If the Old Testament prefigured Church history in chronological order, it could provide a framework for understanding and interpreting contemporary developments within the Church and its relationship with the world.

However, it is important to note that this is a hypothetical scenario, and I couldn't find any information to support it. These are just some possible implications if it were true.

This dialogue with AI (artificial intelligence) demonstrates the conclusions and implications that can be drawn if this assertion is true. AI has seen the logic of the premise and the conclusions that follow. Because AI cannot grasp supernatural truths, it lacks any true Catholic understanding. Being a computer, it is mechanical and cold. Glory be to God, because these parallels are more than just a mechanical sequence of foreshadowed events. Instead, they are a divine poem that weaves together truths of our Faith, extols virtue, inflames our hearts and glorifies God.

The simplicity and straightforwardness of these parallels resemble the "whistling of gentle air" that Elias heard on Mt. Horeb. The Lord was not in the strong wind, the earthquake or the raging fire but in the unassuming whisper. If we remove our attention from the "fires" and "earthquakes" raging in the world today, we can better contemplate the implications derived from these parallels, which are both simple and startling.

Why Is This Important?

I do not claim that these parallels are essential for salvation or that they are required in any way. This book is just a testimony to God's great work. Who would not want to witness more of the works of God? Who would not want to have a deeper insight into the mysteries of God? I say *YES*, I want to see them! We should be prepared to toil as slaves our whole lives if God commands so. How much more should we be eager to pursue these delightful and beautiful ideas if they are true?

Throughout Catholic history, great miracles have stirred the hearts of both fervent and lukewarm Catholics. Those miracles confirmed the doctrines of the Faith and proved the legitimacy of certain people, places and events in the eyes of God. If these prefigurements of Church history are as splendid and astonishing as I claim, and if they follow the same chronological order, then they are truly a miracle.

It is a different kind of miracle than we might be used to hearing about, because this miracle has been taking place every moment since the beginning of Church history. Indeed, these parallels did not happen by accident as they are statistically impossible. God must have done it. So what does this miracle prove? It proves that the Catholic Church is exactly what It has always professed to be. It also sheds light on the current state of the Catholic Church.

Obstacles to Perceiving the Parallels

In my study of these prefigurements, I have encountered different reactions ranging from awestruck to skeptical. Of those who are skeptical, they tend to fall into one of four categories. They may:

1. Lack the necessary knowledge of Church history and the Old Testament to appreciate the parallels.

2. Resist the implications of the parallels for their personal lives.

3. Feel uneasy about this type of analysis and doubt its validity.

4. Judge the information by the author's presentation ability and credentials, rather than by the content.

I do not claim to be a skilled writer, but I have done my best to convey this information in a clear and honest way. I may not have the credentials, the style, or the voice of a professional, but I have the facts and the evidence to support my claims. In today's world, information is often overshadowed by marketing. We are bombarded by the techniques and tricks of persuasive experts. But I urge you to look beyond the delivery style of this information and focus on the content. The parallels are undeniable and have serious implications, regardless of how well or poorly I describe them.

Be Open to the Old and the New

The concept of the Old Testament prefiguring the Church is nothing new. This concept permeates the great work, *The Liturgical Year* by Dom Prosper Louis Pascal Gueranger, as well as so many other authors and saints. The book of Ecclesiastes, chapter 1, says:

> "What is it that hath been? The same thing that shall be. What is it that hath been done? The same that shall be done. Nothing under the sun is new; neither is any man able to say: Behold this is new: for it hath already gone before in the ages that were before us."

This book presents nothing new to you, as it claims that nothing shall happen that has not already happened before. This book tries to demonstrate precisely this: the Catholic Church's history is prefigured by what has already happened in the Old Testament.

While you are reading this book, I implore you to adopt a child's hopefulness, eagerness to believe, and sense of wonder. From the perspective of a child's innocence, can you not see that this sounds like something God would do? A major obstacle to seeing this amazing work of God is our adult skepticism and cynicism. As Catholics who have lived through the great apostasy, we have learned to be very critical. We hold tightly to the Faith and put up imposing mental walls to protect what we have preserved. We are right to do this. This book, therefore, comes to the fortified walls of your Catholic mind and politely knocks on the door.

Introduction

The Old Testament history of Israel prefigures the entire history of the Catholic Church, even in the same chronological order. It is through the use of typology that this phenomenon is made visible. If your understanding of typology is rusty, let's talk about it.

Typology – What Is It?

Biblical typology is truly divine poetry. It masterfully wraps up the truths of the Faith into a digestible story that draws out profound and beautiful meaning.

Typology uses stories and images from the Old Testament as a prefigurement or a foreshadowing of the New Testament. Typology is a method of interpreting the Old Testament used by many saints, Church Fathers, and Our Lord Himself. You may not be familiar with the term *typology*, but you have undoubtedly encountered the concept before. For example, in the Gospel, Our Lord said the following:

> "And as Moses lifted up the serpent in the desert, so must the Son of man be lifted up: That whosoever believeth in him, may not perish; but may have life everlasting."
>
> - John 3: 14-15

Here, our Lord connects the story of Moses raising the serpent on a pole to His own crucifixion. The symbol of the serpent on a pole (and the context around that story) represents a type of Christ and His crucifixion. Therefore, by studying that story in the Old Testament, we can discover something about Our Lord's crucifixion. Likewise, I am sure we all know this passage, also taken from the Gospel of St. John.

> "Our fathers did eat manna in the desert, as it is written: He gave them bread from Heaven to eat. Then Jesus said to

them: Amen, amen I say to you; Moses gave you not bread
from Heaven, but my Father giveth you the true bread from
Heaven. For the bread of God is that which cometh down
from Heaven and giveth life to the world. They said
therefore unto him: Lord, give us always this bread. And
Jesus said to them: I am the bread of life: he that cometh to
me shall not hunger: and he that believeth in me shall never
thirst."

- John 6: 31-35

The manna in the desert is a symbol or a type of the Holy Eucharist. Just
as the manna was given to the Israelites as they wandered in the desert on
their way to the Promised Land, so too does God give us the Holy Eucharist
—that *Heavenly Bread*—as we wander through this valley of tears, awaiting
our entrance into Heaven, the true and ultimate Promised Land.

May I present one more example of typology: the Church as the New
Israel. This specific example will support the idea that the entire history of
the Catholic Church is typified, or prefigured, by the Old Testament in the
same chronological order. St. Augustine wrote:

"The Church is the new people of God, the true Israel, which
is not of this world, but of heaven." (Sermon 96, 7)

The Catholic Church Is the New Israel

Israel typifies the Catholic Church. The Catholic Church is the true Israel,
or we could also say that the Catholic Church is the New Israel. The Catholic
Church is, in essence, the focus of the New Testament. There are many
general similarities between the Church and Old Testament Israel. For
example, both have a priesthood and a Temple (we have basilicas and
cathedrals instead of a Temple.) Both have a *holy of holies* (we have a
tabernacle and sanctuary.) Both have an ark, as Our Lady is widely
recognized as the New Ark. Both have a city where our religion is based and
where the high priest resides. In the Old Testament, this was Jerusalem; in
Church history, this city is Rome.

It is not difficult to see the Catholic Church as the New Israel. This typological connection between Old Testament Israel and the Catholic Church is our launch-off point for the entire premise of this book. Once we have established that the Church is the new Israel, the next step is to demonstrate chronological, typological connections at all the points from beginning to end.

We will see that the Catholic Church has been typified by the Old Testament Israel not only in a general way but in an event-by-event, chronological way. The ups and downs, the victories and defeats, the prophets and villains, the glories and tragedies of the Old Testament all happened to the Church in the same order. And, to make it even more impressive, they also happened in great detail and in mind-boggling artistry and poetry. Let's look at the chronological parallels between Joseph (from the Old Testament) and St. Peter for an example.

Old Testament	New Testament
Joseph was one of the twelve sons of Israel and was his father's favorite.	St. Peter was the chosen Apostle among the twelve.
• He received a signet ring from pharao, who also changed Joseph's name.	• Our Lord gave St. Peter the keys to the kingdom of Heaven and changed his name from Simon to Peter.
• This happened because God revealed to Joseph the meaning of pharao's dream.	• This happened because God revealed to St. Peter the answer to Our Lord's question about Our Lord's identity as the Messias.
• Pharao then appointed Joseph as the second-in-command of Egypt, giving him authority over the whole kingdom.	• St. Peter became the first pope, with authority over the entire Catholic Church (the Kingdom of God on Earth.)
• Joseph moved the Israelites to Egypt, which later became the place of their oppression.	• St. Peter moved to Rome, which later became the place where Christians were persecuted.

This kind of parallel occurs throughout the entire history of the Catholic Church and with even more poetry and detail, all the way until our present day. It is truly a sight to behold!

Micro Verses Macro

Without getting bogged down in details, I would like to acknowledge and document here that the following presentation of Church history and the Old Testament is really just an introduction. It is an analysis of chronological parallels from the widest and largest perspective possible. The events that I chose to include from Church history are of the highest profile. For instance, the papacy is the focus of many parallels throughout this book. The papacy is the highest office in the Church. Likewise, the Byzantine Empire is the focus of many parallels as well, being one of two major Catholic empires in history.

However, there also exists minor or "micro" parallels between the Old Testament and smaller, more regional people and events in Church history. By and large, I have excluded them from this book because they would make this presentation more complicated and, perhaps, confusing. These "micro" parallels can be perceived by shrinking down the frame of reference and viewing the Old Testament story inside a limited framework of Church history. For example, if one were to look only at the history of Ireland, it also parallels the Old Testament in chronological order, all by itself and without reference to the wider context of history. In that "micro" parallel, St. Patrick is like Moses, the Vikings are like the Philistines (and other early enemy tribes of Israel), the McNamaras or the O'Neills are like King Saul, Brian Boru is like King David, the Rock of Cashel is like the Temple, the north-south split of Ireland mirrors the north-south split of Israel, the English occupation of Ireland is like the Babylonian captivity, Home Rule and the Irish Republic are like the decree of Cyrus and so on.

These smaller, regional parallels are present all throughout Church history. Therefore it is possible to have multiple parallels in Church history for any one character in the Old Testament. For example, the middle age saint kings are all likely to share parallels with King David. I mention this because, undoubtedly, you will notice that countless people and events from history are not included in this book. My goal was to summarize the "macro" people and events only, so the big picture can be perceived.

Breakdown of Time Periods

Both Church history and the Old Testament can be challenging to learn. To make them both easier to manage, I have split them into time periods. Remarkably, because the Old Testament is a chronological foreshadowing of Church history, these time periods correspond.

This book will show the parallels across eight time periods. The names reflect the defining characteristics of each period for both the Old and the New. Note that the descriptions of each period below are written in such a way as to apply to both the Old Testament and Church history. Please refer to the chart in **Appendix 2** for Church history dates and Old Testament book references. Those dates and book references also appear at the start of each section. The eight time periods are as follows:

Period 1: Beginning and Foundation – God founds His people on the twelve. The chosen one of the twelve is given a kingdom to rule and takes God's people into an abundant land that will become the place of their persecution.

Period 2: Persecution and Deliverance – A severe and long-lasting persecution ensues for God's people in a pagan land. After ten separate "plagues," God's people are set free.

Period 3: Enemies and Establishment – God's people are led into the wilderness. Once they obtain their own land, they fight enemies to establish themselves. During this time, a vital conversion and ensuing marriage leads to the eventual rise of the great king who arrives in Period 4.

Period 4: Kingdom and Golden Era – After establishing themselves, God's people are protected by their first king, who disobeys God's vicar. God's vicar anoints a new king, who establishes a long-lasting dynasty. The two anointed kings have a complicated relationship of friendship and enmity. God's people fight a series of wars, securing a time of peace in which the great Temple is built, followed by wealth, wisdom, and architecture.

Period 5: Revolt and Separation

– At the height of wealth, wisdom, and grandeur, God's people are corrupted by the introduction of profane ideas. The high standard of living of the king and his immense building projects require a significant funding stream. A rebel leader revolts due to the abuse of revenue collection. This rebel breaks from the covenant, the sacrifice, the king, and the high priest. He starts a new religion in the north and draws a substantial number of God's people into apostasy. A civil war erupts between the north and the south, as the south wants to bring the north back into the fold. Eventually, the north is assimilated by the profane world. The southern kingdom that has kept the true religion faces a powerful new empire that has arisen in the East and threatens its destruction. They are saved by miraculous battles but remain in a weakened position.

Period 6: Invasion and Exile

– A ruthless conquering force captures the holy city and makes God's people exiles in a pagan land. Now they live under secular and foreign laws. The ark is seen in a cave, and a miraculous water springs from the right side of the Temple. The dry bones come to life, giving hope to the weary and demoralized. Through a holy prophet, God gives an example and template for the priesthood. A mysterious message announces the destruction of a kingdom. At the end of this time period, it is proclaimed that God rules in the kingdom of men, and His word is un-contradictable.

Period 7: Autonomy and City-State

– A new pagan king rises to power and allows God's people to return and keep their holy city as a city-state. They must pledge allegiance to the pagan king and pray for him in the Temple sacrifice. This king gives money to God's people and even commands them to teach God's laws to everyone in the land.

Period 8: Temple Takeover

– Yet another empire comes to power. This one is hostile to the holy city and God's people, demanding that they modernize their religion to adapt to the new realities of the world. The sacred Temple of God is infiltrated and the holy religion is changed from inside. A new, second altar is placed over the true altar of God. A new, profane sacrifice is mandated and the traditional sacrifice is outlawed, along with all former religious practices. The house of God is stripped of its ornamentation, and women thrust themselves into the sanctuary. One old priest flees to the mountains to preserve tradition and to launch a counter-offensive. He is old so he passes on the uprising to his sons, who eventually compromise with the enemy. God's people are fractured and scattered.

Now that we have identified the parallel time periods of both the Old Testament and Church history, let's roll up our sleeves and get down to business. For the sake of both credibility and readability, I am aiming for a balance between details and story flow. It will be a tricky balancing act, and I pray that you will make some allowance for any misstep toward either insufficient or too much detail.

This book exclusively features Biblical quotes from the Douay-Rheims Bible.

Period 1

Beginning and Foundation

God's people are founded on the twelve and grow numerous in a pagan empire.

OLD TESTAMENT: Book of Genesis

The Old Testament story begins in the book of Genesis, where God creates Heaven and Earth and all its inhabitants. The great flood resets the Earth, and God enacts a Covenant with Abraham, Isaac, and Jacob. The twelve tribes of Israel go into Egypt and grow numerous.

CHURCH HISTORY: Approximately 1^{AD} to 60^{AD}

The Gospels are the beginning of Church history. Our Lady's "fiat" brings forth Jesus Christ, who chose twelve Apostles, upon whom the Church was founded. Christianity grows quickly in the Roman Empire.

Old Testament	New Testament
God chose Abraham to be the father of God's people because he obeyed God above all else.	Our Lady, chosen by God, said "Yes" to God and brought forth Jesus Christ.
Abraham's wife, Sarah, was visited by angels who announced her imminent, miraculous pregnancy.	Our Lady was visited by an angel who announced her imminent, miraculous pregnancy.
Rebekah gave birth to two sons, Jacob and Esau. Esau was hairy and rough, while Jacob was smooth-skinned and refined.	Our Lady and St. Elizabeth each bring forth a son. St. John the Baptist was rough and dressed in camel hair. Our Lord was superior and received the Father's blessing.

Jacob (Israel) had twelve sons. His favorite son, Joseph, took the entire nation into Egypt.	Our Lord has twelve Apostles. St. Peter was selected from among them and eventually established the Church in Rome.

The Old Testament starts with the words:

> "**In the beginning**, God created Heaven and Earth. And the Earth was void and empty, and darkness was upon the face of the deep, and the spirit of God moved over the waters."
>
> - Genesis 1:1-2

Similarly, the Gospel of St. John starts with the words:

> "**In the beginning** was the Word, and the Word was with God, and the Word was God. "

Our Lady, whose womb was empty before the Annunciation, would soon be filled with God. Just as the Spirit of God moved over the waters in the Old Testament, the Holy Ghost overshadowed Our Lady. The angel Gabriel said:

> "The Holy Ghost shall come upon thee, and the power of the most High shall overshadow thee."
>
> - Luke 1: 35

The new Creation in the New Testament is Christ and His Church. Christ is the new Adam, and Our Lady is the new Eve. The Holy Ghost overshadowed Our Lady, who became the "sea" for the beginning of the new Creation, just as the Spirit of God moved over the waters in the beginning of Genesis. In his masterpiece *True Devotion to Mary*, St. Louis De Montfort states that God brought all the waters together and called it the sea (mare). He brought all the graces together in the New Testament and called it "Maria".[1]

In the Old Testament, God created in the natural order. The Church and everything that comes from Her in later history belongs to the new creation in the supernatural order. The supernatural dogmas and doctrines of the Church are like the stars in the firmament, in the natural order. Doctrines are fixed in place and are used for our navigation to our "Promised Land" much like the stars, in the natural order, are used for navigation. The papacy is like the sun that brightens the Earth with the light of Truth. By comparing the beginning of the Old Testament in the book of Genesis with the beginning of Church history in the Gospels, it emerges that the creation in the New Testament is Christ and His Church.[a]

Water, A Dove And Confounded Speech

In the book of Genesis, the accounts of the Great Flood and the Tower of Babel have striking similarities with the beginning of Church history. When Noe desired to know if the flood waters were receding, he released a dove which returned with an olive branch.

> "And having waited yet seven other days, he again sent forth the dove out of the ark. And she came to him in the evening, carrying a bough of an olive tree, with green leaves, in her mouth. Noe therefore understood that the waters were ceased upon the earth."
>
> - Genesis 8: 10 – 11

Similarly, at the Baptism of Christ, we see Our Lord submerged in the waters of the Jordan River. When He emerged, the skies parted and a dove came to rest on His shoulder.

> "And Jesus being baptized, forthwith came out of the water: and lo, the heavens were opened to him: and he saw the Spirit of God descending as a dove..."
>
> - Matthew 3: 16

The story of the Tower of Babel relates how God confounded the speech of the prideful builders who were then scattered across the face of the earth. However, in the Gospel of St. Luke, St. Zachary was not able to speak until

---

a   St. Vincent Ferrer, in his "Sermon on the Last Judgment on the Gospel of St. Luke 21:25-28" made use of the these creation terms in similar fashion. See *Angel of the Judgment: A Life of Vincent Ferrer*, by S.M.C., Ave Maria Press. Chapter XI, pp. 102-117.

he confirmed the will of God on a writing tablet. His ability to speak was noised abroad to all the surrounding area.

> "Come ye, therefore, let us go down, and there confound their <u>tongue</u>, that they may not understand one another's speech. And so the Lord <u>scattered them from that place into all lands,</u> and they ceased to build the city. And therefore the name thereof was called Babel, because there the language of the whole earth was <u>confounded</u>: and from thence the Lord <u>scattered them abroad</u> upon the face of all countries."

- Genesis 11: 7-9

> "And immediately his mouth was opened, and his <u>tongue</u> loosed, and he spoke, blessing God. And fear came upon all their neighbours; and all these things were <u>noised abroad</u> over all the hill country of Judea."

- Luke 1: 64

The Great Patriarch and the Miraculous Birth
Abraham and St. Joseph

As the Old Testament progresses we encounter Abraham, the great patriarch. His "yes" to God and his unwavering obedience brought God's blessing and promise upon him. His wife, Sarah, was blessed with a miraculous pregnancy. Their son Isaac was to be the long-awaited child of the promise made to Abraham. From him all nations would be blessed, and his descendants would be as numerous as the stars in the sky.

Likewise, in the New Testament, St. Joseph shares many similarities with Abraham. Like Abraham, St. Joseph's wife was also blessed with a miraculous pregnancy. Like Abraham, who sent away his concubine Hagar at God's command, St. Joseph was also going to send away Our Lady when He found her to be with child. Like Abraham, St. Joseph also moved his family to Egypt and back again.

Abraham and Sarah were visited by three mysterious figures, whom one can understand to be angels or perhaps, the three Persons of the Blessed Trinity. These three figures announced the miraculous pregnancy and birth of a son in one year's time. Sarah did not believe the word that was spoken to her and was rebuked. The visitors then gave the child his name, Isaac.

Similarly, Our Lady was visited by the angel Gabriel to announce Our Lord's miraculous conception and birth. The angel Gabriel also announced the name of the child. Unlike Sarah, Our Lady believed the words of the angel, as St. Elizabeth declared:

> "And blessed art thou that hast believed because those things shall be accomplished that were spoken to thee by the Lord."
>
> - Luke 1:45

Later, after His birth, Our Lady was also visited by three mysterious travelers, just like Sarah was. These three travelers, of course, were the three kings.

Isaac married Rebekah and they had twin sons: Jacob and Esau. Esau came out first, with Jacob holding his heel. As the eldest, Esau was set to inherit the birthright and blessing from his father. He was a hairy and rough man, who loved hunting and eating. He did not care much about higher things or his future. Jacob, on the other hand, was a smooth and smart man who stayed at home with his mother. He was cunning and ambitious, and he wanted the birthright and the blessing for himself. He took advantage of his brother's shortsightedness and traded a bowl of stew for Esau's birthright. Later, he deceived his father and stole his blessing.

In these two figures, we can see the two Testaments. Esau represents the Old Testament and Jacob, the New. However, we can also see the persons of St. John the Baptist and Our Lord in Esau and Jacob. Like Esau, St. John the Baptist was born first, but only by six months. He wore rugged clothes and lived in the wilderness, much like how Esau was hairy and an outdoors-man. Remember that Our Lord said:

"Amen I say to you, there hath not risen among them that are born of women a greater than John the Baptist: yet he that is the lesser in the kingdom of heaven is greater than he."

- Matthew 11:11

Thus, we can see that even by the words of Our Lord, St. John the Baptist was the embodiment of the Old Testament, which was meant to prepare the way for the New Testament, just as St. John the Baptist prepared the way for Christ.

To see St. John the Baptist and Our Lord as the new Esau and Jacob, we can also look to the Baptism of Christ, in which the Father's voice was heard, "This is my beloved Son". Likewise, Isaac gave his fatherly blessing to Jacob and not to Esau. The concept of Jacob and Esau as figures for the New Testament and the Old Testament has already been expounded throughout Church history with much more eloquence than I can accomplish.[b]

God's People Founded on the Twelve
Twelve Sons of Jacob and the Twelve Apostles

The twelve sons of Jacob are a type of the twelve Apostles. Remember the parallels between Jacob and Our Lord. Jacob had his name changed to *Israel*, which means "he who wrestles with God". Israel, formerly Jacob, went on to have twelve sons, upon whom the nation of Israel was founded. The descendants of the twelve sons of Israel were called the "Nation of Israel," taking their collective name from him.

Likewise, Our Lord (the new Jacob and the new Israel) is the only man who has ever lived that could contend (wrestle) with God. Because Our Lord is fully God and also fully human, only He could pay the price for the sins of men. He is the one who can "wrestle" with God in that His prayers are heard, and our prayers are heard through Him. We can call God "Father" only

---

b   One example of this can be found in the work of St. Augustine, *The City of God*, Book XVI, Chapter 35.

because Christ did first. Like Israel (Jacob), Our Lord also had twelve "sons". As the nation of Israel in the Old Testament was founded upon the twelve sons of Israel, so was the Catholic Church in the New Testament founded on the twelve Apostles. Finally, just as the Nation of Israel took its name from its founder, so also did Christendom take its name from Christ.

Of the twelve sons of Israel in the Old Testament, Joseph was the favored child, elevated above the other eleven. Similarly, of the twelve Apostles, St. Peter was elevated above the other eleven. Let us look more closely at the two chosen among their respective group of twelve.

Old Testament	New Testament
God gave Joseph the ability to interpret pharao's dream.	Our Lord said that St. Peter answered correctly because the Father gave him direct knowledge.
Pharao changed Joseph's name as a result of his ability to interpret his dream.	Our Lord changed St. Peter's name because he answered Our Lord's question.
Pharao made Joseph ruler of all of Egypt, with only pharao above Joseph. He also gave him a signet ring as a sign of authority.	Our Lord made St. Peter the first pope, in charge of Christ's kingdom on Earth, the Catholic Church. He gave St. Peter the keys.
Joseph brought all of Israel into Egypt to escape the famine. Egypt would later enslave the Israelites and persecute them horribly.	St. Peter traveled to and centered the Church in Rome. The Roman Empire would later go on to severely persecute the Church.

Israel (Jacob) had twelve sons by different wives. His favorite wife, Rachel, was the mother of Joseph and Benjamin. Joseph was, therefore, the favorite son of Israel. His father gave him a unique coat to signify this favor. In Joseph's absence, Benjamin was all the more loved by his father.

The twelve Apostles also came from various ideologies and backgrounds, just as the twelve sons of Israel came from different mothers. St. Peter was a fisherman, and St. Matthew was a tax collector. St. Simon was a zealot (a militaristic Jewish faction that wanted to drive the Romans from Jerusalem.) Of these twelve Apostles, St. Peter was singled out among them. But, in another way, St. John the Evangelist is known as the "Beloved Disciple" and was given a special relationship with Our Lady during the crucifixion of Christ. Both Benjamin and St. John were the youngest of the twelve.

Given Special Knowledge by God

JOSEPH AND ST. PETER

Joseph was sold into slavery and spent time in prison. God gave him the ability to interpret dreams, and because of this, he was brought before pharao. He interpreted the dreams of pharao, who was so impressed that he said to Joseph:

> "Seeing God hath shewn thee all that thou hast said, can I find one wiser and one like unto thee?"

> - Genesis 41: 39

Likewise, at Caesarea Philippi, Our Lord asked the Apostles who they thought He was:

> "Jesus saith to them: But whom do you say that I am? Simon Peter answered and said: Thou art Christ, the Son of the living God. And Jesus, answering, said to him: **Blessed art thou, Simon Bar-Jona: because flesh and blood hath not revealed it to thee, but my Father who is in Heaven**. And I say to thee: That thou art Peter; and upon this rock I will build my Church, and the gates of hell shall not prevail against it. And I will give to thee the keys of the kingdom of Heaven. And whatsoever thou shalt bind upon Earth, it shall be bound also in Heaven: and whatsoever thou shalt loose upon Earth, it shall be loosed also in Heaven."

> - Matthew 16: 15 – 19

St. Peter responded to Our Lord's question, and Our Lord replied that His Father in Heaven gave St. Peter that answer. Just as God gave St. Peter knowledge to answer Our Lord's question, so did God give Joseph the ability to interpret pharao's dream.

Name Is Changed

Our Lord then changed St. Peter's name (which had previously been Simon Bar Jona), just as pharao changed the name of Joseph to "Zaphnath paaneah".

> "And the king said to Joseph: I am Pharao; without thy commandment, no man shall move hand or foot in all the land of Egypt. And he turned his name, and called him in the Egyptian tongue, The saviour of the world (Zaphnath paaneah.)"
>
> - Genesis 41: 44 – 45

Put In Charge Of The Whole Kingdom

St. Peter was given the keys and placed in charge of Christ's kingdom, just as Joseph was given a signet ring and put in charge of the Kingdom of Egypt.

> "Thou shalt be over my house, and at the commandment of thy mouth, all the people shall obey: only in the kingly throne will I be above thee. And again Pharao said to Joseph: Behold, I have appointed thee over the whole land of Egypt. And he took his ring from his own hand and gave it into his hand:"
>
> - Genesis 41:40–42

Into the Land of Their Eventual Persecution

JOSEPH GOES TO EGYPT AND ST. PETER GOES TO ROME

The other eleven sons of Israel and their families were living in the land of Abraham, suffering through a famine. When Joseph was made ruler of all the Kingdom of Egypt, he called for his brothers and their families to join him. Thus, Joseph was responsible for bringing the Israelites into Egypt.

Similarly, after St. Peter escaped prison, he eventually moved his episcopal seat to Rome. Because he was the first pope, he was thus responsible for centering the Catholic Church in Rome, the capital of the Roman Empire, just as Joseph brought Israel to Egypt.

When the Israelites moved to Egypt, they were given the best land for their cattle and herds in the territory of Goshen. The Israelites thus grew considerably. Their numbers multiplied so much that it alarmed the next pharao, who decided to persecute the Israelites. Similarly, the Church grew rapidly in the Roman Empire, especially in the city of Rome. It alarmed the roman emperors, who launched a series of persecutions against the early Church. Both persecutions in the Old Testament and in Church history lasted for hundreds of years.

This concludes my analysis of parallels in the time period of "Beginning and Foundation". The chosen among the twelve Apostles, St. Peter, brings the Church to Rome. Likewise, Joseph, the chosen of the twelve sons of Jacob, brings the Israelites to Egypt. Let's move on to the next time period, "Persecution and Deliverance".

Period 2

Persecution and Deliverance

God's people are severely persecuted in a foreign land and delivered by a prince of the empire.

OLD TESTAMENT: Books of Exodus, Leviticus, Numbers, Deuteronomy, and Josue

In Egypt, the Israelites multiplied to a significant number, attracting the attention of pharao. They were then enslaved and persecuted for hundreds of years. They were delivered from their oppression after the tenth plague and wandered in the wilderness until they reached a land of their own.

CHURCH HISTORY: Approximately 60^{AD} to 400^{AD}

In Rome, the Church grew quickly, attracting the emperor's attention. Christians suffered ten persecutions over a time span of approximately 250 years. Roman Emperor Constantine ended the persecution of Christians. He led them out of Rome and into the wilderness of Anatolia, where he founded the new city of Constantinople.

Old Testament	New Testament
The egyptian pharao was worried about the growth of the Israelites in Egypt and decided to persecute them.	The roman emperor was worried about the growth of Christianity and decided to persecute the Christians.
Israel was enslaved for hundreds of years.	Christian persecution spanned hundreds of years.
Moses, a prince of Egypt, freed Israel after the tenth plague.	Constantine, an emperor of Rome, stopped Christian persecution after the tenth Roman persecution.

A Long and Severe Persecution
EGYPTIAN SLAVERY AND ROMAN PERSECUTION

Joseph brought his father, his eleven brothers and their families to Egypt. Because the pharao favored Joseph, he was able to place his family in one of the best regions of Egypt, the land of Goshen. Their flocks prospered, and the nation of Israel multiplied. In years to come, a new pharao would grow alarmed at the numbers of the Israelites and decided to enslave them before they became a threat to the kingdom of Egypt. The Israelites were slaves in Egypt for hundreds of years until God called Moses to lead His people out of bondage and into the Promised Land. It was after the tenth plague that they were finally set free.

In Church history, after Pentecost, the Apostles preached the Faith throughout the ancient world. However, it was in the Roman Empire that the Church prospered, more so than in other places.

St. Peter centered the Catholic Church in Rome. In the Roman Empire, the Christians began to grow and multiply, so much so that the Roman Empire grew alarmed at their numbers. Many roman emperors saw Christianity as a threat to the state. Thus, the Roman Empire, over the course of about 250 years, perpetrated ten major persecutions of Christians in an effort to limit them or stamp them out all together.[a] After the tenth persecution of Diocletian, Christianity was legalized and the persecutions stopped.

The Prince of the Empire Delivers God's People
MOSES AND CONSTANTINE

After centuries of slavery in Egypt, the Israelites endured further suffering as pharao decreed his worst persecution: newborn Israelite boys were to be thrown into the Nile River. Moses was spared from death by his Hebrew mother who placed him in a basket in the Nile. Pharao's daughter

---

a   The ten Roman Emperors who initiated a major persecution of Christians are generally identified as Nero, Domitian, Trajan, Marcus Aurelius, Septimius Severus, Maximin, Decius, Valerian, Aurelian, and Diocletian.

discovered him and raised him as a prince in pharao's house. Later, to avoid punishment from pharao, Moses fled to the land of the Midianites, where he was given his mission and authority from God at the burning bush. He returned to Egypt to free God's people from their slavery. After the tenth and most severe plague, the death of the firstborn son, pharao finally freed the Israelites.

After about 250 years of on-and-off persecution by the Roman Empire, Emperor Diocletian ordered the final and worst persecution of Christians. When Diocletian retired, a power struggle ensued. Constantine, the heir to junior emperor Constantius Chlorus, was held as a political prisoner by Emperor Galerius. Constantine fled for his life to Britain, where he was made emperor after his father's death.[2] Although Constantine was a roman emperor, he had a devout and holy Catholic mother, St. Helena. This is just like how Moses was prince of Egypt but had a Hebrew mother. And just like how Moses was raised apart from his real mother, so too was Constantine raised away from St. Helena after her husband divorced her. Constantine went on to become the sole emperor and issued the Edict of Milan in 313 which legalized Christianity, stopping the persecution.

Just as Moses fled from pharao and took refuge in Midian, so Constantine fled from Emperor Galerius and took refuge in Britain. Moses received his authority in Midian and returned to free his people. Likewise, Constantine was made emperor in Britain and returned to legalize Christianity.

The actions of Moses after he freed the Israelites from Egypt and the actions of Constantine after he freed the Christians from Roman persecution are very similar. Let's look at what happened to God's Old and New Testament peoples immediately after their freedom.

Old Testament	New Testament
Pharao pursued the Israelites to recapture them and bring them back into slavery.	Maxentius contested Constantine and wanted to reinstate the Christian persecution.

The egyptian army and the Israelites met at the Red Sea, where pharao and his army drowned.	Maxentius and his army met Constantine and his army at the Tiber River. Maxentius and his army drowned.
The Israelites were surely free since pharao and the egyptian army were defeated.	Christians were indeed free since the last pagan emperor and his army were defeated.
Moses led the Israelites out into the wilderness toward a land of their own.	Constantine founded a new Christian city of Constantinople out in the wilderness.
Moses gave the people manna, which was bread from Heaven.	Constantine diverted grain shipments from Egypt so his new city could have free bread.
Moses gave the Israelites water from the rock.	Constantine started construction on a new aqueduct to bring water to his new city (water from a rock.)

The Tyrant Comes Back to Persecute

PHARAO AND MAXENTIUS

After the tenth plague, pharao's will was broken, and he agreed to release the Israelites from their slavery. The Israelites left Egypt, taking much of its wealth. Pharao's heart was hardened again as he realized Egypt had been defeated and humiliated, so he decided to pursue the Israelites to bring them back into bondage in Egypt. He found Moses and the Israelites trapped with their backs to the Red Sea.

At this dramatic point in the story, Moses raised his staff, which he had already used to work many wonders in Egypt. Upon doing so, the Red Sea parted, exposing the dry land in front of the Israelites and forming walls of water on each side of them. Moses and the Israelites crossed the Red Sea, pursued by the Egyptians. Once all the Israelites were safe, God drowned pharao and the Egyptians in the Red Sea by collapsing the waters around

14

them. When the Israelites saw this, they knew that their slavery was definitively over. The Israelites left Egypt with the wealth of the egyptian kingdom.

In the New Testament, Emperor Diocletian had retired in 305, and the empire was thrown into conflict. Constantine desired to rule the whole empire by himself, wanting to do away with the tetrarchy that Diocletian had recently established. The tetrarchy divided the Roman Empire into four parts, with an emperor or "junior" emperor ruling over each of the four divisions.

Constantine came into conflict with Maxentius, the new emperor of Rome. Maxentius was pagan and wanted to perpetuate the persecution of Christians[3], while Constantine wanted to legalize Christianity. The armies of Constantine and Maxentius met outside Rome, near the Milvian Bridge over the Tiber River. Constantine was able to trap Maxentius and his army, who had their backs to the Tiber River. The battle ended when Maxentius and his army drowned in the Tiber River. With the death of Maxentius, the threat of Christians being dragged back into persecution ended. Now the Christians were truly free from the Roman Empire's wrath. In the coming years, Christians would receive the wealth of the empire as Constantine showered the Church with money, lands, and buildings. He also funded the construction of exquisite churches. This is similar to how the Israelites left their bondage with the wealth of the Kingdom of Egypt.

> "And the children of Israel did as Moses had commanded: and they asked of the Egyptians vessels of silver and gold, and very much raiment. And the Lord gave favour to the people in the sight of the Egyptians, so that they lent unto them: and they stripped the Egyptians."

> - Exodus 12: 35-36

Out Into the Wilderness
SINAI WILDERNESS AND FOUNDING OF CONSTANTINOPLE

Moses led the Israelites out of Egypt and headed to the Promised Land, where they would have their own land and could live by God's laws. They would no longer be oppressed by the idolaters in Egypt. In the desert, God provided them with "free bread" from Heaven, *manna*, which fed them every day on their way to the Promised Land. God also gave them water from the rock, when he told Moses to strike it with his staff.[b]

Constantine was the sole emperor of Rome after he defeated Maxentius at the Battle of Milvian Bridge in 312. He ended the persecution of Christians with the Edict of Milan in 313. He decided to move the capital of the empire by building a new city in the wilderness adjacent to the Bosporus Straight. In that remote location, there was no infrastructure or agriculture, and water was scarce and poor.

Constantine called his new city "Nova Roma", but it soon became known as Constantinople, or "Constantine's City". It was the first Christian city in the world—unlike Rome, which was full of paganism. Christians from all over the empire followed Constantine and moved to the Anatolian wilderness.

Constantine solved the food and water problem for his new city by diverting grain shipments from Egypt that used to go to Rome. Thus, he gave the citizens of Constantinople free bread from the emperor. He also started the construction of an aqueduct in 337, which his son Constantius II completed. The aqueduct, made of stone, brought water to the city. The citizens of Constantinople had water from the rock, just like the Israelites.

Old Testament	New Testament
The Israelites took the bones of Joseph into the Promised Land.	Constantine built St. Peter's Basilica over the bones of St. Peter after the persecution was over.

---

b   See Exodus 17 : 5-6

During their time in the wilderness, the Israelites turned back to worshiping false pagan gods during the incident of the golden calf.	In 361, Emperor Julian the Apostate tried to bring the Roman Empire back to the worship of the ancient pagan gods.
The Israelites constructed the ark of the covenant during their time in the wilderness.	The Church defined the first Marian doctrine, that of Theotokos. Our Lady is the "New Ark of the Covenant".
In the wilderness, the Israelites ate and drank relatively little.	After the legalization of Christianity by Constantine, many Christians fled to the egyptian wilderness as "Anchorites" eating and drinking very little.
Moses was away on Mount Sinai, and Israel worshiped the golden calf. Aaron reluctantly capitulated to their request out of weakness.	St. Athanasius was regarded as the pillar of strength in the fight against Arianism. He was exiled; in his absence, Pope Liberius, did not speak boldly against Arianism.

On their way out of Egypt, the Israelites took Joseph's bones with them. Joseph was not only their patriarch but also the one who brought them into Egypt in the first place. They took his bones to give them a proper place of honor once they arrived in the Promised Land.

> "And Moses took Joseph's bones with him: because he had adjured the children of Israel, saying: God shall visit you, carry out my bones from hence with you."
>
> - Genesis 13: 19

Likewise, in Church history, after the persecution of Christianity ended with the Edict of Milan, Constantine was pleased to honor the bones of St. Peter by funding the construction of the first Basilica of St. Peter, built directly over his tomb on Vatican Hill. It was St. Peter who centered the Church in Rome, just like it was Joseph who brought the Israelites into Egypt.

Reverting Back to Their Pagan Ways
The Golden Calf and Julian the Apostate

Even though the Israelites were miraculously delivered by God and led out of slavery in Egypt, they infamously reverted back to pagan beliefs and false worship. This is the story of the golden calf near Mount Sinai. Moses was on Mount Sinai, away from the Israelites at that time. The Israelites began to doubt the true God and wanted to make an image of a false god that they could see, touch, and understand. Thus, they built a golden calf to worship.

Romans throughout the empire converted to Christianity during the Roman persecutions and even more so when it became popular to be a Christian in the time of Constantine. But when Emperor Julian the Apostate came to power in 361, he pressured Romans to return to their old pagan gods. Some Christian Romans succumbed to this pressure and followed their emperor. To them, the emperor (whom they could see with their eyes) was the leader of their religion. If the emperor was Catholic, so were they. If he was pagan, so were they. Perhaps they were scared of a God they could not see, touch, or comprehend and they preferred to have an emperor as a substitute. It was not that long ago, in the experience of early roman Christians, that their ancestors worshipped the emperors as gods.

Thus we can see that the paganism of Egypt ran deep in the Israelites, because of their long exposure to it during their bondage. Likewise, Christianity was a long time under the heavy influence of roman pagan society and many roman Christians had a hard time disassociating the pagan roman understanding of religion from the Catholic belief in a transcendent God.

The Ark Is Constructed
The Ark and the Dogma of Theotokos

The Israelites had demonstrated through the disastrous incident of the golden calf that they desired something visible to represent God. Perhaps that is part of the reason why God commanded Moses to construct the ark of the covenant. The ark was made of incorruptible materials, such as gold and acacia wood. It was immaculate and not to be touched by anyone, signifying that it must not be corrupted by sinful men. The ark was to contain the Ten Commandments, the manna, and the rod of Aaron.

Because of these attributes and many others, the ark is said to be a foreshadowing of Our Lady. Many saints have identified Our Lady as the new ark.[c]

Around the time of Julian the Apostate, Christological heresies challenged the Church. In effect, heretics like Arius and Nestorius were trying to make Christ in the image of their own understanding. (This is like the Israelites wanting to make a god they could understand.) Arius denied the divinity of Christ and Nestorius denied that Christ was one person with two natures. In response to the heresy of Nestorianism and the other heresies, the Church proclaimed the dogma of Mary Theotokos at the Council of Ephesus in 431. *Theotokos* means "God-bearer". Our Lady was God's mother because Our Lord is a person with two natures, one human and one divine. Because Christ cannot be divided and because Our Lady is His mother, she is also the Mother of God.

Just as the Israelites constructed the ark in the wilderness, so too did the Church "construct" the theology of the new ark. The dogma of Theotokos is the foundational Marian doctrine that all other Marian doctrines are built upon. It was the first Marian doctrine proclaimed by the Church. Formally and officially, it gave Our Lady to Catholics as a way to relate to the transcendent God, just as the ark was a way for the Israelites to have a visual reminder of the invisible God.

Penance In The Desert

The Israelites spent forty years wandering in the desert, with only manna (and quail) to eat and water to drink. Similarly, in the Gospels, Our Lord

---

c   See these references for examples of saints referring to Our Lady as the new Ark: Serm. xlii. 6, Int. Opp., S. Ambrosii , Orat. In Deip. Annuntiat, nn. 13, 14. Int. Opp. S. Athanasii , Orat. in Deip. Annunciat. Int. Opp. S. Greg. Thaumaturg

went out into the desert, or wilderness, for forty days. He fasted, neither eating or drinking. Thus, we can see that the forty years in the wilderness was a type or figure of penance for the Israelites.

Similarly, in Church history, after the persecution of Christianity was over, devout Christians could now practice the Faith in a public way. St. Antony of the Desert established communities of hermits in the egyptian desert in 305, living penitentially. They famously ate and drank very little. These devout souls are called the Anchorites.

The Leader Is Absent, And The High Priest Is Weak

Revisiting the story of the Israelites and the golden calf, we see the weakness of Moses' brother, Aaron. Aaron, from the tribe of Levi, was to become the first high priest of Israel. After the golden calf incident, the priesthood was given to the tribe of Levi for their zeal in slaying the worshipers of the golden calf. Since Aaron was both from the tribe of Levi and the brother of Moses, he became the first high priest.

When Moses was away on Mount Sinai for forty days, the Israelites pressed and threatened Aaron to make for them a golden calf. Aaron gave an excuse to Moses later, when he said that he put some gold in the furnace and an idol emerged. This is a puzzling statement on Aaron's part. Probably, Aaron failed to stand against the pagan worship of the Israelites. However, he was not treated as one of the idol worshipers who were slain when Moses returned from Mount Sinai.

> "They said to me: Make us gods, that may go before us: for as to this Moses, who brought us forth out of the land of Egypt, we know not what is befallen him. And I said to them: Which of you hath any gold? and they took and brought it to me: and I cast it into the fire, and this calf came out."
>
> - Exodus 32: 23-24

In 355, during the reign of Emperor Constantius II, Pope Liberius was pressured to capitulate to the Arian heresy. Emperor Constantius II was an

Arian, and he wanted to impose Arianism on the entire Roman Empire. He removed St. Athanasius from his seat as the bishop of Alexandria and sent him into exile. St. Athanasius was the leading voice defending Nicene (Catholic) Christianity. With St. Athanasius away, the Christians lacked a strong leader. Emperor Constantius II brought Pope Liberius to Thrace, where he was tortured and threatened. There is a controversy that exists to this day as to whether Pope Liberius actually capitulated and signed a vaguely worded statement in support of Arianism. There are various contemporary accounts, one from St. Ambrose, that denied Pope Liberius' defection from the Faith. Pope Liberius never endorsed Arianism, nor did he deny Nicene Christianity (Catholicism) as Pope Pius IX told us in his encyclical Quartus Supra of 1873. [4]

However, both Aaron and Pope Liberius failed to raise their voice in loud rebuttal. Aaron did not strongly oppose the golden calf and so it seems Pope Liberius did not strongly oppose Arianism. Moses came back to save Aaron and restore worship to the true God. Likewise, St. Athanasius eventually returned from exile in 362, and was once again the strong and leading voice in denouncing Arianism.

This concludes my analysis of the time period "Persecution and Deliverance". Now that the time of persecution of God's people has come to an end, they are both looking to a bright and hopeful future where they will have a land of their own. What lies in store for them in their "Promised Land"?

Period 3
Enemies and Establishment

God's people arrive in their land, beset on all sides by enemies.
Only through difficult struggle will they establish themselves.

OLD TESTAMENT: Books of Josue, Ruth, and Judges

The Israelites crossed the Jordan River into the Promised Land. There, they had to contend with many enemy tribes. The Judges defended Israel through battles and miracles. Over time, the enemy tribes were eradicated or suppressed, and the Kingdom of Israel was established in the Promised Land.

CHURCH HISTORY: Approximately 400^{AD} to 700^{AD}

The Catholic Faith became the state religion of the Roman Empire in 380. Christians now had a land of their own. However, heresies relentlessly arose, challenging the Faith. Church Fathers (including Pope St. Leo the Great and Pope St. Gregory the Great) waged a series of theological battles against them. Over time, the heresies were defeated, and the doctrines of Faith were firmly established. There were also hostile barbarian tribes threatening the Church in this period as well, just like in the Books of Judges and Josue.

Old Testament	New Testament
The twelve tribes of Israel crossed the Jordan River into the Promised Land. The Chanaanites were very afraid.	Multiple barbarian tribes crossed the Rhine River into the Roman Empire in 406. Romans were very afraid.
The Israelites went on to sack the city of Jericho, giving them full access to the Promised Land.	The barbarians went on to sack the city of Rome in 410, giving them an unreserved hand in the Roman Empire.

Judges arose to defend Israel against the many neighboring enemy tribes.	Church Fathers arose to defend Christianity from heresies. Pope St. Gregory the Great and Pope St. Leo the Great saved Rome from hostile barbarian tribes.
King Eglon had a gruesome and embarrassing death in a bathroom.	Heretic Arius had a gruesome and embarrassing death in a bathroom.
Ruth converted and married Booz. King David is their descendant, whose dynasty ruled Israel for centuries.	The Frankish king, Clovis, married St. Clothilda and converted. Because of this conversion, Charlemagne's later dynasty ruled Europe for centuries.

Tribes Cross the River Into the Promised Land

THE TRIBES OF ISRAEL CROSS THE JORDAN AND TRIBES OF BARBARIANS CROSS THE RHINE

The Israelites had wandered in the wilderness for forty years. Now they were ready to cross the Jordan River into the Promised Land. The Promised Land was overflowing with milk, honey, green grass, and prosperity. This was the land in which the Israelites would establish their nation.

The Chanaanites, who inhabited the land, were very afraid of the Israelites. The Israelites had great numbers and were determined to wipe them out in order to claim the land for themselves.

> "Now when all the kings of the Amorrhites, who dwelt beyond the Jordan westward, and all the kings of Chanaan, who possessed the places near the great sea, had heard that the Lord had dried up the waters of the Jordan before the children of Israel, till they passed over, their heart failed them, and there remained no spirit in them, fearing the coming in of the children of Israel."
>
> - Josue 5: 1

"And they went forward and encamped in the plains of
Moab, over against Jericho, situated beyond the Jordan. And
Balac the son of Sephor, seeing all that Israel had done to the
Amorrhite, And that the Moabites were in great fear of him,
and were not able to sustain his assault. He said to the elders
of Madian: So will this people destroy all that dwell in our
borders, as the ox is wont to eat the grass to the very roots."

- Numbers 22: 1-4

We can see the fear that the inhabitants of the Promised Land had for the
twelve tribes of Israel. In Church history, where do we see anything like the
fear the Chanaanites had for the twelve tribes of Israel? The counterpart to
the Israelites in this particular parallel takes an unexpected twist. In 406,
about a dozen barbarian tribes gathered on the northern shore of the Rhine
River in the middle of winter. The river froze over, enabling them to cross the
otherwise natural barrier between them and the Roman Empire to the south.
[5]

Depending on how the tribes are categorized, they can be identified as the
Vandals, the Alans, the Suebi, the Burgundians, the Gepids, the Goths, the
Herules, the Franks, the Alemanni and the Saxons.

The citizens of the Roman Empire greatly feared these tribes. From the
Roman perspective, the numbers of barbarians were seemingly endless. To
the barbarians, the Roman Empire was the promised land. When the
barbarians crossed the Rhine River in 406, the Romans would have had the
same reaction as the Chanaanites did in the book of Josue 5:1. As it says,
"their heart failed them, and there remained no spirit in them, fearing the
coming in of the children of Israel".

But, you may protest, the barbarians are not the new Israel. Isn't it so that
we are comparing the old Israel to the new Israel? The old Israel was God's
chosen people who came out of Egypt. The barbarians were pagans or
Arians. So, how can we compare them? That is a good question. Let's see
how they relate.

24

Circumcised And Baptized In The Promised Land

Recall that the children of Israel were given a sign for their covenant with God. The sign, which was given to Abraham, was that of circumcision. Circumcision was the physical mark that indicated membership in the Israelite nation; being counted as one of God's chosen people. Catholics also have a mark that admits us to membership in the Catholic Church. However, this mark is not visible, but an indelible mark on our soul. This mark, of course, is the sacrament of Baptism.

The Israelites were circumcised in Egypt before they fled into the wilderness. However, as they wandered for forty years, they did not circumcise their sons. Then, just as they were crossing the Jordan River to enter the Promised Land, Josue commanded that there was to be a second circumcision of the Israelites, of the children of the first generation of Israelites to come out of Egypt. This quote from the book of Josue and the footnotes from the Douay-Rheims Bible give context and commentary:

> "At that time the Lord said to Josue: Make thee knives of stone, and circumcise the second time the children of Israel."
>
> - Josue 5: 2
>
> ### Douay-Rheims footnote
>
> "The second time": Not that such as had been circumcised before were to be circumcised again, but that they were now to renew and take up again the practice of circumcision, which had been omitted during their forty years' sojourning in the wilderness; by reason of their being always uncertain when they should be obliged to march.

The second-generation Israelites were to be circumcised upon their crossing of the Jordan River into the Promised Land. After circumcision, they were officially God's chosen people and would go on to found the nation of Israel in the Promised Land.

Compare the barbarian tribes who crossed the Rhine River to the twelve tribes of Israel who crossed the Jordan River. The pagan barbarians eventually would submit to Baptism in coming decades. The Arian barbarians would later convert to Catholicism. These barbarian tribes, after their baptisms and conversions, would go on to found Christendom. If you are a Catholic of Western European descent, you are likely a descendant of these barbarian tribes.

As the Israelites were circumcised and entered the Promised Land, so too were the barbarians baptized after they entered the Roman Empire's land. As the Israelites would go on to found the Kingdom of Israel in the Promised Land, so too did the barbarians go on to found Christendom in the land they conquered from Rome.

The City In The Way

After the Israelites crossed into the Promised Land, they were confronted with the fortified city of Jericho. To have the run of the land, the Israelites had to sack that city.

The Israelites sent spies into Jericho, whom Rahab, a woman in the city, hid. To reward her, they promised to spare her and anyone who took shelter in her house during the sack of the city by the Israelites.

> "And let this city be an anathema, and all things that are in it, to the Lord. Let only Rahab the harlot live, with all that are with her in the house: for she hid the messengers whom we sent."

-Josue 6: 17

Likewise, for the barbarians who crossed the Rhine River in 406, the fortified city of Rome stood in the way of the barbarian domination of Western Europe. The inhabitants of Rome were terrified of the barbarians yet could not imagine it possible for Rome to be sacked. In 410, the barbarian Alaric sacked Rome with the help of people from inside the city who opened up for him the Salarian Gate.[6] Because Alaric was an Arian and not a pagan, he agreed not to harm anyone who took refuge in St. Peter's Basilica or St. Paul's Basilica.[7]

The sack of Jericho cleared the path for the Israelites to occupy the Promised Land, just as the sack of Rome cleared the way for the barbarians to dominate the Roman lands. The Israelites were helped by people inside the city of Jericho, just as Alaric was helped by sympathizers inside of Rome. All inside Rahab's house were spared from the slaughter at Jericho just as those who took sanctuary in St. Peter's and St. Paul's Basilica were likewise spared.

Ad Hoc Defenders of God's People

THE JUDGES ARISE TO PROTECT ISRAEL; THE CHURCH FATHERS DEFEAT EARLY HERESIES

In the Old Testament, the period of the Judges was situated between the time of egyptian slavery and the rise of the first king of Israel. The first judge to rule over the Israelites was Moses. In the desert, the Israelites asked him to act as a judge or arbitrator between different quarreling parties. The next judge was Josue. Once the Israelites took possession of the Promised Land, other Judges would arise, mainly to serve as protectors and authority figures in Israel. No set formula or procedure determined who was considered a judge.

For example, the judge *Aod* killed the Moabite king, Eglon. This act of bravery gave him the status of a judge since all of Israel looked up to him. Samson was another judge because of his miraculous strength. He destroyed the temple of the Philistines along with many of their people. Gedeon was a judge chosen by God to defend Israel against the oppression of the Midianites.

Using the lens of foreshadowing and prefigurement, we can see that the period of the Church Fathers has many parallel characteristics with the Old Testament period of the Judges. Instead of fighting enemy tribes, as the Judges did in the Old Testament, the Church Fathers fought, ad hoc, against heresies and heretics (enemies of the Faith). Just as there was no official way to become a judge in the Old Testament, there is no official procedure, office, or mechanism for someone to be classified as a Church Father.

Various Church Fathers, both in the East and the West, arose to fight specific and dangerous heresies in this time period. For example, St. Athanasius fought the heresy of Arianism. St. Cyril of Alexandria was a great opponent of the heresy of Nestorianism, while St. Augustine wrote against the heresy of Pelagianism. The Church Fathers were shining lights in a time of confusion for Catholics, just as God raised up the Judges to protect the Israelites in the time before Israel had a king.

The period of the Judges and the period of the Church Fathers both had a cyclical nature. The Israelites would start to worship some pagan false god (usually Baal) and then would be oppressed by some enemy tribe. A judge would arise to defend and liberate the Israelites, and then the cycle would start again. This is similar to the period of the Church Fathers, as heresy would arise after heresy. The heretics would draw many Catholics to themselves with their false beliefs. A Church Father (and/or a council) would arise to condemn the heresy and the cycle would start again with a new heresy.

Not Yet Established, Do What Is Thought Best
No King Yet in Israel; Doctrine Is Not Yet Established

When I describe the book of Judges to my children, I like to tell them that it was like the "Wild West" of the Old Testament. The uniform application of law was still being worked out and as a result, there was a sense that self-assertion was an unspoken law unto itself. As is evidenced many times throughout history, social cohesion is significantly strengthened by uniform rules, expectations and goals. In the Old Testament, the king provided these guidelines. But in the time of the Judges, Israel did not yet have a king. Thus, the book of Judges tells us twice:

> "In those days there was no king in Israel, but every one did that which seemed right to himself."

> - Judges 17 : 6

"In those days there was no king in Israel: but every one did
that which seemed right to himself."

- Judges 21 : 25

Likewise, during the early centuries of Church history, particularly
during the time of the Church Fathers, there was a similar situation. After the
Roman Persecution, the Church was free to publicly discuss theology. It took
time for doctrine to be established, and in the early days immediately after
the persecution, barely any doctrine was officially declared. As a result,
many bishops taught what they thought was best. Of course, this got many
of them into trouble. What many of these bishops thought was best turned
out to be heresy! Of course this underscores the importance for defined
doctrine and catechism. To condense this situation, perhaps we could phrase
it this way:

"In those days there was no defined doctrine in the Church,
but every bishop taught which seemed right to himself."

Of course this is a bit of a hyperbole, because after each successive
council, Christological doctrine was further established. Nonetheless, this
general and overall idea is similar to the period of the Judges in the Old
Testament.

Gruesome Death in a Bathroom
King Eglon and Heretic Arius

King Eglon was the exceedingly fat leader of the Moabites. The judge Aod
gained a private audience with the king and proceeded to stab him in the
stomach. The shock of the blow caused Eglon to lose his insides, as they were
spilled onto the floor through his "secret parts". Aod then closed and locked
the door to Eglon's chamber, giving the impression that Eglon was relieving
himself.

"And Aod put forth his left hand, and took the dagger from
his right thigh, and thrust it into his belly, With such force

that the haft went in after the blade into the wound, and was closed up with the abundance of fat. So that he did not draw out the dagger, but left it in his body as he had struck it in. And forthwith by the secret parts of nature the excrements of the belly came out. But Aod carefully shutting the doors of the parlour and locking them, Went out by a postern door. And the king's servants going in, saw the doors of the parlour shut, and they said: Perhaps he is easing nature in his summer parlour. And waiting a long time till they were ashamed, and seeing that no man opened the door, they took a key: and opening, they found their lord lying dead on the ground."

- Judges 3: 21-25

In the time of the Church Fathers, there were likewise spiritual tyrants who oppressed the faithful. These were the heresiarchs, or arch-heretics, most notorious of whom was Arius, the founder of Arianism. The story of Arius' death is perhaps not well known, but it was undoubtedly a sign to early Christians. In 336, Arius was summoned to Constantinople to meet with Constantius II, who was an Arian heretic himself.

Before he reached the imperial palace, he stopped at a public restroom in the city to relieve himself. His friend and colleague waited outside for a long time, thinking that Arius was lost in thought. His friend went into the restroom and found Arius dead on the floor. The insides of his bowels had amazingly and spontaneously spilled out through his "secret parts," and he died.[a]

What a coincidence. In both cases, they were presumed to be taking a long time in the bathroom only to be discovered dead from the same, unexpected, unheard of, and embarrassing cause. Recall that they both appear at the same point in their chronologically aligned time periods.

---

a The death of Arius is recorded in *The Ecclesiastical Histories of Socrates Scholasticus,* a seven volume work of the fifth century Greek historian, Socrates of Constantinople (See chapter 38 "The Death of Arius").

Heresies And Stories From The Book Of Judges

Some of these early heresies seem to be mysteriously encoded into the stories of the Judges in the Old Testament. Consider the story of Gedeon, a judge of Israel. Gedeon was told to defend Israel from the enemy tribe of Midianites. He gathered an army of about 32,000 men to fight. However, God commanded that 22,000 of them return home. If Israel had defeated the army of Midianites, they would have given credit for their victory to their strength and great numbers instead of to God.

> "And the Lord said to Gedeon: The people that are with thee are many, and Madian shall not be delivered into their hands: lest Israel should glory against me, and say: I was delivered by my own strength."

> - Judges 7: 2

Douay-Rheims footnote

"Lest Israel": By this, we see that God will not choose for his instruments in great achievements, which depend purely on his grace, such as, through pride and self-conceit, will take the glory to themselves.

Thus, we can see that God wanted Israel to attribute their victory to His might and not theirs. In other words, it is God who saves and not men.

In the 380s, the heresy of Pelagianism arose to plague the faithful. Pelagius falsely taught that men could attain Heaven on their own, without Christ's sacrifice on the Cross. The heresy of Pelagianism denied original sin. In other words, Pelagianism stated that men could save themselves, and did not need God to save them. So it seems that the rebuttal to the heresy of Pelagianism is written into the story of Gedeon.

Another story concerning Gedeon is that of the golden ephod (a priestly garment), which Gedeon made to glorify God. Despite the pious reason for its creation, the Israelites turned it into an idol and started to worship the ephod.[b] This story has all the elements of the eighth century Byzantine

---

b   See Judges 8:27

heresy of Iconoclasm. Iconoclasm argued that icons were idols and sought to eliminate them all together from churches. In the case of both the golden ephod and also the icons, the religious objects were meant to glorify God. However, they were either used as a false god (in the case of the ephod) or were mistaken for a false god (in the case of the icons.) The story of Gedeon is filled with other vivid and perplexing images. Perhaps there are more treasures to find. It is something to study, pray about and contemplate.

A Pivotal Conversion with Long-Lasting Effects

Ruth Converts, Becomes an Ancestor of King David and Clovis Converts, Preparing the Way for Charlemagne

During the time of the Judges, a wealthy landowner named Booz married a Moabite woman who converted to the God of Israel. Ruth was one of two daughters-in-law to the Israelite woman Naomi. Upon the death of Naomi's husband and sons, Naomi moved back to Bethlehem. Ruth accompanied her mother-in-law and, in the process, converted to the true God of Israel. Booz decided to marry Ruth in order to lift Naomi and Ruth out of poverty and produce heirs for Naomi.

The story of Ruth is pivotal to the Old Testament because without the union of Ruth and Booz, King David would never have been born. Ruth and Booz had a child named Obed, who was the father of Jesse, who was the father of King David. Thus, the central monarchical dynasty of the Old Testament, the Davidic dynasty, could not have come about without the conversion of Ruth and her marriage to Booz.

In Church history, in the time of the Church Fathers, there was also an extremely significant conversion that laid the necessary foundation for the eventual rise of the great Catholic monarch, Charlemagne.

In the decades following the fall of the Western Roman Empire in 476, the barbarians chaotically ruled over Western Europe. The barbarians were generally not friendly to the Church and had no allegiance or fidelity to the pope. At that time, there was a barbarian princess of the small tribe of the

Burgundians who was a Catholic. Her father died, and her mother and sister moved to Geneva. In 486, around that same time, the Frankish tribes were being united by Clovis, thus becoming the largest barbarian tribe in Western Europe. Clovis' first wife had died, and he sought friendship with the Burgundians, so he proposed marriage to St. Clothilda. Clovis was either a pagan or an Arian— and so were all of the Franks. Upon her marriage to Clovis, St. Clothilda found herself to be the only Catholic in the entire Frankish realm.

The virtues of St. Clothilda won the heart of Clovis. After a victory in battle which he attributed to his wife's God, he submitted to baptism by St. Remigius. His baptism led to the conversion of the entire Frankish tribe. The Church now had a new ally in Clovis and his Catholic Frankish empire.

More importantly, however, are the later effects of Clovis' conversion. Because the Franks were the dominant tribe, mighty and centrally located, their conversion paved the way for the rise of Charlemagne some centuries later.[c] Charlemagne was the great Frankish Catholic monarch. He founded the Holy Roman Empire, and his zeal for the Faith led to the conversion of large swaths of other barbarian tribes.

King David's dynasty was only possible because of the conversion of Ruth, just like Charlemagne's dynasty was only made possible because of the conversion of Clovis. Just like King David, whose descendants sat on the throne in Jerusalem until the last king was deposed, so too did the descendants of Charlemagne rule the Holy Roman Empire until the last emperor was deposed.

The last Davidic king was Sedecias, whom the Babylonian king Nabuchodonosor deposed. Likewise, the last Holy Roman Emperor, Francis II, was deposed in 1806 by Napoleon. We will see in Period 5 that

---

[c] Clovis' conversion to Nicene (Catholic) Christianity created the potential for future alliances between the Franks and the papacy. In the 500s, the pope was surrounded by Arian barbarian tribes, such as the Goths. In future centuries, when the papacy was looking for a new protector, Charlemagne and the Franks were the natural choice. Thus, Clovis' conversion set the stage for Charlemagne's coronation as emperor in 800 by Pope Leo III.

Nabuchodonosor and Napoleon parallel each other, as do the events surrounding their lives. God is so amazing!

There are still further parallels between the book of Ruth and the story of St. Clothilda and King Clovis. Clovis is credited with the creation of Salic Law, which was the basis for inheritance law in Europe throughout the Middle Ages and into the modern world. One of the tenants of Salic Law was that women could not inherit land.[8] Remarkably, in the story of Ruth, there is also a plot thread that deals with the inheritance of land by women and its application in Mosaic Law. Amid the story of Naomi, Ruth, and Booz, it is revealed how land is inherited and obtained. Booz could only buy the field of Naomi if he also agreed to marry Ruth, who came with the land.

> "If thou wilt take possession of it [the field] by the right of kindred: buy it and possess it: but if it please thee not, tell me so, that I may know what I have to do. For there is no near kinsman besides thee, who art first, and me, who am second. But he answered: I will buy the field. And Booz said to him: When thou shalt buy the field at the woman's hand, thou must take also Ruth the Moabitess, who was the wife of the deceased: to raise up the name of thy kinsman in his inheritance."
>
> - Ruth 4: 4-5

An End To This Time Period

The period of the Judges came to an end with Samuel, the last judge of Israel. Samuel's tenure as a judge overlapped with the reign of King Saul, the first king of Israel. Similarly, the period of the Church Fathers does not have an officially pronounced end date. Generally, the period of the Church Fathers is considered to have extended from the time of St. Ignatius of Antioch in the second century until the eighth century with St. John of Damascus in the East.[d]

---

d   The identity of the last Church Father is not unanimously agreed upon. Some consider St. Bede as a candidate for this title. The role of the Patristic declined once doctrine was established.

As the period of the Church Fathers was winding down, the byzantine emperors were starting the tradition of accepting their crowns from the patriarch of Constantinople (who was still part of the Catholic Church at that time.) As the period of the Judges was coming to an end in the time of King Saul, so too did the period of the Church Fathers come to an end during the early days of the Byzantine Catholic Empire.

In this way, Christendom had its first empire-protector, just as King Saul was the first king of Israel. Both of them would be overtaken by a second line of kings who would establish a long-lasting dynasty. The Carolingians would establish the Holy Roman Empire in the West even when there already was the Byzantine Empire in the East. The Holy Roman Empire would eventually outlast and overtake the Byzantine Empire. Likewise, David was anointed even while Saul was king of Israel. David would grow in power and fame while Saul was killed in battle. Let's explore that time period now: "Kingdom and Golden Era".

Period 4
Kingdom and Golden Era

God's people battle back their enemies and establish a great dynasty and kingdom to protect themselves. They grow into their golden era only to later become corrupted.

OLD TESTAMENT: Books of 1 Kings, 2 Kings and 3 Kings

Saul was the first king of Israel but fell from grace. Samuel anointed David, who established his dynasty to rule over Israel. David's wars secured his kingdom. His son, Solomon, built the Temple but also corrupted Israel by allowing the worship of false gods. Jeroboam complained about unfair taxes and threatened to split the twelve tribes.

CHURCH HISTORY: Approximately 700[AD] to 1500[AD]

The Byzantine Empire first protected Christianity but fell from grace. The pope crowned Charlemagne to establish a new line of holy roman emperors in the West. The Crusades defended Christendom. St. Peter's Basilica was built during the Renaissance, a time when Christendom was being corrupted with ancient and humanistic pagan Roman and Greek ideas. Martin Luther complained about the "sale" of indulgences and threatened to split Christendom.

Overview of Period 4

This period, entitled "Kingdom and Golden Era," is a significant portion of the Old Testament and, similarly, takes up the most extensive singular time period of Church history. The central theme is consistent: the self-rule of God's people by their own kings. Many threads, subplots, and changing circumstances permeate this period and make for all the more amazing parallels. If such a complex series of events occur in the same chronological order, in both the Old Testament and in Church history, with similar context, then all the more does it underscore the attribution of authorship of these parallels to God Almighty. This chart is a summary of the parallels in this time period:

Old Testament	New Testament
Saul was anointed by the prophet Samuel. He disobeyed God, and Samuel anointed David.	The Byzantine emperors were the first to receive their crowns from the Church, but they disobeyed the pope. Therefore the papacy sought a new protector and crowned the Carolingians as holy roman emperor.
King David established Israel's dominance and united the twelve tribes.	The Carolingians (descendants of Charlemagne) established Christian dominance in Europe.
David's son, Solomon, built up Jerusalem. His reign was characterized by relative peace, prosperity, architecture, art, and corruption.	Wealth, relative peace, architecture, and art all characterized the Renaissance, along with a focus on pagan Greek and Roman "wisdom," corrupting Christendom.
Jeroboam, an Israelite, complained about Solomon's high taxes. He led the ten northern tribes into revolt and apostasy.	Martin Luther, an Augustinian friar, complained about the "sale" of indulgences. He led northern Europe into revolt and apostasy.

The First King

Saul was the first king of Israel, chosen by God and anointed by Samuel. He was a handsome and tall man who looked like a king. He was also proud and self-confident, which led to his ruin. Saul struggled to unite the twelve tribes under his authority and protection, particularly the tribe of Juda.[a] Saul

---

a   *Old Testament Essays*, Shaul Bar, University of Memphis, *Saul's wars against Moab, Ammon, Edom, and Zobah*, 2014, Paragraph B "The Wars Against The Phillistines and the Amalakites"

fought bravely against the enemies of Israel, but he also disobeyed God's commands. Before a battle with the Philistines, he offered a sacrifice in the place of the priest, Samuel. Because of this action, Samuel informed Saul that he had lost God's favor.

> "And Samuel said to Saul: Thou hast done foolishly, and hast not kept the commandments of the Lord thy God, which he commanded thee. And if thou hadst not done thus, the Lord would now have established thy kingdom over Israel forever. But thy kingdom shall not continue. The Lord hath sought him a man according to his own heart: and him hath the Lord commanded to be prince over his people, because thou hast not observed that which the Lord commanded."
>
> - 1 Kings 13: 13-14

Because Saul took upon himself the role of the priest, he was told that his kingdom would not be established forever but would come to an end. God would find another king, after His own heart. This new king would be David.

Similarly, the first empire to receive its crown from the Church and vow to protect Christianity was the Byzantine Empire. The Byzantine Empire, however, did not enjoy the allegiance of all Christians, particularly since it was not able to adequately protect all of them from their oppressors. This was most evident in Italy, where Christians lived under the rule of the Lombards and the Ostrogoths. Just as Saul struggled to protect Juda, so too did the Byzantines struggle to protect Italy. The tribe of Juda would later contain the city of Jerusalem, the religious and political capital of Israel. Likewise, the city of Rome is situated in Italy, the religious and political capital of Europe throughout much of European history.

The Byzantine Empire's origins go back to the ancient Roman Empire. As a result, the Byzantine Empire had a high opinion of itself. This is most evidenced by the byzantine emperor's belief that he was the head of the

38

Church.[9][b] Like King Saul, the byzantine emperor, sometimes and unofficially, took on the role of a religious leader. In the Old Testament, this displeased the judge, priest and prophet Samuel, who found another to anoint in place of Saul. In Church history, this displeased the pope, who was the real head of the Catholic Church. In a short time, the pope would find another "to anoint," one after "his own heart". This occurred in 800 when Pope Leo III crowned Charlemagne as the holy roman emperor.

The Second King Is Established

To continue with our summary, let us skip over many details for now and see how the first king fell and the second king arose. We'll come back to those details in later pages.

In the Old Testament, the first king was Saul; in Church history, the first "king" was the Byzantine Empire. In the Old Testament, the second king was David, and in Church history, the second "king" was the Carolingian dynasty (holy roman emperor), descendants of Charlemagne.

In the Old Testament, after Saul disobeyed God's command, as given by the prophet Samuel, Saul began to experience more difficulties in battle. At the same time, Samuel went to anoint David, who was surprised by such an unexpected honor. David proved himself in battle, winning victory after victory, making Saul jealous. Israel was turning to David as their protector instead of Saul. David and Saul parted ways when David realized that Saul would not stop trying to kill him.

Saul and his son Jonathan perished in battle against the Philistines at Gilboa, after which there was a brief attempt to raise Saul's other son, Isboseth, to the throne. After a massacre of Saul's men by David's forces, and some other ensuing events, David was eventually proclaimed king of the twelve tribes of Israel. David then went on various war campaigns that secured the borders of Israel. After David had secured his kingdom, the story of King David turned inward and focused on his family.

---

b   The Byzantine emperor's notion of his role in Church hierarchy is not explicitly stated, as far as I know. Byzantine emperors' actions and words over centuries have been described as caesaropapism, meaning both the king and religious leader combined.

In Church history, the pope excommunicated the byzantine emperor for the iconoclastic heresy in the 700s. After repeated episodes and disagreements between the pope and the Byzantine Empire, the pope decided to crown the Frankish king, Charlemagne, as the holy roman emperor. Charlemagne was called to Rome on Christmas Day in 800 and was crowned by surprise, just as King David was anointed by Samuel by surprise. Charlemagne was militarily successful and subdued the Church's enemies in Western Europe. Holy Roman Emperor Otto II successfully defeated and converted the Magyars in 955. These violent and troublesome people were geographically situated between the Holy Roman Empire to the west and the Byzantine Empire to the east. The Byzantine Empire could not defeat and subdue the Magyars, but the Holy Roman Empire could. Thus, Christians started to turn towards the Holy Roman Empire as their protector, just as the Israelites turned towards King David. The Byzantines felt threatened by the Holy Roman Empire, just as Saul felt threatened by David. We will examine these parallels in more detail later.

The Schism of 1054 was the formal break between the East and the West and parallels the final separation of David and Saul. The Byzantine Empire would eventually experience a crushing defeat by the Muslim Turks at the Battle of Manzikert in 1071.[10] This battle was the beginning of the end for this empire, just as the Battle of Gilboa (the death of Saul and Jonathan) was the beginning of the end for the House of Saul. The Byzantine Empire was slipping and waning. After the Massacre of the Latins in the city of Constantinople, the West (Holy Roman Empire) lost much respect for the Byzantine Empire. The Byzantine Empire was taken over by the Christian West in 1204 when the Crusaders sacked the city of Constantinople and set up a Latin kingdom.

Just as David fought wars to secure the borders of Israel, the West launched the Crusades, giving security to Western Christendom. After the Crusades, the main story line of Christian history turns inward, with events like the Avignon Papacy, the Hundred Years War, and the Papal Schism. These events mirror the troubles in David's household, starting with Bathsabee and the rebellion of his son, Absalom, as we will examine later.

<u>Wisdom, Riches, Architecture, And Corruption</u>

With the death of King David, Israel was ruled by his heir and son, King Solomon. Solomon started his reign with integrity and pure intentions. God asked what Solomon desired, and Solomon asked for wisdom to know how to rule God's people. God was pleased by this request and granted Solomon both riches and wisdom. Solomon's wisdom was legendary. King Solomon is most well known for the construction of the Temple in Jerusalem. The Temple was opulent, beautiful, and glorious. However, it was also expensive.

The money in the time of King Solomon flowed like a river, but it did not last long. The bill came due after Solomon's death. In time, the Israelites, especially those of the northern tribes, began to complain about high taxes. These taxes were used to fund the Temple and the opulent lifestyle of the king. The seeds of revolt were being sown.

In Church history, after the Avignon Papacy and the Papal Schism, Pope Nicholas V reigned in Rome, a city in a state of disrepair. In 1450, he decreed the building of a new St. Peter's Basilica. This was the start of the Renaissance in Italy, which is characterized by all the same elements present in the time of King Solomon. The Renaissance started more pure and innocent than it ended, just like the reign of King Solomon did.

During the Renaissance, there were great thinkers and inventors like Leonardo da Vinci and Michelangelo. The banking family of the Medici funded artists with their incredible wealth, which flowed like a river. Magnificent architecture sprang up throughout Italy and beyond, culminating in the exquisite and glorious St. Peter's Basilica in Rome.

At this same time, the Renaissance popes were living in great luxury, and sadly, some were accused of misconduct in grave matters. Similarly, King Solomon also broke the laws of Moses by marrying hundreds and hundreds of wives, many of them pagan. Pope Leo X, who was known to live opulently, needed to secure adequate financing for the construction of St. Peter's Basilica. His campaign of generating revenue from indulgences soured the opinion of the papacy and the Roman hierarchy in the eyes of

Martin Luther. This began the first stage of a revolt that would eventually split Christendom in two.

The North Revolts And Splits With The Covenant

This time period of "Kingdom and Golden Era" ends with the revolt of the North and their separation from the covenant. In the Old Testament, Jeroboam led a revolt of the ten northern tribes, initially because the taxes were too high. He objected to the abusive use of taxes to fund the king's lifestyle and building projects in Jerusalem. The ten northern tribes did not see the benefit for themselves of these high taxes.

Similarly, Martin Luther led northern Christendom into revolt from the Catholic Church and the Holy Roman Empire. His initial reason for starting his evil revolt was that Pope Leo X was "selling" indulgences to raise money for the construction of St. Peter's Basilica and fund his opulent lifestyle. The Council of Trent, while upholding the goodness of indulgences, would later condemn the practice of issuing indulgences in abusive ways.

It is not inherently immoral to offer indulgences in exchange for donations. For example, during the Crusades, some faithful who could not join the holy war received indulgences by donating money instead. Like indulgences, taxes are likewise morally and rationally acceptable. However, both taxation and indulgences can be abused and exploited. Therefore, the comparison between Jeroboam and Luther is all the more striking, and we will explore it more thoroughly in a future section.

Now that we have finished our summary of events, lets go back to the beginning of this time period.

Into The Details

Let's look at the early days of King Saul and the early days of the Byzantine Catholic Empire. The Byzantine Empire, starting with the Leonid dynasty in 457, received its crown from the patriarch of Constantinople. This is comparable to Saul being anointed by Samuel.

Old Testament	New Testament
Philistines took the ark of the Covenant.	Persians took the relic of the True Cross.
Saul fought against the Philistines and inserted himself into religious matters.	Byzantine-Persian wars and the byzantine emperor's interjection of himself into religious matters.
God rejected Saul through Samuel.	The pope excommunicated the byzantine emperor.
Saul ripped away at the cloak of Samuel, who went to anoint another, per God's will.	The byzantine emperor "tore" lands away from the pope after his excommunication; the pope crowned a new emperor.

The Holiest Relic/Artifact Is Taken
PHILISTINES TAKE THE ARK AND PERSIANS TAKE THE TRUE CROSS

The book of 1 Kings starts with the story of Anna, who was crying before the Lord because she was barren. She was given a son, Samuel, whom she dedicated to the service of the Lord under the care of Heli, the high priest. While Samuel was growing up and serving the Lord in the sanctuary, he became aware of the evil ways of the high priest's sons, Ophni and Phinees. As part of the punishment for Heli's negligence to correct his sons' behavior, God allowed the Philistines to capture the most holy object that Israel possessed.

The Philistines were constantly at the borders of Israel, threatening their security, killing and robbing. It would not be until the days of King David that the Philistines would be subdued. During the time of Heli and his corrupt sons, the Philistines launched a large attack in which they captured the ark of the covenant, Israel's most holy object. This was a complete disaster, unimaginable to the Israelites. It was a great profanation of such a sacred object for it to fall into the hands of infidels. However, the ark of the covenant would return to Israel after briefly staying among the Philistines.

"So the Philistines fought, and Israel was overthrown, and every man fled to his own dwelling: and there was an exceeding great slaughter; for there fell of Israel thirty thousand footmen. And the ark of God was taken: and the two sons of Heli, Ophni and Phinees, were slain."

- 1 Kings 4: 10-11

Similarly, the Persian Empire persistently threatened the Byzantine Empire in the 500s and 600s, capturing territories along their eastern border. During the Persian conquest of Jerusalem in 615, they took the relic of the True Cross, the most holy relic in Christendom. It had been residing in Jerusalem since the time of St. Helena in the 300s.[11] It was a devastating blow to Christians, but just like the ark, it was also returned. In 631, it was brought back to Constantinople.

The Persian Empire, which took the relic of the True Cross in 615, would not exist much longer. Islam was soon to rise in the mid-600s and engulf the Persian Empire and surrounding lands. Keep an eye on the parallels between the Philistines in the Old Testament and the Muslims in Church history. The Philistines were the infamous archenemy of the Israelites. The Philistines were a constant and severe problem from the time of the Judges until the days of King David. Likewise, the Muslims serve as their primary parallel in Church history, as they are often recognized as the one persistent and severe threat to Christendom from their inception in the 600s until the waning of the Ottoman Empire in the late 1600s. This parallel will pop up a lot in later pages.

The First King
KING SAUL AND THE BYZANTINE EMPIRE

Actions Of The Newly Crowned King

Both Saul and the Byzantine Empire were "crowned" or anointed in wartime. In 1 Kings 11, the newly anointed King Saul fights against the Ammonites to protect the Israelites of Jabes Galaad. After the battle, Saul was re-confirmed as king. In 457, Leo I was the first byzantine emperor to be crowned by the patriarch of Constantinople (a gesture that demonstrated his deference to the Church.) Leo I's reign was plagued by the menace of the Ostrogoth barbarians and the Huns, who threatened Christendom. The next emperor (not counting the 10-month reign of Leo II) was Emperor Zeno, crowned in 474. Like Saul who was victorious over the Ammonites, Zeno stabilized the Byzantine Empire by driving back the barbarians.

Some of his subjects opposed Saul's kingship, just as parts of the Western Roman Empire opposed Zeno's rule. In 1 Kings 10, the "children of Belial" (disloyal Israelites) opposed Saul as their king. After the victory of Saul against the Ammonites, the children of Israel wanted to kill the "children of Belial" for rejecting Saul as their king. However, Saul acted with clemency and refused to kill those who opposed his kingship. In Church history, Emperor Zeno had his authority opposed by Marcian, the son of the deposed western roman emperor. After putting down Marcian's revolt, he refused to have Marcian killed but instead exiled him to a monastery. Later, he freed Marcian to return to Italy.

Neither Saul nor the byzantine emperors had any legitimate religious authority. Yet both of them clumsily assumed that their authority and leadership as temporal rulers gave them the authority to make decisions regarding religious matters. The Byzantines had an unformulated, nebulous belief, expressed through their actions, that they were co-head of the Church, sharing spiritual authority (in some vague way) with the patriarch of Constantinople or the pope in Rome.

Saul acted in a similar manner. As Philistines continued to threaten the Israelites, Saul and his army readied themselves for battle. Saul's men lacked conviction, and his soldiers began to slip away and desert him. To rally them together, Saul offered a holocaust. Offering sacrifice was not a function of a king, but of a priest. Upon hearing this, Samuel the prophet reproved Saul for not obeying the Lord's commands.

> "And Samuel said to him: What hast thou done? Saul answered: Because I saw that the people slipt from me, and thou wast not come according to the days appointed, and the Philistines were gathered together in Machmas, I said:

Now will the Philistines come down upon me to Galgal, and I have not appeased the face of the Lord. Forced by necessity, I offered the holocaust. And Samuel said to Saul: Thou hast done foolishly, and hast not kept the commandments of the Lord thy God, which he commanded thee. And if thou hadst not done thus, the Lord would now have established thy kingdom over Israel for ever. But thy kingdom shall not continue."

- 1 Kings 13: 11-14

Likewise, Emperor Zeno inserted himself into theological matters (infringing upon the authority and role of the papacy) when he tried to settle the theological dispute between the Chalcedonians (Catholics) and Monophysites (heretics.) In 482, he issued a decree called the "Henotikon,"[12] which tried reconciling the opposing theological positions. He did this to unite his empire and stop the Monophysites from slipping away from imperial influence. (The Monophysites were primarily centered in the East, in Syria and Palestine.) The pope rejected Zeno's interference in theological matters. This affair initiated the tension between byzantine emperors and the papacy, as the Byzantine Empire demonstrated in future events that it considered itself commissioned and competent to legislate on theological matters.

It will not be long before God rejects both Saul in the Old Testament and the byzantine emperor in Church history.

Rejected By God's Representative

Because Saul disobeyed God's command given by Samuel, and because the byzantine emperor did not acknowledge the pope as God's vicar on earth and disobeyed him, then God rejected Saul and the byzantine emperor. Consider the following:

Saul was directed by the prophet Samuel to attack the Amalecites, who were a sworn enemy of Israel and who were pressing into Israelite lands. Samuel instructed Saul to slay all of the Amalecites, along with all of their livestock. God did not want one trace of Amalecite influence left but wanted them destroyed. Saul fought the Amalecites but did not obey the word of Samuel. Instead, Saul kept the Amalecites' livestock and let the Amalecite King Agag live as a prisoner.

In the 700s, the Iconoclastic heresy plagued the Byzantine Empire. Iconoclasm was a heresy in which the use of religious images was said to be idolatry and against the First Commandment. One hypothesis regarding the origin of this heresy supposes that it may have been inspired by Islamic beliefs. Islam teaches that a religious image is a form of idolatry. Because the Byzantine Empire did not wholly defeat the Arab Muslims but instead interacted with them, their religious influences could have contaminated byzantine religious thought. The Iconoclastic heresy, sponsored by Emperor Leo III, possibly arose from Muslim influence in the East.[c] Indeed, the eighth century witnessed substantial trade and the exchange of ideas between the two neighboring civilizations of the Byzantine Empire and Muslim Caliphates. Many Greek works were translated and absorbed by Muslim philosophers during this time.

This is akin to the danger to the Israelites of contamination of belief and worship posed by the Amalecites. God commanded Saul to wipe out the Amalecites completely. God had commanded the Israelites to eliminate all pagan tribes from their land so as not to be influenced by their beliefs and practices.

> "But shalt kill them with the edge of the sword, to wit, the Hethite, and the Amorrhite, and the Chanaanite, the Pherezite, and the Hevite, and the Jebusite, as the Lord thy God hath commanded thee: Lest they teach you to do all the abominations which they have done to their gods: and you should sin against the Lord your God."
>
> - Deuteronomy 20: 17-18

Emperor Leo III sponsored the Iconoclastic heresy with the full weight of his authority. Popes Gregory II and Gregory III fiercely opposed Byzantine Emperor Leo III for his heresy and disobedience to papal authority.

---

c   Leo III is accused of being "Saracen-minded" by Theophanes the Confessor, a ninth century byzantine chronicler, indicating Leo III's sympathies with Islam and Islamic culture. [13]

Ironically, the byzantine emperor was declaring it idolatry to venerate icons, and in the Old Testament, Samuel told Saul that disobedience was like the sin of idolatry.[d] Thus, in disobeying the popes, the byzantine emperors were committing a sin "like the sin of idolatry" in his misguided and erroneous attempts to avoid idol worship.

As a result of Saul's disobedience, Samuel rejected him on God's behalf.

> "And Samuel said: Doth the Lord desire holocausts and victims, and not rather that the voice of the Lord should be obeyed? For obedience is better than sacrifices: and to hearken rather than to offer the fat of rams. Because it is like the sin of witchcraft, to rebel: and like the crime of idolatry, to refuse to obey. Forasmuch therefore as thou hast rejected the word of the Lord, the Lord hath also rejected thee from being king."
>
> - 1 Kings 15: 22-23

Similarly, the pope rejected the byzantine emperor for his refusal to obey. In 730, Pope Gregory III excommunicated Byzantine Emperor Leo III for his persistence in the iconoclastic heresy.

The Rejected King Tears Away At God's Representative

In the Old Testament, Samuel turned to leave after having rejected Saul. Saul was distraught and grabbed ahold of Samuel's robe to stop him from leaving. However, in grabbing Samuel's mantle, he tore it. Samuel saw the tearing of his mantle as a sign from God.

> "And Samuel turned about to go away: but he laid hold upon the skirt of his mantle, and it rent. And Samuel said to him: The Lord hath rent the Kingdom of Israel from thee this day, and hath given it to thy neighbour who is better than thee. But the triumpher in Israel will not spare, and will not be moved to repentance: for he is not a man that he should repent."

---

d   1 Kings 15: 23

- 1 Kings 15: 27-29

In Church history, the Byzantine Emperor Leo III reacted to his excommunication by Pope Gregory III by ripping away the southern Italian lands of Sicily, Calabria, and Illyria from the papacy. He did this ironically to strengthen his kingdom since, in his mind, the pope had divided his empire into two opposing groups, those against and those adhering to the Iconoclastic heresy. Those lands, under the nominal rule of the Byzantine Empire, were geographically nearer to Rome than to Constantinople. Thus, they tended towards the Latin Rite and submission to the papacy. Perhaps Byzantine Emperor Leo III thought he could put pressure on Pope Gregory III to change his mind. However, as Samuel stated *"the triumpher in Israel will not spare, and will not be moved to repentance: for he is not a man that he should repent"*. The pope would not repent of his decision to excommunicate the byzantine emperor because he was not acting as just a man, but as the Vicar of Christ. The pope is the "triumpher in Israel".

I'd like to highlight the poetry of juxtaposing these two parallel stories together. Samuel says that the tearing of his mantle by Saul signifies that the kingdom will be taken from him and given to another. This was fulfilled in time when David became king. In Church history, after Leo III is rejected, he tears away at the papal lands to build up his kingdom (which Saul was told he would lose). However, the Byzantine Empire would follow Saul's fate because it would also lose its "kingdom" in the coming centuries when the Latins conquered Constantinople and then later when the Ottoman Turks vanquished Constantinople and the whole Byzantine Empire in 1453. As Samuel told Saul, "If only you would have obeyed the Lord God *(paraphrased)"*.

> "And Samuel said to Saul: Thou hast done foolishly, and hast not kept the commandments of the Lord thy God, which he commanded thee. And if thou hadst not done thus, the Lord would now have established thy kingdom over Israel forever."
>
> - 1 Kings 13: 13

God commands Samuel to anoint another, David, who will eventually take Saul's kingdom. Similarly, the pope is on the lookout to anoint a new emperor, one that is pious and obedient to the papacy, to replace the role of the Byzantine Empire. Let us examine those parallels with a new chart and the following details.

The Second King Is Anointed by Surprise
KING DAVID AND THE CAROLINGIAN DYNASTY

Old Testament	New Testament
Goliath, the giant warrior, threatened Israel.	The hardened soldiers of the Umayyad dynasty threatened Western Christendom.
David won an unlikely victory, as King Saul was reluctant to fight.	Charles Martel won an improbable victory as the Merovingian king did not fight.
David's popularity after his victory propelled him to become the king.	Charles Martel was famous for his victory; his descendants were first made kings and then holy roman emperors.

The Giant Enemy Attacks

In the Old Testament, after Saul was rejected, Samuel traveled to Bethlehem to anoint David. A bit later, the Philistines presented themselves in battle formation against Israel's army. They had been a constant threat to the Israelites since the time of the Judges, and it was Saul's task, as the king of Israel, to defend the Israelites. The Philistines had a secret weapon, the giant Goliath. They faced off with the Israelites for forty days, with Goliath calling out for someone to fight him, specifically mocking King Saul and the God of Israel. For his part, King Saul was most likely afraid to face Goliath. At this time, David was serving as Saul's armor-bearer.[e] David was outraged

---

e   See 1 Kings 16:21

at the giant's blasphemy against God and went out to fight Goliath, even though he was severely outmatched.

In Church history, the Muslim Umayyad dynasty grew and spread across North Africa and Spain and, in the early 700s, was threatening the kingdom of the Franks. The Byzantine Empire failed to contain and suppress the Muslims in the East, allowing them to spread to Western Europe through North Africa. The Muslim army was battle-hardened and well-equipped, especially with cavalry. The sizes of the Frankish and Muslim armies are disputed. Charles Martel probably had around 30,000 men while the Muslims probably had around 80,000.[14][15] During this time, the Merovingian dynasty—the direct descendants of Clovis—ruled the Franks. They were known as the *do-nothing kings*[16][f] as they were essentially figureheads. Charles Martel had the position of *Mayor of the Palace* for the Merovingian kings and was charged with the actual defense of the Frankish realm. This is like how David was the armor bearer for King Saul.

Charles Martel gathered his forces and met the advancing Muslim army at Tours, France, in 732. For seven days, the Muslim Army called out for Martel to descend from his position, but Martel refused. Martel was severely outmatched as the Muslims had more experience, better equipment, and larger numbers.[14][15] He waited until the enemy came to him. Despite being severely outmatched, Martel defeated the Muslim army in a remarkable upset. This victory was pivotal as it halted the spread of Islam into Western Europe.[17] If it were not for Charles Martel, Christendom might have been replaced with a European Islamic Caliphate. The victory of Charles Martel at Tours in 732 is like the victory of David over Goliath.

Popularity Is Launched

Because of David's victory over Goliath, he was universally acclaimed throughout Israel and was considered a hero. Saul had promised that David could marry his daughter because of his victory, even though Saul was

---

f   In reference to the Merovingian king, the eighth century Frankish scholar, Einhard writes: "There was nothing left the King to do but to be content with his name of King, his flowing hair, and long beard, to sit on his throne and play the ruler..." -translated by S. E. Turner, 1880

jealous of David. The people of Israel acclaimed that "Saul killed thousands, but David killed tens of thousands," which only made Saul more jealous and angry.[8] From this point, Saul saw David as a threat to his reign as king.

David's victory over Goliath gave him popularity and recognition in Israel. It also set him on a collision course with King Saul. He needed David to help him defend Israel, because David never lost a battle, but at the same time, Saul was plotting against David. David would come to recognize Saul's malevolence as events unfolded.

Similarly, after the victory of Charles Martel over the Muslim army at the Battle of Tours in 732, he was universally acclaimed as the savior of Christendom. His popularity launched his house into European-wide fame. Within one generation, his lineage was established as the new royal family, becoming the kings of the Franks, supplanting the old Merovingian dynasty. Charles Martel's line was called the Carolingian dynasty. It would be from the Carolingian line that Charlemagne would arise a few decades later. Charlemagne would be crowned holy roman emperor by the pope on Christmas day in 800, in St. Peter's Basilica. This angered the Byzantine Empire, who was threatened by this new Catholic empire. Just as there were two anointed in Israel there were now two emperors in Christendom.

We will see that the Byzantines later gave one of their princesses to marry the holy roman emperor, just as King Saul gave his daughter to David in marriage. We will also see later that the Byzantine Empire requested the help of the Carolingian kings and the Holy Roman Empire to defend their realm against the Muslim Turks; but at the same time, the Byzantines betrayed the Franks during the first three Crusades. In like manner, this is also what Saul did to David, as he needed David to help defend Israel but also tried to kill him on several occasions.

---

g   See 1 Kings 18: 6-9

Relationship Between the First and Second Kings

RELATIONSHIP BETWEEN SAUL AND DAVID AND BETWEEN THE
BYZANTINE AND HOLY ROMAN EMPIRES

Old Testament	New Testament
David married Michol, King Saul's daughter.	A byzantine princess married a holy roman emperor.
David was betrayed by Saul, and they eventually parted ways.	The Schism of 1054 separated East and West; Byzantines betrayed the Crusaders.
Saul and Jonathan were killed at the Battle of Gilboa, leaving only weak heirs of King Saul.	The Byzantine Empire suffered a crushing loss at the Battle of Manzikert, leaving their empire extremely weak.

The Princess Marries The Young, Victorious Warrior

After David's victory over Goliath, he was renowned as the great defender of Israel. He was also made a captain in King Saul's army, returning victorious against the enemies of Israel. King Saul was in a bind. On the one hand, he knew that David was going to threaten his authority eventually, but on the other hand, he needed David, who was a great asset in the defense of Israel. On a personal level, Saul was jealous of David's fame and success.

Saul decided to give his daughter, Michol, to David in marriage. One purpose of this marriage was to unite David's house with Saul's house, thus deflecting or lessening any rivalry between them that loomed in the future. But also, Saul's stated purpose of this marriage was that Michol should cause David difficulty and perhaps keep a closer eye on him. As the saying goes, keep your friends close but your enemies closer. David was a "frenemy" of King Saul.

"But Michol the other daughter of Saul loved David. And it was told Saul, and it pleased him. And Saul said: **I will give her to him, that she may be a stumbling-block to him, and**

that the band of the Philistines may be upon him. And Saul said to David: In two things thou shalt be my son in law this day. And Saul commanded his servants to speak to David privately, saying: Behold thou pleasest the king, and all his servants love thee. Now therefore be the king's son in law. And the servants of Saul spoke all these words in the ears of David. And David said: Doth it seem to you a small matter to be the king's son in law? But I am a poor man, and of small ability. And the servants of Saul told him, saying: Such words as these hath David spoken. _And Saul said: Speak thus to David: **The King desireth not any dowry, but only a hundred foreskins of the Philistines, to be avenged of the king's enemies. Now Saul thought to deliver David into the hands of the Philistines.**"

- 1 Kings 18: 20-25

Notice, at the end of this passage, King Saul's request to produce one hundred philistine foreskins as a dowry for his daughter, Michol. We will come back to this point soon.

Let us look at Church history, to the newly formed Holy Roman Empire. Remember that Charlemagne was crowned as the first holy roman emperor by surprise in 800 in Rome by the pope. Upon Charlemagne's coronation, Christendom had two emperors. The Byzantine Empire was in the East, and the Holy Roman Empire was in the West. This is akin to having two of God's anointed in Israel simultaneously, King Saul and David. The Byzantines became threatened by the Holy Roman Empire just as Saul was of David.

In the 900s, a group known as the Magyars emerged as a menace and danger to Christendom. The Magyars lived in present-day Hungary, which was geographically situated between the Holy Roman Empire and the Byzantine Empire. The Byzantines were not able to defeat them, and Christians in the East suffered from Magyar raids and attacks. However, in 955, Holy Roman Emperor Otto I crushed the Magyars at the Battle of Lechfeld. This ended the Magyar menace and gave Otto I the reputation as the defender of Christendom.[18] This growing popularity of the Holy Roman Empire was threatening to the Byzantine Empire. To further upset the Byzantines, the Magyars adopted Latin Christianity instead of Greek Christianity when they converted in the tenth century.

The victory of Otto I also secured Italy under his reign and dominion, which was awkward because the Byzantine Empire still claimed Southern Italy as part of its empire, even though they could not sustainably project their power there. To resolve this situation and smooth things over with the Byzantine Empire, Otto I arranged the marriage of his son, Otto II, to the Byzantine Princess Theophanu. This marriage brought the two empires together, just like how the marriage of Saul's daughter Michol to David smoothed over any tension between David and Saul.

Now, let's return to the topic of the foreskins that David brought back as a dowry for marrying Saul's daughter, Michol. In the Old Testament, circumcision was the sign of belonging to God's chosen people. Circumcision was the cutting away of the foreskin of males, and it was necessary to be part of the Old Testament covenant. In like manner, the sacrament of Baptism is necessary to become a member of the Catholic Church, the "New Israel".

After the Battle of Lechfeld in 955, the Magyar leader, Géza and his family were baptized and received into the Catholic Church in 974. Géza's son was St. Stephen, the first king of Hungary. He led his whole kingdom into the Catholic Church. Thus, shortly after the Battle of Lechfeld, the Magyars were baptized. This resonates with the "forced circumcising" of the Philistines by David as a dowry to marry Michol. The victory at Lechfeld made the political alliance between the Holy Roman Empire and the Byzantine Empire all the more necessary. The later conversion of the Magyars to Latin Christianity (instead of the Eastern Rite) only served to legitimize and magnify the prestige of the Holy Roman Empire in the eyes of Christians, to the chagrin of the Byzantines.[19][h]

---

h The conversion of the Magyars to Latin Christianity evoked a mixed response from the Byzantines. They welcomed the end of Magyar attacks and a friendly partner against the northern Bulgarians, but they resented the increasing power of the Holy Roman Empire and the Latin West.

The Two Anointed Part Ways

Even though David was united with Saul through his marriage to Saul's daughter, Michol, Saul was still jealous and threatened by David. David fled from Saul to save his life. From that point, David and Saul were never united again and parted ways. However, Saul would ask David to come back and fight for him again because Saul needed help in defeating Israel's enemies.

> "And Saul said: I have sinned, return, my son David, for I will no more do thee harm "
>
> - 1 Kings 26: 21

David did not return to King Saul but lived in the wilderness and then among the Philistines. Saul would later be threatened again by the Philistines, who had invaded deep into Israel's territory. At the Battle of Gilboa, Saul's lineage was dealt a crushing blow as he lost the battle and was killed along with his warrior son, Jonathan.[i]

Just as David and Saul were united through Michol, the Holy Roman Empire and the Byzantine Empire joined politically through marriage with Otto II and Theophanu in 974. However, this union was not meant to last. It was inadequate to bring about true union of the empires since they were divided by substantial political, cultural, and religious differences. In the great Schism of 1054, the Byzantine Empire and the Latin West (Holy Roman Empire) effectively and officially parted ways.

In 1071, the Seljuk Turks invaded the byzantine heartland of Anatolia and inflicted a devastating blow on the byzantine army at the Battle of Manzikert, weakening the empire's footprint and paving the way for Turkish settlement in Anatolia. The Byzantine Empire was severely weakened. This is similar to how Saul and Jonathan were killed at the Battle of Gilboa, which critically weakened Saul's lineage and their hold on the royal crown.

Just as King Saul later regretted his actions towards David and asked David to come back to him, so too did the Byzantine Emperor Alexios I

---

i   1 Kings 31

Komnenos also request the help of the Latin West when he petitioned the pope in 1095 for help against the Seljuk Turks. The Byzantines were unable to defeat the Turks by themselves.

The Crusaders came to the aid of the Byzantine Empire, who nonetheless betrayed the Crusaders by not sending military aid, even when the Crusaders were in danger of death.[j] Their actions in the First Crusade were much like King Saul, who sent David to fight the Philistines, hoping that in doing so, David would be killed and the Philistines weakened.

Sensing their betrayal, the Crusaders established a Latin kingdom in Jerusalem in 1099 instead of handing control of Jerusalem over to the Byzantines. The kingdom of Jerusalem was surrounded by Muslim kingdoms. (If you recall from previous pages the parallels between the Philistines and the Muslims.) This is akin to David fleeing from Saul and living among the Philistines because he felt threatened and betrayed by Saul.

> "And David said in his heart: I shall one day or other fall into the hands of Saul: is it not better for me to flee, and to be saved in the land of the Philistines, that Saul may despair of me, and cease to seek me in all the coasts of Israel? I will flee then out of his hands. And David arose and went away, both he and the six hundred men that were with him, to Achis the son of Maoch, king of Geth (a Philistine king.)"
>
> - 1 Kings 27: 1-2

In the Second Crusade, the Holy Roman Emperor Frederick Barbarossa intentionally held back his forces from taking revenge on the Byzantine Empire when they attacked him in 1147, as he was on his way to fight in the Holy Land. Emperor Frederick Barbarossa repelled the byzantine forces only and refrained from attacking them, just as David refrained from fighting against King Saul despite Saul's attempt to kill him.

> "And David said to Abisai: Kill him not: for who shall put forth his hand against the Lord's anointed, and shall be

---

j   Byzantine Emperor Alexios Komnenos did not send urgently needed troops and supplies to the Crusaders at the siege of Antioch in 1097-1098.

guiltless? And David said: As the Lord liveth, unless the Lord shall strike him, or his day shall come to die, or he shall go down to battle and perish: The Lord be merciful unto me, that I extend not my hand upon the Lord's anointed. But now take the spear, which is at his head, and the cup of water, and let us go."

- 1 Kings 26: 9-11

The Second King Rules the Kingdom

SAUL'S LINEAGE IS SEVERELY WEAKENED; DAVID RULES ISRAEL: THE BYZANTINE EMPIRE IS WEAKENED; THE HOLY ROMAN EMPIRE IS DOMINANT

Old Testament	New Testament
David rebuked his servants for killing Saul's descendant.	The pope rebuked the Crusaders for sacking Constantinople in 1204.
David waged wars to secure Israel.	The Crusades established a time of peace and security in Western Christendom.
David killed his mighty warrior Urias so David could marry his wife, Bathsabee.	French King Phillip IV destroyed the Knights Templar, confiscating their lands and nullifying his debt with them.
David's son, Absalom, claimed to be king even while David was still alive.	During the Papal Schism, there were two papal claimants in Christendom.

A Massacre, Followed By The End Of The First King's House

After Saul's and Jonathan's deaths, Saul's house and lineage were severely weakened and few in number. Saul's two most prominent male descendants, his son Isboseth and his grandson (Jonathan's son) Miphiboseth, were weak and unpopular heirs. Saul's general, Abner, met David's general, Joab. This meeting resulted in the slaughter of Abner's men. In a complicated story from the Old Testament, Abner realized that his loyalty to Saul's son, Isboseth, was in vain. Abner declared that he would give the throne to David.

Later, in reaction to the death of Abner and the collapse of Saul's legacy, some of Saul's former servants murdered Isboseth, thinking it would please David. However, David rebuked them and put them to death, even though by eliminating Isboseth, David was established as the sole ruler in Israel. In all its complexity, this story can be read in the book of 2 Kings, chapters 1 through 4.

Likewise, in Church history, after the Battle of Manzikert in 1071, the Byzantine Empire was irreparably weakened. In Constantinople at this time, there were many Venetian and other Latin Rite Christians. In 1187, tens of thousands of them were suddenly and summarily slaughtered by the Byzantines. This is known as the *Massacre of the Latins*.

Shortly after this massacre, the Crusaders were approached in 1202 by Alexius IV Angelus, the son of the deposed byzantine emperor. The Crusaders were on their way to fight in the Fourth Crusade but were in need of money to pay their debts to the Venetians. Alexius IV Angelus requested help to reclaim the byzantine throne. If the Crusaders would help him, he promised to give them a large sum of money. The Crusaders accepted his offer and traveled to Constantinople. The plan to restore Alexius IV Angelus went bad, and the Crusaders ended up sacking the city of Constantinople in 1204. The Crusaders then established a Latin kingdom in Constantinople, deposing byzantine rule. Pope Innocent III decried the siege and excommunicated the Crusaders for this action.

Just as Abner went to David, so did the Byzantines go to the Crusaders, who ended the byzantine rule of Constantinople just as David's servants killed Saul's last son and heir, Isboseth. David rebuked and killed these servants for this murder, just as the pope rebuked and excommunicated the Crusaders for sacking Constantinople. The murder of Isboseth made David the sole ruler of Israel just as the establishment of a Latin kingdom in Constantinople did the same for the Christian West.

Mighty Men And Wars To Secure The Borders

Even though some descendants of King Saul were still alive, they were weak and scattered, posing no threat or hindrance to David. Once David was crowned king over all of Israel, he went on to fight many wars with the help of his mighty men. Together, they fought and won against the Philistines, Jebusites, Amalecites, Moabites, Edomites, and the Ammonites. King David and his mighty men were victorious time and time again. See 2 Kings chapters 5, 8, 9 & 10.

> "And king David dedicated them to the Lord, together with the silver and gold that he had dedicated of all the nations, which he had subdued: Of Syria, and of Moab, and of the children of Ammon, and of the Philistines, and of Amalec, and of the spoils of Adarezer the son of Rohob king of Soba."
>
> - 2 Kings 8: 11-12

King David's mighty men, his inner core of warriors, are particularly interesting due to their most astonishing and heroic deeds in battle. For example, there was Jesbaham who "killed eight hundred men at one onset" (2 Kings 23:8). Eleazar, who "stood and smote the Philistines till his hand was weary, and grew stiff with the sword" (2 Kings 23:10). Semma, who "stood in the midst of the field, and defended it, and defeated the Philistines" (2 Kings 23:14). Abisai, who "lifted up his spear against three hundred whom he slew" (2 Kings 23:18). Banaia, who "slew the two lions of Moab" (2 Kings 23:20). These mighty men were special and unique in Israel and credited with many of David's victories. They, along with the rank-and-file army, subdued the enemies of Israel and calmed the borderlands. A time of peace and tranquility ensued for David's kingdom. From this point, the story of King David shifts away from his outward role as king and towards the interior life of his maturing family.

After the Battle of Manzikert in 1071 and the Sack of Constantinople in 1204, the Byzantine Empire was vanquished. The scattered outlying byzantine provinces still survived, but the restoration of the Byzantine Empire looked increasingly unlikely. By contrast, the Holy Roman Empire was at the height of its strength and influence. During the twelfth and thirteenth centuries, Crusades had been waged against the enemies of Christ. It was not just Muslims who were targets of the Crusades, but also the remaining pagan kingdoms in Lithuania and Estonia and the Mongols for a short time. Like the wars of David, the Crusades pacified the borders of Western Christendom and subdued all the surrounding enemies.

Similar to King David, the pope and the kings of Europe also had "mighty men" who formed the core of their war campaigns. During these centuries, a new kind of monk, the warrior monk, was introduced into Christendom. There were dozens of military orders of monks, such as the Knights Templar, Knights Hospitaller, and Teutonic Knights, among others. Like David's mighty men, these military orders are known for exceptional feats on the battlefield. For example, at the Battle of Montgisard in 1177, five hundred Knights Templar, and a small band of regular infantry, defeated an army of 26,000 Muslim soldiers.[20][21]

By the beginning of the fourteenth century, the Crusades were winding down. From this point, the story of Western Christendom turns inwards to internal events that both shaped and shook the realm.

The Sin of the King

DAVID KILLS URIAS AND TAKES BATHSABEE WHILE KING PHILIP IV DESTROYS THE KNIGHTS TEMPLAR AND TAKES THEIR WEALTH

Near the end of his war campaigns, David stopped going out to battle with his soldiers. His army commanders were concerned that David would needlessly die in battle and advised him to stay in Jerusalem. It also may be the case that David had grown used to luxury.

> "And it came to pass at the return of the year, at the time when kings go forth to war, that David sent Joab and his servants with him, and all Israel, and they spoiled the children of Ammon and besieged Rabba: **but David remained in Jerusalem**. In the meantime, it happened that David arose from his bed after noon and walked upon the roof of the king's house, and he saw from the roof of his

house a woman washing herself over against him, and the woman was very beautiful. And the king sent and inquired who the woman was. And it was told him that she was Bathsabee, the daughter of Eliam, the wife of Urias the Hethite."

- 2 Kings 11: 1-3

David's attention turned away from doing God's will. His concupiscence tempted him to lust after the wife of one of his mighty men. That mighty man was Urias the Hethite, and his wife was Bathsabee. David committed adultery with Bathsabee, who conceived a son. To cover up his sin, he called Urias back from the battlefront. David wanted Urias to go home and be intimate with his wife, Bathsabee, to cover up her conception with David. However, Urias did not want to go home to the comforts of a wife; he wanted to remain diligent and focused on his role as a soldier. David could not get Urias to swerve from his dedication and duty.

David, therefore, sent Urias back to the battlefront with a letter to the army commander, Joab. Urias did not open the sealed letter but handed it to Joab. He read the letter from David, instructing him to put Urias on the front line and then have the army pull back. In this way, David killed one of his mighty men in order to cover up his sin and also so that he could take Bathsabee for his own.

"And when the morning was come, David wrote a letter to Joab: and sent it by the hand of Urias, writing in the letter: Set ye Urias in the front of the battle, where the fight is strongest: and leave ye him, that he may be wounded and die."

- 2 Kings 11: 14-15

Just as King David remained in Jerusalem towards the end of his war campaigns, so did the kings of Europe stop going on Crusade by the end of the thirteenth century. The First Crusade featured the nobles of Europe coming together to capture Jerusalem in 1099. The Third Crusade saw King Richard the Lionheart, King Philip II of France, and King Frederick I of Germany fight against Muslim forces in the Holy Land in 1192. St. King

Louis IX of France and King Edward I of England went on the Ninth Crusade, which ended in 1272. After the Ninth Crusade, the kings and nobles of Europe no longer went on Crusade. The military orders, such as Knights Templar, were stationed around the Mediterranean, desiring to launch another Crusade to re-take Jerusalem again.

At this time, in the late 1200s and early 1300s, the ruthless and covetous King Philip IV reigned in France. His desire for money, land, and power broke away from the limits imposed by Catholic piety and deference to the Church. He is infamous for kidnapping and abusing Pope Boniface VIII. Philip IV owed a large sum of money to the Knights Templar[22], which he borrowed to fund wars, financial maneuvers and other ambitions. The Knights Templar were very wealthy after having accumulated lands and tributes from pious Christian donors throughout the crusading years. They did not indulge in their wealth but remained vigilant and disciplined, just like Urias did not indulge in the pleasures of his wife and household.

In 1296, Jacques DeMolay, the Grand Master of the Knights Templar, was out in the field with his fighting knights. He was called back from the crusading effort by Pope Clement V in 1307. This was the time of the Avignon Papacy. Pope Clement V was considered to be highly influenced by King Philip IV[23]. Thus, we have a situation much like that of King David, Urias, and Bathsabee. Like King David, King Philip IV of France was covetous of what belonged to one of his mighty men. David was covetous of Bathsabee, and King Philip was covetous of the money and lands of the Knights Templar. Urias was called back from the war front just like Grand Master Jacques DeMolay was called back from the war front.

The pope and King Philip IV wanted to know if Jacques DeMolay would agree to a merger of his order, the Knights Templar, with another order, the Knights Hospitaller. This merger would place Philip IV as the new head of the merged organization.[24] This would have effectively wiped out Philip's debts to the Templars and given him access to their money and land. The Knights were wealthy but did not enjoy their wealth; they lived austerely, so they could stay sharp and focused on the conquest of the Holy Land for Christ and His Church. Jacques DeMolay politely rejected the proposition of a merger for fear that it would weaken his order.

The Templar's wealth is similar to Urias' wife. David wanted to find a way to cover his sin with Bathsabee and her conception of a child. King Philip IV wanted to find a way to erase his debts to the Templars. Urias was zealous for his duty as a soldier and inadvertently foiled David's plan by refusing to go home to his wife, Bathsabee. Likewise, in refusing to merge the Templars and Hospitallers, Jacques DeMolay, who was similarly zealous in carrying on the Crusades, foiled King Philip's plan to erase his debts to the Templars and gain access to their assets. David responded by having Urias killed, and King Phillip IV acted in a likewise despicable manner.

Philip IV decided to eradicate the Knights Templar and take their money by force. He sent out sealed letters to his men in France, with orders to open them on a specified day.[25] On October 13, 1307, the king's men opened the letters and immediately carried out the arrest of all the Templar Knights in France. They made confessions under torture, saying that they committed outrageous acts of immorality and blasphemy. The pope, based on these confessions, ended the order of the Knights Templar.[k] King Philip IV kept the monetary assets of the Templars. Jacques DeMolay was burnt at the stake in Paris in 1314, all the while declaring his innocence before God and retracting the confession he made under torture.[26]

As an end note, Nathan, the prophet, confronted David over this great sin. David had murdered one of his mighty men and taken his wife. Similarly, this destruction of the Knights Templar took place in the time and context of the Avignon Papacy, in which the popes were living in France, but belonged in Rome. Just as Nathan confronted King David and brought him out of his sinful mindset, so too did St. Catherine of Sienna humbly confront and beg the Avignon popes to return to their rightful place in Rome, ending the scandal of the Avignon Papacy.

---

k   The Knights Templar were disbanded and charged with terrible crimes by Pope Clement V's bull, *Vox in Excelso*, in 1312. I do not question the pope's authority or decision. I simply observe the similarities between the Templars and Urias, without making claims concerning the Templars' innocence or guilt.

Two (Then Three) Kings in Israel at the Same Time

ABSALOM CLAIMS DAVID'S THRONE, CONFUSING ALL OF ISRAEL AND
THE PAPAL SCHISM CONFUSES CHRISTENDOM

After David repented of his sin with Bathsabee, God told him that, as a punishment, the sword would never leave his house.

> "Why therefore hast thou despised the word of the Lord, to do evil in my sight? Thou hast killed Urias the Hethite with the sword, and hast taken his wife to be thy wife, and hast slain him with the sword of the children of Ammon. Therefore the sword shall never depart from thy house, because thou hast despised me, and hast taken the wife of Urias the Hethite to be thy wife. Thus saith the Lord: Behold, I will raise up evil against thee out of thy own house..."
>
> - 2 Kings 12: 9-11

This was fulfilled when the sons of King David, who were now coming of age, fought each other for power. It started with the violation of David's daughter Thamar by David's son, Amnon. David punished Amnon but did not have him killed. This angered Thamar's brother, Absalom, who felt that David was lenient with Amnon. (Amnon was from a different mother than Thamar and Absalom.) Absalom then killed Amnon for this foul act and to avenge the shame of his sister.[1] Soon after, Absalom challenged David and claimed the throne of Israel even though David was still living.

In the late 1300s, France and England were maturing and becoming self-aware of their identities as nation-states.[27] In 1337, they were plunged into the Hundred Years War. Because the popes resided in Avignon, the Church appeared to favor the kingdom of France over all Her other "children". However, when the King of England invaded and ravaged France, Pope Benedict XII was unable to stop the attack on France.[28] Thus, both France and England felt slighted by the papacy for different reasons.

---

1   The events of Amnon, Thamar and Absalom are found in 2 Kings 13.

Just as Amnon violated his half-sister Thamar, so too did the king of England ravage the kingdom of France. The monarchies of England and France were ancestrally related. In 1328, the French King Charles IV died without a male heir. In 1316, France had established a law that women could not claim the throne.[29] Edward III was related to the French King Charles IV because Edward's mother, Isabella, was his sister. Therefore, King Edward III of England sought to claim the French throne for himself.[30] This degree of relation between the French and English monarchies is like the relationship between Amnon and Thamar, who were half brother and sister.

On June 22, 1340, England launched an invasion of France. The English, sailing into the English Channel, cleverly deceived the French by feigning retreat.[m] When they struck, it was a near-decisive blow, severely damaging the French navy. In 1346, the English continued their onslaught, wreaking havoc in battle after battle across France.

The papacy, which was in Avignon at the time, was perceived as weak and unable to properly broker peace between the two "children" of the Church. Like King David, who appeared weak in his response to Thamar's violation, the papacy was unable to stop the invasion of France[28]. Also, of noteworthiness is the animosity that persisted between France and England after the Hundred Years War[31], similar to the hatred that Amnon had for Thamar after he violated her.

> "But he would not hearken to her prayers, but being stronger overpowered her and lay with her. Then Amnon hated her with an exceeding great hatred: so that the hatred wherewith he hated her was greater than the love with which he had loved her before, And Amnon said to her: Arise, and get thee gone."
>
> - 2 Kings 13: 14-15

St. Joan of Arc, a central figure in the Hundred Years War, led the French forces to victory against the English. However, she was eventually betrayed and captured. During her notorious trial, the English attempted to condemn

---

m   Similar to the feigning of retreat by the English, Amnon pretended to be sick in bed in order to lure Thamar close to him. See 2 Kings 13:6-10.

her on charges of heresy. Her unwavering witness to the Truths of the Faith prevented this outcome. Instead, they placed St. Joan in a men's prison, subtly threatening her with the forced physical violation of her virginity.[n] She pleaded to be transferred to a women's prison, as was her right. To protect herself, she wore men's clothing, but this act led to accusations of grave misconduct against her. The English forced her into an impossible situation: either break her will through physical violation or condemn her for her attire.[32] Remarkably, she was threatened with the same fate that was suffered by Thamar at the hands of Amnon.

Two Kings In Israel

Pope Gregory XI returned to Rome in 1376, ending the Avignon Papacy. A group of French cardinals regretted their election of Pope Urban VI in 1378, so they returned to France and "elected" an antipope, Clement VII, who would reside in Avignon again. Thus, there were two papal claimants: one true pope in Rome and an antipope in Avignon. Clement VII persuaded half of Christendom that he was the real pope.[33] Similarly, Absalom was recognized by the Israelites in Jerusalem and most of the army as the rightful king, after having usurped the throne from his father David.

Absalom took over King David's harem and had relations with David's concubines.[o] In like manner, the antipopes of Avignon would assume command of papal assets. Both antipope Clement VII and antipope John XXIII controlled significant portions of the Papal States, collected revenues that belonged to Rome and otherwise assumed papal actions that were the purview of the real pope only.

---

n   While I do not assert that St. Joan of Arc suffered actual physical violation, I acknowledge that such a threat loomed over her. St. Joan is an intrinsic and important figure in the Hundred Years War, which already demonstrates parallels with the story of Amnon and Thamar. The mere mention of violation in St. Joan's narrative weaves yet another strand connecting her to this Old Testament story.

o   This occurs in 2 Kings 16: 21 – 22. Absalom went into David's concubines in a tent visible to the public. This fulfills God's promise to David concerning his punishment spoken by Nathan the prophet: "I will take thy wives before thy eyes and give them to thy neighbour, and he shall lie with thy wives in the sight of this sun"- 2 Kings 12: 11.

The concubines of David were a type or a figure for these assets of the pope. The concubines produced offspring for David, and the papal lands produced wealth and armies. By controlling papal assets, it lent credibility to their papal claims. By administering over them, it made them de facto rulers. By comparison, Absalom's actions with David's concubines also gave him an air of de facto legitimacy.

The Papal Schism persisted for decades. In the end, there was even a third papal claimant who lived in Pisa, Italy. Similarly, the rebellion of Absalom was a major ordeal in King David's life. It took a major effort for King David to regain the throne from Absalom. Christendom was divided and confused in their allegiance, not knowing who the true pope was, just as Israel was likewise misguided in their allegiance between David and Absalom.

> "And there came a messenger to David, saying: All Israel with their whole heart followeth Absalom."
>
> 2 Kings 15 : 13

Absalom's rebellion caused many in Israel to have a diminished opinion of the Davidic dynasty. Likewise, the Avignon Papacy and the Papal Schism damaged the papacy's reputation in the hearts and minds of Catholics.

The End of Wars and Start of Great Wealth

King David's Reign Ends, Giving Way to King Solomon; the Middle Ages Come to an End and the Renaissance Begins

Old Testament	New Testament
David faced his first real threat to his dynasty, the rebellion of Seba.	The rebellion of Jan Hus was the first real threat to a united Christendom.
Saul's descendants were handed over by David, except for one.	The definitive end of the Byzantine Empire except for one tiny province.

68

The end of David's reign and the start of King Solomon's reign.	The end of the Middle Ages and the start of the Renaissance.

First Big Threat To The Unity Of The Kingdom

The rebellion of Absalom confused the entire nation of Israel, as they did not know who the real king was. This scandal and that of David and Bathsabee caused many in Israel to have a lower opinion of the Davidic dynasty. Not only did they lose faith in King David personally, but they also lost faith in the right of David and his heirs to rule them.

A man named Seba, who was not of the tribe of Juda, blew a trumpet and said that Israel had no part in the kingship of David. He told all of Israel to return to their dwellings and to stop following David. Most of the tribes of Israel listened to Seba. However, the men of Juda still followed David as their king.

> "And there happened to be there a man of Belial, whose name was Seba, the son of Bochri, a man of Jemini: and he sounded the trumpet, and said: We have no part in David, nor inheritance in the son of Isai: return to thy dwellings, O Israel. And all Israel departed from David, and followed Seba the son of Bochri: but the men of Juda stuck to their king from the Jordan unto Jerusalem."

\- 2 Kings 20: 1-2

King David sent soldiers after Seba to stop him from leading a rebellion. However, David did not send his trusted general Joab to lead the forces but instead gave command of his troops to another man, named Amasa. David's choice of sending this new commander instead of his general, Joab, stems from the intuition that Joab was growing increasingly manipulative and powerful. It was Joab who killed Abner against David's wishes and killed Absalom against David's explicit instructions. He later commanded King David to stop mourning for Absalom.[p] In the minds of Israel, Joab appeared

---

p   2 Kings 19: 5- 7, Joab gives David a veiled threat and in so doing, demonstrates his growing power as either a kingmaker or a direct rival to David's rule.

solid and powerful. By contrast, David appeared weak due to his sin and the rebellion of his son, Absalom.

The Avignon Papacy and the Papal Schism (1378-1417) caused confusion throughout Christendom. During the Papal Schism, Christians of goodwill were divided in their allegiances between the two papal claimants. The heresy of Conciliarism arose from this confusion, teaching that a Church council had authority over the pope or that the pope could even be deposed by such a council. The papacy appeared weak enough for the proposition of the heresy of Conciliarism to have gained traction in such a time as the Middle Ages.

During this time Jan Hus was a Catholic priest and professor at the Charles University of Prague. In 1408, he began teaching that the pope was not the head of the Church and that the Bible had authority over Church teaching.[q] Jan Hus was a follower of John Wycliffe[34], who in 1376 started a theological rebellion in England. He taught that the Avignon Papacy constituted the reign of antichrist and then denied the temporal authority of the papacy. Pope Gregory XI issued multiple papal bulls condemning the teachings of Wycliffe in 1377.[35] The Avignon Papacy and the Papal Schism eroded the papacy's credibility among certain Christians, who followed heretics like Wycliffe and Hus, just as David's scandals weakened his perceived authority over Israel, causing many to follow Seba.

In the countryside of Bohemia, Jan Hus gathered a large following. He became a symbol of Bohemian national identity. This was important to the Bohemians because they were ruled over mainly by ethnic Germans, associated with the holy roman emperor.

Jan Hus and his heretical teachings were tolerated at the university for a time until the Church officially condemned the writings of John Wycliffe. Wycliffe's writings were ordered to be burned. Nonetheless, Jan Hus only intensified his public and heretical teaching.

---

q   Later, Luther adopted this false dichotomy that attempted to detach the Bible from Church authority, then to place the Bible over Church authority.

At that time, the Papal Schism was causing much division in Europe. The Bohemian King Wenceslaus IV was afraid that Pope Gregory XII in Rome would block his attempt at being crowned the holy roman emperor. In anticipation of this, King Wenceslaus IV ordered all the Bohemian clergy to stay neutral in the Papal Schism.[36] However, the clergy sided with Rome instead of Avignon, and only the university staff, including Jan Hus, remained neutral. Then, King Wenceslaus' brother, Sigismund, gained the Bohemian crown by supporting an uprising against Wenceslaus. Sigismund made himself the leader in the effort to bring down Jan Hus and had him burned at the stake for heresy at the Council of Constance in 1415.[37] Sigismund likely did this to strengthen his position and influence in the Church and among other European monarchs, as well as from a desire to stamp out heresy in his realm.

Returning to the Old Testament, Joab gained control of David's forces and led the campaign to put down Seba's revolt. Then Joab went on to kill David's choice of commander, Amasa. This gave David no practical way of separating from Joab, since David had need of a proven commander. Similarly, Sigismund led the campaign to stop Jan Hus' rebellion by unseating his brother Wenceslaus. Since the Jan Hus affair was of such a high profile in Europe, and since Jan Hus was attacking the institution of the papacy directly, then if Sigismund could be seen as the leader in the fight against Jan Hus and the Hussites, it would significantly bolster his efforts to be crowned holy roman emperor. Likewise, because Seba's revolt against David was so dire, if Joab could lead the campaign against Seba, he would gain public honor and restore his position as leader of King David's army.

In the Old Testament, what followed was that Seba and his forces retreated to a walled city. Joab and his army approached the city. The inhabitants of the city did not want to be destroyed simply because Seba was taking refuge there. The city's people gladly gave up Seba, wanting to stay loyal to King David. They did not want any trouble and just wanted to be left in peace. The city responded by beheading Seba and throwing his head over the wall towards Joab. Remarkably, this city was also home to an academy or an institution of learning, as per the footnotes from the Douay-Rheims Bible for verse 19 (see below):

"Am not I she that answer truth in Israel, and thou seekest to destroy the city, and to overthrow a mother in Israel? Why wilt thou throw down the inheritance of the Lord? And Joab answering said: God forbid, God forbid that I should, I do not throw down, nor destroy."

- 2 Kings 20: 19-20

Douay-Rheims footnote

"Ver. 19. <u>Truth</u>. Hebrew, "I am peaceable, faithful in Israel." (Haydock) --- I am one of the cities most inclined to peace, and to the king's service, noted for lessons of loyalty. (Calmet) --- **Probably there was an academy here.**"

Similarly, the university in Prague, where Jan Hus was a professor, was ordered by the Holy See to put down the Hussites. All copies of Wycliffe's writings were burned. The Hussites responded by burning a papal bull, openly defying papal authority. The university responded by beheading three Hussites for their open opposition.[38] The university did not want any trouble, willingly beheading the followers of Jan Hus.

As a final note and a foreshadowing of a future rebellion, I would like to offer a last set of parallels between Jan Hus and Seba.

Seba's rebellion was quelled when his head was severed and cast over the city walls. However, the quelling of Seba's revolt did not erase the reasons that had led the tribes of Israel to follow him in the first place. The motivations that had sparked their rebellion against their king persisted. Subsequently, after Solomon's death, these tribes rallied behind a new leader, Jeroboam. This time, their revolt was not suppressed but was actualized. The rebellion of Seba paved the way for the later successful rebellion led by Jeroboam.

In 1415, Jan Hus was presented to the Council of Constance by Sigismund and was subsequently executed. Despite the failure of Hus' rebellion, the spirit of dissent against the papacy and the Holy Roman Empire remained alive among many Bohemians. A small faction even maintained their loyalty to Hus' cause for the next century. About a hundred years later, a revolt echoing Hus' rebellion emerged, led by Martin Luther. This time, the revolt succeeded, with Luther affirming, "Ja, ich bin ein Hussite" ("Yes, I am a Hussite").[r]

We will see the amazing parallels between Jeroboam and Martin Luther in Period 5.

The Final Days Of The First King's Descendants

After the deaths of King Saul and Jonathan in the Battle of Gilboa and the death of Saul's son Isboseth, the remnants of Saul's lineage were sparse, dispersed, and lacked political influence. The concluding part of 2 Kings documents the demise of the last of Saul's descendants.

In 2 Kings 21, Israel was hit by a famine, which David learned from God was due to Saul's transgressions against the Gabaonites. To redress their grievances, David approached the Gabaonites, who demanded the execution of Saul's descendants. David complied, but spared Mephibosheth, Jonathan's lame son. Mephibosheth was welcomed into David's court and dined at his table for the remainder of his life.[s]

The Battle of Manzikert in 1071 dealt a significant blow to the Byzantine Empire, robbing the empire of its territorial heartland, Anatolia. Growth was no longer a realistic goal. Its definitive end occurred with the fall of Constantinople in 1453. Following this event, the only remaining province of the Byzantine Empire was a small region known as Morea, situated on the Peloponnese Islands off the coast of Greece.

When the Ottoman Turks laid siege to Constantinople in 1453, the Holy Roman Empire did not intervene with military aid or offer any other substantial measures to prevent its demise.[39][t] However, the ruler of Morea,

---

r   Luther made this audacious claim at the Leipzig disputation of 1519.

s   The biblical passages necessary to demonstrate this are lengthy and therefore not included in the text of this book. See 2 Kings 21: 1 – 7.

t   After centuries of schism, the Christian West was not inclined to aid the Byzantine Empire without their conversion and submission to the pope. Thus, the Christian West effectively handed the Byzantines over to the Ottomans for their execution.

the remaining byzantine province on the Peloponnese Islands, was rescued and transported to Rome.[40] There, he lived under the pope's protection until his death. This situation mirrors the biblical account of Mephibosheth, Saul's lame grandson who was spared and welcomed by David.

Going back to the story of the execution of Saul's descendants by the Gabaonites in the Old Testament, Respha, Saul's former concubine, stood by his dying descendants, offering solace during their final hours. She gave them water and shielded them from scavenging birds and wild creatures while they were bound to poles, exposed to the relentless sun, until their death.

> "And Respha the daughter of Aia took haircloth, and spread it under her upon the rock from the beginning of the harvest, till water dropped upon them out of heaven: and suffered neither the birds to tear them by day, nor the beasts by night."
>
> - 2 Kings 21: 10

Likewise, the dying city of Constantinople got some relief and aid from Italian merchant states. The Venetians made a lot of money over the centuries by trading with the Byzantine Empire. In this way, they were like the concubine of King Saul, Respha. Other Italians sent food and various provisions. Archers and an elite unit of soldiers were also sent, specializing in defending the walls of Constantinople from enemy attack.[41] Other small, token relief efforts were made.

The Venetian archers picking attackers off the walls of Constantinople is like Respha preventing the birds of prey from picking at the dying descendants of King Saul. She gave them water just as the Venetians sent food and supplies to the dying city.

Finally, and notably, there is a unique and intriguing connection between the fall of Constantinople, the death of Saul's descendants, and a full moon.

The death of Saul's descendants occurred during harvest time. In ancient Israel, the harvest was always done during the full moon so the harvesters could work into the night. Therefore, a full moon was in the sky during the death of Saul's descendants.

> "And gave them into the hands of the Gabaonites: and they crucified them on a hill before the Lord: and these seven died together **in the first days of the harvest** when the barley began to be reaped."
>
> - 2 Kings 21: 9

There was an ancient byzantine prophecy, supposedly spoken by Constantine himself, that said the fall of Constantinople would coincide with a great sign of the full moon[42]. In May 1453, only days before the city's fall, the moon rose as a crescent when it should have been full. No clouds were in the sky, and the air was crystal clear. Then, to the amazement of the Muslim Turks and the Byzantines, the moon turned from a crescent to a full moon within a few hours. This was a great sign, and it fulfilled the ancient prophecy about the fall of this great city. This sign is attributed to a partial lunar eclipse one week before Constantinople fell to the Turks.[43]

Time Of Peace, Wealth, Construction And Corruption

After the long reign of King David, whose story spanned the first and second books of Kings, his son Solomon was crowned king. King Solomon began his reign desiring to rule Israel with wisdom and righteousness. God gave him the unique gifts of incomparable wisdom and wealth.

> "And the Lord said to Solomon: Because thou hast asked this thing, and hast not asked for thyself long life or riches, nor the lives of thy enemies, but hast asked for thyself wisdom to discern judgment, Behold I have done for thee according to thy words, and have given thee a wise and understanding heart, insomuch that there hath been no one like thee before thee, nor shall arise after thee. Yea and the things also which thou didst not ask, I have given thee: to wit riches and glory, as that no one hath been like thee among the kings in all days heretofore. And if thou wilt walk in my ways, and keep

my precepts, and my commandments, as thy father walked,
I will lengthen thy days."

- 3 Kings 3: 11-15

King Solomon's reign is remarkably similar to the Renaissance. The Old
Testament, with verbose stories and rich character development, clearly
distinguishes between the qualities of King David and King Solomon.
Likewise in Church history, there is a marked difference in character
between the Middle Ages and the Renaissance. The Middle Ages are largely
comparable to King David's reign, while the end of the Middle Ages and the
beginning of the Renaissance is like the transition from David to Solomon's
reign in the Old Testament. Solomon's reign was characterized by immense
wealth, beauty, grandiose and stunning architecture, art, wisdom, relative
peace, expansion of influence, and corruption: the same defining
characteristics as the Renaissance.

It's important to remember that King Solomon broke the law of Moses by
marrying not one, but potentially hundreds of idol worshiping pagan
women.[u] These pagan wives of Solomon caused him to make sacrifices to
their false gods, which ultimately led to his downfall and the division of his
kingdom after his death. Despite his religious corruption, Solomon still ruled
his kingdom with unprecedented wisdom. The crowning achievement of
Kind Solomon was undoubtedly the construction of the Temple, which
defined the Israelites throughout the rest of their history.

Now consider the Renaissance and its striking similarities to Solomon's
reign. During this transformative period, the Medici family, hailing from
Italy, played a pivotal role. Alongside other affluent banking dynasties, the
Medicis laid the groundwork for the amassing of immense wealth across
Christendom. Their patronage extended to artists—masters like
Michelangelo, Raphael, and Leonardo da Vinci—who, under their
sponsorship, crafted masterpieces that continue to captivate us today.

In the realm of architecture, the Renaissance stands as an unparalleled
era. In Florence, Filippo Brunelleschi achieved the seemingly impossible with

---

u   See 3 Kings 11: 1-5

his magnificent dome atop the Church of Santa Maria del Fiore in Florence. It was during the Renaissance and, in particular, the Renaissance Papacy (the popes from 1417 to 1565), such as Pope Alexander VI and Pope Innocent VIII that Rome was built up to be a magnificent city. But the crown jewel and the most significant building project in all of Christendom was the construction of St. Peter's Basilica, starting in 1506. St. Peter's Basilica could easily be described as the most beautiful building in the world. Upon completion, it instantly became an icon of Catholic identity. St. Peter's Basilica and the Vatican would be the focal point for many upcoming events in Catholic history, just as the Temple was to Israel in the Old Testament.

Additionally, just like the reign of King Solomon, the Renaissance saw great leaps in the sciences, matching the wisdom of King Solomon's reign. The Holy Roman Empire and the Papal States swelled to their largest size during the Renaissance[44], just as the Kingdom of Israel grew to its largest size under the reign of Solomon.[v] However, the Renaissance departed from the piety of the Middle Ages. During this time, Christendom was tainted, and one may even say infected, with moral and spiritual corruption through the introduction of humanistic, pagan "wisdom" from the past.

The Renaissance was launched, in part, by the rediscovery of ancient pagan Roman and Greek manuscripts.[45] The rediscovery of ancient pagan "wisdom" led to the introduction of humanism into the heart of Christendom. This corruption manifested in the personal immorality of many of the Renaissance popes. Paintings by Renaissance artists depicted nude or otherwise suggestive subjects. Many paintings had pagan gods or goddesses as their themes. Alchemy and astrology grew in popularity and practice. Queen Catherine de Medici of France devised plays and musical events depicting ancient Roman and Greek gods, often drawing morals and lessons from their mythical stories. She was famous for sponsoring the Ballet Comique de la Reine and the Festival of Fontainebleau, both of which fit the above description.

There are also many minor parallels between events in the Renaissance and the reign of King Solomon. Let's examine some of them briefly.

---

v   3 Kings 4: 20-21

During the Renaissance, Spain sailed across the Atlantic and discovered gold in South America, bringing riches and gold back to Europe. Similarly, King Solomon commissioned exploration vessels that sailed to the mysterious land of Ophir and brought back large amounts of gold.

> "And King Solomon made a fleet in Asiongaber, which is by Ailath on the shore of the Red Sea in the land of Edom. And Hiram sent his servants in the fleet, sailors that knew the sea, with the servants of Solomon. And they came to Ophir and brought from thence to King Solomon four hundred and twenty talents of gold."
>
> - 3 Kings 9: 26-28

Another striking parallel between the Renaissance and the reign of King Solomon is the famous story of his wisdom in which he settled the argument of two women, both claiming to be the mother of the same infant. King Solomon threatened to split the child in half. He did this to reveal which was the real mother by seeing which woman expressed selfless concern.[w]

Likewise, after Christopher Columbus's exploration in 1492, the New World became a coveted prize for Portugal and Spain. They both started to argue about who could claim the lands in the New World as their own. Like the two women who took their disagreement to Solomon to render his judgment, so too did Portugal and Spain take their disagreement to Pope Alexander VI that he would render his judgment. He resolved the issue by splitting the world in two. He drew a line down the middle of the known world. All the land west of the line would be for Spain, and all of the land east would be for Portugal. This is known as the Treaty of Tordesillas of 1494.[46]

Summary of Period 4

We have now come to the end of this time period. In the Old Testament, we started with King Saul's rise and then David's anointing. Saul and David

---

w   3 Kings 3: 16-28

had a complex relationship, with Saul being jealous and acting with animosity towards David. In Church history, the Byzantine Empire was the first Christian empire to receive its crowns from the Church. Because of the Byzantine Empire's lack of fidelity, the pope crowned a new emperor, Charlemagne, even when a byzantine emperor reigned in Constantinople. The Holy Roman Empire of Charlemagne and his descendants had a complex relationship with the Byzantine Empire, who were threatened by its growing success and popularity. There was mistrust and betrayal of the Crusaders by the Byzantine Empire, just as King Saul acted towards David.

Saul was killed in battle, and Saul's descendants, who were weak, lost their throne to David. Likewise, the Byzantines were dealt a crushing blow at the Battle of Manzikert in 1071, which marked the beginning of the end for the Byzantine Empire. In 1204, the Crusaders established a Latin kingdom in Constantinople.

David allowed Saul's scattered descendants to live in Israel for a time until he delivered them to their execution at the hands of the Gabaonites. Similarly, the Christian West allowed the weakened and scattered territories of the Byzantine Empire to live on, even after the Schism of 1054 and despite all the animosity accumulated during the Crusades. However, the Christian West did not intervene to stop the siege and conquest of Constantinople in 1453 at the hands of the Ottoman Turks.

David and his mighty men fought wars to secure the borders of Israel, while the Crusades fought back the enemies of Christendom. David betrayed his mighty warrior, Urias, to take his wife Bathsabee, just as King Philip IV betrayed the Knights Templar to take their wealth and lands. David's son Absalom then claimed the throne of David, and Israel did not know who was the real king. Similarly, the Papal Schism began after the Avignon Papacy and all of Christendom did not know who the real pope was, the one in Rome or the one in Avignon.

David regained his throne only to be confronted with the rebellion of Seba. In Church history, near the end of the Papal Schism, the pope and the Holy Roman Empire faced the rebellion of Jan Hus. David's son, Solomon, took the throne after his death. Solomon's reign was nearly identical to the Renaissance, which followed the Middle Ages.

Now, let us move on to the next time period[x] in which an earth-shattering revolt manages to split the kingdom in two. This revolt (of Jeroboam in the Old Testament and Martin Luther in Church history) is strikingly similar to the failed revolts of Seba and Jan Hus respectively. The glory days of Solomon and the magnificent period of the Renaissance wane and dim. Now the bill comes due for all the luxuries and superfluous living. Brutal and devastating civil war is on the horizon. Worse still is that millions of God's people will be ripped away from the covenant and led into apostasy.

---

[x] Before we move on, I would like to include some miscellaneous parallels for this time period. St. Teresa of Ávila was known for her ecstasies of love for God. Her heart was mystically pierced. At a cursory glance, this seems to resonate with the Canticle of Solomon, filled with love language. St. Teresa of Ávila lived at the end of the Renaissance, and King Solomon is credited with writing the Canticle of Solomon. Another parallel of interest is the book of Ecclesiastes, also attributed to King Solomon. The book starts with the famous line "vanity of vanities, and all is vanity". In the Douay-Rheims Bible, the heading for chapter 2 is entitled "The vanity of pleasures, riches, and worldly labours". During the latter stages of the Renaissance, a priest named Savonarola on February 7, 1497, held the "Bonfire of the Vanities". Savonarola preached against the excesses of the Renaissance, convincing many Florentines to burn their vanities. A notable participant at that bonfire was Italian Renaissance painter Botticelli, who threw some of his immodest and pagan works into the fire.

80

Period 5
Revolt and Separation

God's people are split, and the north rebels against the holy city and God given authority. The rebels change their religion and forget their origins.

OLD TESTAMENT: Books of 3 Kings, 4 Kings, and Tobias

The reign of King Solomon was marked by the building of the Temple in Jerusalem, wisdom, beauty, wealth, but also moral and religious corruption. Solomon raised taxes to pay for the construction of the Temple and also for his opulent lifestyle. As a member of the tribe of Juda, which encompassed Jerusalem, Solomon's tax policies disproportionately favored his own people. Meanwhile, the northern tribes of Israel, burdened by these taxes, began questioning the fairness of this system.

Upon Solomon's death, a man named Jeroboam led a revolt of the ten northern tribes. He approached King Roboam (Solomon's son) with an ultimatum. Either King Roboam would lessen the taxes, or the ten northern tribes would revolt. The revolt of Jeroboam and the ten northern tribes was a reawakening of the sentiments and protests from the failed revolt of Seba during the last years of King David's reign. This time, the tribes of Israel were more upset and more primed for a revolt than they had been under Seba. Times had changed.

We will discuss the revolt of Jeroboam in detail and also its aftermath. In summary, however, the revolt of Jeroboam set up a new political and religious system for the ten northern tribes. They broke with the Mosaic Law, the Temple sacrifice and the Davidic kingdom. But the rebellion in the north did not stop with Jeroboam. Someone overthrew him, and in turn, that man was overthrown in a cycle of revolt. The ten northern tribes eventually were conquered and assimilated by the Assyrians. The two southern tribes kept the Law of Moses, at least officially. The Davidic kingdom continued to rule over the two southern tribes, which became known as the Kingdom of Juda, to distinguish itself from the ten northern tribes who retained the name Israel.

Ultimately, the Babylonians laid waste to Jerusalem, bringing an end to the Davidic dynasty's reign over Juda. They then forcibly exiled the Jews to Babylon. This action by the Babylonians will mark the end of Period 5 and will commence Period 6.

CHURCH HISTORY: Approximately 1500[AD] to 1800[AD]

The Renaissance was marked by the building of St. Peter's Basilica in Rome, as well as invention, beauty, wealth, and the introduction of the corrupting forces of classical humanism into Christendom. Pope Leo X issued indulgences to fund the construction of St. Peter's Basilica and also to support his opulent lifestyle. Just like the excessive taxes levied by Solomon, this program of funding with indulgences upset many. Taxes are a legitimate source of funding, and likewise, indulgences can be granted in exchange for a financial contribution, as was done during the crusading years. However, the method and extent of Pope Leo X's program for issuing indulgences[a] was likely an abuse, just as King Solomon's taxes were abusive.[b] The funding obtained from indulgences in Germany and Bohemia disproportionately benefited Rome and Italians connected with the Holy See.

A German monk, Martin Luther, objected to using indulgences to fund Rome's projects and lifestyles. He infamously nailed his *95 Theses* to the church door in Wittenberg, Germany. Luther's revolt mirrored in many ways the failed revolt of Jan Hus only decades before. Martin Luther would later exclaim, "Ich bin ein Hussite" (I am a Hussite).

We will discuss the revolt of Luther and its aftermath in detail. In summary, however, Luther's revolt established a new political and religious system for northern Europe. It broke with the Catholic Faith and abandoned the Holy Mass. But the rebellion in the north did not stop with Luther.

---

a   The Council of Trent was convened in response to the Protestant Revolt. Trent reaffirmed the practice of granting indulgences but condemned any abusive practice in this regard. See the Council of Trent, 25th session, 3rd decree.

b   3 Kings 12: 4

Luther's example of rebellion inspired others to rebel against him. Protestantism fractured and split until it was eventually absorbed into the "Age of Enlightenment" and then into mainstream secularism.

The kingdoms in southern Europe kept the Catholic Faith. Allegiance to the papacy and the reign of the Holy Roman Empire and other Catholic monarchies continued. Before Luther's revolt, Europe generally was referred to as "Christendom". However, after Luther, the Protestants to the north retained the name "Christian," so the southern European countries adopted the identity "Roman Catholic" to differentiate themselves from the Protestants. The first known use of the word "Catholic" was by St. Ignatius of Antioch in the first century. It was not widely used as an identification until the Protestant Revolt. Before Luther, the name "Christian" and "Christendom" were widely used instead of the terms "Roman Catholic" and "Roman Catholicism".[47]

Eventually, the French Revolution ended the French Catholic monarchy in 1793 (except for a brief and weakened period of the *citizen-kings*) and also ended the Holy Roman Empire in 1806. The French Revolution spread secular republics and atheism across Europe. Catholics found themselves living in exile in their own lands, as they no longer were living under Catholic rulers and Catholic laws. The Papal States were taken from the Holy See in 1870, and the popes referred to themselves as *prisoners in the Vatican*. The French Revolution and its aftermath will be covered in Period 6.

Overview of Period 5

Let's look at an overview of Period 5 in the following chart. Afterward, we'll examine the parallels in more detail. They are fascinating, especially those between Jeroboam and Luther.

Old Testament	New Testament
Jeroboam revolted and led northern Israel into apostasy.	Luther revolted and led northern Christendom into apostasy.

Baasa and Amri led revolts, unseating Jeroboam.	Zwingli and Calvin dissented from Luther.
Civil war ensued between the ten northern tribes and the southern Kingdom of Juda.	The Wars of Religion ensued between the Protestant north and the Catholic south.
The Assyrian Empire took advantage of a fractured Israel. It grew in power, eventually swallowing up the ten northern tribes.	The Ottoman Empire took advantage of a fractured Christendom. It grew and eventually swallowed up much of Eastern Europe.
Isaias had his lips purified with a hot coal to prepare him for his role as prophet.	St. Margaret Mary had her heart purified with divine fire to prepare her to be the Apostle of the Sacred Heart.
Jeremias was suppressed and imprisoned by the king of Jerusalem. He was seen as a threat to the kingdom.	European kings suppressed and imprisoned the Jesuits who were seen as threats to their authority and interests.
The angel saved Jerusalem from invasion and destruction by the Assyrians.	The angel-winged Hussars saved Vienna from invasion and destruction by the Ottoman Turks.

The Rebel Leader that Splits God's People in Two
Jeroboam and Martin Luther

The unity and strength of Israel won by King David and celebrated by King Solomon were destroyed by the revolt of Jeroboam. Likewise, in Church history, the Middle Ages forged Christendom politically under the Holy Roman Empire and other Catholic kingdoms. Intellectually and spiritually, Christendom matured and developed through the examples and writings of great saints like St. Thomas Aquinas, St. Dominic, St. Francis of Assisi and countless others. Militarily, Christendom was united and focused towards a common cause during the Crusades. During the Renaissance,

Christendom enjoyed the material benefits that flowed from the great struggles and victories of the Middle Ages. However, the corruption of the Renaissance and scandals from the late Middle Ages weakened Christendom to such a degree that Martin Luther's revolt was able to shatter its unity. Let's explore the dazzling similarities between Jeroboam and Luther.

Old Testament	New Testament
Initially, Jeroboam's revolt was a protest against abusive taxes.	Initially, Luther objected to the "sale" of indulgences.
Jeroboam was a man of rank and influence in Israel before revolting.	Luther was a provincial vicar and a professor of theology before revolting.
After launching his revolt, Jeroboam fled to Egypt for safety.	After launching the Protestant Revolt, Luther hid in Wartburg Castle for safety.
The ten northern tribes united under Jeroboam, making a new political and military alliance in the north, separate from the Kingdom of Juda.	Northern Europe came together under Luther's theological revolt. They formed the Protestant Schmalkaldic League and Protestant Union.
Jeroboam's revolt eventually took on a more religious nature, opposed to the Mosaic Law and Temple Sacrifice.	Luther's revolt deepened religiously as he further refined his heresies. He was particularly opposed to the Mass; denying It is the Sacrifice of Calvary.
Jeroboam claimed that two golden calves were the real gods who brought Israel out of the land of Egypt.	Luther claimed that his ideas of "sola scriptura" and "sola fidei" were believed by early Christians, including the Church Fathers.
Jeroboam invented a new feast day to break the ten northern tribes from their former religious practices.	Reformation Day was established to celebrate the Protestant separation from the Catholic Church.

Man Of Rank Opposes Abusive Method Of Funding

Jeroboam was a captain in King Solomon's army and a foreman for his building projects. He was a man of responsibility and reputation in Israel.

As I have outlined in previous pages, Jeroboam's initial objection to the king was the high taxes levied on the tribes of Israel. These high taxes were used to fund the construction of the Temple and support the king's high standard of living. When Jeroboam approached King Roboam to petition for more reasonable taxes, he was given a harsh response.

After seeking counsel with his young advisors, King Roboam rejected Jeroboam's demand. Despite having access to his father's aged and wise advisors, King Roboam listened to young friends, who encouraged him to reject Jeroboam's grievances and assert his authority as king.

> "And they sent and called him: and Jeroboam came, and all the multitude of Israel, and they spoke to Roboam, saying: **Thy father laid a grievous yoke upon us: now, therefore, do thou take off a little of the grievous service of thy father, and of his most heavy yoke, which he put upon us, and we will serve thee.** And he said to them: Go till the third day and come to me again. And when the people was gone, King Roboam took counsel with the old men, that stood before Solomon his father while he yet lived, and he said: What counsel do you give me, that I may answer this people? They said to him: If thou wilt yield to this people today, and condescend to them, and grant their petition, and wilt speak gentle words to them, they will be thy servants always. **But he left the counsel of the old men, which they had given him, and consulted with the young men, that had been brought up with him,** and stood before him. And he said to them: What counsel do you give me, that I may answer this people, who have said to me: Make the yoke which thy father put upon us lighter? And the young men that had been brought up with him, said: Thus shalt thou speak to this people, who have spoken to thee, saying: Thy

father made our yoke heavy, do thou ease us. Thou shalt say to them: My little finger is thicker than the back of my father."

"And now my father put a heavy yoke upon you, but I will add to your yoke: my father beat you with whips, but I will beat you with scorpions. So Jeroboam and all the people came to Roboam the third day, as the king had appointed, saying: Come to me again the third day. And the king answered the people roughly, leaving the counsel of the old men, which they had given him, And he spoke to them according to the counsel of the young men, saying: My father made your yoke heavy, but I will add to your yoke: my father beat you with whips, but I will beat you with scorpions."

- 3 Kings 12: 3 – 14

Like Jeroboam, Martin Luther was also a person of responsibility and reputation in his enclave of Christendom. He was the provincial vicar of the Augustinian order for Saxony and Thuringia, as well as a teacher of theology at the University of Wittenberg. He held these positions before he began his revolt in 1517. The incident that sparked Martin Luther's revolt was the papal-sanctioned campaign of Fr. Johann Tetzel to preach indulgences to raise funds for the construction of St. Peter's Basilica. (The Council of Trent would later go on to affirm the issuance of indulgences, but to condemn any abusive or evil practices in doing so.)[48][c] Luther expressed himself in his eighty-sixth thesis, which was one of the ninety-five that he nailed to the door of the Church in Wittenberg.

"Why does the Pope, whose wealth today is greater than the wealth of the richest Crassus, not build the Basilica of St. Peter with his own money rather than that of the poor faithful?" (Thesis 86) – Martin Luther

---

c   *Decree on Indulgences,* trans. J. Waterworth, (London: Dolman, 1848): "...and being desirous that the **abuses which have crept therein**, and by occasion of which this honourable name of Indulgences is blasphemed by heretics, be amended and corrected, It ordains generally by this decree, **that all evil gains for the obtaining thereof**,--whence a most prolific cause of abuses amongst the Christian people has been derived,--**be wholly abolished**."

In the meantime, Pope Leo X was living a rather opulent lifestyle in Rome.[49] Of the many different extravagances, he was known for holding lavish feasts with exotic food several times per month. When Pope Leo X learned of Martin Luther, he took counsel about how to handle him and this budding revolt. Some of his advisers included Guglio D'Medici and Luigi de Rossi, who were cousins and lifelong friends of Pope Leo X. Like them, Pope Leo X was also a Medici by birth.

The papacy had many financial commitments that required Leo X to secure substantial sources of income. He incurred a great deal of expense with his war against France, patronizing the arts, building St. Peter's Basilica, and preparing a Crusade against the Turks. Thus is was difficult to stop the issuance of indulgences as a funding source. Pope Leo X reacted to Luther by reasserting papal authority and defending the papal right to issue indulgences in his bull *Exsurge Domine*.

Although it was the right of King Roboam to issue taxes and to assert his kingly authority, it can be argued that a more diplomatic approach could have satiated the objections of Jeroboam and the ten northern tribes, potentially averting disaster. However, that course of action also could have set a dangerous precedent for the future. Similarly, the reforms that were introduced at the Council of Trent, one of which was the recognition that indulgences can be issued in an abusive manner, could have been recognized and enacted earlier by Pope Leo X, thus satiating some of Luther's initial, albeit arrogant, objections.

The Rebel Flees To Safety, And The Holy City Is Sacked

At one point, Jeroboam fled to Egypt to avoid being captured or killed by King Solomon. This occurred just before Solomon's death. Jeroboam returned to Israel after King Solomon died. In the fifth year of Roboam's reign, the city of Jerusalem was sacked by King Sesac of Egypt. The sack took many priceless works of art and gold from King Solomon's Temple.

> "And when the kingdom of Roboam was strengthened and fortified, he forsook the law of the Lord, and all Israel with him. And in the fifth year of the reign of Roboam, Sesac king

of Egypt came up against Jerusalem (because they had sinned against the Lord) With 12 hundred chariots and threescore thousand horsemen: and the people were without number that came with him out of Egypt, to wit, Libyans, and Troglodites, and Ethiopians."

- 2 Paralipomenon 12: 1-3,

"So Sesac king of Egypt departed from Jerusalem, taking away the treasures of the house of the Lord, and of the king's house, and he took all with him, and the golden shields that Solomon had made."

- 2 Paralipomenon 12: 9

"And he took away the treasures of the house of the Lord, and the king's treasures, and carried all off: as also the shields of gold which Solomon had made."

- 3 Kings 14: 26

Similarly, Martin Luther was declared an outlaw by Holy Roman Emperor Charles V, after the Diet of Worms in 1521. As a result, Luther fled to Wartburg Castle and hid there for ten months to avoid being captured or killed. He came out of hiding in 1522 and returned to Wittenberg, Germany to lead the nascent Protestant Revolt.

Just as the city of Jerusalem was sacked five years after Jeroboam returned from his hiding place in Egypt, so too was Rome sacked five years after Luther returned from his hiding place in Wartburg Castle. Luther returned in 1522[50], and Rome was sacked by rebellious soldiers (many of them Lutherans) of Emperor Charles V in 1527. Countless and priceless works of art, historical artifacts, and objects of otherwise great value were stolen, defaced, or destroyed during the Sack of Rome in 1527.[51] One memorable defacement of artwork was the graffiti scratched onto a fresco of Raphael's masterpiece *Disputation of the Holy Sacrament* in the Vatican Palace. The graffiti said "Luther".

The Rebellion Deepens Religiously And Politically

Jeroboam became the ruler of Israel's ten northern tribes, who formed a separate political system in the north.

> "And Israel revolted from the house of David, unto this day. And it came to pass when all Israel heard that Jeroboam was coming again, that they gathered an assembly, sent and called him, and made him king over all Israel, and none followed the house of David but the tribe of Juda only."
>
> - 3 Kings 12: 19-20

Likewise, the northern Protestant states also separated themselves politically from the Holy Roman Empire. In 1531, the Protestants formed an alliance called the Schmalkaldic League[52], a military alliance of Lutheran princes and cities within the boundaries of the Holy Roman Empire. It was formed to defend themselves against Emperor Charles V, who wanted to strike Luther's heresies from his realm. Northern Protestant states organized themselves into an entirely separate political entity. They followed Martin Luther as an almost de facto "pope" who advised the Protestant princes and leaders.

The Protestant Revolt's most critical and devastating characteristic was not a political but rather a theological and a religious rebellion. Martin Luther's initial and impious objections evolved and deepened over time, taking on more substantial theological significance. He became the leader of an entirely new religion, retaining only trace elements of Catholicism. Martin Luther came to oppose to the Holy Mass and insisted that it was not the Sacrifice of Our Lord on Calvary. He also insisted that the pope was not the head of the Church. Not only did Luther disparage the Holy Mass and the papacy, but he constructed a substitute system of "theology" to take the place of the Catholic Faith in the hearts and minds of Christians under his heretical influence.

Luther claimed that instead of the papacy and the Church's Magisterium, Sacred Scripture was the only authority for Christians. He called this "sola scriptura," claiming that Scripture alone was all that was necessary to know the truth revealed by God. He rejected the idea that the Church gave us the canon of Scripture and that the Church alone had the authority and ability to interpret Sacred Scripture infallibly. Luther also concocted the idea of "sola fidei", positing that works were unnecessary for salvation. Luther instead taught that "faith" alone was necessary. Luther's concept of faith was false since he rejected the teachings of the Catholic Church.

Thus, Luther gave Christians two new doctrines, "sola scriptura" and "sola fidei", (or "sola gratia") to detach them from Catholic theology.[53]d Luther also then claimed that the early Church believed these new ideas and that he, Luther, was restoring the Church to its original state. Of course, this is false, but this was Luther's position.

Like Luther's revolt, Jeroboam's revolt evolved into a religious movement as well. Jeroboam erected two golden calves, one in the northern tribe of Dan and one bordering the southern Kingdom of Juda. He intended to stop Israelites from traveling to Jerusalem to offer sacrifice in the Temple. He established the calves as substitute gods to which sacrifice could be offered. He also devised a new priesthood that was not of the sons of Levi. (In the Old Testament, a true priest could only be a descendant of Levi, of the tribe of Levi.) And finally, to pry the people from their religious feast days, Jeroboam devised a new one for his new religion.

> "And Jeroboam said in his heart: Now shall the kingdom return to the house of David, If these people go up to offer sacrifices in the house of the Lord at Jerusalem: and the heart of this people will turn to their lord Roboam the king of Juda, and they will kill me, and return to him. And finding a device, he made two golden calves and said to them: Go ye up no more to Jerusalem: **Behold thy gods, O Israel, who brought thee out of the land of Egypt.** And he set the one in Bethel, and the other in Dan: And this thing became an occasion of sin: for the people went to adore the calf as far as

d   Today's Protestants recognize five "solas": sola scriptura, sola fidei, sola gratia, solus Christus, and soli Deo gloria. These five pillars of Protestantism were not clearly articulated until the 19th or 20th centuries. The early Protestants only distinctly articulated two of these five solas.

Dan. And he made temples in the high places and priests of the lowest of the people, who were not of the sons of Levi. **And he appointed a feast in the eighth month, on the fifteenth day of the month, after the manner of the feast that was celebrated in Juda.** And going up to the altar, he did in like manner in Bethel, to sacrifice to the calves, which he had made: and he placed in Bethel priests of the high places, which he had made."

- 3 Kings 12: 26-32

Thus, Jeroboam and Luther were both prying the people away from the "sacrifice" and their allegiance to the "king". Jeroboam was stopping his subjects from going to the Temple in Jerusalem to offer sacrifice, and Luther opposed the Holy Mass, the Sacrifice of Calvary. Jeroboam was establishing himself as the new king and wanted to sever the people's allegiance to the house of David, the king of Israel, just as Luther cut his subjects from their allegiance to the papacy and Church hierarchy. Jeroboam established two golden calves as substitute gods, which he falsely claimed were the gods that brought Israel out of Egypt. Luther gave his subjects the two new "doctrines" of "sola scriptura" and "sola fidei" (or "sola gratia"), which he claimed were believed by the early Church.

Jeroboam made a new line of "priests" that were not true priests, since they did not come from the tribe of Levi. Luther disregarded Catholic ordination rites and episcopal lineage and took ministers for his new religion from the general population.

Finally, Jeroboam gave his people a new feast day to celebrate, on the fifteenth day of the eighth Jewish month.[e] On a Jewish calendar, the eighth month is called *Cheshvan* and coincides with Oct-Nov on a Gregorian calendar. Thus, the fifteenth day of Cheshvan is approximately the end of October or early November. Amazingly, by comparison, the only new "feast day" celebrated by Protestants is *Reformation Day*, which celebrates Luther's break from the Church. Reformation Day is celebrated on October 31. Thus,

---

e   See 3 Kings 12: 32.

the "feast day" invented by Jeroboam and Luther's "feast day" both occur on approximately the same calendar day!

Now, let's list more parallels between the Protestant Revolt and the revolt of the ten northern tribes of Israel. In both cases, the separation between the north and south was permanent, never healed.

A Civil War in the Kingdom

JEROBOAM'S REVOLT RESULTS IN CIVIL WAR AND LUTHER'S REVOLT RESULTS IN THE WARS OF RELIGION

Old Testament	New Testament
The apostate north retained the name of *Israel*. Southern tribes went by the name *Kingdom of Juda*.	Protestants retained the name of *Christian*. The name *Roman Catholic* is emphasized to distinguish Catholic from Protestant.
Civil war erupted between the apostate Kingdom of Israel and the southern Kingdom of Juda.	Civil war erupted in Christendom with the *Wars of Religion* between the Protestants and the Catholics.
New rebel leaders arose and deposed Jeroboam.	New Protestant rebels revolted against Luther.
Amri established the capital city of Samaria for the apostates.	John Calvin established Geneva as the capital of Calvinism.
Jehu massacred the Amrides (descendants of Amri).	St. Bartholomew's Day Massacre in France killed thousands of French Calvinists (Huguenots).
King Josaphat sent out judges in his kingdom to educate and judge on religious matters.	Roman Inquisition was established to guard against heresies, judge, and educate. Jesuits were formed, to educate Catholics in the Faith after the laxities of the Renaissance.

The Rebels Retain The Name

Before Jeroboam's revolt, the twelve tribes of Israel were united under the Davidic king. The twelve tribes were collectively known as the Nation or Kingdom of Israel, and all the members of this kingdom were called *Israelites*. However, after Jeroboam broke from the covenant, from the Temple sacrifice and from allegiance to the Davidic king, he formed the ten rebellious tribes into a new kingdom. They retained the name *Israelites*, calling themselves the *Kingdom of Israel*. To distinguish themselves from the ten rebellious tribes, the southern tribes called themselves the *Kingdom of Juda*. To be clear, only the Kingdom of Juda in the south was the true Israel. The ten northern rebellious tribes, who abandoned all their traditions to follow Jeroboam, were no longer the true Israel. Nonetheless, they stole the name *Israel* and forced the south to re-brand in order to distinguish themselves from the northern apostates.

Likewise, in Church history, before Luther's revolt, all of Western Europe was collectively known as *Christendom*. From Sweden to Ireland to Switzerland to Italy to Spain to Denmark, they all just called themselves Christians. However, after Luther's revolt, the Protestants retained the name *Christian* even though they no longer followed Christ's vicar in Rome, no longer attended Holy Mass, and rejected Christ's Mystical Body, the Church. They were no longer Christians and effectively stole the name. To differentiate and distinguish themselves, the Christians in the south began to identify as *Catholic Christians*, or just as *Catholics*. The name *Catholic* goes back to St. Ignatius of Antioch, but it was not the primary name used to identify followers of Christ before Luther's revolt. However, after Luther, the name *Roman Catholic* [47] became increasingly used by those who still were joined to the true Church of Christ.

Wars Of Religion Between The North And The South

King Roboam did not immediately respond to the revolt of the ten northern tribes. However, his successors, King Abia and King Asa, both responded militarily to bring back the ten northern tribes. This sparked a civil war between the apostate north (Kingdom of Israel) and the south (Kingdom of Juda). Even though both sides won battles, neither side could dominate the other. Thus, the fighting was sustained and very destructive. Here is the account of the battle between King Abia and Jeroboam.

"...and there was war between Abia and Jeroboam. And when Abia had begun battle and had with him four hundred thousand most valiant and chosen men, Jeroboam put his army in array against him, eight hundred thousand men, who were also chosen and most valiant for war. And Abia stood upon mount Semeron, which was in Ephraim, and said: Hear me, O Jeroboam, and all Israel: Do you not know that the Lord God of Israel gave David the kingdom over Israel forever, to him and to his sons by a covenant of salt?

And Jeroboam the son of Nabat, the servant of Solomon the son of David, rose up: and rebelled against his lord. And there were gathered to him vain men, and children of Belial: and they prevailed against Roboam the son of Solomon: for Roboam was inexperienced, and of a fearful heart, and could not resist them. And now you say that you are able to withstand the kingdom of the Lord, which he possesseth by the sons of David, and **you have a great multitude of people, and golden calves, which Jeroboam hath made you for gods. And you have cast out the priests of the Lord, the sons of Aaron, and the Levites: and you have made you priests, like all the nations of the earth:** whosoever cometh and consecrateth his hand with a bullock of the herd, and with seven rams, is made a priest of those who are no gods. But the Lord is our God, whom we forsake not, and the priests who minister to the Lord are the sons of Aaron, and the Levites are in their order.

And they offer holocausts to the Lord, every day, morning and evening, and incense made according to the ordinance of the law, and the loaves are set forth on a most clean table, and there is with us the golden candlestick, and the lamps thereof, to be lighted always in the evening: for we keep the precepts of the Lord our God, whom you have forsaken.

95

Therefore God is the leader in our army, and his priests who sound with trumpets, and resound against you: O children of Israel, fight not against the Lord the God of your fathers, for it is not good for you. While he spoke these things, Jeroboam caused an ambushment to come about behind him. And while he stood facing the enemies, he encompassed Juda. who perceived it not, with his army. And when Juda looked back, they saw the battle coming upon them both before and behind, and they cried to the Lord: and the priests began to sound with the trumpets. And all the men of Juda shouted: and behold when they shouted, God terrified Jeroboam, and all Israel that stood against Abia and Juda.

And the children of Israel fled before Juda, and the Lord delivered them into their hand. And Abia and his people slew them with a great slaughter, and there fell wounded of Israel five hundred thousand valiant men. And the children of Israel were brought down, at that time, and the children of Juda were exceedingly strengthened, because they had trusted in the Lord the God of their fathers. And Abia pursued after Jeroboam, and took cities from him, Bethel and her daughters, and Jesana with her daughters, Ephron also and her daughters. And Jeroboam was not able to resist any more, in the days of Abia: and the Lord struck him, and he died."

- 2 Paralipomenon 13 : 3-20

In Church history, the Protestant Revolt prompted the Holy Roman Empire to take military action. Their aim was to reconcile the wayward Protestants to the Catholic Church. The Thirty Years War, fought between the Protestant north and the Catholic south, stood as the bloodiest conflict in Christendom up until that time.

A New Cycle of Rebellion

REBEL OVERTHROWS REBEL IN ISRAEL; PROTESTANT LEADERS BREAK
FROM EACH OTHER

The Apostate Rebel Is "Dethroned"

By leading a rebellion against the Davidic king and the law of Moses,
Jeroboam set an example for all the people in the ten northern tribes to
follow. It was not long before Jeroboam had someone rebelling against his
authority, with the pattern repeating ad nauseam. Thus, the ten northern
tribes experienced revolt after revolt until their eventual assimilation by the
Assyrian Empire.

The first revolt against the authority of Jeroboam was by a man named
Baasa. Sacred Scripture gives little detail about Baasa; the little it offers is
enlightening, as we see parallels with Huldrych Zwingli. Here are the verses
concerning Baasa:

> "But Nadab, the son of Jeroboam, reigned over Israel in the
> second year of Asa king of Juda, and he reigned over Israel
> for two years. And he did evil in the sight of the Lord, and
> walked in the ways of his father, and in his sins, wherewith
> he made Israel to sin. And Baasa, the son of Ahias of the
> house of Issachar, conspired against him and slew him in
> Gebbethon, a city of the Philistines, for Nadab and all Israel
> besieged Gebbethon. **So Baasa slew him in the third year of
> Asa king of Juda and reigned in his place**."
>
> - 3 Kings 15: 25 – 28

When Baasa reigned in place of Nadab, the son of Jeroboam, Baasa
constructed a fortification north of Jerusalem. He created this city so "that no
man might go out or come in, of the side of Asa king of Juda". In other
words, Baasa was blockading Jerusalem and cutting it off. His efforts failed
as the king of Juda broke the blockade.

"And Baasa king of Israel went up against Juda and built Rama that no man might go out or come in, of the side of Asa king of Juda."

- 3 Kings 15: 17

In like manner, Martin Luther's revolt against Church authority and rejection of the Catholic Faith set an example for Protestants. New Protestant leaders arose to challenge Luther's ideas, just as Luther had rebelled against the Church. The blueprint for Protestantism became that of a revolution and usurpation.

It is therefore unsurprising that no sooner had Luther asserted his erroneous interpretation of Sacred Scripture, he was supplanted by others who thought their erroneous interpretations were better than his. The first to confront Luther was Huldrych Zwingli. Zwingli also rejected Catholic Church teaching just as Luther had done before him. He started his rebellion in Switzerland by instigating the *eating of sausages* [54] during Lent, instead of abstaining from meat. He then moved to ban the Mass in Zurich and much more.

Switzerland, at the time, was not united as one nation. The land was divided into *cantons*, fiercely independent regions. Many of the Swiss cantons became Protestant and followed Zwingli. However, five cantons remained Catholic. Zwingli advocated for a plan that called for a food blockade to be carried out against the five Catholic cantons in order to starve them into submission.[55] The Catholic cantons responded by launching a military attack against the Protestant cantons, which caught them completely by surprise. Thus, the blockade was ended, and the Catholic cantons were relieved. To summarize, Baasa blockaded Jerusalem and Zwingli blockaded Catholics in Switzerland. Neither were successful.

The Next Rebellion Spreads Far And Wide

In the Old Testament, the house of Baasa did not last long. Baasa's son was assassinated by one of his army commanders, named Zimri. Zimri was himself overthrown by Amri. Amri spread his influence and progeny across the northern kingdom to an extent greater than his predecessors. Amri is also known for surpassing the apostasy and evil that Jeroboam unleashed on the ten northern tribes. Amri introduced more wicked and false gods, deepening the apostasy of the ten northern tribes.

> "And Amri did evil in the sight of the Lord and acted wickedly above all that were before him. And he walked in all the way of Jeroboam the son of Nabat, and in his sins wherewith he made Israel to sin: to provoke the Lord the God of Israel to anger with their vanities."
>
> - 3 Kings 16: 25-26

Amri's dynasty included King Achab, Ochozias, and Athalia. Athalia married into the southern Kingdom of Juda and ruled over it for a time as queen regent. The rule of Athalia over the southern Kingdom of Juda shows that the northern and southern kingdoms were beginning to grow weary of war and opposition. Athalia's marriage to the southern King Joram was an attempt to broker peace between the two kingdoms. We will see the same phenomenon occur when a Protestant married into the French royal family. We will come to that parallel in a short time.

In Church history, the next prominent Protestant rebel to challenge Luther and Zwingli was John Calvin. Unlike Zwingli, who established no significant and lasting Protestant movement, Calvin's influence spread far and wide.

John Calvin went beyond the heresies of Martin Luther. Luther set up the two false doctrines of "sola scriptura" and "sola fidei" (or "sola gratia"). All subsequent Protestant leaders kept these two principle errors of Luther in their teachings. These two Lutheran teachings are like the two golden calves that Jeroboam set up and which all subsequent kings of Israel would also worship, even though they would go further than Jeroboam and worship other false gods as well.

John Calvin surpassed Luther by taking the Protestant Revolt even further away from Catholicism. Calvin developed new heretical ideas that even Luther thought were going too far. For example, the Lutheran "liturgy" was closer to Catholicism than the Calvinist "services". Thus, like Amri, who "acted wickedly above all that went before him," so too did Calvin exceed in his departure from Catholic truth more than Luther who came before him.[f]

Finally, like Amri, whose influence spread far through his many descendants, Calvin's influence also spread far. Calvinism spread to Scotland, France (with the Huguenots), England, and Plymouth in the New World and particularly to Switzerland, where Calvin set up his headquarters in the city of Geneva. This brings us to our next topic.

Capital City For The Apostates

Amri established his capital city of Samaria in the northern Kingdom of Israel on top of a flat topped mountain. In the Old Testament, the prophet Eliseus visited this apostate city of Samaria, attempting to restore the worship of the true God. Remember the relationship between the prophet Eliseus and the city of Samaria because we will see parallels between Eliseus the prophet and St. Francis de Sales, as well as between the city of Samaria and the city of Geneva, Switzerland.

The Assyrians later conquered the city of Samaria, and brought many foreign peoples into the land, making it diverse and multicultural.[56] It also became a center of Greek power and culture after Alexander the Great conquered the ancient world, stationing many Macedonian soldiers there. [57] If you can mark this paragraph, we will see that Geneva undergoes the same events in parallel that Samaria underwent further along in Old Testament history. Geneva became known as an international city in the 1900s, with hundreds of global businesses, the headquarters of the League of Nations, and the Geneva Convention all based there.

Massacre Of The Amrides (Calvinists)

When Amri became king of Israel, he instituted the worship of the pagan god Baal. This evil was much worse than the evil of Jeroboam, who initiated the worship of the two golden calves. Amri founded the Amride dynasty in

---

f Calvinism emphasizes predestination, while Luther taught that salvation is freely offered to all who believe in Jesus Christ and is received through grace. Both of them reject the necessity of the Catholic Church but Calvin's ideas deviate more.

the northern Kingdom of Israel, having many descendants who ruled the northern kingdom after him. Amri's influence would also spread into the southern kingdom as his granddaughter, Athalia, became queen regent of Juda.

The evil that was brought about through Amri and his descendants angered God very much. The worship of the pagan god Baal was growing. Therefore, God had his prophet anoint a new king in Israel, Jehu. He was zealous for the true God of Israel and was determined to rid the land of the influence of Baal.

Originally from France, John Calvin was caught up in the Protestant Revolution while studying at university. He fled to Geneva, where he founded a new Protestant movement, which can generally be called *Calvinism*. This new body of heresy incorporated the two main errors of Luther ("sola scriptura" and "sola fidei"). Still, Calvin went much further than Luther did in his apostasy from Catholic truth. Calvin's teachings spread all across Europe, and particularly in France. The followers of John Calvin in France called themselves the *Huguenots*, and their population grew to a substantial size. It was a startling development when even many of the French nobility converted to this new and more poisonous heresy.[58] The diffusion of Calvinism in France did not go without opposition by devout Catholics. A French noble family, the House of Guise, zealously opposed the spread of Calvinism.[59]

Allow me to keep things straight by briefly outlining the parallels so far. John Calvin parallels Amri, while Calvinists across Europe are like the descendants of Amri. Calvin kept Luther's two principle errors of "sola scriptura" and "sola fidei", just like Amri kept the two golden calves of Jeroboam. Calvin introduced worse heresies than Luther, just as Amri introduced the northern kingdom to the greater evil of Baal worship. Now, let's continue by moving back to the Old Testament story of Jehu and the massacre of the Amrides.

King Achab, a descendant of Amri, had a pagan wife from Sidon[g] named Jezabel. When Jehu entered the city, Jezabel was looking out of her window at Jehu. Jehu spoke to the servants standing behind her and ordered them to throw her out the window, which they did.

> "And Jehu came into Jezrahel. But Jezabel hearing of his coming in, painted her face with stibic stone, and adorned her head, **and looked out of a window** at Jehu coming in at the gate, and said: Can there be peace for Zambri, that hath killed his master? And Jehu lifted up his face to the window, and said: Who is this? And two or three eunuchs bowed down to him. And he said to them: **Throw her down headlong: and they threw her down,** and the wall was sprinkled with her blood, and the hoofs of the horses trod upon her."

- 4 Kings 9: 30-33

Then, Jehu went on to kill the rest of Jezabel's and Achab's friends in the city. Jehu went even further when he ordered all seventy sons of Achab (son of Amri) to be beheaded, and their heads sent to him. Jehu then gathered all the priests of Baal into one place to celebrate a great feast to Baal. When they were all together, he had them all slaughtered, thus the worship of Baal was stricken from the land.

> "And Jehu gathered together all the people, and said to them: Achab worshipped Baal a little, but I will worship him more. **Now therefore call to me all the prophets of Baal, and all his servants, and all his priests: let none be wanting, for I have a great sacrifice to offer to Baal: whosoever shall be wanting shall not live. Now Jehu did this craftily, that he might destroy the worshippers of Baal.** And he said: Proclaim a festival for Baal. And he called, and he sent into all the borders of Israel, and all the servants of

---

g   Sidon was north of Israel, in present day Lebanon. It was a Phoenician city and a center for Baal worship. Jezabel was from Sidon, whose end came when her dead body was devoured by dogs. Compare that story to the Gospel account of the woman from Sidon who pleaded with Our Lord by saying even the dogs eat the crumbs that fall to the ground. See Matthew 15.

Baal came: there was not one left that did not come. And they went into the temple of Baal: and the house of Baal was filled, from one end to the other. And he said to them that were over the wardrobe: Bring forth garments for all the servants of Baal. And they brought them forth garments. And Jehu and Jonadab the son of Rechab went to the temple of Baal, and said to the worshippers of Baal: Search, and see that there be not any with you of the servants of the Lord, but that there be the servants of Baal only. And they went in to offer sacrifices and burnt offerings: **but Jehu had prepared him fourscore men without, and said to them: If any of the men escape, whom I have brought into your hands, he that letteth him go shall answer life for life. And it came to pass, when the burnt offering was ended, that Jehu commanded his soldiers and captains, saying: Go in, and kill them, let none escape.** And the soldiers and captains slew them with the edge of the sword, and cast them out: and they went into the city of the temple of Baal, and brought the statue out of Baal's temple, and burnt it, And broke it in pieces. They destroyed also the temple of Baal, and made a jakes in its place unto this day. **So Jehu destroyed Baal out of Israel:"**

- 4 Kings 10 : 18-28

Switching now to our story line in Church history, recall that the French noble family, the House of Guise, were staunch Catholics, outraged that the heresy of Calvinism had made its way into French nobility. On the occasion of the Calvinist Henry III of Navarre's marriage in 1572 to Margaret of Valois (a Catholic and sister to King Charles IX), almost all of the country's Huguenot nobility came to Paris to celebrate the marriage. For the Huguenots, this was a significant development to have the king's Catholic sister marry a Calvinist Huguenot.[60] For the Catholics of Paris, this was an outrage, a dire situation and a pivotal moment. The marriage took place on August 24, 1572, the feast of St. Bartholomew.

After the marriage took place, there was an attempted assassination of the Huguenot leader, Gaspard de Coligny. It is suspected that someone in the

House of Guise ordered the assassination. The assassination failed, but it led to a great slaughter of the Huguenots in Paris, with Gaspard de Coligny being thrown from a window.[61] Compare this to Jezabel also being thrown out a window at Jehu's orders. This has come to be known as the St. Bartholomew's Day Massacre.

The St. Bartholomew's Day Massacre grew into an immense slaughter of Huguenots in Paris and the surrounding countryside.[62] It is estimated that 10,000 to 70,000 Huguenots were massacred, completely crippling the Huguenot movement in France, especially since most of their nobility were killed. Many Huguenots left France after this, and Calvinism was stricken from the land.

Educators and Judges Fortify True Religion
Josaphat's Judges and the Catholic Reformation

King Solomon's idol worship was sadly inherited by the southern kings of Juda. Roboam, the first king of the southern kingdom, was a feeble king who failed to react appropriately to Jeroboam's revolt. His son Abia attempted to reunite the northern tribes by force of arms. The next king of Juda, Asa, removed the false gods from the southern kingdom, but it was King Josaphat who finally brought about positive change and religious reform.

King Josaphat launched a two-phase reform of the southern kingdom. His first phase was to establish traveling judges who would go from city to city throughout the southern kingdom. King Josaphat was insistent that these judges realized the seriousness and weight of their role in relation to the people of Juda. He warned his judges that they were not giving the judgments of men, but the judgments of the Lord. For this reason, they were very careful not to accept any gifts or bribes or to favor any man over another but sought only the truth and fair judgment.

The second phase of the reform of Josaphat was to appoint priests in Jerusalem. For the first time in a long time, common people were given an intentional knowledge of their religion.

"And Josaphat dwelt at Jerusalem: and he went out again to the people from Bersabee to mount Ephraim, and brought them back to the Lord the God of their fathers. And he set judges of the land in all the fenced cities of Juda, in every place. And charging the judges, he said: Take heed what you do: for you exercise not the judgment of man, but of the Lord: and whatsoever you judge, it shall redound to you. Let the fear of the Lord be with you, and do all things with diligence: for there is no iniquity with the Lord our God, respect of persons, or desire of gifts. In Jerusalem, also Josaphat appointed Levites, priests, and chiefs of the families of Israel, to judge the judgment and the cause of the Lord for the inhabitants thereof. And he charged them, saying: Thus shall you do in the fear of the Lord faithfully, and with a perfect heart. Every cause that shall come to you of your brethren, that dwell in their cities, between kindred and kindred, wheresoever there is question concerning the law, the commandment, the ceremonies, the justifications: shew it them, that they may not sin against the Lord, and that wrath may not come upon you and your brethren: and so doing you shall not sin."

- 2 Paralipomenon 19: 4-10

Likewise, in Church history, the Catholic Reformation was initiated with the same goals that King Josaphat sought to achieve by sending priests and judges to his kingdom.

The Catholic Reformation did not occur immediately as a response to Martin Luther and the Protestant Revolt. Luther was swiftly condemned and excommunicated by 1521, but the Catholic Counter-Reformation did not begin in earnest until the reign of Pope Paul III in 1534.[63]

The first significant step taken in the Catholic Reformation was the creation of new religious orders. These new orders had a strong focus: to teach the Faith. Chief among these new orders were the Jesuits, founded by St. Ignatius of Loyola. The Jesuits quickly became a legendary force, building schools and universities across Catholic Europe, zealously educating the people. Jesuits brought many Protestants back to the Faith and gave lay Catholics intellectual weapons to defend themselves against Protestant heresies. They were directly under the authority of the pope, just like King Josaphat's priests and judges took orders directly from the king.

Another major part of the Catholic Counter-Reformation was the establishment of the Inquisition. The Inquisition was a traveling legal court that would visit Catholic cities (it did not function in Protestant lands) and judge the people of that city who were charged with heresy. Despite the myths and false allegations about the Inquisition, it was a very meticulous and faithful legal court. It grasped the seriousness of its decisions in delivering the judgment of the Catholic Church. There were some excesses, but, for the most part, the inquisitors (judges) were honest and pious men of the Church who took their role seriously.

We can see the clear parallels between Josaphat's judges and educators who went through his southern kingdom and the Jesuits and the Inquisition who did the same in Catholic kingdoms in Church history. Both were in response to revolts, those of Jeroboam and Luther, respectively.

After setting up a framework of parallels for the events of the Protestant Revolt and the events of the ten northern tribes' revolt in the Old Testament, let us return and fill in some more details.

Old Testament	New Testament
The bald prophet Eliseus went to Samaria to bring the apostates back to the worship of the true God.	St. Francis de Sales, noticeably bald, went to Geneva to bring Calvinists back to the Church.
A demon killed Sarah's seven husbands.	Henry VIII, inspired by a demon, killed his "wives".
The Assyrians arose to threaten Jerusalem and the Kingdom of Juda.	Ottoman Turks arose to threaten Christendom, with their goal to conquer Rome.

King Ezechias went before the ark, and his kingdom was miraculously delivered from the Assyrian threat by an angel.	King Jon Sobieski prayed to Our Lady and delivered Vienna from the Ottomans with his winged Hussars.
Isaias had his lips purified by a burning coal so he could be a prophet for God.	St. Margaret Mary had her heart purified by divine fire so she could be an Apostle of the Sacred Heart.
Ezechias' sundial and Passover	Gregorian calendar of Pope Gregory XIII

The Bald Prophet Is Sent to the Apostates

ELISEUS GOES TO SAMARIA AND ST. FRANCIS DE SALES GOES TO GENEVA

Eliseus was a prophet to the ten northern tribes. He was the protégé and successor to the great prophet Elias (Elijah). The stories in the Old Testament about Elias are phenomenal. He alone opposed the worship of Baal in the ten northern tribes. As of the writing of this book, I have not yet written nor explored possible parallels between Elias and the Jesuit martyrs of England. But at first glance, there are a lot of parallel points. King Henry VIII and Queen Elizabeth share many parallels with King Achab and Queen Jezabel in the Old Testament. Queen Jezabel was fanatical about tracking down Elias and having him killed, just as Queen Elizabeth hunted down the Jesuits. Further, King Henry VIII coveted and stole the convents and monasteries throughout England, just as King Achab coveted and stole the vineyard and garden of Naboth.[h]

I write this about Elias and the English persecution of Catholics only because I did not want to omit the stories of Elias completely in this book. There are several places in Old Testament/Church history in which I have not sufficiently "discovered" nor recorded a parallel. Elias is perhaps the most notable topic yet overlooked. Nonetheless, Elias is a key character in this time period. With all that being said, I would like to articulate some striking

h King Achab unjustly confiscates the vineyard and gardens of Naboth in 3 Kings 21.

parallels between the protégé and later successor of Elias (Elijah), the prophet Eliseus (Elisha).

The prophet Eliseus was chosen by the prophet Elias to follow and succeed him. Before Elias was taken up into Heaven in a fiery chariot, they were both standing on the Jordan River's bank. There, Eliseus asked to be like Elias (have a double portion of his spirit), and it was granted to him.

Eliseus was notably bald. There is a story where some children made fun of his baldness, and he cursed them. Bears came out of the forest and tore at the children.

> "And he went up from thence to Bethel: and as he was going up by the way, little boys came out of the city and mocked him, saying: Go up, thou **bald head**; go up, thou bald head. And looking back, he saw them, and cursed them in the name of the Lord: and there came forth two bears out of the forest, and tore of them two and forty boys."

\- 2 Kings 2: 23-24

St. Francis de Sales was named after the great St. Francis of Assisi. In fact, his parents had a whole room in their house devoted to this great saint; St. Francis de Sales was born in that room. Later in life, St. Francis de Sales would choose St. Francis of Assisi as his patron saint. One day, when St. Francis de Sales was by the shores of Lake Geneva, St. Francis of Assisi appeared to him and said the following: "You would like to die as a martyr, just like I longed for martyrdom. But, like me, you will not obtain martyrdom. You must become a means of your own martyrdom[64]". Thus just like Eliseus was handed a mission by Elias when they were both standing by the Jordan River, so was St. Francis de Sales handed his mission by St. Francis of Assisi when they were by Lake Geneva.

Also, I must point out that St. Francis de Sales is notably bald, just like Eliseus.

Another parallel point between Eliseus and St. Francis de Sales is their relationship with their natural fathers and their rejection of an inheritance. They both chose instead to follow the Lord's calling.

When Eliseus was called by Elias (and by God) to follow him, Eliseus rejected the inheritance of his father and chose to follow Elias. This is evidenced by his actions of killing his oxen and burning his plow. He then returned and said goodbye to his mother and father and followed Elias. Later, before Elias was taken up in the fiery chariot, Eliseus would ask for a double portion from Elias. This indicates the manner of inheritance that the firstborn son would receive from a father. In the natural relationship of a father and son, it was customary for the father to give a double portion of his estate to his firstborn son.[i] The fact that Eliseus called Elias his "father" further underscores this. It suggests that Eliseus could have been the firstborn son of his natural father and rejected his double portion of inheritance to follow Elias. Then, because Elias was his "spiritual father," he requested a double portion of Elias.

> "And Elias departing from thence, found Eliseus the son of Saphat, ploughing with 12 yoke of oxen: and he was one of them that were ploughing with 12 yoke of oxen: and when Elias came up to him, he cast his mantle upon him. And he forthwith left the oxen and ran after Elias, and said: Let me, I pray thee, kiss my father and my mother, and then I will follow thee. And he said to him: Go, and return back: for that which was my part, I have done to thee. And returning back from him, he took a yoke of oxen, and killed them, and boiled the flesh with the plough of the oxen, and gave to the people, and they ate: and rising up he went away, and followed Elias, and ministered to him."
>
> - 3 Kings 19 : 19-21

Eliseus asks for a double portion from Elias in this passage.

---

i   Deuteronomy 21:17: "But he shall acknowledge the son of the hated for the firstborn, and shall give him a double portion of all he hath: for this is the first of his children, and to him are due the first birthrights."

"And when they were gone over, Elias said to Eliseus: Ask what thou wilt have me to do for thee, before I be taken away from thee. And Eliseus said: I beseech thee that in me may be thy **double spirit**. And he answered: Thou hast asked a hard thing: nevertheless if thou see me when I am taken from thee, thou shalt have what thou hast asked: but if thou see me not, thou shalt not have it. And as they went on, walking and talking together, behold a fiery chariot, and fiery horses parted them both asunder: and Elias went up by a whirlwind into heaven. And Eliseus saw him, and cried: My father, my father, the chariot of Israel..."

- 4 Kings 2 : 9-12

Douay-Rheims footnote

"**Double spirit**": A double portion of thy spirit, as the eldest son and heir: or thy spirit which is double in comparison of that which God usually imparteth to his prophets.

Similarly, St. Francis de Sales' father opposed his calling to the priesthood. His family was wealthy, and his father wanted to send him to the best schools to become a magistrate.[65] St. Francis de Sales was the oldest of six children and, as such, was set to inherit the most. However, he signed over his inheritance to his younger brother and followed God instead.[j]

To wrap up our comparison of the prophet Eliseus and St. Francis de Sales, I would like to call attention again to the parallels discussed earlier between the city of Samaria in the Old Testament and the city of Geneva. Remember that both became the capital city for the apostates. Amri built Samaria in the northern Kingdom of Israel, and John Calvin made Geneva into the headquarters for Calvinism.

With that in mind, consider that Eliseus was the only prophet of God to visit the apostate city of Samaria. He entered the city of Samaria and interacted with the king and nobles of the city. Through a miracle, Eliseus

---

j   On the Wikipedia page for St. Francis de Sales, it states that St. Francis signed his title and right of succession over to his younger brother, Louis, before he was ordained. However, the source link for this information is broken and unable to be confirmed.

brought about the destruction of Israel's enemies and a significant influx of goods into the city for the benefit of the people. See 4 Kings 6-7.

By comparison, at the pope's request, St. Francis de Sales entered the city of Geneva to meet with the "Protestant Patriarch" Theodore Beza. Beza was the handpicked successor to John Calvin. Beza and St. Francis de Sales had a conversation, after which Beza was visibly troubled. It is thought that Beza wanted to convert to the Catholic Faith, but he found it too difficult, given his position and reputation in the city.[66] However, a great many common people converted away from Calvinism and back to the Catholic Faith because of the work of St. Francis de Sales.

The Demon Kills the Spouses
SARAH'S HUSBANDS ARE KILLED BY ASMODEUS AND HENRY VIII KILLS HIS "WIVES" BECAUSE OF THE DEMON OF LUST

The book of Tobias takes place during this time period of "Revolt and Separation". If you recall, the northern Kingdom of Israel was eventually conquered and taken into exile by the Assyrian Empire. The book of Tobias occurs inside the Assyrian Empire when and where the Israelites were in captivity.

The book of Tobias revolves around a set of definite themes woven throughout the story. Those themes are:

1. Marriage / consummation of marriage

2. Difficulty in producing offspring

3. Avoiding lust, especially as a reason to marry

In this instance, the parallels between the Old and New have an unexpected and inverse quality about them. The book of Tobias has a happy ending and a clear moral lesson. However, in the story from Church history, the outcome is tragic. Nonetheless, I think you will agree that the parallels between the Old and New are striking.

111

The book of Tobias starts with the story of an old man named Tobias, who lived in exile in Assyria. The northern Israelites were all taken into exile, including Tobias. However, Tobias was not a typical northern-kingdom Israelite because, despite his nation's apostasy, he had refrained from worshiping the golden calves of Jeroboam and went to the Temple in Jerusalem to offer sacrifice. While in exile, he kept the Law of Moses by burying the dead and giving alms.

Tobias got in trouble with his pagan overlords for burying the dead, and all his kinsmen told him he was going to get killed for his piety. However, Tobias did what was right, even if it meant his death. He was widely recognized for his piety and virtue. Even though he was virtuous and good, he was further tested by God by being blinded.

Tobias and his wife only had one son, also named Tobias. They sent him to a distant town to recover some money owed to them. God heard the prayers of this poor, pious family and sent an angel disguised as a man to help Tobias on his journey. The angel was St. Raphael.

At the same time, another tragedy was unfolding elsewhere in the Assyrian Empire. Another exiled Israelite named Sarah had just lost her seventh husband. Every time she married, and just before the new couple could consummate, a demon named Asmodeus killed her husband. Thus, Sarah remained a virgin despite having been married seven times. Keep in mind that for the Israelites, having children was considered a great blessing from God, and remaining childless was considered to be a great curse.

The angel Raphael directed young Tobias to Sarah, and Tobias approached her father and asked to marry her. He was told by Raphael that before they consummated the marriage, they were to wait three days and pray to Almighty God.

> "But thou when thou shalt take her, go into the chamber,
> and for three days keep thyself continent from her, and give
> thyself to nothing else but to prayers with her."

"And when the third night is past, thou shalt take the virgin with the fear of the Lord, moved rather for love of children than for lust, that in the seed of Abraham, thou mayst obtain a blessing in children."

- Tobias 6: 18, 22

Sarah's father peeked in on the newly married couple and was delighted to see that Tobias had not been killed like the previous seven husbands. He gave the new couple half of his possessions. Tobias and Sarah traveled back to Tobias' parents, who, at this time, were worried about his long delay. Tobias was their only son, and they were scared to lose him and be left childless. Tobias arrived home with his new wife and many possessions, causing great joy. As an extra blessing to Tobias (the elder), he was cured of his blindness through the wisdom of the angel Raphael.

Let's look now at Henry VIII and his "wives."

In 1501, the sixteen year-old Princess Catherine of Aragon married the young English Prince Arthur, Henry VIII's older brother. Catherine was a pious woman, seeking the will of God in her life, fasting and praying often. The pope even told her to lessen her fasts because they were too severe. Within a year of their marriage, Arthur died.

Since the kings of England and Spain still wanted to create an alliance between their two kingdoms, Catherine of Aragon was betrothed to Arthur's brother, Henry VIII.[67] Because Catherine had been the wife of Henry VIII's brother, she was related to him by marriage and needed a papal dispensation to marry him according to canon law. The pope granted the dispensation, and the marriage was permitted.

Over several years, Henry VIII and Catherine tried to produce a male heir. Catherine suffered through a horrific number of miscarriages, stillbirths, and children dying as infants. She had a total of six mishaps, with only one child surviving, Mary Tudor.

Henry VIII kept mistresses during this time. He had a son, Henry Fitzroy, by one of his mistresses. He was acknowledged by Henry VIII and given a dukedom. Still, Henry VIII was growing restless and impatient with Catherine because she was not producing a male heir. Henry VIII famously divorced Queen Catherine, without an annulment from the pope, and broke with the Catholic Church. His lust was so great that he went through five different "wives," getting rid of some by killing them and others by divorcing them. He covered up his lust with the excuse of looking for a woman who could give him a son.

Now that we have established some basic facts in the stories of Tobias and Henry VIII, let us explore the remarkable parallels between these stories.

In the Old Testament, Sarah lost seven husbands to a demon of lust named Asmodeus.[k] Before they could consummate the marriage with her, they were all struck dead. Later in the book of Tobias, it is explained that these men only lusted after Sarah and did not marry her for the godly reason of bringing up offspring in the fear of the Lord.

> "Then the angel Raphael said to him: Hear me, and I will shew thee who they are, over whom the devil can prevail. For they who in such manner receive matrimony, as to shut out God from themselves, and from their mind, and to give themselves to their lust, as the horse and mule, which have not understanding, over them the devil hath power."
>
> -Tobias 6: 16-17

By comparison, Henry and Catherine tried to produce offspring in their marriage, but Catherine lost six children. She was unable to produce a male heir for Henry. In the Old Testament, Sarah's husbands were struck dead before they could consummate the marriage with her. Additionally, it is noted that Sarah was a pious and devout young Israelite woman. By comparison, Catherine's first husband, Arthur, died before they consummated their marriage.[68] Catherine was a pious and devout young Catholic woman.

---

k   Many ancient cultures linked Asmodeus to lust, a vice he embodied. The 1486 medieval book *Malleus Maleficarum* also named him as the demon of lust.

Finally, there are some details concerning the events around Catherine and Henry VIII that I have not explored, but on the surface, they also have parallels with the book of Tobias. For example, Catherine's father was reluctant to pay a dowry[67] to her first husband's father, King Henry VII. In contrast, Sarah's father agreed to pay a large dowry to Tobias after his marriage to Sarah.

> "And when Raguel had pressed Tobias with many words, and he by no means would hearken to him, he delivered Sara unto him, and half of all his substance in menservants, and womenservants, in cattle, in camels, and in kine, and in much money, and sent him away safe and joyful from him."
>
> - Tobias 10: 9

Let us leave behind the story of Tobias and King Henry VIII for now and move on to another topic of parallels: the rise of the Assyrian Empire in the Old Testament and the Ottoman Empire in Church history. They both arose at the same corresponding time in their respective histories. The Assyrian Empire emerged to threaten Israel after the rebellion of the ten northern tribes, and the Ottoman Turks threatened Christendom during and after the Protestant Rebellion. They both were a brutal scourge.

A Brutal Enemy Empire Arises and Displaces Israel
THE ASSYRIANS AND THE OTTOMAN TURKS

The rebellion of the ten northern tribes and the establishment of the northern apostate kingdom was disastrous for the united Kingdom of Israel. The Nation of Israel during the reigns of King David and King Solomon was strong and united. Because of its later division and civil war in the times of Jeroboam and subsequent rebels, the surrounding pagan empires were able to grow in power. Such was the case with the Assyrian Empire.

The Assyrian Empire was growing throughout the books of 3 and 4 Kings, contemporaneous with the ten tribes' rebellion. They grew to overpower the northern kingdom completely[1] and would have also conquered the southern Kingdom of Juda were it not for God's intervention. The Assyrians could field a vast army, far greater than the northern and southern kingdoms could match. When the Assyrians laid siege to Jerusalem, they came with an army of 185,000. They seemed like an unstoppable force.

Europe was a stronghold of Catholicism and enjoyed a period of strength and cultural flourishing during the Middle Ages and the Renaissance. However, this unity was shattered by the Protestant Revolt, which began in 1517 and sparked a series of religious wars and conflicts that lasted for more than a century. As a result, Christendom was weakened and divided, and faced a formidable enemy: the Ottoman Empire. The Ottomans were a Muslim dynasty that ruled over a vast territory in Asia, Africa, and Europe. They had conquered Constantinople, the former capital of the Byzantine Empire, in 1453, and expanded their influence into the Balkans and Eastern Europe. The Ottoman Empire was a military and political powerhouse that posed a serious threat to the survival of Christian Europe. The Ottomans had a huge army, a powerful navy, abundant resources, and expansive territory. They seemed to be an unstoppable force that would eventually overrun Europe, just as the Assyrians had done to the Israelites in ancient times. The Ottomans took advantage of the division of Christendom[m], just as the Assyrians did with the division of Israel.

Both the Assyrians and the Ottomans were unspeakably cruel. The Assyrian Empire led the northern Israelites away into slavery by putting rings through their lips and then attaching chains to the rings from which they would pull them along the road into exile.[n] There are many more examples of their cruelty. The Assyrians also practiced a policy of forced population relocation. They took the Israelites out of their land and moved in peoples from other pagan lands to settle.[56] Thus, northern Israel (known as

---

l   4 Kings 17: 1-18

m   The Ottoman Turks allied with the Calvinists, who shared their hostility towards the Holy Roman Empire. The Wars of Religion in Europe distracted and drained the Christian powers, making Ottoman expansion into Eastern Europe easier.

n   Isaias 37:29: "When thou wast mad against me, thy pride came up to my ears: therefore I will put a **ring in thy nose, and a bit between thy lips**, and I will turn thee back by the way by which thou camest."

Samaria) became a mixture of different peoples and languages. Another result of this policy was that the ten tribes lost their identity in exile, being assimilated into myriads of foreign peoples.

Likewise, the Ottoman Turks were especially cruel in the way they treated conquered populations. They employed bizarre and horrible tortures and also engaged in a policy of forced population relocation. This was known as deportation (sürgün) or resettlement (iskân). This policy scattered native populations across their vast empire as a way to dominate them and eliminate any possibility of revolt against the Ottoman Empire.[69] As a result of this policy of population displacement, so many poor Christians just became absorbed into the cultures and religions of their new locations, forgetting their identity and religion. Take, for example, the Ottoman Janissaries.

The Janissaries were the elite unit of soldiers of the Ottoman Empire. They were entirely composed of formerly Christian men who were taken from their Christian families when they were just young boys. The Ottomans indoctrinated them with Islam and trained them to fight against Christians as a way to further demoralize conquered territories.[70]

Before the Assyrian Empire grew to dominate the region, near the beginning of the ten tribes revolt, both the northern and southern kingdoms would make alliances with the Assyrian Empire at different times. The king of Juda, Achaz, made a deal with the Assyrians that was seen as an abomination by the devout Jews in his kingdom. This outrage was voiced by the prophet Isaias, who spoke against this unholy alliance and prophesied that it would come back to harm the Kingdom of Juda later.

> "And Achaz sent messengers to Theglathphalasar king of the Assyrians, saying: I am thy servant and thy son: come up, and save me out of the hand of the king of Syria, and out of the hand of the king of Israel, who are risen up together against me."
>
> - 4 Kings 16 : 7

And likewise, in Church history, unholy alliances were made with the Ottoman Empire.

Starting at the beginning of the Protestant Revolt and well into the seventeenth century, the Ottoman Empire was sought after by both Catholic and Protestant powers for alliances against their enemies. The most notable was the Franco-Ottoman alliance, which King Francis I of France was so shamefully responsible for. This alliance was seen as an abomination throughout Catholic Europe.[71] It was unthinkable for a Catholic king to offer weapons, money, and trade to the Christian-killing Muslim Ottoman Empire. However, France and the Ottomans had a common enemy, Charles V and the Holy Roman Empire. Europe's religious and political disunity created a situation in which the Ottoman Empire could expand and grow powerful. This is still heartbreaking to consider. What would have been the outcome if France and the Holy Roman Empire, both powerful Catholic monarchies, had put aside their differences and fought alongside each other? Instead, France chose to ally with the Muslim Ottoman Turks against the Holy Roman Empire. It is almost unimaginable.

As the Assyrians grew in power, and after they conquered the northern apostate Kingdom of Israel and forcibly displaced the land's inhabitants, they turned their attention to the southern Kingdom of Juda and the capital city of Jerusalem. The Assyrians came up against Jerusalem with 185,000 soldiers to conquer the southern kingdom and dominate the entire region. However, the Lord sent an angel that night into the Assyrian camp, who killed all 185,000 of the Assyrian army. The Lord saved His holy city from destruction. This happened because of the faithfulness of King Ezechias, the king of Juda. He piously went before the ark to beg God's intervention.

By comparison, the Ottoman Turks conquered much of Eastern Europe, including both Catholic and Protestant lands. They were still looking to expand further, even into Western Europe. However, the fortified Catholic city of Vienna stood in their way. In many ways, Vienna was the capital of the Holy Roman Empire. If Vienna fell to the Ottoman Turks, Western Europe would have been opened up to Ottoman expansion. Rome would have been a future target for the Muslims. The Turks, however, tried but failed to conquer Vienna. The winged Polish cavalry, the Hussars, saved Vienna from destruction.[72]

Now let us examine more closely the amazing parallels between the Battle of Vienna in 1683 and the Assyrian-slaying angel from the book of 4 Kings, chapter 19.

The Winged Savior Delivers God's People
THE ANGEL KILLS THE ASSYRIAN ARMY AND THE WINGED HUSSARS
DEFEAT THE OTTOMAN TURKS – BATTLE OF VIENNA 1683

In the Old Testament, King Ezechias ruled over the southern Kingdom of Juda when the Assyrian Empire was at its peak. The southern Kingdom of Juda paid tribute to the Assyrians so they would not attack Jerusalem. But King Ezechias stopped paying this tribute, which eventually caused the Assyrian Empire to bring its large army to attack Jerusalem.° The Assyrians came to Jerusalem with a massive army of 185,000 soldiers to lay siege to the city. The Jews in Jerusalem could not come close to matching the size of such a force. The Assyrians sent a man named Rabsaces to approach the walls of Jerusalem and shout up to the men, telling them they should surrender. Rabsaces said they had no chance of victory, and if they surrendered, they would be treated well. King Ezechias refused to surrender.

> "Then Rabsaces stood, and cried out with a loud voice in the Jews' language, and said: Hear the words of the great king, the king of the Assyrians. Thus saith the king: Let not Ezechias deceive you: for he shall not be able to deliver you out of my hand. Neither let him make you trust in the Lord, saying: The Lord will surely deliver us, and this city shall not be given into the hand of the king of the Assyrians. Do not hearken to Ezechias. For thus saith the king of the Assyrians: Do with me that which is for your advantage, and come out to me: and every man of you shall eat of his own vineyard, and of his own fig tree: and you shall drink water of your own cisterns"

o   4 Kings 18: 7

119

- 4 Kings 18: 28 – 31

Taunted by the Assyrians and confronted with the overwhelming force, King Ezechias went before the Lord in the Temple and prayed before the ark.[p] That night, an angel of God came down unexpectedly and killed the entire Assyrian army of 185,000. The Assyrian king was devastated and was forced to retreat in defeat. The city of Jerusalem was safe, and God miraculously saved his people from destruction.

> "And it came to pass that night, that an angel of the Lord came, and slew in the camp of the Assyrians a hundred and eighty-five thousand. And when he arose early in the morning, he saw all the bodies of the dead."
>
> - 4 Kings 19: 35

In the 1500s and 1600s, the Muslim Ottoman Empire was at the peak of its power and influence. Various regions of Hungary were paying tribute to the Ottomans so they would not invade and conquer. The Holy Roman Empire, Hapsburg Hungary, and other smaller principalities joined together in an alliance to oppose the Ottoman Turks in 1683, at which time tribute was halted to the Ottomans. These actions were met with a landmark encounter between the Ottoman Turks and the Catholic coalition.[73]

In July of 1683, the Ottomans approached the walls of Vienna, the capital of the Holy Roman Empire at that time. The Ottomans had between 90,000 and 300,000 soldiers[73][74], while the Viennese defended their city with only 15,000 to 70,000.[75]

Before the battle started, an Ottoman representative was sent to the walls of Vienna to ask for surrender. In response, the leader of the Catholic army in Vienna, Count Ernst Rudiger von Starhemberg, said they would "fight to the last drop of blood".

---

p   See 4 Kings 19:14. The ark was located in the "holy of holies" in the Temple. When King Ezechias is said to have went before the Lord, it implies that he went to the ark, since that is where the Lord was present.

In anticipation of the Ottoman siege, Vienna had reached out to the Polish King, John Sobieski III for help. John Sobieski made a public and very pious petition to Our Lady of Częstochowa, and he entrusted his entire kingdom to her.[76] (Remember that Our Lady is the new Ark.) Afterwards, he departed for the defense of Vienna.

On September 12, 1683, the Polish army emerged from the forest to the cheers of the men on the walls of Vienna. The Polish army included highly effective cavalry units called the *Winged Hussars*, armed knights that wore large angel wings on their backs. King John Sobieski III led over 18,000 mounted Hussars in a crushing cavalry charge against the Ottoman Turks. This was the largest cavalry charge in recorded history. The Ottoman Turks were defeated thanks to the Hussars and Vienna was saved.

Vienna's fall to the Ottoman Turks would have made Western Europe and Rome easier to conquer. Vienna was saved from the Ottomans, thanks to Our Lady and the brave Polish King, John Sobieski (and his Winged Hussars). Because they saved Christendom from further Muslim conquest, the pope made a new feast day for all to celebrate: the Feast of the Holy Name of Mary.

Thus, in both stories, God's people appealed to the ark and were delivered from the Assyrian and Ottoman Empire respectively at the last minute by the "winged savior". Remarkable!

Now, let's shift gears and move to a more mystical story in the Old Testament about the seraphim angel purifying the lips of Isaias the prophet. There are beautiful parallels between Isaias the prophet and St. Margaret Mary.

Purified by Divine Fire to Speak for God
ISAIAS THE PROPHET AND ST. MARGARET MARY

Isaias prophesied in Jerusalem in the time after the revolt of the ten northern tribes but before the Babylonian conquest and exile (which marks the start of our next time period). Isaias declared that he was unworthy to be

God's messenger because he was a man of unclean lips coming from a people of unclean lips. God sent a "burning one,"[q] a seraphim angel, to Isaias with a hot coal from the altar in Heaven. The angel pressed the hot coal to Isaias' lips, purifying them.

St. Margaret Mary Alocoque lived in the mid-to-late seventeenth century. She lived in the time after the Protestant Revolt but before the French Revolution (which marks the parallel for the Babylonian conquest and exile and the start of our next time period). She received apparitions from Our Lord, starting in 1673 and ending in 1674. Fire was a dominant theme throughout these apparitions.

St. Margaret Mary was asked by Our Lord to spread devotion to His Sacred Heart, to be the *Apostle of the Sacred Heart*. She expressed her unworthiness for such a task. But instead of her lips being purified, as in the story of Isaias, it was her heart that was purified. Our Lord took the heart of St. Margaret Mary and immersed it in the "burning furnace" of His Sacred Heart. He then returned her heart, all ablaze with divine love; thus, she was purified for her mission.[77][r] Her autobiography is filled with strong language describing her burning love for God. She wanted to make a return to Our Lord for His love, but she felt she could not do enough.

At the beginning of the book of Isaias, he saw a vision of the throne of God in Heaven. This is a unique and extraordinary privilege. During this vision, a seraphim descended with a hot coal from the altar in Heaven and placed it on the lips of Isaias. This action purified his lips so he could speak for God.

> "And one of the Seraphim flew to me, and in his hand was a live coal, which he had taken with the tongs off the altar. And he touched my mouth and said: Behold this hath touched thy lips, and thy iniquities shall be taken away, and thy sin shall be cleansed. And I heard the voice of the Lord,

---

q   The word *seraphim* comes from the Hebrew word for "burning" or "fiery".

r   See page 45 of *The Autobiography of St. Margaret Mary* (noted in the Bibliography citation next to this footnote above.)

saying: Whom shall I send? and who shall go for us? And I said: Lo, here am I, send me."

- Isaias 6 : 6-8

It is fascinating that in the Old Testament, it was just the lips that were purified, but in the parallel history of the Church, it is the heart that is purified. This speaks eloquently to how Our Lord came to write the law of God on our hearts. The Old Testament was an exercise in externally following God's laws, thus the focus on the mere lips of Isaias. However, Our Lord wants our hearts to be converted, for as we know, it is from the fullness of the heart that the mouth speaketh. Did not God say, "This people honoureth me with their lips: but their heart is far from Me?"[s]

The parallels between the Old Testament story of Isaias and the story of St. Margaret Mary are stunning and meaningful, particularly because of the lesson contained in the messages of the Sacred Heart devotion. When we see these juxtaposed to the story of Isaias, even greater meaning is given to us. He wants our hearts converted to Him, not just outward practices and words. Our hearts must burn with love for Him, and our lips will easily follow. He sacrificed ALL of Himself on the cross and the only appropriate response is for us to give ourselves totally back to Him.

During the apparitions of Our Lord to St. Margaret Mary Alocoque, Our Lord purified St. Margaret Mary for her mission as the *Apostle of the Sacred Heart*. He asked for her heart, which she willingly gave Him. He then placed her heart, which appeared tiny, into the burning furnace of His divine Heart. After her heart was aflame, Our Lord placed her heart back where it came from. He gave her a new heart that would "burn her up" and be a little spark of the hot flames of His divine Heart. He promised that she would experience humiliation and suffering more than relief. Finally, he called her the beloved disciple of His Sacred Heart.[77][t]

---

s   Our Lord spoke these words in Matthew 15:8. He was referring to Isaias 29:13 where it is written "Forasmuch as this people draw near me with their mouth, and with their lips glorify me, but their heart is far from me". Here is another point of connection between the Sacred Heart and the book of Isaias.

t   See page 45 of *The Autobiography of St. Margaret Mary* (noted in the Bibliography citation next to this footnote above.)

Another remarkable similarity between Isaias and St. Margaret Mary is that they both approached the king, indicating problems in the kingdom. In both instances, the result was the end of the kingdom that had been so long established over God's people. In the Old Testament, it was the end of the Davidic kingdom; in Church history, it was the end of the French monarchy. We will cover these particular parallels in the following time period. I will just touch upon them here in as much as they are relevant to Isaias and St. Margaret Mary.

Isaias prophesied to King Ezechias that his kingly descendants would be taken as captives into Babylon. This happened when the Babylonians invaded Jerusalem during the days of King Sedecias. This event ended the rule of the kings of Juda, who never again were able to re-establish their kingdom. Isaias started his prophecy around the year 740 BC and is thought to have lived into the reign of King Manasses, dying, most likely, around the year 670 to 690 BC. This means that Isaias died approximately one hundred years before the end of the Davidic kingdom at the hands of the Babylonians in 597 BC.

> "Behold the days shall come, that all that is in thy house, and that thy fathers have laid up in store until this day, shall be carried away into Babylon: there shall not any thing be left, saith the Lord. And of thy children, that shall issue from thee, whom thou shalt beget, they shall take away, and they shall be eunuchs in the palace of the king of Babylon."
>
> - Isaias 39: 6-7

As for our paralleled story in Church history, Our Lord famously requested, through St. Margaret Mary Alocoque, that the king of France consecrate France to His Sacred Heart. It is well known that one hundred years after the request of Our Lord was made known, the French monarchy was overthrown by the French Revolution in 1789, and never again would an autonomous sovereign king reign from the French throne. There would be a few other kings of France after the French Revolution but they were limited, having to share power with the people.

Finally, I want to point out another parallel, somewhat more abstract but wonderful and edifying. The book of Isaias contains the beautiful and astonishing prophecy of Our Lord's suffering and death. This prophecy is known as the *Suffering Servant* and is a remarkable description of the Passion of Christ. Here are the passages from the book of Isaias:

> "Despised, and the most abject of men, a man of sorrows, and acquainted with infirmity: and his look was as it were hidden and despised, whereupon we esteemed him not. Surely he hath borne our infirmities and carried our sorrows: and we have thought him as it were a leper, and as one struck by God and afflicted. But he was wounded for our iniquities, he was bruised for our sins: the chastisement of our peace was upon him, and by his bruises we are healed. All we like sheep have gone astray, every one hath turned aside into his own way: and the Lord hath laid on him the iniquity of us all."
>
> - Isaias 53: 3-6

Likewise, how Isaias prophesied about Our Lord being a suffering servant, Our Lord Himself mentioned as much to St. Margaret Mary. Throughout her life, she was a suffering servant. She had accepted physical ailments, humiliations, and even mystical penances all because she wanted to imitate Our Lord, the suffering servant.

During the apparitions of Our Lord to St. Margaret Mary, Our Lord told her about His sufferings for the sins of men. He described the abundance of love in His heart for mankind. He gave everything on the Cross, but has only received coldness and indifference from the vast portion of mankind. Our Lord expressed to her that He was hurt more by this indifference than by the pains of His passion. Our Lord indicated to her that He would look for more ways to suffer and give to mankind if it would mean they would offer Him a little love in return.[77][u] Thus, through the words in St. Margaret Mary's autobiography, Our Lord was clearly portraying Himself as a suffering servant.

---

u   See page 46-47 of *The Autobiography of St. Margaret Mary* (noted in the Bibliography citation next to this footnote above.)

Not only are these parallels between the Old Testament and Church history chronologically ordered with extensive details, but they also contain poetry. The stories in the Old Testament, when compared to their counterparts in Church history, can bring out the truths of the Catholic Faith and highlight Catholic piety and devotion. Indeed, the Incarnation fundamentally changed our relationship with Our Heavenly Father, as is evidenced by the differences between the Old Testament and Church history.

Now let us move on to the last subject in this time period. It is the parallels between the sundial of Ezechias and the Gregorian calendar. I think you will appreciate this one also.

The Great King Resets Time by Ten
THE SUNDIAL OF KING EZECHIAS AND THE GREGORIAN CALENDAR

In 4 Kings 18, the good king Ezechias went before the ark of the Lord to ask God to save the city of Jerusalem, which was about to be conquered by the Assyrian army. God sent an angel that night who killed all the Assyrians, saving Jerusalem. Shortly after the defeat of the Assyrians, Ezechias fell sick and was dying. The prophet Isaias told him that God would work a miracle and heal him.

It just so happened that King Ezechias' father gave him a sundial. This is the only reference to a sundial in the whole of the Old Testament. King Ezechias asked that the sundial retreat ten steps backward. For the sundial to retreat ten steps back, the sun would have to miraculously retreat across the sky.

> "And Ezechias had said to Isaias: What shall be the sign that the Lord will heal me, and that I shall go up to the Temple of the Lord the third day? And Isaias said to him: This shall be the sign from the Lord, that the Lord will do the word which he hath spoken: Wilt thou that the shadow go forward ten lines, or that it go back so many degrees? And Ezechias said: It is an easy matter for the shadow to go forward ten lines: and I do not desire that this be done, but let it return back

ten degrees. And Isaias the prophet called upon the Lord, and he brought the shadow ten degrees backwards by the lines, by which it had already gone down in the dial of Achaz."

- 4 Kings 20: 8-11

This is not the only story about King Ezechias pertaining to the altering of time. In another story, King Ezechias was preparing a great Passover feast in Jerusalem. Passover was the most important feast day for the Jews, for it marked their deliverance from slavery in Egypt. However, Ezechias noticed that his people were not ready for the Passover on the prescribed day. Passover was always celebrated on the new moon in the first month of Nisan. Ezechias made a bold decision to move the date of Passover back one month. Note that in the citation below, the word "phase" indicates "Passover".

"And Ezechias sent to all Israel and Juda: and he wrote letters to Ephraim and Manasses, that they should come to the house of the Lord in Jerusalem, and keep the phase to the Lord the God of Israel. For the king, taking counsel, and the princes, and all the assembly of Jerusalem, **decreed to keep the phase the second month.**[v] For they could not keep it in its time; because there were not priests enough sanctified, and the people was not as yet gathered together to Jerusalem. _And the thing pleased the king, and all the people. _And they decreed to send messengers to all Israel from Bersabee even to Dan, that they should come, and keep the phase to the Lord the God of Israel in Jerusalem: for many had not kept it as it is prescribed by the law."

- 2 Paralipomenon 30: 1 – 4

In Church history, in 1571, Pope St. Pius V pleaded with God for a victory over the Ottoman Turks, who were launching a naval invasion force. Through the intercession of Our Lady (the new Ark), God delivered Europe through a historic victory of the Catholic navy at the Battle of Lepanto. This

---

v   Passover was to be kept in the first month of Nissan. But in this text, King Ezechias decreed to keep Passover in the second month of Iyar. Thus, King Ezechias is moving back the celebration of Passover by one month.

miraculous victory echoes the deliverance of Jerusalem by the angel, as a result of the prayers of Ezechias before the ark.

Shortly after this, in 1582, Pope Gregory XIII was faced with the problem of revising the universal calendar. The Julian calendar, which had been in use since the days of Julius Caesar in 46 BC, contained an inaccuracy relating to how the leap year was calculated. Because of this, over the course of sixteen-hundred years of Christian history, the date of the spring equinox was migrating slowly, creating a difference of ten days between the actual date of the spring equinox and its supposed date on the calendar. This was important because it affected the date on which Easter was celebrated. The rule was that the full moon preceding Easter was not to precede the spring equinox. The discrepancy of ten days was making this rule impossible to follow.[78]

Pope Gregory XIII, therefore, revised the calendar to make it more accurate. In doing so, it was necessary to delete ten days from the calendar. The calendar took effect in October. The day before the calendar took effect was Thursday, October 4, 1582. The calendar immediately skipped ten days, and the first day of the new calendar was Friday, October 15, 1582, even though it was, in reality, only a day later than October 4. Thus, instead of skipping backward ten degrees, like the miracle of the sundial of Ezechias, the calendar skipped forward ten days.

The changing of the calendar by Pope Gregory XIII also changed the date of Easter. From that point on, Easter was celebrated on a different date in Catholic countries than in Protestant lands. Easter is comparable to the Old Testament Passover. The Easter Triduum is our celebration of our deliverance from the slavery of sin, Satan, and death. The Old Testament Passover required the slaughter of an innocent lamb, whose blood was to be spread on the doorposts. In the New Testament, Our Lord was the innocent Lamb who was killed and whose Precious Blood covered the cross on which He died.

This concludes my presentation of Period 5. Before we move on, I would like to include a parallel that did not mange to find a place in prior pages. It pertains to an Old Testament compilation of various writings concerning Holy Wisdom and its New Testament counterpart.

The book of Proverbs is mostly attributed to King Solomon but has several sections attributed to numerous authors over varying time periods. The earliest collection of proverbs dates to about 700 BC, which is the time of the divided kingdoms of Israel and Juda (after Jeroboam but before the Babylonian captivity). The book of Proverbs is a collection of wisdom compiled into one book. If we, as Catholics, have read the footnotes in our missals, we would be aware that Holy Wisdom in the Old Testament is a figure of Our Lady.

> "The Lord possessed me in the beginning of his ways, before he made any thing from the beginning."

> - Proverbs 8:22

> "I am the mother of fair love, and of fear, and of knowledge, and of holy hope. In me is all grace of the way and of the truth, in me is all hope of life and of virtue. Come over to me, all ye that desire me, and be filled with my fruits. For my spirit is sweet above honey, and my inheritance above honey and the honeycomb. My memory is unto everlasting generations. They that eat me, shall yet hunger: and they that drink me, shall yet thirst. He that hearkeneth to me, shall not be confounded: and they that work by me, shall not sin. They that explain me shall have life everlasting."

> - Ecclesiasticus 24: 24-31

At this same respective time in Church history, during the time of divided Christendom (after Martin Luther but before the French Revolution), St. Alphonsus Liguori wrote *The Glories of Mary*, which is a compilation of stories about Our Lady's intercession, miracles and mercy for her children. Its a compilation of writings glorifying Our Lady, just like the book of Proverbs is a compilation of wisdom.

Now, let us move on to Period 6, "Invasion and Exile".

Period 6
Invasion and Exile

After war with the apostate north, God's people are weakened. A powerful, unholy empires arises. It besieges and subjugates God's people.

OLD TESTAMENT: Books of 4 Kings, Daniel, Jeremias, and Ezechiel

The twelve tribes of Israel were united under the leadership of King David and King Solomon. After King Solomon's death, Israel's united kingdom was ripped in two by the rebellion of Jeroboam. The northern apostate Kingdom of Israel and the southern Kingdom of Juda were never reunited. After so much internal chaos and relentless waves of apostasy, the northern kingdom was eventually assimilated by the Assyrian Empire.

The southern Kingdom of Juda remained intact, even though it was greatly weakened. The last king of Juda, King Sedecias, was deposed by the Babylonian Empire and their king, Nabuchodonosor. The Jews were brought into exile into Babylon, where they lived under secular and pagan laws. There was immense pressure from the dominant Babylonian culture, which tested their belief in the one true God. At this time, God raised up prophets like Jeremias, Daniel, and Ezechiel. The Jews remained in exile for seventy years until the Persian King Cyrus allowed them to return to Jerusalem. Upon their return, they governed Jerusalem as a city-state inside the larger Persian Empire. Their return marks the end of Period 6 and the start of Period 7.

CHURCH HISTORY: Approximately 1800^{AD} to 1929^{AD}

Christendom had been united during the Middle Ages and the Renaissance under the rule of Carolingian kings, descended from Charlemagne. At the end of the Renaissance, Christendom was ripped in two by the revolt of Martin Luther. Much of northern Christendom followed Luther's Protestant Revolt. Luther set the example of rebellion from Church authority, so wave after wave of Protestant movements came and went in the centuries following Luther. By the end of the eighteenth century, Protestantism had assimilated many secular and "enlightenment" ideas, drifting far from the heretical ideas of which Luther had originally started.

The Catholic kingdoms to the south remained sovereign and intact, even though they were weakening. The world was becoming increasingly hostile to religion. The French Revolution broke out, and the king of France, Louis XVI, was beheaded. Emperor Napoleon deposed the last Holy Roman Emperor, Francis II, only years later. Catholics were now living in exile, albeit in their own lands. Secular and worldly governments, ideologies, and movements pressured Catholics to give up their religious convictions as they were tested to hold fast to the Faith.

At this time, God sent His Mother to appear throughout France. Famous and beloved apparitions such as Lourdes, LaSalette, Pontmain, and Rue du Bac, among others, gave Catholics hope. In 1870, the Holy See had its land stolen by the Freemasonic Kingdom of Italy. For the first time since 756, the pope no longer ruled an actual territory. In 1929, the Lateran Treaty was signed with the Holy See, granting it the city-state of Vatican City. Inside Vatican City, the Holy See could once again live by Her own laws.

Here is a summary chart of the parallels presented in this time period. Each section of this summary chart will be expanded in subsequent pages.

Old Testament	New Testament
The Babylonians conquered the Kingdom of Juda, deposed the last king, and took the Jews into exile.	The French Revolution conquered the French monarchy, deposed King Louis XVI, and spread secularism throughout Europe.

After the Babylonian conquest, the Jews spread throughout the ancient world; this is known as the diaspora.	Catholic immigration in the 1800s spread Catholics throughout the New World.
God came to dwell with His people, as evidenced through the vision of Ezechiel and the words of the prophets.	Our Lady appeared, comforting and healing Catholics in many well-known Marian Apparitions throughout France.
Daniel is taken from Jerusalem and put in a Babylonian school for boys. He had a gift for interpreting dreams.	St. John Bosco started a boys school for orphans and likewise had a gift of dreams and interpretation.
The Babylonians took the land of the Jews and brought them into Babylon as prisoners.	The Freemasonic Kingdom of Italy took the land of the Holy See, and the popes were prisoners in the Vatican.

The Babylonian Conquest Of Juda And The French Revolution

The French Revolution was a gigantic turning point in the history of Europe and Western Civilization. It marked the beginning of the end of Catholic monarchy in Europe and the destruction of the last vestiges of the Catholic Church's temporal authority.[a] It was a tragedy, a disaster, and a great evil on a monumental scale. The black cloud of the French Revolution casts its shadow onto the rest of the history of the Catholic Church going forward, as we are still experiencing its effects today.

Likewise, the destruction of Jerusalem and the Temple in the Old Testament was a tragedy for the Jews that shook them to their foundations. It marked the end of the Kingdom of Juda, as never again would a Judean king

---

a   Before the French Revolution, most Catholic countries in Europe were ruled by absolute or constitutional monarchies that upheld the Church's authority and privileges; in decades following the Revolution, Catholic countries adopted republican, imperial, or democratic forms of government that challenged or reduced the Church's influence and power.

sit on the temporal throne of David.[b] It was a gigantic turning point in the Jews' history and changed how they thought about themselves and their place in the world. The parallels between these two cataclysmic events are numerous and quite impressive.

After summarizing the parallels between the Babylonian conquest of Juda and the French Revolution in the following chart, we'll examine more closely the parallels for these pivotal events.

Old Testament	New Testament
The southern Kingdom of Juda had grown weak and was overshadowed by a powerful empire.	Catholic kingdoms had grown weak with the rise of powerful new ideologies like secularism, atheism, scientism, etc.
Just prior to the invasion of the Babylonians, the Jews had silenced the prophet Jeremias.	Just prior to the French Revolution, Catholic kings and the pope suppressed the Jesuits.
King Sedecias was getting help from abroad and later fled through his garden.	King Louis XVI was getting help from Austria and later fled through the Tuileries Gardens of Paris.
King Sedecias tried to flee and was caught and punished.	King Louis XVI tried to flee and was caught and punished.
The walls of Jerusalem were symbolically demolished to make a point.	The Bastille and Cluny Abbey were demolished, brick by brick, to make a point.
The Temple was looted and destroyed, halting the practice of the Jewish religion.	Notre Dame was desecrated, assets stolen, and Catholic priests were driven into hiding.

---

b   By "temporal throne" I mean the earthly Kingdom of Israel. Our Lord inherited the kingdom of David, His father. Our Lord's kingdom is Heavenly. But because Our Lord reigns also through the Church, then perhaps the Church's authority can also be seen as an extension of the Davidic kingdom.

133

God's Kingdom Has Grown Weak

The northern Kingdom of Israel and the southern Kingdom of Juda existed side by side for centuries. The northern kingdom was carried away and scattered, losing their identity. The southern Kingdom of Juda lasted longer, keeping their Temple and their kingdom, but were reduced to a small, powerless state. The Babylonian Empire rose to dominance during this time, conquering the Jews, destroying their Temple, and bringing them into exile in Babylon.

Likewise, Protestants and Catholic countries existed side by side in Europe for centuries after Luther's revolt. During the "Age of Enlightenment," Protestants were carried away by new secular ideas, as formerly Protestant governments became increasingly secular. Protestantism lost its cohesiveness and became scattered in its theology, being absorbed into the modern world.

Catholic kingdoms lasted much longer, keeping their identity, led by the pope in Rome. Nonetheless, Catholic authority lost influence as secular ideas grew and spread across Europe. These ideologies manifested into political movements that ultimately overcame the Catholic monarchies and transformed Europe into a neo-pagan land. The French Revolution marked the beginning of this new era. Catholics became exiles in their own lands.

The Silencing of the Holy Man
JEREMIAS IS SUPPRESSED BY THE KING AND THE JESUITS ARE SUPPRESSED

Just Before The Conquest, The Holy Man Is Silenced

Just prior to the conquest of Jerusalem by Babylon, Jeremias was prophesying in Juda. He urged the Jews to change their ways, be kind to the strangers among them, take care of the fatherless and widows, and obey God's laws. If they heeded these words, God would allow them to stay in Jerusalem. If not, God was going to destroy the city and the Temple and allow them to be taken into captivity. The Jews hated Jeremias and had him silenced.

> "Thus saith the Lord of hosts, the God of Israel: Make your ways and your doings good: and I will dwell with you in this place. Trust not in lying words, saying: The Temple of the Lord, the Temple of the Lord, it is the Temple of the Lord. For if you will order well your ways, and your doings: if you will execute judgment between a man and his neighbor, If you oppress not the stranger, the fatherless, and the widow, and shed not innocent blood in this place, and walk not after strange gods to your own hurt, I will dwell with you in this place: in the land, which I gave to your fathers from the beginning and for evermore."
>
> - Jeremias 7: 3-7

In the 1760s, the Industrial Revolution was beginning. Children were exposed to unspeakable abuses and the most horrible working conditions. It was a time of "oppression of the fatherless".

Further, throughout the 1700s, the New World was being settled both in North America and South America. The native peoples were often mistreated by European settlers, as were African slaves. Often the best friends that the native peoples had in Catholic colonies were the Jesuits. They founded settlements called "reductions," also known as "missions". The native peoples were given the ability to work and keep much of their earnings, protected from the exploitation of other Europeans. The Jesuits also instructed the natives in the Catholic Faith. Just as Jeremias admonished the Jew to be kind to the stranger, the fatherless, and the widow, and shed not innocent blood, so too did the Jesuits do the same.

King Sedecias was torn and undecided about Jeremias. He was under great pressure from the princes of Juda to get rid of him. However, King Sedecias believed Jeremias' prophecies came from God. In an effort to please God and avert His just wrath, King Sedecias made a proclamation to free the slaves in his kingdom. The people of Juda ultimately did not obey the decree and kept their slaves anyway.

> "The word that came to Jeremias from the Lord, after that king Sedecias had made a covenant with all the people in Jerusalem making a proclamation: That every man should let his manservant, and every man his maidservant, being a Hebrew man or a Hebrew woman, go free: and that they should not lord it over them, to wit, over the Jews their brethren. And all the princes, and all the people who entered into the covenant, heard that every man should let his manservant, and every man his maidservant go free, and should no more have dominion over them: and they obeyed, and let them go free. But afterward, they turned: and brought back again their servants and their handmaids, whom they had let go free, and brought them into subjection as menservants and maidservants."

- Jeremias 34: 8-1

In amazing fashion, just as Jeremias was telling the Jews to release their slaves, so too did the pope issue an encyclical criticizing slavery.

Just prior to the French Revolution, the Jesuits were persecuted by the Catholic monarchs of Europe.[c] The Catholic monarchs and rulers of Europe were upset with the Jesuits, abused them horribly, and expelled them from their realms. They were pressuring the papacy to terminate the Jesuit order completely.[79] In 1741, Pope Benedict XIV released a papal bull, *Immensa Pastorum Principis*, which spoke against the enslavement of the native peoples of the Americas and elsewhere. This papal bull was largely ignored, particularly in Brazil. The natives remained enslaved despite the best efforts of Jesuits in Brazilian reductions.[80]

There are many other parallels between the silencing of Jeremias and the suppression of the Jesuit order. They both were delivered to the angry

---

c   The Jesuits were treated harshly by Catholic monarchs just before the French Revolution, as they were expelled from many countries, suppressed by the pope, and accused of political interference.

nobles, who had them beaten and imprisoned.[d] They both were accused of treason.[e] Finally, they both were vindicated and released/reinstated. King Sedecias reluctantly handed Jeremias over to the angry nobles but later ordered him to be released. Likewise, the Jesuits were reluctantly suppressed by Pope Clement XIV in 1773 and their order was reinstated by Pope Pius VII in 1814.

The Holy City Is Taken and the Kingdom Is Ended
BABYLONIAN CONQUEST OF JERUSALEM AND THE FRENCH REVOLUTION

The Besieged King Gets Covert Help From Abroad

Before the destruction of Jerusalem and the abolishment of the Davidic kingdom, the Babylonians forced the Jews' submission and demanded a tribute of gold. The king of Juda, Sedecias, agreed to this tribute and obeyed King Nabuchodonosor of Babylon. However, Sedecias was also secretly requesting the help of Egypt, whom he hoped would come to aid Jerusalem against the Babylonians. King Sedecias' plan did not work, and the Babylonians besieged Jerusalem.

The Babylonians broke through the walls of Jerusalem and entered the city. The Babylonian force was so great that the Jewish army was unable to protect the king. The Jewish soldiers fled by way of the king's garden and left the king defenseless.

> "And a breach was made into the city: and all the men of war fled in the night between the two walls by the king's garden, (now the Chaldees besieged the city round about,) and Sedecias fled by the way that leadeth to the plains of the wilderness. And the army of the Chaldees pursued after the

d   Jeremias was cast down a well in Jeremias 38:1-13. The Jesuits were likewise imprisoned in Lisbon dungeons from 1759 onward.

e   Jeremias was accused in Jeremias 38:4. In Portugal, the Jesuits were accused of treason by Marquis of Pombal, the powerful minister of King Joseph I of Portugal. In England, the Jesuits were also accused of treason.

king, and overtook him in the plains of Jericho: and all the
warriors that were with him were scattered, and left him."

- 4 Kings 25: 4-5

In Church history, just as King Sedecias was covertly getting help from
Egypt, so did the French King Louis XVI do likewise. From 1789 to 1792
(before the abolishment of the French monarchy by the French Revolution on
September 22, 1792) King Louis XVI of France lived as a virtual prisoner in
Paris. He was forced to sign his rights away to the Revolution through a
series of documents and acts. However, he was also secretly sending word to
Austria, requesting assistance to defeat the revolutionaries who were forcing
their will upon him.[81]

On August 10, 1792, the people of the Revolution brought armed forces to
the Tuileries Palace in Paris, where the king was residing, having been forced
to leave Versailles in October of 1789. Before the suspected attack, the king
was confident that his troops could defend the palace. However, on the day
of the attack, many of his troops declared they would not fire on fellow
Frenchmen. Thus, the king was left without a strong defense. He did still
have a group of Swiss soldiers who stood to defend the palace, but they were
overwhelmed. The king gave the order to flee through the Tuileries Gardens
at the rear of the palace.[82] The king of France submitted himself to the
National Assembly of the Revolution and was later brought to trial and
judged to be guilty.[81]

The King Flees, Is Caught, And Is Punished.

King Sedecias realized that he was in great danger, having defied King
Nabuchodonosor of Babylon. After he fled, the Babylonians pursued him
and caught him. They took him prisoner and brought him to be judged by
Nabuchodonosor.

> "...and Sedecias fled by the way that leadeth to the plains of
> the wilderness. And the army of the Chaldees (Babylonians)
> pursued after the king, and overtook him in the plains of
> Jericho: and all the warriors that were with him were
> scattered, and left him: So they took the king and brought

138

him to the king of Babylon to Reblatha, and he gave judgment upon him."

- 4 Kings 25: 4-6

Sedecias was brought before King Nabuchodonosor, who pronounced judgment on him. The sons of Sedecias were all killed before him; then, he was blinded and taken to Babylon, where he died in prison.

On June 21, 1791, the French king and queen fled Paris in disguise. They felt increasingly threatened and were fearful for their lives. They left under the cover of darkness for Austria, where they could take refuge with the queen's family. However, the king and queen were discovered and detained before they could cross the French border. They were arrested and brought back to Paris, where he stood trial on December 26, 1792.[81] King Louis XVI was found guilty before the National Convention of the Revolution and sentenced to death. He was infamously beheaded on January 21, 1793.

The Walls Are Demolished To Make A Point

After the Babylonians broke through the walls and destroyed the city, they came back and completely tore down the walls of Jerusalem.

"And all the army of the Chaldees, which was with the commander of the troops, broke down the walls of Jerusalem round about."

- 4 Kings 25: 10

"And all the army of the Chaldeans that were with the general broke down all the wall of Jerusalem round about."

- Jeremias 52: 14

Likewise, during the French Revolution, the revolutionaries made a point to come back and tear down iconic buildings that were symbols of the Catholic monarchy. On July 14, 1789, the forces of the Revolution stormed the Bastille. The Bastille was a prison fortress with high defensive walls; a symbol of the monarchy. The revolutionaries would soon return to the Bastille and dismantle the whole structure, brick by brick.[83]

Similarly, the revolutionaries descended on the Abbey of Cluny, which had been a beacon for papal authority and religious purity and renewal throughout the history of Catholic France. After its initial demolition, the remains of Cluny were used as a quarry, sending its historic and holy bricks throughout France.[84] This was a deliberate symbolic act by the revolutionaries, signifying their conquest of Catholicism and the monarchy. They had demolished and scattered its proponents and strongholds.

Property Is Plundered, And Worship Of God Is Disrupted

After the trial of the king, the Babylonians destroyed the Temple and killed the high priest and other high-ranking persons. However, before they did, they plundered the Temple of everything of value and carried it back to Babylon to enrich their empire. By destroying the Temple, the Babylonians halted the Jews' ability to offer sacrifice.

After the trial and death of King Louis XVI sometime in 1793, the goal of de-Christianization became increasingly important to the Revolution. They confiscated Church lands, money, and all other assets. They tried to eliminate Catholicism. This is evidenced by the so-called *Reign of Terror* that swept through France in 1793 and 1794. During this time, so many clergy were butchered in cold blood by the French Revolution.[85]

The Great Emperor Arises
NABUCHODONOSOR AND NAPOLEON BONAPARTE

Nabuchodonosor is the main Babylonian character in the Old Testament. He appears in the books of Jeremias and 4 Kings, but he has a larger role in the book of Daniel. The book of Daniel shows us what Nabuchodonosor thought and felt, not just what he did. Nabuchodonosor was the first great conqueror of the ancient world, who came to power by overthrowing the Assyrians.

140

Nabuchodonosor had a complicated relationship with the Jews and the God of Israel. He destroyed their Temple and brought them into exile, but he also made sweeping, empire-wide proclamations attesting to the God of Israel, forbidding any to speak badly of Him. Although he captured and imprisoned two kings of Juda, in the end, Nabuchodonosor publicly professed belief in the God of Israel.

In Church history, there is a character from the French Revolution who likewise played a prominent role in some of the initial battles but then went on to dominate the story line. This is the towering (yet small in stature) Napoleon Bonaparte. Let's explore the amazing parallels between Nabuchodonosor and Napoleon.

Just like Nabuchodonosor and the Jews, Napoleon also had a complicated relationship with the Catholic Church. He signed the *Concordat of 1801* with Pope Pius VII, allowing Church authority to return to France. But he also invaded the Papal States, kidnapping Pope Pius VI and allowing him to die in exile. Later, he would kidnap Pope Pius VII, whom he imprisoned for years. On the day of his death, May 5, 1821, Napoleon asked for the last rites and reconciled himself to the Church.

Here is a chart displaying some of the more prominent parallels, and then we'll go on, as usual, to fill in the details for each section of the following chart.

Old Testament	New Testament
Coup led to a new, capable leader, Nabuchodonosor.	Coup led to a new, capable leader, Napoleon.
The empire of Nabuchodonosor greatly expanded.	The empire of Napoleon greatly expanded.
Nabuchodonosor took two kings of Juda into exile.	Napoleon took two popes into exile.
Opulent gardens for his wife	Opulent gardens for his wife

Constructed the iconic arch-gate of Ishtar	Constructed the iconic Arc de Triomphe
Nabuchodonosor had a conversion at the end of the book of Daniel.	Napoleon received the last rites on his deathbed.

A Coup Leads To A New Capable Leader

Nabuchodonosor's father was an official in the Assyrian Empire who rebelled and made himself king of Babylon in 626 BC. Nabuchodonosor proved himself to be a capable military leader and gained much credit when he fought alongside his father against the Egyptians and Assyrians around the year 605 BC. Nabuchodonosor inherited the Babylonian kingdom from his father during the Assyrian Empire's decline.

Early on in the reign of Nabuchodonosor, in approximately 595 BC, there was a short but serious uprising that he had to quell before his position and power were made secure. The rebellion involved elements of the army who were dissatisfied with his rule. He was able to quell the revolt and resume his campaigns in Syria.

By comparison, Napoleon started out as an artillery officer in the French Revolutionary Army in 1789. He quickly rose through the ranks of the army, becoming a general in 1793. Like Nabuchodonosor's father, Napoleon engineered a coup in November of 1799, making himself *First Consul of the Republic*. Five years later, he became emperor, thus founding the Napoleonic French Empire.[86]

In 1798, he led a military campaign in Egypt and Syria.[86] These campaigns were fought in the territories of the Ottoman Empire during the time of its decline. Remember from previous pages the parallels between the Assyrian Empire in the Old Testament and the Ottoman Empire in Church history. Nabuchodonosor fought the Assyrians and Napoleon fought the Ottomans.

Just as Nabuchodonosor put down a rebellion, so did Napoleon. In 1795, there was a rebellion against the French Revolution in Paris. This rebellion was carried out by royalists who wanted to restore the French monarchy and the hegemony of the Catholic Church. The royalist rebellion, called *13 Vendémiaire*, was a serious threat to the new French Republic. The royalists outnumbered the forces of the Republic six to one. The Republic called a young general, Napoleon, into action to quell the rebellion. Napoleon placed forty cannons in strategic places and loaded them with grapeshot instead of a cannonball. (Grapeshot is a large load of tiny lead balls, about the size of marbles or grapes.) He blasted this murderous grapeshot into the royalist forces, thus quickly crushing the rebellion. This was a ruthless act, but it was efficient and expedient.[86]

The Empire Greatly Expands

In the years following the rebellion, King Nabuchodonosor went on to expand the Babylonian Empire, extending it all the way to Anatolia (present-day Turkey). He became the undisputed king of a vast empire, and all authority rested with him. Here are the words of Daniel, speaking to King Nabuchodonosor:

> "Thou art a king of kings: and the God of heaven hath given thee a kingdom, and strength, and power, and glory: And all places wherein the children of men, and the beasts of the field do dwell: he hath also given the birds of the air into thy hand, and hath put all things under thy power."

- Daniel 2:37-38

Likewise, in Church history, following 1795, Napoleon rose higher and higher in the ranks of the French Revolution until he seized power and crowned himself emperor in 1804. He went on to expand the French Empire to the four corners of Europe. He retained absolute power over his empire. [86]

Two Kings Are Taken Into Exile

Nabuchodonosor is famous for conquering Jerusalem and taking two kings into exile in Babylon. The first Jewish king that Nabuchodonosor took was Joachin.[f] Then, some years later, Nabuchodonosor came back to Jerusalem and took Sedecias into exile.[g] It was after he took Sedecias that Nabuchodonosor destroyed Jerusalem and the Temple.

Napoleon was involved in the capture of two popes, who were both taken into exile in the French Empire. In 1796, Napoleon led forces into the Papal States, conquering and occupying them. When Pope Pius VI refused to renounce his temporal authority, he was kidnapped and brought into exile in Grenoble, where he died shortly after. The next pope, Pius VII, was abducted by Napoleon in 1812 and was held against his will in the Palace of Fontainebleau in France until 1814.[87]

Opulent Gardens For His Wife

Nabuchodonosor is also known for the construction of the *Hanging Gardens of Babylon*. There is still debate about whether the gardens actually existed, but it is a well-established story, nonetheless. The Hanging Gardens were thought to have contained plants and animals from all over the vast Babylonian Empire, not only as a way to show the vastness and power of the empire but also as a gift for his wife, Queen Amytis.[88]

Napoleon Bonaparte's first wife, Josephine de Beauharnais, was an avid gardener and collector of plants and animals. She turned their estate of Malmaison, which she bought in 1799, into a botanical wonderland that displayed her exotic specimens from various parts of the world. She hired skilled gardeners to create the gardens in the English style, with winding paths, bridges, temples, and cottages. She also built a large orangery and a greenhouse to house her tropical plants, such as pineapples, orchids, and magnolias. She obtained many of her plants from the botanists who accompanied Napoleon on his military campaigns throughout Napoleon's vast empire. There was no garden like it anywhere in Europe.[89]

---

f   See 4 Kings 24: 8-16.

g   See 5 Kings 25: 1-7.

Constructs The Iconic Arch-Gate

The *Gate of Ishtar*, deep blue in color and imposing in structure, was an iconic monument in the ancient city of Babylon. It was built by King Nabuchodonosor around 575 BC, and dedicated to the goddess Ishtar, the patron of the city. The gate was decorated with glazed bricks in blue, yellow, and white, depicting dragons, bulls, and lions, which symbolized the gods Marduk, Adad, and Ishtar, respectively.[90]

The gate was part of a grand ceremonial road, called the *Processional Way*, which led into the city. It was used for religious and military parades. The processions would pass through the gate, which was also adorned with reliefs of animals and flowers. The gate and the Processional Way were meant to display the power and glory of Babylon, as well as the favor of the gods. The gate survived the fall of Babylon to the Persians and the Greeks, and was considered one of the wonders of the world.[90]

The Arc De Triomphe, a famous Parisian monument, was commissioned by Napoleon in 1806. It symbolizes the French Revolution's ideals. Many European armies have marched through the Arc, such as the Nazis and the Americans in World War II. Later in this book, we will see how the Allied Nations parallel Alexander's Greek Empire. Alexander used the Gate of Ishtar in Babylon to parade his victorious troops, just as the Nazis and the Allies did with the Arch De Triomphe. The Arc De Triomphe stands at the center of a large roundabout at the end of the Champs-Elysees, a long and wide avenue that leads to the Arc. It has hosted many ceremonial events that were enhanced by the presence of the Arc in the background.[91]

The Gate of Ishtar honored the Babylonian goddess Ishtar, who ruled over war and victory. The gate also featured the image of Marduk, the chief god of Babylon. These two deities represented the identity and values of the Babylonian people. Walking through this gate, especially in a ceremonial manner, was a way of showing respect and allegiance to the gods and the ideals of Babylon. There were other gates in the city, but the Gate of Ishtar was markedly different and special.[92]

The Arc De Triomphe has several reliefs that show scenes from the French Revolution and the Napoleonic Empire. These reliefs include various gods and goddesses as symbols of the French Republic's ideals. One relief has the "goddess of Liberty" helping the Revolution overthrow the monarchy. Another relief has the "goddess of Victory" crowning Napoleon as the emperor.[93] Therefore, the sculpture and art on the Arc De Triomphe were dedicated to pagan gods and goddesses just like the Gate of Ishtar.

Cast Out Among the Nations
Jewish Diaspora and Catholic Emigration

The diaspora refers to the scattering of the Israelites, and affected both the Israelites (ten northern tribes) and later the Jews (southern kingdom) in the Old Testament. Similarly, both Protestants and later Catholics were scattered from Europe in the course of Church history. To understand this event better, we have to return to previous time periods to see how it unfolded in the histories of both people, old and new. The Jewish diaspora began with the revolt of the ten northern tribes against God's law, and similarly, emigration from Europe began after the Protestant Revolt.

> "And I will disperse thee in the nations, and will scatter thee among the countries, and I will put an end to thy uncleanness in thee. And I will possess thee in the sight of the Gentiles, and thou shalt know that I am the Lord."
>
> - Ezechiel 22: 15 – 16

Old Testament Diaspora

In the previous time period, we learned that the ten northern tribes rebelled against the Davidic kingdom and formed their own kingdom in the north. The southern tribes remained loyal to the Davidic king, assuming the name *Kingdom of Juda*. The term *Jew* comes from the name *Juda*. The Old Testament diaspora can be divided into two phases: the Israelite diaspora and the Jewish diaspora.

The Israelite diaspora occurred when the northern Kingdom of Israel was conquered and exiled by the Assyrians. The ten northern tribes walked away from the Old Testament covenant and worshiped false gods. God allowed them to be conquered by the Assyrian Empire and forcibly relocated. They lost their identity and were assimilated into the pagan cultures around them. This was the first diaspora.

The second diaspora, the Jewish diaspora, occurred when the southern Kingdom of Juda was conquered and exiled by the Babylonians. The Jews had also sinned against God, but they had some faithful remnant who preserved their identity and hoped for a restoration. This was the second diaspora, and it took place more than a century after the first diaspora of the ten northern tribes of Israel.

Church History Diaspora

In Church history, the Protestant Revolt divided Christendom, just like Jeroboam divided the twelve tribes of Israel. The Protestant countries in northern Europe adopted new doctrines and beliefs that were contrary to the Catholic Faith. The first wave of European immigrants who left for the New World were mostly Protestants, such as the Pilgrims, Puritans, and Quakers. Thus the first diaspora of Christendom occurred with the apostate north[h], just like it occurred in the Old Testament with the apostate ten northern tribes.

The Catholic countries in southern Europe, such as Spain, France, Italy, and Portugal, stood firm against the "Age of Enlightenment" more than the Protestant countries in northern Europe, such as England, Germany, and Sweden. This was because they had a unity of Faith and the guidance of the papacy, which defended Catholic doctrine against the rationalist and secularist ideas of the "Enlightenment". Political Catholicism, which was based on the alliance of the Church and the monarchy, preserved its stability for a longer time, but it eventually succumbed to the forces of the French Revolution, the Napoleonic Wars, and the emergence of secularism and nationalism in Europe. Catholicism was marginalized and weakened in the

---

h   I am not referring to the Europeans who came to the New World to enrich or expand their kingdoms, but instead to settle and relocate.

147

political arena. Catholics had to endure the oppression of secular governments, just as the Jews had to suffer the domination of pagan Babylon.

Many Catholics chose to leave Europe in the second half of the 1800s because of difficulties in their countries. The Irish were the first to move in large numbers because of the potato famine. Later, in the 1870s, about thirteen million Italians emigrated as southern Italy faced poverty and injustice. Polish and German Catholics also left in great numbers during this time. These Catholic emigrants left for different parts of the western world, especially the United States, where they looked for a better life.

Most Never Returned To Their Homeland

In the Old Testament, most of the Jews who were exiled or fled from their land never came back. This was true for the Jews who escaped to Egypt after the Babylonian exile and for those who stayed in Babylon.

In Church history, most of the Catholics who emigrated from Europe never returned to their countries, even when the situation improved. They settled in their new lands. If you are a Catholic living in South or North America or Australia, you are probably a descendant of these Catholic immigrants. You are part of the *Catholic Diaspora* in Church history.

So far, we have seen the tragic events that reduced God's once prosperous and pious kingdom (both Old and New) into an exiled and demoralized band who were being punished for their unfaithfulness. After God's people had been brought low, He sent them great consolations through visions and prophets. Following is a chart of parallels between some of those consolations and visions in the Old Testament and in Church history for this time period.

Old Testament	New Testament
Ezechiel's prophecy of the dry bones coming back to life	The discovery of St. Philomena's bones

The prophecy of the reunification of Israel by Ezechiel, the branches came together	Oxford Movement led by Cardinal John Henry Newman and his "branch theory", the "branches" came together
Jeremias, the weeping prophet	Our Lady of LaSalette, weeping for the Church
The life of the prophet Ezechiel	St. Jean Vianney
Jeremias hid the ark in a cave, and Ezechiel prophesied about the water from the Temple.	Our Lady of Lourdes
The mysterious handwriting on the wall	The vision of Pope Leo XIII

The Dry Bones Revive God's People

Ezechiel's Vision of the Dry Bones; the Relics of St. Philomena Are Discovered

Ezechiel was a Jewish prophet who lived in exile in the Babylonian Empire. The book of Ezechiel contends with the destruction of Jerusalem but also with the restoration of the people, the Temple, and the city. It is full of vivid imagery.

One of Ezechiel's fascinating visions was the valley of dry bones in Ezechiel 37:1-14. In this vision, Ezechiel was taken by the Spirit of the Lord to a valley full of dry bones. The Lord told Ezechiel to prophesy to the bones and say:

> "Ye dry bones, hear the word of the Lord. Thus saith the Lord God to these bones: Behold, I will send spirit into you, and you shall live. And I will lay sinews upon you, and will cause flesh to grow over you, and will cover you with skin: and I will give you spirit, and you shall live, and you shall know that I am the Lord."

- Ezechiel 37: 4-6

Ezechiel obeyed the Lord and prophesied to the dry bones. The bones came together and formed skeletons, and were covered with sinews, flesh, and skin. However, they were still lifeless. The Lord told Ezechiel to prophesy and say:

> "And he said to me: Prophesy to the spirit, prophesy, O son of man, and say to the spirit: Thus saith the Lord God: Come, spirit, from the four winds, and blow upon these slain, and let them live again. "

- Ezechiel 37: 9

Ezechiel did as the Lord commanded and the wind blew over the bodies. The spirit entered them and they came to life, standing up to form a great army.

The Lord then explained to Ezechiel the meaning of this vision:

> "And he said to me: Son of man: All these bones are the house of Israel: they say: Our bones are dried up, and our hope is lost, and we are cut off. Therefore prophesy, and say to them: Thus saith the Lord God: Behold I will open your graves, and will bring you out of your sepulchres, O my people: and will bring you into the land of Israel. And you shall know that I am the Lord, when I shall have opened your sepulchres, and shall have brought you out of your graves, O my people: And shall have put my spirit in you, and you shall live, and I shall make you rest upon your own land: and you shall know that I the Lord have spoken, and done it, saith the Lord God:"

- Ezechiel 37: 11-14

In summary, the vision of the dry bones represented the condition of the people of Israel in exile, having lost their hope and life. The Lord promised to restore them and to bring them back to their land. He would give them His Spirit and make them live again.

A similar story of dry bones and revival of spirit can be found in the history of the Church. On May 24, 1802, a new tomb was discovered in the Catacomb of St. Priscilla in Rome. The tomb was sealed with three ceramic tiles on which was written: *Lumena Pax Te Cum Fi*, meaning *Peace to you, Philomena*. Inside the tomb were the dry and dusty bones of a young girl, along with a small glass vial of her blood. After their discovery, the bones were taken to the Vatican for safekeeping.[i]

A few years later, in 1805, a priest named Francesco De Lucia from the small town of Mugnano in southern Italy was saddened by the lack of fervor in his parish. He asked the Vatican for the relics of the newly discovered and unknown young martyr, Philomena. He hoped the relics would inspire his parish with renewed fervor. The Vatican agreed and the bones of St. Philomena were brought to Mugnano.

As soon as the bones of St. Philomena entered the town, miracles abounded. Many sick, lame, and blind were cured in an explosion of miracles overwhelming this little parish in southern Italy. The news of the miracles spread quickly throughout Italy and beyond. Faithful came to Mugnano to venerate the relics of St. Philomena and ask for her intercession. Across Europe, fervor and devotion in the hearts of Catholics was being revived and renewed due of the bones of this newly discovered martyr.[j]

In 1835, a friend of Pope Gregory XVI, Pauline Jaricot, became gravely ill and was near death. She decided to travel to Mugnano, Italy to seek a cure from St. Philomena. On August 10, she was carried into the church where the saint's relics were venerated. She was too weak to walk and was dying. However, at the moment of Benediction, she felt a sudden surge of energy and life in her body. She was completely cured of her illness and was able to walk again. She went to Rome to thank the pope and to testify to the miracle. The pope was so impressed by her story that he started the process of canonization for St. Philomena. She was declared a saint in 1837.[k]

---

i   https://www.vaticannews.va/en/saints/08/13/saint-philomena.html

j   https://www.philomena.org/patroness.asp

k   https://www.philomena.org/foundress.asp

Because of these miracles, the relics of St. Philomena were highly sought after. The Holy See retained the bones and decided to just send out the bone dust. In this process, they noticed that the amount of dust from the bones did not decrease at all, no matter how much was sent. In fact, it increased. This was another miracle! Now, let's analyze the parallels between these two accounts of dry bones, both in the Old and New Testaments.

Loss Of Hope

Old Testament: The dry bones of Ezechiel's vision represented the Jews in exile, who had lost hope after the destruction of Jerusalem and the Temple. They lived in a foreign land, surrounded by pagan religions and cultures. They felt hopeless.

Church History: Catholics in Europe in the early 1800s were also downtrodden. They had witnessed the French Revolution, which persecuted the Church in France, and the rise of a new, pagan emperor who conquered Europe and oppressed the Church. Father Francesco De Lucia wanted to revive the fervor of his small parish in Mugnano.

Come Back To Life

Old Testament: God restored the bones with flesh and gave them His Spirit, making them come alive again. He promised to bring them back to their land and renew His covenant with them.

Church History: God also restored the people through the miracles of St. Philomena, whose bones were brought to Mugnano. Many people were healed physically, but more importantly, spiritually. They regained fervor and hope and their outlook improved. Pauline Jaricot was an example, as she was cured of her terminal illness when she prayed to St. Philomena in the church in Mugnano.

Bones Out Of The Sepulcher

Old Testament: God said to the bones:

> "Behold I will open your graves, and will bring you out of
> your sepulchers, O my people: and will bring you into the

land of Israel. And you shall know that I am the Lord when I shall have opened your sepulchers, and shall have brought you out of your graves, O my people:"

- Ezechiel 37: 12-13

Church History: St. Philomena's bones were taken out of her tomb in the catacomb of St. Priscilla. This led to the revival of many Catholics, who were inspired by the miracles of St. Philomena. They saw her as a sign of hope and God's power.

The Branches Come Together

Ezechiel's Prophecy of the Sticks, Ephraim Returns to Juda, and the Oxford Movement and Branch Theory of Cardinal John Henry Newman

God instructed Ezechiel to perform various symbolic actions to convey His message to the people. For example:

1. He made a miniature replica of the Temple and besieged it with a siege wall, a ramp, and battering rams. This signified that the Temple would be attacked and destroyed by the Babylonians. - Ezechiel 4: 1-3

2. He shaved his head and beard and divided his hair into three parts. He burned one part, chopped another part with a sword, and scattered the last part to the wind. This represented the fate of the people of Jerusalem: some would die by fire, some by sword, and some by exile. - Ezechiel 5: 1-4

3. He took two sticks and wrote *Juda* on one and *Ephraim* on the other. (Ephraim was one of the ten northern tribes that had separated from Juda.) He joined the two sticks together, and they became one in his hand. This indicated that God would reunite the apostate tribe of Ephraim under the rule of the Davidic king.

> "And the word of the Lord came to me, saying: And thou son of man, take thee a stick: and write upon it: Of Juda, and of the children of Israel his associates: and take another stick and write upon it: For Joseph the stick of Ephraim, and for

all the house of Israel, and of his associates. And join them one to the other into one stick, and they shall become one in thy hand."

"And I will make them one nation in the land on the mountains of Israel, and one king shall be king over them all: and they shall no more be two nations, neither shall they be divided any more into two kingdoms."

"And my servant David shall be king over them, and they shall have one shepherd: they shall walk in my judgments, and shall keep my commandments, and shall do them."

- Ezechiel 37: 15-17, 22, 24

Now, let us switch over to the mid-1800s. The Anglican Church, or the Church of England, was founded by King Henry VIII in the 1500s when he broke away from the Catholic Church. In the early 1800s, the Anglican Church was divided into different factions, influenced by the Protestant Reformation and the "Age of Enlightenment". Some Anglicans were liberal, some were evangelical, and some were *high church*, meaning that they retained more rituals and traditions from the Catholic Church (in other words, they lost less beauty than the other sects by comparison). The high church Anglicans were centered at Oxford University.[94]

A group of high church Anglicans started the Oxford Movement, which aimed to restore ancient and Catholic heritage to the Anglican Church. The leader of this movement was John Henry Newman, an Anglican clergyman. At this time, the Anglican rites had become invalid according to the Catholic Church. Pope Leo XIII declared that Anglican orders were null and void in 1896.[94]

Newman and his followers adopted *Branch Theory*, which claimed that the Anglican Church and the Catholic Church were two branches of the same original Church. Newman traced the origin of the split to King Henry VIII's break with Rome. However, he later realized that this theory was not satisfactory and that the Anglican Church was not a true branch but a separate entity altogether.[95]

Newman's studies and writings led him to the conclusion that the Catholic Church was the one true Church and that he had to join it. He converted to Catholicism in 1845 and brought many other Anglicans with him, including clergymen, lawyers, novelists, scholars, theologians, poets, and others. He was ordained as a Catholic priest and later became a cardinal. He is now known as Cardinal John Henry Newman.[96]

Newman's conversion had a huge impact on the religious landscape of Britain, as he was the most prominent figure of the Oxford Movement. He also fulfilled an Old Testament prophecy, which said that the tribe of Ephraim, one of the ten lost tribes of Israel, would reunite with the tribe of Juda under the rule of the Davidic king. Newman and his fellow converts became part of the Catholic Church, under the authority of the pope. Newman, as a cardinal, was especially close to the pope.

It is interesting to note that the Anglican Church was the closest to the Catholic Church in terms of beliefs and practices among the various Protestant sects. Therefore, the conversion of the Anglicans was not a long theological journey. Similarly, the tribe of Ephraim was the closest to the tribe of Juda among the northern tribes in terms of geography and culture. Therefore, their reunion was not a difficult journey.

The Weeping Prophet
JEREMIAS THE WEEPING PROPHET AND OUR LADY OF LASALETTE

Prophecies Before Invasion

Old Testament: Jeremias was a prophet who warned the Jews about the Babylonian invasion of Jerusalem. The Babylonians captured Jerusalem, confiscated the land of the Jews, and exiled them to Babylon. The first exile happened in 597 BC, and the second and final exile happened in 587 BC.

Church History: Our Lady of LaSalette appeared in 1846, shortly before the Italian nationalists invaded and confiscated the Papal States in 1860 (first wave) and again in 1870 (final wave). After 1870, the Holy See lost all its land, even the land under its feet. The popes called themselves *prisoners in the Vatican*, not leaving the Vatican during this time.

Wept And Cried

Old Testament: Jeremias was called the *weeping prophet* because he cried for the future of his people, their pride, and their sins.

> "But if you will not hear this, my soul shall weep in secret for your pride: weeping it shall weep, and my eyes shall run down the tears, because the flock of the Lord is carried away captive."
>
> - Jeremias 13:17

Church History: On September 19, 1846, Our Lady appeared to two children, high up in the Alps, and wept bitterly almost the entire time.

Not Keeping God's Day Holy

Old Testament: One of the ways that the Jews offended God, according to Jeremias, was that they did not keep the Sabbath day. They worked on the Sabbath, disobeying the Lord's command.[1]

> "And it shall come to pass: if you will hearken to me, saith the Lord, to bring in no burdens by the gates of this city on the Sabbath day: and if you will sanctify the Sabbath day, to do no work therein:"
>
> - Jeremias 17:24

Church History: One of the ways that the Catholics offended God, according to Our Lady of LaSalette, was that they did not keep Sunday holy. Many did not attend Mass and worked on Sundays. This was one of the main rebukes of Our Lady of LaSalette. Here are some of her words about keeping Sunday holy:

> "Only a few old women go to Mass; in the summer, the rest work all day Sunday, and in the winter, when they are at a

---

[1]   See chapter 17 for the full admonishment of Jeremias concerning the Sabbath.

loose end, they only go to Mass to make fun of religion. During Lent, they go to the butcher's like hungry dogs."[97][m]

A Great Famine Is Sent

Old Testament: One of the punishments that God sent to the Jews was famine. Jeremias prophesied about this in chapter 14.

> "When they fast I will not hear their prayers: and if they offer holocausts and victims, I will not receive them: for I will consume them by the sword, and by famine, and by the pestilence."

> "And the people to whom they prophecy, shall be cast out in the streets of Jerusalem because of the famine ..."

> "If I go forth into the fields, behold the slain with the sword: and if I enter into the city, behold them that are consumed with famine ..."

> - Jeremias 14: 12, 16, 18

Church History: Our Lady of LaSalette foretold the upcoming potato famine in Europe (with Ireland and France being the worst affected). Our Lady of LaSalette appeared in September of 1846. The potato famine began in 1845, and Our Lady predicted its continuation. The potato famine was devastating, lasting until about 1852.

> "If the harvest is spoiled, it does not seem to affect you. I made you see this last year with the potatoes. You took little account of this. It was quite the opposite when you found bad potatoes, you swore oaths, and you included the name

---

m   There are some alleged versions of the words and secrets offered by Our Lady of LaSalette that never received approval by the Catholic Church. Some were actually put on the Index of Forbidden Books. However, this particular excerpt is part of the approved messages of Our Lady of LaSalette. It was given an imprimatur by Bishop Zola of Lecce in 1879.

of my Son. They will continue to go bad and at Christmas, there will be none left."[97][n]

Now, let's go on to look more closely at the life of the prophet Ezechiel and see how it mirrors the life of St. Jean Vianney in many ways.

Sent to a Stiff-Necked People
EZECHIEL AND ST. JEAN VIANNEY

Priests And Prophets Of God

Ezechiel was a priest who became a prophet in exile. He was captured by the Babylonians when he was twenty-five years old and he began his prophetic ministry when he was thirty years old.[o] Ezechiel was prevented from exercising his priesthood in the Temple because the Law of Moses required that priests could not begin their official duties until the age of thirty.[p] He was taken into exile before he came of age.

> Now it came to pass in the **thirtieth year**, in the fourth month, on the fifth day of the month, when I was in the midst of the captives by the river Chobar, the heavens were opened, and I saw the visions of God. On the fifth day of the month, the same was the **fifth year** of the captivity of king Joachin, The word of the Lord came to Ezechiel the priest the son of Buzi in the land of the Chaldeans, by the river Chobar: and the hand of the Lord was there upon him.
>
> - Ezechiel 1: 1-3

> **"The thirtieth year"**: Either of the age of Ezechiel; or, as others will have it, from the solemn covenant made in the eighteenth year of the reign of Josias. 4 Kings 23.

---

n   This particular excerpt is part of the approved messages of Our Lady of LaSalette. It was given an imprimatur by Bishop Zola of Lecce in 1879.

o   He was thirty when he first saw the visions of God, but was taken into exile five years prior to this vision. Thus, he was twenty-five when he was taken into exile in Babylon.

p   Numbers 4:3,23,30

God gave him many commands that he had to perform as signs for the people. For example, he had to lie on his right side for forty days and on his left side for three hundred ninety days, symbolizing the sins of Juda and Israel, respectively.[q] He also had to eat bread baked with ashes and dung, representing the famine and defilement that would afflict the people. God also warned him that the people were stubborn, hard-hearted, and rebellious.[r]

St. Jean Vianney was a holy priest who transformed his parish through penance, prayer, and preaching, becoming the role model for parish priesthood everywhere. He lived in France after the French Revolution and the Napoleonic Wars, when the Church was oppressed and persecuted. He had a desire to be a priest since his youth, but he had to stop his studies when he was conscripted into Napoleon's army. He managed to escape and was ordained, even though he had difficulties with his studies. St. Jean Vianney was assigned to the small town of Ars in rural eastern France, about twenty miles north of Lyon. The people of Ars were sinful and hard-hearted. St. Jean Vianney touched their hearts with his prayers, preaching, sacrifices, and example. He became a renowned confessor and spiritual director, drawing thousands of pilgrims to Ars. He also had the gift of prophecy, as he could read souls and predict the future.[98][s]

Now, let's go on to identify some substantial parallels between them.

Priesthood Interrupted

Old Testament: Ezechiel was a Levite and a priest but he was exiled to Babylon when he was twenty-five years old before he could offer his first sacrifice in the Temple. The Law of Moses required that a priest be thirty years old to start his ministry. God would give him a way to function as a priest in exile by doing penances for his people.

---

q   See Ezechiel 4. Note that *Israel* was the northern kingdom that was dispersed by the Assyrians, and *Juda* was the southern kingdom that was exiled to Babylon.

r   See Ezechiel 2:4-5

s   This source, Butler's *Lives of the Saints*, mentions St. Jean Vianney's life. The bibliography cites page 236, which refers to his enlistment in Napoleon's army. This is a key detail to draw a parallel with Ezechiel.

Church History: St. Jean Vianney wanted to be a priest but he had to stop his studies when he was twenty-three years old because he was drafted into Napoleon's army for his war against Spain. He escaped and was ordained.

Sent To The Hard-Hearted

Old Testament: God sent Ezechiel to a stubborn, obstinate, and hard-hearted people.

> "And saying: Son of man, I send thee to the children of Israel, to a rebellious people, that hath revolted from me, they, and their fathers, have transgressed my covenant even unto this day. And they to whom I send thee are children of a hard face, and of an obstinate heart: and thou shalt say to them: Thus saith the Lord God: If so be they at least will hear, and if so be they will forbear, for they are a provoking house: and they shall know that there hath been a prophet in the midst of them."
>
> - Ezechiel 2: 3-5

Church History: St. Jean Vianney came to the little town of Ars in 1818. He was a holy priest who wanted to help people love God. But the Catholics in France had forgotten their religion. The French Revolution had destroyed many churches and killed many priests. The people of Ars did not care about God or the Church. They did not go to Mass or pray. They drank too much and reveled in debauchery. They would not hear the teachings of the Church, nor were they interested in amending their lives.[99][t]

Penance By Sleep And Food

Old Testament: Since Ezechiel was a priest but could not offer sacrifice in the Temple, God gave him a way to make atonement for his people. Ezechiel had to lie on his side, bound with cords, for over a year. He could not move. This was very uncomfortable. He also had to eat meager rations of food and bread made with dung and ashes.

---

t   This portrayal of the people of Ars can be seen clearly in the 1949 French film *Le Sorcier Du Ciel*.

Church History: St. Jean Vianney said:

> "The devil is not greatly afraid of the discipline and other instruments of penance. That which beats him is the curtailment of one's food, drink, and sleep. There is nothing the devil fears more. Consequently, nothing is more pleasing to God."[u]

He lived this out by sleeping very little and fasting a lot. When he did sleep, it was usually only a few hours. He did these penances for his flock to bring about their conversion.

The Dry Bones Come Alive

Old Testament: In Chapter 37 of the book of Ezechiel, there is the famous vision of the dry bones. These bones came back to life, symbolizing the despair of Israel in exile and their later restoration by God.

Church History: St. Jean Vianney had a great devotion to St. Philomena. The bones of St. Philomena were discovered in his lifetime, and miracles of St. Philomena spread throughout Europe. St. Jean Vianney attributed all the healing and miracles in his parish to the intercession of St. Philomena. He had a side altar in his church dedicated to her.

Sober Warning To The Faithful

Old Testament: God told Ezechiel to warn the Jews about their sins. He said: If they listen to you and stop sinning, they will live. But if they ignore you and keep sinning, they will die. You will live because you warned them. But if you do not warn them, they will die in their sins, and I will blame you.

> "If, when I say to the wicked, Thou shalt surely die: thou declare it not to him, nor speak to him, that he may be converted from his wicked way, and live: the same wicked man shall die in his iniquity, but I will require his blood at thy hand."

---

u   Taken from this website: https://www.olrl.org/lives/vianney.shtml , a listing of quotes attributed to St. Jean Vianney.

- Ezechiel 3:18

Church History: St. Jean Vianney did not hesitate to tell his parish about the great danger they were in because of their unbelief and sin. He thundered to them about Hell and eternal damnation, not simply to scare them but to give them a warning. As their parish priest, it was his responsibility to warn them and guide them onto the path of Heaven. One of my favorite quotes from St. Jean Vianney goes something like this:

> "Even if I was certain that I would be killed for preaching certain things from the pulpit, then so much more is my responsibility to preach those Truths to the people."[v]

> "A priest goes to Heaven or a priest goes to Hell with a thousand people behind."[w]

Restoration Of The Priesthood

Old Testament: The book of Ezechiel focuses on the destruction and restoration of the Temple and the priesthood. The priests could not offer sacrifice without the Temple, so they lost their function in exile. However, God also wanted the priests and the people to have a change of heart, not just a change of place. Before the exile, the priests were corrupt and unfaithful to God, for which Jeremias rebuked them. But their time in exile humbled the Jews and enkindled a desire for God once again. When they returned to Jerusalem, the priests had a new spirit and a new zeal for God's laws. This is seen in the books of 1 and 2 Esdras.

Church History: St. Jean Vianney is the patron saint of parish priests. He revived the true spirit of the priesthood, which had been tainted and weakened by the French Revolution. Before the French Revolution, the clergy were powerful and respected. But after the Revolution, the Church was persecuted and oppressed. The clergy were humbled and demoralized. St. Jean Vianney was sent by God at the right time to restore the dignity of the priesthood and to be an example of priestly holiness in a secular world.

---

v   I first heard this quote on a Catholic recording many years ago, and it has never left my mind. Even though I do not know where it came from, it perfectly captures the passion and sense of duty that St. Jean Vianney embodied.

w   https://www.sainttherse.com/25-quotes-from-st-john-vianney/

So, it seems that St. Jean Vianney is the "New Ezechiel". St. Jean Vianney died in 1859. Just one year before his death, Our Lady so famously appeared in Lourdes in 1858. The apparitions of Our Lady at Lourdes are filled with vivid imagery, such as the grotto and the miraculous spring. Let's look at some stunning parallels between the apparitions of Our Lady at Lourdes and events and prophecies from Ezechiel and Jeremias.

The Ark in a Cave
JEREMIAS HIDES THE ARK IN A CAVE; OUR LADY OF LOURDES

The period of exile was transformative for the Jews in many ways. It had profound psychological effects on them as a people, living in a pagan world that was not under their control. The shock caused by the destruction of their city and Temple along with their exile caused them to deeply contemplate the sins of their people, leading to a conversion of heart. This just punishment from God was harsh. But in His mercy, God also comforted His people. During their exile the Jews were given consoling promises and prophecies through His prophets. Two major prophets of the exile period were Jeremias and Ezechiel.

Jeremias prophesied in Jerusalem before its destruction. He foretold the exile of the Jews and their eventual return. Not only did he prophesy, but he also looked after the holiest object of the Jews, the ark of the covenant. Since Jeremias knew the Babylonians were coming to destroy the Temple, he took the ark of the covenant and hid it in a cave so the Babylonians would not take it or destroy it.

> "It was also contained in the same writing, how the prophet, being warned by God, commanded that the tabernacle and the ark should accompany him, till he came forth to the mountain where Moses went up, and saw the inheritance of God. And when Jeremias came thither he found a hollow cave: and he carried in thither the tabernacle, and the ark, and the altar of incense, and so stopped the door."

- 2 Machabees 2: 4-5

Ezechiel prophesied in Babylon. One of the largest sections of the book of Ezechiel is his description of the new Temple. Ezechiel goes into minute details about the physical attributes and measurements of this new Temple. He also describes a river that flows from the threshold of the Temple that heals and gives life wherever it flows. What is curious about this description of the Temple by Ezechiel is that when the Jews did eventually rebuild the Temple, it did not resemble Ezechiel's description. The prophecy of Ezechiel about the new Temple would have given the Jews in Babylon tremendous hope.

The Ark In A Cave Before The Invasion

Old Testament: Jeremias took the ark of the covenant and hid it in a cave near Mount Nebo before the Babylonians came to destroy the city and carry away the Jews into exile. This happened twice: the first wave of exiles was taken in 597 BC, and then, ten years later, in 587 BC, the remaining exiles were taken, and the city was destroyed.[100]

Church History: Our Lady appeared in a cave in 1858 at Lourdes, France, only two years before the Spoliation of the Papal States.[x] In 1860, the emerging Kingdom of Italy confiscated two-thirds of the Papal States. Then, in 1870, ten years later, the Kingdom of Italy confiscated the remaining one-third. The Holy See was left without any land. Even the very land under the pope's feet was claimed by the king of Italy. From this point, the popes referred to themselves as *prisoners in the Vatican* and, under protest, would not leave the Vatican.

Just as there were two waves of exile and destruction by the Babylonians in 597 and 587 BC, so were there two waves of spoliation of the Papal States in 1860 and 1870. In both cases, the two waves were separated by ten years.

The Ark Is Kept Safe

Old Testament: Jeremias hid the ark of the covenant in order to keep it safe from the Babylonians. The ark of the covenant was pure and holy, to be treated with the greatest reverence. Babylonian control of the ark would have

---

x   The term "Spoliation of the Papal States" is a term used to describe the confiscation of the Papal States.

been a profound evil, a sacrilege, and a desecration. By God's grace, the ark was kept safe.

Church History: In the years preceding the theft of the Papal States, the popes consistently asserted their need for independent territory directly governed by the Holy See. Pope Pius IX demonstrated this in an allocution given on April 29, 1848 entitled *Non-Semel*. He indicated that the Holy See was not interested in expanding its land holdings but instead was interested in expanding the Kingdom of Christ, the Church. However, he thanked God for the Papal States nonetheless because they secured the "free exercise of the Supreme Apostolate".[101]

The Papal States gave the Church a source of income independent from any foreign government. This kept the Holy See free to teach, govern, and proclaim doctrine without the threat of loss of livelihood. Without this territorial independence, various powers throughout history would have tried to leverage the dependency of the Holy See to obtain political objectives with the pope's authority.

Pope Pius IX proclaimed the *Dogma of the Immaculate Conception* in his papal bull, *Ineffabilis Deus*, in 1854. He did this only six years before the Kingdom of Italy took two-thirds of the Papal States in 1860. Pope Pius IX was well aware of the Freemasons' plans to take away the Papal States, as it was not secret. It had been discussed openly for a long time, especially by a man named Giuseppe Mazzini in the mid-1800s.[102]

Could it be that Pope Pius IX finally dogmatized the Immaculate Conception because he feared outside influences would pressure him once the Papal States were taken? So, the words of Our Lady of Lourdes, "I am the Immaculate Conception," seem to indicate that Our Lady was announcing that she was now in a safe place because she spoke these words from a cave before the Spoliation of the Papal States. In the Old Testament, the ark was safe in the cave, and so too does it seem that the dogma of the Immaculate Conception was also safely proclaimed to the world, and Our Lady indicated this from the cave at Lourdes.[y]

---

y   I do not know of any previous conjecture or study that shows a connection between the dogma of the Immaculate Conception and the loss of the pope's temporal power in this

The Secret Is Kept

Old Testament: When Jeremias went to hide the ark in a cave, he was followed by some Jews who wanted to mark the spot where it was hidden. Jeremias rebuked them and said that the location of the ark would remain a secret. To this day, nobody knows where the ark is hidden. Jeremias seems to have kept this secret well.

> "Then some of them that followed him came up to mark the place, but they could not find it. And when Jeremias perceived it, he blamed them, saying: The place shall be unknown, till God gather together the congregation of the people, and receive them to mercy."
>
> - 2 Machabees 2: 6-7

Church History: Our Lady of Lourdes appeared to a young girl named Bernadette Soubirous in a series of eighteen apparitions from February 11, 1858, to July 16, 1858. During these apparitions, St. Bernadette was given three secrets by Our Lady. Amazingly, St. Bernadette never wrote down the three secrets, nor did she tell them to anyone. To this day, nobody knows what they are.[103] I am unaware of any other apparition of Our Lady in which the secrets conveyed to the seer were not intended for revelation to the faithful at some point.

Ark, Altar, And Sacred Fire

Old Testament: When Jeremias hid the ark in the cave, he also hid the altar of incense from the Temple. Another great concern for Jeremias was the sacred fire from the Temple, which was supposed to be kept burning at all times. Jeremias put the ark and the altar in a cave and commanded that the sacred fire stay lit, even in captivity.

> "Now it is found in the descriptions of Jeremias the prophet, that he commanded them that went into captivity, to take the fire, as it hath been signified, and how he gave charge to them that were carried away into captivity."
>
> - 2 Machabees 2: 1

manner. But based on the parallels, I offer my opinion as stated.

Church History: Upon looking at a picture of the Grotto at Lourdes, there are three things that immediately stand. The first is a statue of Our Lady of Lourdes that is situated in a cave, marking the spot where Our Lady appeared. Secondly, one can see the altar that is below and to the left. Thirdly, there are always large candles lit and present near the altar and the statue. These candles are a famous attribute of the grotto, and it is striking to see just how many and how large they are. Thus, just as Jeremias hid the ark and the altar and ordered the sacred fire to stay lit, so too at Lourdes is the new Ark in a cave; the altar is present, and so is the fire lit.

Blocked Up And Restricted

Old Testament: Jeremias blocked up the cave so it could not be found later.

> "And when Jeremias came thither he found a hollow cave: and he carried in thither the tabernacle, and the Ark, and the altar of incense, and so stopped the door. "
>
> - 2 Machabees 2: 5

Church History: St. Bernadette was not able to approach the grotto during the last apparition of Our Lady because the local police had blocked up the grotto. St. Bernadette was only able to see Our Lady from a distance and, after that, received no more apparitions.

A Place of Refuge and Healing
THE DESCRIPTION OF EZECHIEL'S TEMPLE MATCHES THE SANCTUARY OF LOURDES, INCLUDING HEALING WATER

Miraculous Font Of Water

Old Testament: Ezechiel's prophecy about the Temple and the font of water is recorded in the book of Ezechiel, chapters 40 to 48. A whole eight chapters are dedicated to this vision—a substantial amount of text. In these chapters, the measurements are given with a voluminous amount of detail. One of the most striking features of the new Temple is a spring of water that issues forth from the base of the Temple. The water starts off small but grows bigger, giving life wherever it flows. The direction of the spring's flow and its relationship to the Temple are described in detail. The spring of water flows east, which is the same direction that the front of the Temple faces. The water issues forth on the right side of the Temple from the threshold or the foundation. The spring of water flows on the altar's south side.

> "And he brought me again to the gate of the house, and **behold waters issued out from under the threshold of the house toward the east: for the forefront, of the house looked toward the east: but the waters came down to the right side** of the Temple **to the south part of the altar.** And he led me out by the way of the north gate, and he caused me to turn to the way without the outward gate to the way that looked toward the east: **and behold there ran out waters on the right side.** And when the man that had the line in his hand went out towards the east, he measured a thousand cubits: and he brought me through the water up to the ankles. And again he measured a thousand, and he brought me through the water up to the knees. And he measured a thousand, and he brought me through the water up to the loins. And he measured a thousand, and it was a torrent, which I could not pass over: for the waters were risen so as to make a deep torrent, which could not be passed over. And he said to me: Surely thou hast seen, O son of man. And he brought me out, and he caused me to turn to the bank of the torrent. And when I had turned myself, behold on the bank of the torrent were very many trees on both sides. And he said to me: These waters that issue forth toward the hillocks of sand to the east, and go down to the plains of the desert, shall go into the sea, and shall go out, **and the waters shall be healed.** And every living creature that creepeth whithersoever the torrent shall come, shall live: and there shall be fishes in abundance after these waters shall come thither, and they shall be healed, and all things shall live to which the torrent shall come."

> - Ezechiel 47: 1-9

Church History: Perhaps the most famous aspect of Our Lady's apparitions at Lourdes is the spring of water that St. Bernadette unearthed at Our Lady's command. It started as a trickle but soon grew bigger. Today the spring produces as much as forty liters per minute.

This spring bears uncanny similarities with the water in Ezechiel's vision. The water comes forth from the right side of the church, at its foundation. The church faces east, and the water flows east. The taps for the water are east of the source of the spring. The spring flows behind, on the south side of the grotto's altar. The spring water is miraculous and has healed countless people. Amazingly, the description of the Temple and flow of water in the book of Ezechiel exactly match the description of the basilica and miraculous spring of water at Lourdes.[z]

The Temple Described

Old Testament: The book of Ezechiel gives a detailed description of this Temple:

1. The Temple faces towards the east. - Ezechiel 47: 1

2. The Temple has an outer court which could only be accessed through three gates. - Ezechiel 40: 5-19

3. The Temple also has an inner court.

4. The Temple's annex has three chambers, built vertically, on top of each other. See the below reference to Ezechiel 42: 5-6.

5. There is a description of winding stairs that give access to the upper chamber. Here are some selected verses from this description:

> "Where were the store chambers lower above: because they bore up the galleries, which appeared above out of them from the lower parts, and from the midst of the building. **For they were of three stories,** and had not pillars, as the pillars of the courts: therefore did they appear above out of the

---

z I owe my life to Our Lady of Lourdes! Although I was not healed physically, I did have a conversion of heart that brought me back to the Catholic Faith.

lower places, and out of the middle places, fifty cubits from the ground."

- Ezechiel 42: 5-6

"And there was a broad passage roundabout, going up by **winding stairs**, and it led into the upper loft of the Temple all round: therefore was the Temple broader in the higher parts: and so from the lower parts they went to the higher by the midst."

- Ezechiel 41: 7

Church History: Below is a description of the grounds and the Basilica at Lourdes, France. Google Maps makes these descriptions easy to verify. Compare these descriptions below to the description of Ezechiel's Temple previously provided.

1. The Basilica of Lourdes faces east.

2. The Sanctuary of Lourdes has a large outer courtyard accessed through three gates. These are St. Michael's Gate in the east, St. Joseph's Gate in the south, and the Crypt Gate.

3. The Basilica grounds also have an inner courtyard partially enclosed by the curved ramps that extend from the mid-level of the Basilica and wrap around to the ground at the inner courtyard below.

4. The Basilica of Lourdes is three churches built on top of each other. The bottom level is the Basilica of the Holy Rosary. The mid-level is the Crypt. Finally, the top level is the main Basilica of the Immaculate Conception.

5. There are rounded, winding steps that lead from the bottom level to the mid-level of the Basilica. Also, rounded ramps extend from the bottom to the mid-level of the Basilica.

Beyond the mere physical description of the Temple lies a much more important concept. The Temple was vital to the Jews, therefore Ezechiel's prophecy about the Temple was a great source of hope. The Temple was the place where Heaven and Earth met.

For Catholics living in the 1800s, the apparitions of Lourdes and the miraculous Lourdes water were a tremendous sign of hope. The world was becoming more secular and evil year by year. God and Our Lady are so gracious to give us such miracles at Lourdes. We are reminded that God is with us and has not abandoned us. Our Lady descended from Heaven to instruct us, give us hope, and show the great love she has for her children. Thank God for Our Lady!

The apparitions of Our Lady of Lourdes and the miraculous spring gave great consolation to the Catholics of that time. Lourdes is sweetness. However, as we enjoy the comfort that God sends us, we must not assume that consolation and sweetness are the usual state of affairs. As a Father, He also sends bitterness to draw us closer to Him. In the late 1800s, only decades after the apparitions at Lourdes, bitterness was looming on the horizon. A mystical event was about to unfold that would confound Catholics with a dreadful mystery. I am referring to the vision of Pope Leo XIII, when he reportedly overheard Satan asking God to allow him to destroy the Church.

In the Old Testament, we have the parallel story of the mysterious handwriting on the wall during the blasphemous feast of the Babylonian King Baltasar, as recounted in the book of Daniel. Let us compare the two events below.

The Mysterious Message
THE HANDWRITING ON THE WALL; THE VISION OF POPE LEO XIII

Summary Of The Feast Of King Baltasar - Daniel: 5

In this Old Testament account, the Jews were still in exile in Babylon. Nabuchodonosor died, and his son took his place as king of Babylon. He was unlike Nabuchodonosor, who learned to respect the God of the Jews and even professed belief in Him in the fourth chapter of Daniel. King Baltasar, on the other hand, had no respect for the God of the Jews.

The fifth chapter of the book of Daniel begins with a feast that King Baltasar was giving for his nobles. King Baltasar was drunk and commanded that the sacred vessels from the Temple in Jerusalem be brought to him and used for his feast. This was a great sacrilege. Here are the words from Sacred Scripture:

> "And being now drunk he commanded that they should bring the vessels of gold and silver which Nabuchodonosor, his father had brought away out of the Temple that was in Jerusalem, that the king and his nobles, and his wives and his concubines, might drink in them."
>
> - Daniel 5: 2

Shortly after King Baltasar did this, a hand appeared over the candlestick and started to write words on the palace wall. The king's countenance changed, and he became very afraid.

> "Then was the king's countenance changed, and his thoughts troubled him: and the joints of his loins were loosed, and his knees struck one against the other."
>
> - Daniel 5: 6

After the incident, the king immediately called for his wise men to come and interpret the words written on the wall, but nobody knew what they meant. The king then called for Daniel. He promised to make Daniel one of the three princes in his kingdom if Daniel could interpret the words for the king.

> "But I have heard of thee, that thou canst interpret obscure things, and resolve difficult things: now if thou art able to read the writing, and to shew me the interpretation thereof, thou shalt be clothed with purple, and shalt have a chain of gold about thy neck and shalt be the third prince in my kingdom."
>
> - Daniel 5: 16

Daniel proceeded to give the interpretation to the king. First, Daniel rebuked King Baltasar for his pride and arrogance in profaning the sacred vessels of the Temple. Then, Daniel interpreted the writing on the wall, telling the king that the days of his reign are numbered. Baltasar was not found worthy, and his kingdom would be divided and given to another.

> "And this is the interpretation of the word. MANE: God hath numbered thy kingdom, and hath finished it. _THECEL: thou art weighed in the balance, and art found wanting. PHARES: thy kingdom is divided, and is given to the Medes and Persians. Then by the king's command Daniel was clothed with purple, and a chain of gold was put about his neck: and it was proclaimed of him that he had power as the third man in the kingdom. The same night Baltasar the Chaldean king was slain."
>
> - Daniel 5: 26-30

Vision Of Pope Leo XIII

At some time in the 1880s, the exact year is unknown, Pope Leo XIII was attending Mass with his cardinals and some key staff members in the Vatican. At the end of Mass, he suddenly froze and his face turned ashen white. He stared for ten minutes at the wall in front of him.

In 1933, the German newspaper *Neues Europa* printed an unsubstantiated story of this account. Then in 1947, an eyewitness came forward publicly. This is a summary of the 1933 newspaper story.

On October 13, 1884, after Pope Leo XIII had finished celebrating Mass in the Vatican Chapel, attended by some Cardinals and staff, he stopped at the foot of the altar. He stood there for about ten minutes, his face pale white. Afterwards, he went straight to his office and wrote the prayer to St. Michael. He gave instructions that it be said after all Low Masses throughout the Church. He said he heard two voices, one gentle and the other harsh. The guttural voice of Satan said "I can destroy your Church". The gentle voice of Our Lord replied "You can? Then go ahead and do so". Then Satan said "To do so, I need more time and more power". Our Lord followed with "How much time? How much power?" Then Satan said "75 to 100 years, and a greater power over those who will give themselves over to my service". Our

Lord then replied "You have the time, you will have the power. Do with them what you will".[104][aa]

As was previously stated, in 1947 an eyewitness came forward and offered his account. His name was Fr. Domenico Pechenino, a priest who worked at the Vatican during the time of Leo XIII. In his account, published in the 1955 Roman journal *Ephemerides Liturgicae* V. LXIX, pp 54–60, he stated that Pope Leo XIII was attending a Mass of Thanksgiving after having already offered Mass himself earlier (as was his daily custom). The witness then saw him suddenly raise his head and stare at something above the priest's head, who was saying Mass. Pope Leo XIII's face expressed his horror and awe at what he was seeing or hearing as he stood motionless. Then suddenly, coming to his senses, he quickly went to his private chambers and composed the prayer to St. Michael.[105]

Finally, before we examine the parallels between the two stories, there is a portion of the St. Michael Prayer that I would like to include. As a side note, please remember that during this time in Church history, the Holy See had Her lands and properties seized by the Kingdom of Italy in 1870. The new Kingdom of Italy had financial problems, and it sold off many stolen Church assets to raise money. Some of the sacred properties were not respected, but were put to use for common and profane purposes.

With that in mind, here is a portion of the St. Michael Prayer composed by Pope Leo XIII. This is part of the extended prayer. We are all familiar with the short version of the prayer.

> "These most crafty enemies have filled and inebriated with
> gall and bitterness the Church, the spouse of the immaculate
> Lamb, and have laid impious hands on her most sacred
> possessions. In the Holy Place itself, where the See of Holy

aa The alleged conversation between Our Lord and Satan during this mystical moment witnessed by Pope Leo XIII is strikingly similar to the conversation between God and Satan in the book of Job. In the book of Job 1: 6 – 12, Satan requested permission from God to strip Job of all his possessions, which was granted by God. However, despite losing everything, Job still blessed God. The implication is that even if the Church is stripped of all Her material possessions (buildings, honors and other benefices) the Church will never lose the Faith.

Peter and the Chair of Truth has been set up as the light of the world, they have raised the throne of their abominable impiety, with the iniquitous design that when the Pastor has been struck, the sheep may be scattered."

Now that the stories are recounted and summarized, let's explore their amazing parallels.

Feast For His Nobles And A Vision

Old Testament: King Baltasar was giving a feast for his nobles when he saw a vision of a hand, writing words on a wall. His countenance changed, and he became noticeably distraught as he watched.

> "Then was the king's countenance changed, and his thoughts troubled him: and the joints of his loins were loosed, and his knees struck one against the other."

> - Daniel 5: 6

Church History: Pope Leo XIII was attending Holy Mass with his cardinals and Vatican staff when he saw a vision or heard a conversation between Our Lord and Satan. Pope Leo's countenance changed, and he became distraught while staring intently for ten minutes.

> "...he stopped at the foot of the altar. He stood there for about ten minutes, his face pale white."

Sacred Possession Taken

Old Testament: King Baltasar was drunk and called for the sacred vessels to be brought to him so he could use them in his feast.

> "And being now drunk he commanded that they should bring the vessels of gold and silver which Nabuchodonosor, his father had brought away out of the Temple that was in Jerusalem, that the king and his nobles, and his wives and his concubines, might drink in them."

> - Daniel 5: 2

Church History: The Kingdom of Italy laid hold of and sold properties belonging to the Church. Many of the properties were consecrated and sacred. In his prayer, Pope Leo XIII wrote the following concerning the Italian government stealing Church property. He even referred to being inebriated (drunk):

> "These most crafty enemies have filled and inebriated with gall and bitterness the Church, the spouse of the immaculate Lamb, and have laid impious hands on her most sacred possessions..."

Immediate Reaction

Old Testament: Upon seeing the vision of the handwriting on the wall, King Baltasar immediately called upon his wise men to interpret the words of the vision.

Church History: Upon hearing Our Lord and Satan converse, Pope Leo XIII immediately went to his chambers and composed a prayer to St. Michael to come to the aid of the Church.

Kingdom To Be Destroyed

Old Testament: Daniel told Baltasar that because of his pride, his kingdom would come to an end and be given to another.

Church History: In the vision of Pope Leo XIII, Satan asked for more power in order to destroy the Catholic Church. Remarkably, in the vision, Our Lord told Satan that he could have seventy-five to one hundred years and all the power that Satan requested in order to destroy. The Catholic Church is the Kingdom of God on Earth. The pope is the king of this kingdom. Was this vision of Pope Leo XIII referring to the destruction from the Second Vatican Council that would come about seventy-five to one hundred years from the papacy of Pope Leo XIII? It is difficult to say.

In the Old Testament, it was only Daniel who interpreted the mysterious writing on the wall. In future writings, I will demonstrate that in light of these parallels, the book of Daniel unlocks a mysterious connection between the Old Testament prophecies concerning the abomination of desolation and the events of the Second Vatican Council and the Novus Ordo rite of Paul VI.

As a final note, and one that is more humorous than convincing, Pope Leo XIII was the first pope to have been filmed.[106] The very first films invented were silent films. Instead of audio, written words were displayed between scenes. The effect for everyone worldwide who watched those early silent movies in the late 1800s was that writing would appear on the walls as the films were projected for viewing.

In the Old Testament, words mysteriously appeared on the wall, and in Church history, for the first time in history, words were being projected on a wall. Amazing!

Boys, Dreams, and a Pagan King
DANIEL THE PROPHET AND ST. JOHN BOSCO

Now, let's move on to a more uplifting account. In the Old Testament, Daniel was gifted with the interpretation of dreams. In Church history, we are all familiar with the famous dreams of St. John Bosco. Here are some parallels between St. John Bosco and Daniel.

School For Young Boys

Old Testament: Daniel was a young boy when he was taken from Jerusalem as a captive of Nabuchodonosor. He was placed in a special Babylonian school for young boys and taught the ways of the Babylonians. A eunuch, a castrated male servant of the king, was placed in charge of the school of boys to make sure they were progressing, kept healthy, and made presentable to King Nabuchodonosor. King Nabuchodonosor saw something unique in Daniel and chose him to serve at court.

> "In the third year of the reign of Joakim king of Juda, Nabuchodonosor king of Babylon, came to Jerusalem and besieged it. And the king spoke to Asphenez the master of the eunuchs, that he should bring in some of the children of

Israel, and of the king's seed and of the princes, Children in whom there was no blemish, well favoured, and skillful in all wisdom, acute in knowledge, and instructed in science, and such as might stand in the king's palace, that he might teach them the learning, and the tongue of the Chaldeans. And the king appointed them a daily provision, of his own meat, and of the wine of which he drank himself, that being nourished three years, afterward they might stand before the king."

-Daniel 1: 1,3-5

Church History: St. John Bosco was born in northern Italy in 1815 and is well known for his prophetic dreams. He was only nine years old when he had his first prophetic dream about converting boys and convincing them to honor virtue and detest vice. St. John Bosco grew up poor. It was difficult for the poor at the time to attend school.

However, a young priest, Fr. Giuseppe Cafasso, recognized something special in St. John Bosco and supported his schooling. In 1846, St. John Bosco was ordained a priest in the diocese of Turin, northern Italy. St. John Bosco recognized the desperate situation and horrible conditions for orphaned boys living in the streets. These conditions were created by the Industrial Revolution, in which children would perform difficult work in horrible working conditions, being beaten and discarded to fend for themselves.[ab]

St. John Bosco would befriend these boys, win their trust, and take them under his care. He fed them and taught them the Catholic Faith and how to behave in civilized society. St. John Bosco did not have a wife and children because he was a priest and, therefore, could devote his whole heart and attention to these young boys. The eunuch in charge of the Babylonian school of boys parallels this. The eunuch, since he was castrated, also did not have a wife and family and could devote all his attention to the young boys in the Babylonian school.

---

ab   https://www.donboscoyouth.net/don-bosco.html

Prophetic Dreams

Old Testament: Daniel is famous for his ability to interpret dreams and for very mysterious prophecies. Many of Daniel's prophecies concern both the persecution of Antiochus in the Books of the Machabees but also Antichrist and the end of the world.[ac] Daniel's visions, recorded in the book of Daniel, chapters 7-12, are shrouded in mysterious language. Despite this mysterious language, they have long captivated those who have studied them.

Church History: St. John Bosco is famous for his prophetic dreams. Throughout his life, he had vivid dreams about both the present and the future. Many of his dreams are shrouded in mysterious language. Some of his prophetic dreams of the future are thought to be predictions of the events that await the Church at the end of time.

Walking A Fine Line

Old Testament: Daniel had to walk a fine line due to his position in the king's court in Babylon. Daniel was a faithful Jew who never denied his holy religion. However, he had to obey the king of Babylon, a pagan. Despite Daniel being a Jew, Nabuchodonosor saw his wisdom and raised him high in his kingdom. Throughout the book of Daniel, we see various advisors to the king who tried to have Daniel killed.

There is another group that might have thought badly of Daniel as well, and that would have been other Jewish exiles. From their point of view, they could have seen Daniel as a 'sellout' who denied his Jewish religion to gain a position of power and influence in the king's court. These Jews would not have been privileged to the private events of the king's court, so they would not have known Daniel's true intentions.

Church History: In northern Italy in the mid to late 1800s, the government was anti-clerical and secular. St. John Bosco lived in the kingdom of Piedmont, ruled over by King Victor Emmanuel II. This was the same king

---

ac   See the footnote for Daniel 11:21 in the Douay-Rheims Bible: "Antiochus Epiphanes, who at first was despised and not received for king. What is here said of this prince, is accommodated by St. Jerome and others to Antichrist; of whom this Antiochus was a figure."

who would later conquer the Papal States in 1860 and 1870. Thus, St. John Bosco had to walk a fine line with the civic authorities in Turin. They opposed clerics, especially public religious works like those of St. John Bosco.

However, the local government authorities saw value in what St. John Bosco was doing on a natural level. Even while the authorities were creating laws to suppress religious orders, those same civic authorities would secretly advise St. John Bosco about how to get around the new laws. This was the case with Justice Minister of Piedmont, Urbano Rattazzi. In addition to the government, some of St. John Bosco's fellow clergy also opposed him. St. John Bosco was accused of stealing the youth from their parishes and of unorthodox catechism methods.[ad]

There were multiple attempts to kill St. John Bosco, including a stabbing, bludgeoning, and a shooting. He was delivered from all these attempted murders, often through miracles.

Admonishing The Pagan King

Old Testament: Daniel stands out as the one person who could admonish King Nabuchodonosor for his pride and arrogance. All the other ministers of the king were like lap dogs and "yes" men. Because of his love for the true God, wisdom, and personal holiness, Daniel had gained King Nabuchodonosor's respect. Consequently, Nabuchodonosor heard Daniel's admonishment without getting upset. However, the king did not abide by Daniel's advice, which resulted in disaster for King Nabuchodonosor. He would spend seven "times" away from his kingdom, living like an animal because he failed to give glory to God.

Church History: Despite being a devout Catholic priest, St. John Bosco gained the respect of secular authorities. In November of 1854, St. John Bosco wrote a letter to King Victor Emmanuel II, admonishing him to stop the confiscation of Church property and suppression of religious orders. St. John Bosco warned that he saw "great funerals at court," indicating divine chastisement if the king did not alter his course.[107] The king did not listen to the admonishments of St. John Bosco, and within a short period of time,

---

ad   https://www.galwaycathedral.ie/news/saint-month-st-john-bosco

the king's family suffered several deaths. The king's mother, wife, newborn son, and his only brother all died.[107]

This wraps up our analysis of the parallels between the mystical prophecies and events of Ezechiel, Daniel, and Jeremias. Before we examine Period 7, let us circle back and pick up a few odds and ends that still exist to be discussed in Period 6. Following is a chart of those remaining parallels.

Old Testament	New Testament
The golden idol of Nabuchodonosor	Darwin's theory of evolution
Babylonian conquest of Jerusalem	Spoliation of the Papal States and attack on Rome
Conversion of Nabuchodonosor and his admission of the true God	Vatican I and papal infallibility
Darius' Law	Pope St. Pius X and Modernism

Let's dive in and see some astonishing parallels between the large golden idol of Nabuchodonosor and Darwin's theory of evolution.

When the Jews were taken to Babylon, some found favor with the king. This was the case with Daniel and his Jewish companions, Sidrach, Misach, and Abdenago. Daniel was made the governor over all the provinces of Babylon, and chief of the magistrates over all the wise men of Babylon. Daniel "requested of the king, and he appointed Sidrach, Misach, and Abdenago over the works of the province of Babylon".[ae]

God's People In The Ruling Class Under A Pagan King

Old Testament: King Nabuchodonosor recognized the God of the Jews and made professions of belief in Him. He had enough respect and trust in the Jews that he set up Sidrach, Misach, and Abdenago as governors over Babylon. Despite his profession of belief in the God of Israel (see Daniel 2:

---

ae   See Daniel 2: 46-49

47), King Nabuchodonosor chose to erect a giant golden idol. Nabuchodonosor then called all the nobles, governors, magistrates, and other officials to come and worship the golden idol he had erected. Anyone who did not worship the statue would be thrown into the fiery furnace. Of course the Jews could not and would not worship a pagan idol.

> "Now there are certain Jews whom thou hast set over the works of the province of Babylon, Sidrach, Misach, and Abdenago: these men, O king, have slighted thy decree: they worship not thy gods, nor do they adore the golden statue which thou hast set up."
>
> - Daniel 3: 12

Church History: In Prussia in the mid-1800s, the Catholic Church had a close relationship with the ruling classes. The term for the connection between Church and State was called "Thrun und Altar,"[af] and even though the king of Prussia, Frederick William IV, was not Catholic, much of the ruling class of Prussia was Catholic.[108]

However, the position of the Catholic Church in Prussia was about to change drastically, starting in 1859, when Charles Darwin published his work *On the Origin of Species*. This work taught that, among other things, humans evolved from animals. Darwin's work was exceptionally well received by the Prussian intellectual elite, commanding submission on the part of upper-class society.[109]

Will Not Bow to the Idol
NABUCHODONOSOR'S IDOL AND DARWIN'S THEORY OF EVOLUTION

Old Testament: Sidrach, Misach, and Abdenago refused to worship the golden idol that Nabuchodonosor had set up. They were the only ones who refused to bow down to the statue among all the other nobles and rulers of Babylon.

---

af   *Thrun und Altar* is a German phrase that means "throne and altar". It is often used to refer to the alliance between the monarchy and the Church in the nineteenth century, especially in Germany and Austria. The phrase implies a conservative and traditionalist worldview that opposes liberalism and secularism.

Church History: In 1860, only one year after Darwin publicized his theory, a regional council was called in the Archdiocese of Cologne. The council was acknowledged by the Vatican. At the end of the Council of Cologne, the bishops issued a formal statement in which they completely and totally rejected Darwin's theory that humans evolved from animals.

Statement from the Council of Cologne:

> "The first parents were created directly by God. Therefore, we declare the opinion of those who fear not to assert, that through a spontaneous transformation from a less perfect to a more perfect nature, this human body emerged, is clearly contrary to Sacred Scripture and the Faith."[110][ag]

Statement Of Defiance

Old Testament: Because Sidrach, Misach, and Abdenago refused to worship the golden idol, some native Babylonian officials went to Nabuchodonosor and accused them of disobedience to the king's decree. The three Jews responded to Nabuchodonosor: "We have no occasion to answer the king in this matter."

> "Sidrach, Misach, and Abdenago answered and said to king Nabuchodonosor: We have no occasion to answer thee concerning this matter. For behold our God, whom we worship, is able to save us from the furnace of burning fire, and to deliver us out of thy hands, O king. But if he will not, be it known to thee, O king, that we will not worship thy gods, nor adore the golden statue which thou hast set up."
>
> - Daniel 3: 16-18

Church History: The statement from the Council of Cologne in 1860 directly contradicted the rapidly growing acceptance of Darwin's theory of evolution among Prussia's ruling class, which was heavily influenced by the Prussian intellectual class. Although many privately had reservations about

---

ag   Translated by online translation services from the original Latin text cited from the above bibliographical citation.

Darwin's theory, the pressure grew, influencing many not to express their reservations publicly.

The Vatican approved the regional Council of Cologne. The pope was given full knowledge of the subject of the council, and he received the final statement of the council. He gave no signs of disagreement with the council's theological statement. Furthermore, in upcoming years, the Vatican would censure the writings of various Catholic priests who were trying to join the theory of evolution with the Catholic Church's teachings. The writings of Leroy, Zahm, and Bonomelli would be placed on the Vatican's *Index of Forbidden Books* because they favored Darwin's theory.[110]

However, even though the Vatican gave definite signs that it agreed with the Council of Cologne, it never made any official statement or issued any official teaching directly against Darwin's theory. Thus, just as the Jews did not answer Nabuchodonosor for their refusal to worship the statue, so too did the Vatican give no answer.

Make It Seven Times As Hot

Old Testament: Upon hearing that the three Jews would not submit and worship his idol, King Nabuchodonosor's countenance changed, and he ordered that the fiery furnace be heated up seven times as hot and that the Jewish governors be thrown into the furnace. Although the Jews should have died in the furnace, they were preserved from the flames by an angel.

> "Then was Nabuchodonosor filled with fury: and the countenance of his face was changed against Sidrach, Misach, and Abdenago, and he commanded that the furnace should be heated seven times more than it had been accustomed to be heated. And he commanded the strongest men that were in his army, to bind the feet of Sidrach, Misach, and Abdenago, and to cast them into the furnace of burning fire."
>
> - Daniel 3: 19-20

Church History: In 1871, the new prime minister of Germany, Otto von Bismarck, came to power in Prussia. He allied himself with the liberals, who opposed the Church's power in Germany. The liberals in Germany were using Darwin's theory of evolution as a way to dislodge Catholics from social influence, positions of authority and sway over education. The liberals used the theory of evolution to justify their progressive and nationalist agenda, and to portray the Catholics as backward and reactionary. Compare this to the Babylonian officials who were using the three Jews' refusal to worship the golden idol as a way to dislodge them from their positions in Babylon.

In 1871, under the new anti-Catholic leadership of Otto von Bismarck, the "Kulturkampf" was launched against the Catholic Church. The "Kulturkampf" was a period of about seven years in which twenty-two laws were passed to weaken and sideline the Church's power in Germany. However, paradoxically, despite the persecution of the "Kulturkampf" and despite losing many bishops and clergy to prison and exile, the Church in Germany did not weaken. In fact, it is said to have gotten stronger. The Church gained considerable political power due to the rise of the German Centre Party. Catholic organizations flourished at the end of Otto von Bismarck's persecution.[111]

Unharmed And Astonished

Old Testament: Upon noticing that the Jews were still alive in the furnace and that they were unharmed by the flames, the king ordered them to come out. Nabuchodonosor was astonished and again professed belief in the God of the Jews.

Church History: In 1880, the persecution ended when Otto von Bismarck halted the "Kulturkampf" against the Church and made peace with Pope Leo XIII. Otto von Bismarck was astonished at the resiliency of the Catholic Church in Germany to withstand about seven years of a deliberate campaign to destroy the power of the Church. The new *Mitigation and Peace Laws* passed in Germany reflected the peace that Bismarck made with the Vatican and restored many of the rights of the Church that were taken away during the years of persecution.[112]

All Creation Bless The Lord

Old Testament: While Sidrach, Misach and Abdenago were in the fiery furnace, they praised God with a litany found in Daniel 3: 52-90. The litany of praise calls upon God's creation, in all its various forms, to praise God. Here is an excerpt:

> "O ye whales and all that move in the waters bless the Lord: praise and exalt him above all forever. O all ye fowls of the air, bless the Lord: praise and exalt him above all forever. O all ye beasts and cattle, bless the Lord: praise and exalt him above all forever. O ye sons of men, bless the Lord, praise and exalt him above all forever."

Thus, the Jews were specifically calling on God's creation to offer praise to their Creator. All the works of God reflect His goodness and power.

Church History: Darwin's theory of evolution was at odds with the story of Creation from the book of Genesis. It took away from the praise and glory that is due to God by attributing the creation of the natural world to a random set of genetic mutations. Therefore, how amazing that in the story of Nabuchodonosor's golden idol, the three Jews affirm God as the Creator while they are in the fiery furnace.

Animals Do Not Choose To Die As Martyrs

Old Testament: The three Jewish governors would rather have died than worship the statue.

Church History: In the Old Testament story about King Nabuchodonosor and his golden statue, everyone was bowing down to the idol on their hands and knees, like animals on all fours. Only the three Jewish governors were standing erect. The three Jewish governors acted in a way that only human beings are capable of acting by choosing death instead of denying their beliefs. This altruistic act is directly contrary to Darwin's theory of natural selection because it shows that human beings are capable of something greater than a mere animal instinct to survive. Therefore, it is ironic that the "golden statue" to be worshiped in Church history is a theory that proposes we are nothing but animals who have evolved through natural selection and survival instincts.

Now, let's move on to the next set of parallels. Let's look more into the Spoliation of the Papal States as foreshadowed by the Babylonian conquest of Jerusalem.

Land and Sovereignty Is Taken in Two Installments
BABYLONIANS COME TO JERUSALEM TWICE AND THE FREEMASONS TAKE THE PAPAL STATES IN TWO INSTALLMENTS

Old Testament: The Jews were taken into exile in two installments. The first wave of exiles were taken by Nabuchodonosor in 597 BC. Then, ten years later, in 587 BC, the Babylonians came and destroyed the city and the Temple, taking the rest of the Jews into exile.

Church History: The Papal States were lands in north-central Italy that belonged explicitly to the pope. Charlemagne's father, Pepin, gave them to the pope in 756 in an event called *The Donation of Pepin*. The Papal States belonged to the Holy See (under the pope's direct control) from 756 all the way until 1870, when they were finally and totally stolen by the emerging Kingdom of Italy.

The French Revolution and the subsequent conquest of Napoleon planted liberal seeds in the hearts of Europeans across the continent. The 1800s were a time of great upheaval across Europe as nations struggled within themselves. The social conservatives wanted to maintain the old order of monarchy, nobility, and class structure. Liberals were fighting politically and sometimes using force to form republics based on suffrage.

As the 1800s progressed, the concept of *nationalism* emerged. Europeans sought to form themselves into secular states centered around a shared sense of cultural identity. During this time, in the mid-late 1800s, the forces of nationalism, backed by Freemasons, wanted to unite Italy into one country. This was known as the *Risorgimento*, which means *resurgence*.

Risorgimento sought to unite the myriads of smaller Italian kingdoms and lands into one country. The major obstacle to this goal was the Papal States and the pope. It was certain that the Papal States, governed by the pope, would never submit to being part of a larger, secular country. The line in the sand was drawn immediately. The pope would never surrender Church sovereignty to anyone, let alone Freemasons!

Consequently, in 1860, the Italian nationalists attacked the papal armies and defeated them. They then confiscated two-thirds of the Papal States and joined them to the newly forming Kingdom of Italy. Then, in 1870, the Italian army attacked again, taking the rest of the Holy See's land. They claimed everything, even the very land under the Vatican, St. Peter's Basilica, and all the other Church's properties in Rome. The pope was left with precisely zero. [44]

Ark In A Cave Just Prior

Old Testament: Before the invasion of the Babylonians, the destruction of Jerusalem, and the exile of the Jews in Babylon, the prophet Jeremias hid the ark of the covenant in a cave on Mount Nebo. (See the pages about Our Lady of Lourdes for more details, and also see 2 Machabees 2.)

Church History: Before the Spoliation of the Papal States, Our Lady of Lourdes appeared in a cave in 1858. Of course, Our Lady is the new ark of the covenant.

Defensive Walls Breached

Old Testament: The Babylonians were able to breach the walls of Jerusalem and then poured into the city to conquer it. (See 4 Kings 25:4.)

Church History: Various walls surrounded Rome for protection. The Aurelian Walls, built in 275, were a complete set of walls that encircled the city, well before the invention of the cannon. On September 20, 1870, the Italian Republican Army blasted a hole in the walls near Porta Pia. This day is memorialized in Italy. In virtually every sizable Italian town, there is a street called *Via XX Settembre* or, in English, *Road of 20th September*. This is a celebration of the day that the Holy See had its land forcibly taken.[113]

Taken For Seventy Years

Old Testament: King Cyrus, a Persian who defeated the Babylonians, became the new ruler of Babylon. After seventy years of captivity, King Cyrus made a decree that allowed the Jews to leave and to possess Jerusalem once again, but only as a city-state. They no longer could have an army and were no longer a temporal power.[ah]

Church History: The Holy See had its land taken first in 1859-60 and then again in 1870. The pope and the Church in Rome were without land until 1929, when Mussolini signed the Lateran Treaty with the Holy See. The Lateran Treaty gave back a tiny portion of the Holy See's stolen land in the form of present-day Vatican City; a city-state.

From 1870 until 1929, the popes called themselves *prisoners in the Vatican.* They never left the Vatican in protest. The period between 1859 and 1929 is seventy years, which is the same period of time the Jews were in exile in Babylon.

After the Lateran Treaty, the Holy See was no longer a temporal/military power like it was in the past. We will look into the Lateran Treaty of 1929 in much greater detail in the following time period.

Strange And Evil New, Pagan Land

Old Testament: While in exile, the Jews lived among profane religions, customs, and practices. Before the exile, they could control what would enter their city of Jerusalem, but in exile, they had a much diminished power over their surroundings.

Church History: Once Rome was conquered by the Italian nationalists, whose leaders were self-professed Freemasons, the Church no longer had any control over what was allowed into Rome. The Church was engaged in open warfare against Freemasonry during this time period. Popes wrote encyclicals directly against Freemasonry.[ai] What was once a city governed by

---

ah   The decree of Cyrus will be covered at length in Period 7, therefore no Old Testament passages will be offered here.

ai   For Example, *Humanum Genus*, issued on April 20, 1884, by Pope Leo XIII.

codified moral and religious laws had become a city of vice. Houses of immorality went up around the city, as did buildings dedicated to other religions.

The final confiscation of the Papal States took place in 1870 while the First Vatican Council was in session. The First Vatican Council was never concluded because of this invasion. The First Vatican Council proclaimed the doctrine of papal infallibility, which also has an astonishing parallel in the Old Testament. Let's move onto that subject next. To do so, we need to take a closer look into Nabuchodonosor.

Kingdom Taken For "Seven" Times

Nabuchodonosor is a prominent and complex character. He was responsible for destroying Jerusalem, abducting two kings of Juda, and exiling the Jews into a strange and pagan land. Yet, through his contact with the Jews, especially Daniel, he came to honor the God of Israel and raised up the Jews in his kingdom. Finally, the last story of Nabuchodonosor in the Old Testament is the account of what seems like Nabuchodonosor's complete conversion to the God of Israel.

In Church history, the time after the French Revolution in Europe is also complex. The first treatment of Catholicism by the Revolution was overtly hostile. Napoleon later abducted two popes, and France set up a Roman Republic in what was previously the Papal States. Secular laws were enacted across Napoleon's European-wide empire, and Catholics found themselves subjugated in their own lands. Yet, as time passed, the Catholic Church achieved a privileged status in secular Europe. Seventy years after France's confiscation of the Papal States in 1800, the Catholic Church convened in Rome for the First Vatican Council.

Old Testament: In Chapter 4 of the book of Daniel, Nabuchodonosor was troubled by another disturbing dream. He saw a large tree that covered the whole earth and gave shade and food to all the earth's creatures. An angel came down from Heaven and said to cut down the tree but to keep the stump in the ground. Take particular note of the verse, **"The Most High ruleth in the kingdom of men"**.

"Nevertheless leave the stump of its roots in the earth, and let it be tied with a band of iron, and of brass, among the grass, that is without, and let it be wet with the dew of heaven, and let its portion be with the wild beasts in the grass of the earth. Let his heart be changed from man's, and let a beast's heart be given to him, and let seven times pass over him. This is the decree by the sentence of the watchers, and the word and demand of the holy ones; till the living know that the most High ruleth in the kingdom of men; and he will give it to whomsoever it shall please him, and he will appoint the basest man over it."

- Daniel 4: 12-14

Church History: In one sense, the papacy fits the description of the great tree that gave shade and fruit to the whole earth. The fact that the tree was cut down and brought to a low state for "seven times" (see Daniel 4: 13) is similar to what happened to the papacy in 1870 (starting in 1859), when the papacy had the Papal States taken away. The papacy was brought to a low and humble position for seventy years (seven times). This can be calculated using two dates: the first confiscation of two-thirds of the Papal States in 1859 and the Lateran Treaty in 1929, when the papacy finally received land and a kingdom again. If you subtract 1859 from 1929, it equals seventy. Thus, just like Nabuchodonosor, the papacy lost its kingdom for a period of seven times.

To add further mystery and interest, the papacy is the means in which **"The Most High ruleth in the kingdom of men"**. Remember the words of Our Lord to St. Peter: **"He who hears you, hears Me"**. In other words, Christ rules men through the papacy.

Faith and Reason, and No One Can Tell Him "Nay"
NABUCHODONOSOR ADMITS THE TRUE GOD AND PAPAL INFALLIBILITY

Old Testament: Nabuchodonosor's dream became reality. Because of his pride, God punished Nabuchodonosor by removing his human heart and

191

giving him the heart of a beast until he admitted that God was sovereign over all. Nabuchodonosor lost his reason and spent seven "times"[aj] like a beast in the wilderness, eating grass and acting like an animal. During these seven "times," he was away from his throne, abased, and humiliated.

Finally, at the end of seven "times," Nabuchodonosor proclaimed the sovereignty of God:

> "Now at the end of the days, I Nabuchodonosor lifted up my eyes to heaven, and my sense was restored to me: and I blessed the most High, and I praised and glorified him that liveth for ever: for his power is an everlasting power, and his kingdom is to all generations. And all the inhabitants of the earth are reputed as nothing before him: for he doth according to his will, as well with the powers of heaven, as among the inhabitants of the earth: and there is none that can resist his hand, and say to him: Why hast thou done it? At the same time, my sense returned to me, and I came to the honour and glory of my kingdom: and my shape returned to me: and my nobles and my magistrates sought for me, and I was restored to my kingdom: and greater majesty was added to me. Therefore I Nabuchodonosor do now praise, and magnify, and glorify the King of heaven: because all his works are true, and his ways judgments, and them that walk in pride he is able to abase."

> - Daniel 4: 31-34

To summarize this point, Nabuchodonosor lost his reason until he proclaimed that God was sovereign over the kingdom of men. Further, he declared that no one can tell God "no" and contradict Him.

Church History: The First Vatican Council was convened in 1870 and gave us two documents, *Dei Filius* and *Pastor Aeternus*.

---

aj   Sacred Scripture does not indicate if seven "times" is seven days, seven months or seven years. We are given the general description of seven "times."

Dei Filius dealt with the relationship between faith and reason. It stated that reason could not contradict the truths given to us by faith. This is so because God is the Author of both faith and reason, and God is not self-contradictory. Faith is above reason but is not opposed to it. Our reason can lead us to truth, but it can never arrive at the revealed truths given to us by the Church, which we can only possess by means of our faith.[114]

The French Revolution explicitly rejected faith and set up something called *The Cult of Reason*. They literally worshiped reason in a ceremony inside Notre Dame Cathedral in Paris.[115]

Pastor Aeternus gave us the dogma of papal infallibility. It sets up the conditions when papal infallibility applies. But, most importantly, it stated that the pope can, by himself, give definitive statements which no one can contradict. Certain definitions given by the pope are "immutable by themselves".[116]

Thus, we see the two concepts of faith and reason present at the First Vatican Council, and we see those same two concepts present in the narrative about King Nabuchodonosor. Also, we see the concept of a final, supreme authority over the "kingdom of men," which is also present in both the Old and the New Testament narratives. Nabuchodonosor states that God has the last word, and the dogma of papal infallibility states the same thing about the pope.

Spying to Enforce the King's Law
Daniel Defies the Law of Darius; the Oath Against Modernism

Now, leaving behind the stories of Nabuchodonosor and the First Vatican Council, let's move forward in time in both the Old Testament and Church history. We are nearing the end of this time period. In this last set of parallels, let's look at the law of Darius and the battle against Modernism by Pope St. Pius X.

This parallel is a bit different from most of the other ones so far. One reason for this is the slight twisting of roles. Nonetheless, the parallels are still clear to observe. In reading Daniel chapter 6, we are presented with tricky political situation for Daniel. He was excelling in the king's service, above and beyond the native nobles and governors of Babylon. His worst enemies were closest to him, embedded in the same government and administration, hiding behind a smile and flattering words.

Such was the situation in the Vatican during this time. Because of the intense pressure exerted on the Vatican in the late 1800s by secular forces, political/ideological differences became more serious. Many clergy had adopted dangerous new ideas contrary to the Faith. These "ideas" would later be identified as Modernism. At this time, God gave us one of the greatest pope-saints in latter Church history, Pope St. Pius X.

Three Raised Above

Old Testament: King Darius appointed three princes over his kingdom to oversee the governors. Daniel was one of these three.

> "It seemed good to Darius, and he appointed over the kingdom a hundred and twenty governors to be over his whole kingdom. And three princes over them, of whom Daniel was one: that the governors might give an account to them, and the king might have no trouble."
>
> - Daniel 6: 1-2

Church History: Pope Leo XIII died on July 20, 1903, triggering a conclave to elect the next pope. The favorite to win the election (commonly thought by most historians) was Cardinal Secretary of State Mariano Rampolla. However, two others were also viable candidates for election: Cardinal Girolamo Maria Gotti and Cardinal Giuseppe Melchiorre Sarto (soon to be Pope St. Pius X).

Thus, three were effectively set above the rest by the support they received in the conclave of 1903.[117]

Excelled Over The Other Two

Old Testament: Daniel excelled over all the princes, and King Darius chose, therefore, to set him over the whole kingdom. The other princes of Babylon resented Daniel's appointment.

> "And Daniel excelled all the princes and governors: because a greater spirit of God was in him. And the king thought to set him over all the Kingdom."

> - Daniel 6: 3-4

Church History: The conclave of 1903 was famous for what occurred during the voting process. Initially, Cardinal Rampolla was receiving the majority of the votes. To win a papal election, a two-thirds majority vote was needed. This rule was established by Pope Gregory XV in 1621.

Just as it looked like Cardinal Rampolla would receive the required votes to win, something unexpected occurred. The cardinal-bishop of Krakow, Cardinal Kosielsko, presented a veto on behalf of the Austrian Emperor Franz Joseph I. This veto was a relic of the Holy Roman Empire and was considered an artifact of a bygone age; however, the veto power, called *jus exclusivae*, was technically still a privilege of the Austrian Emperor.

The veto by the Austrian Emperor turned the direction of the conclave. After the seventh ballot, the conclave elected Cardinal Sarto. Cardinal Rampolla protested the veto. After his election, Cardinal Sarto took the name of Pope Pius X.

There are various theories on why the Austrian Emperor used his veto privilege against Cardinal Rampolla. One theory suggests that Cardinal Rampolla favored France over Austria, thus provoking the emperor to stop his election. Another theory states that the emperor was presented with evidence that Cardinal Rampolla was a Freemason and Grand Master of the Ordo Templi Orientis. There is much speculation and argument, even to this day, concerning the reason for the veto. However, it is interesting to note that the Ordo Templi Orientis claims Cardinal Rampolla as one of their members[118].

Pope St. Pius X was chosen and placed over the entire kingdom. But, he had enemies in high places who resented his new position.

Attempt To Uproot By Means Of Law

Old Testament: The governors and princes were crafty and scheming. They devised a law designed to remove Daniel from his position by focusing on his devout prayer to God. They deceived the king as to their motives for suggesting a law that appeared to flatter the king but was really a law that was meant to target Daniel.

> "Then the princes and the governors craftily suggested to the king and spoke thus unto him: King Darius, live forever: All the princes of the Kingdom, the magistrates, and governors, the senators, and judges have consulted together, that an imperial decree and an edict be published: That whosoever shall ask any petition of any god, or man, for thirty days, but of thee, O king, shall be cast into the den of lions. So king Darius set forth the decree and established it."
>
> - Daniel 6: 6-7, 9

Church History: Pope St. Pius X launched a crusade to eliminate Modernism from the Catholic Church. In short, Modernism is loosely defined as the belief that truth is not objective but, instead, is changeable. Pope St. Pius X called Modernism "the synthesis of all heresies" because it embraced all heresies by denying the existence of religious truth. Thus, Modernists were amorphous by nature and, as a group, did not have shared beliefs. Modernism had been slowly and stealthily growing among Catholic clergy in various quarters of the Church. It was strongly influenced by the growing secular nature of the world and the diminishing political power of the Catholic Church. Remember, the popes at this time were still without any land due to the Spoliation of the Papal States in 1870.

Many inside the Vatican did not adhere intentionally to Modernism. Vigilance was needed to guard against it. However, there were some who intentionally and purposefully accepted and promoted Modernism.

Like Daniel who was alone at the top of Babylonian government, Pope St. Pius X was known to have made the following statement to express how he felt alone in the fight against Modernism. *"De gentibus non est vir mecum."* - *"Among all men that surround me there is no one with me."*[119]

Pope St. Pius X took various measures in his valiant attempt to combat Modernism in the Church. In 1907, he wrote a letter, *Lamentabili Sane Exitu*, in which he officially identified and condemned sixty-five modernist errors. Later, he wrote an encyclical, *Pascendi Dominici Gregis*, which further identified and condemned Modernism.

Finally, in 1910, Pope St. Pius X instituted an oath that all clergy were required to take. This was his *Oath Against Modernism*, a top-down oath that effectively made it illegal to profess any modernist beliefs. The effect was to drive Modernists underground and out of the open forum.[120]

In summary, Pope St. Pius X identified Modernists as crafty and duplicitous, not stating their true intentions but accomplishing their goals through trickery and deceit. Therefore, Pope St. Pius X devised a law (an oath) that would force them to publicly renounce Modernism as a way to target and trap them.

Spies Watch For Religious Infractions

Old Testament: Daniel knew about the law that forbade praying, but he chose to open his window and pray in plain sight. His enemies were spying on him, waiting for him to break the new law. When he did break the law, they immediately reported it to the king.

> "Now when Daniel knew this, that is to say, that the law was made, he went into his house: and opening the windows in his upper chamber towards Jerusalem, he knelt down three times a day, and adored, and gave thanks before his God, as he had been accustomed to do before. Wherefore those men carefully watching him, found Daniel praying and making supplication to his God. And they came and spoke to the king concerning the edict…"

- Daniel 6: 10-12

Church History: Many of those who tended towards modernist beliefs recanted. After all, most were trying to find the path of least resistance and did not want to sacrifice their careers for any ideology. However, some, especially in the French clergy, were cemented in their modernism and refused to "go underground". They kept on professing modernist beliefs in public.[121]

Pope St. Pius X accepted the formation of the *Sodalitium Pianum*. Monsignor Umberto Benigni formed this group, a type of secret police force, that would search out suspected Modernists and then closely monitor them. If they noticed any infractions of the Oath Against Modernism, this group would report to St. Pope Pius X.[122]

In summary, the proud Modernists, who were not ashamed of their beliefs, chose to still openly profess Modernism. A secret organization was formed to spy on them and report back to the pope with any infractions of the oath, just like the Babylonians who were spying on Daniel, waiting for him to break the law not to pray.

Put Underground Yet Stays Alive

Old Testament: The king did not want to have Daniel thrown to the lions for breaking the new law, but the king could not change the law. Thus, Daniel was thrown to the lions. He spent the night in the lions' den, untouched. He came back out of the lions' den alive and well.

> "Then the king commanded, and they brought Daniel and cast him into the den of the lions. And the king said to Daniel: Thy God, whom thou always servest, he will deliver thee. My God hath sent his angel and hath shut up the mouths of the lions, and they have not hurt me."
>
> - Daniel 6: 16, 22

Church History: Thus, by the efforts of Pope St. Pius X and the Sodalitium Pianum, Modernists were driven underground. They would remain underground during the pontificate of Pope St. Pius X. However, their time underground did not cause the movement to perish. It remained, patiently waiting out the time until it could re-emerge.

Persecution Reversed

Old Testament: When Daniel came out of the lions' den alive, King Darius ordered the men who had just accused Daniel to be thrown into the lions' den. Thus, a complete reversal occurred: Daniel came out and his enemies went in.

> "And by the king's commandment, those men were brought that had accused Daniel: and they were cast into the lions' den..."
>
> - Daniel 6: 24

Church History: After the death of Pope St. Pius X, Pope Benedict XV was elected. Pope Benedict XV was the protégé and personal assistant to Cardinal Rampolla. When Cardinal Rampolla was appointed secretary of state for the Vatican on June 2 1887, he made Giacomo della Chiesa (future Pope Benedict XV) his personal assistant.[ak] Upon the election of Pope Benedict XV, he reversed many of the measures and appointments of Pope St. Pius X. Most notably, he stopped the crusade against the Modernists. He abolished the Sodalitium Pianum,[122] taking the pressure off.

That concludes my analysis of the parallels in this time period, which spanned the Old Testament books of 4 Kings, Jeremias, Ezechiel and Daniel and in Church history, from the French Revolution in 1789 until the Lateran Treaty in 1929. The next time period will start with the Lateran Treaty signed between the Kingdom of Italy and the Holy See.

---

ak   Cardinal of the Holy Roman Church
     https://web.archive.org/web/20190628161227/https://webdept.fiu.edu/~mirandas/
     bios1914.htm

Period 7

Autonomy and City-State

After being without their land for seventy years, God's people go back to their holy city which they govern as a city-state inside a larger pagan empire.

OLD TESTAMENT: Books of 1 & 2 Esdras, Esther

King Cyrus and his Mede-Persian Empire conquered the Babylonian Empire, taking its territories. The Jews were exiled in Babylon for seventy years when the Persian King Cyrus granted them to return to Jerusalem and keep it as a city-state. Cyrus gave money and resources to rebuild the Jewish Temple and decreed that Jews were to live by their own religious laws.

Some Jews, such as Esther, decided to stay in the Persian Empire. As Jews returned to Jerusalem, the story of Queen Esther took place at the same time in the Persian capital city of Susan.

CHURCH HISTORY: Approximately 1929^{AD} to 1950^{AD}

Upon the signing of the Lateran Treaty in 1929, the Holy See received land from the Italian government, resulting in the creation of the city-state of Vatican City. The Lateran Treaty granted financial support to the Holy See, established Catholic laws across Italy, and ensured the Holy See's autonomy within Vatican City's borders.

Throughout the 1800s, Catholics were pressured to accept secularism and agnosticism. It was important to the secular authorities that "religious" citizens, especially Catholics, learned to see their world through the eyes of the modern world and not through the eyes of their Faith.

Using allegory, we can make a comparison. Just as many Jews decided to stay in Persia yet still believe in the one true God, so too did many Catholics in this time choose to retain their worldly outlook yet still remain Catholic. In the story of Queen Esther, she kept her Jewish identity a secret. The Jews were part of a larger multicultural society and were pressured to keep their religion a private affair. Similarly, in the 1800s, especially in the aftermath of the French Revolution in France or the Risorgimento in Italy, citizens were encouraged to view their religion as a private affair.

Old Testament	New Testament
Decree of Cyrus	The Lateran Treaty
The Jews rejected co-worship with the Samaritans.	Pope Pius XI rejected the ecumenical movement.
Religious purification by Esdras	Mandatory Catholic education and Decree Against Communism
Nehemias rebuilt the walls of Jerusalem.	The Marshall Plan rebuilt Europe.
A large crowd was taught by Esdras.	Pope Pius XII drew large crowds after World War II.
Esther, Mardochai,and Aman	The Vatican, German resistance, and the Nazis

God's People Return to Their City-State
Decree of Cyrus and the Lateran Treaty

Old Testament: In 587 BC, the Babylonians destroyed the Jewish Temple and brought the Jews into exile. The Jews remained in captivity until the Persians conquered the Babylonian Empire. King Cyrus, the Persian king, made a decree in 537 BC that permitted Jews to return to Jerusalem and rebuild their Temple. Once back in Jerusalem, the Temple reconstruction started and was completed in 517 BC. Jerusalem became a city-state with Jewish laws, yet under the dominion of the Persian Empire.

Jeremias prophesied that the Jews would be exiled for seventy years. It was seventy years between the destruction of the Temple in 587 BC and its reconstruction in 517 BC.[a] There are other propositions as to how the seventy years is to be calculated. However, it is sufficient to simply quote the prophecy of Jeremias[b] to establish the seventy year exile:

> "And all this land shall be a desolation, and an astonishment: and all these nations shall serve the king of Babylon seventy years. And when the seventy years shall be expired, I will punish the king of Babylon, and that nation, saith the Lord, for their iniquity, and the land of the Chaldeans: and I will make it perpetual desolations."
>
> - Jeremias 25: 11-12

Church History: In 1859-60, the emerging Kingdom of Italy confiscated two-thirds of the Papal States. The Papal States had been in the possession of the Church from the days of Charlemagne, when they were given to the Church as a gift by Pepin in 756.

In 1870, the Kingdom of Italy confiscated the remaining one-third of the Papal States. The Kingdom of Italy sent armed troops into Rome and fought against the papal army, abruptly ending the First Vatican Council. From that point onward, the popes referred to themselves as *prisoners in the Vatican*. The Holy See had all of their land taken; even the land under the pope's feet was technically confiscated, even though no move was made by the Italian state to evict the pope. The new secular government allowed a wave of immorality to flood into Rome. The Holy See was now living in a strange, new, pagan land. In the Old Testament, the Jews were brought to Babylon. In our history, "Babylon" was brought to the Church.[c]

---

a   There is debate about the precise years of the Jewish exile in Babylon, the Edict of Cyrus and the Temple restoration, within one or two years. However, we do not need to know the exact dates to understand the parallels.

b   Note that the heading for Jeremias 25, in the Douay Rheims Bible is "The prophet foretells the **seventy years captivity**; after that the destruction of Babylon, and other nations".

c   St. Peter referred to Rome as "Babylon". Thus, from the time of St. Peter in Rome until the Spoliation of the Papal States in 1870, the Church has come full circle, back in "Babylon" again. See 1 Peter 5:13 "The church that is in Babylon, elected together with you, saluteth you".

Then, in 1929, Mussolini, who had usurped control of Italy from the Italian king, signed the Lateran Treaty with the Holy See. The Lateran Treaty gave the Holy See a small portion of Its land back with the creation of the city-state of Vatican City.[123] Like the Jews who spent seventy years in exile, so too did the Church spend seventy years. This can be calculated from the first wave of confiscation in 1859-60 until the signing of the Lateran Treaty in 1929.[d]

Given A Large Sum Of Money From The Pagan King

Old Testament: Not only did King Cyrus release the Jews from their captivity, but he also gave them a large sum of money to help them rebuild in Jerusalem.

> "And let that Temple of God be built by the governor of the Jews and by their ancients, that they may build that house of God in its place. I also have commanded what must be done by those ancients of the Jews, that the house of God may be built, to wit, that of the king's chest, that is, of the tribute that is paid out of the country beyond the river, the charges be diligently given to those men, lest the work be hindered."
>
> - 1 Esdras 6: 7-8

Church History: The Lateran Treaty of 1929 consists of three parts.[e]

The three parts of the Lateran Treaty are:

- *The Treaty of Conciliation* gave land and sovereignty back.

- *The Financial Convention* gave money to the Holy See.

- *The Concordat* established the relationship between the Vatican and Italian State.

The Lateran Treaty not only gave the Holy See a small portion of its land back (the city-state of Vatican City), but the treaty also established an

---

d   I have never encountered any source indicating the Holy See spent seventy years without land. This is my own interpretation of events. Nonetheless, the parallels are remarkable.

e   The Vatican organizes the treaty into two parts instead of three. The Vatican places the second and the third parts of the treaty together. But either way, it's the same information.

ongoing annuity, payable to the Holy See, plus a one-time lump sum payment to the Holy See at the time of the signing of the Lateran Treaty. Here are the relevant articles from the Lateran Treaty that established the Italian government's payments to the Holy See:

Article 1 of the Financial Convention:

> Italy undertakes to pay to the Holy See, upon exchange of the ratifications of the Treaty, the sum of 750,000,000 Italian lire, and to hand over simultaneously to the Holy See. This aforesaid such a sum in Italian 5% Consolidated Bearer Bonds, with coupon payable on June 30 of the current year attached, as shall represent the nominal value of 1,000,000,000 Italian lire.[124]

Required To Pray For The Pagan King At The Sacrifice

Old Testament: Being a great benefactor to the Jews, King Cyrus thought it prudent to require the Jews to pray for him once their Temple was rebuilt. King Cyrus commanded (not requested) that the Jews offer prayers for him and the Persian Empire during the Jewish sacrifice in the Temple.

> "And let them offer oblations to the God of heaven, and pray for the life of the king (Cyrus) and of his children."
>
> - 1 Esdras 6: 10

In addition to the Bible, the first century Jewish historian, Josephus, also records that the Jews were required to pray for the Persian Empire. In his work *Antiquities of the Jews*, he states that as the priests offer sacrifices in the Temple in accordance with the laws of Moses, "that they should pray for the preservation of the king, and of the Persians".[125]

Church History: The Italian government, under Mussolini, was generous with the Holy See in giving back land, limited sovereignty, and a great deal of money. But the Lateran Treaty also contained a legal requirement (not a request) that specific prayers be offered during Mass for the welfare of the Italian State. Here are the relevant articles from the Lateran Treaty:

Article 12 of the Concordat

On Sundays and days of obligation, the priest celebrating the Chapter Mass shall, in all churches possessing a Chapter, chant a prayer for the prosperity of the King of Italy and the Italian State, according to the usual rules of the holy liturgy. [124]

Owed Their Allegiance To The Pagan King

Old Testament: Although the Jews were free to return to Jerusalem and rebuild, it was understood that they were still part of the Persian Empire. They could not return to the days of the past when the Kingdom of Israel was a world power in its own right. They were completely free to legislate in matters of religion but could not interject themselves in the political affairs of the Persian Empire. The Jews in Jerusalem were at the complete mercy of the Persian Empire.

Church History: The Holy See had no land or reliable revenue between 1870 and 1929. By contrast, in the centuries prior, the Holy See commanded armies and was the leading political and religious force in Christendom for hundreds of years during the Middle Ages and Renaissance. However, by 1929, It has been reduced to a city-state that was legally relegated to exercising only "moral and spiritual power".[f]

With the signing of the Lateran Treaty, the Italian government inserted an article that forbade the Holy See from interjecting itself into international politics. It was to be understood that the Holy See was free to legislate in matters of religion but was required to stay out of political/military affairs of the state. Here is the relevant article from the Lateran Treaty:

Article 24 of the Conciliation Treaty

"In regard to the sovereignty appertaining to it also in international matters, the Holy See declares that it desires to take, and shall take, no part in any, temporal rivalries between other States, nor in any international congresses

---

f   "Moral and spiritual power" is the language used in Article 24 of the Conciliation Treaty describing the limits of the Holy See's authority, per the Lateran Treaty. In truth, the pope has supreme authority on Earth, since he is the Vicar of Christ.

called to settle such matters, save and except in the event of such parties making a mutual appeal to the pacific mission of the Holy See, the latter reserving in any event the right of exercising its moral and spiritual power. The Vatican City shall, therefore, be invariably and in every event considered as neutral and inviolable territory."[124]

Most striking of all, and to drive the point home, here is another article from the Lateran Treaty that requires Italian bishops to swear an oath of allegiance to the Italian State before they take up their new diocese.

Article 20 of the Concordat

Previous to taking possession of their Sees, Bishops shall swear allegiance to the Head of the State, using the following form of oath, viz:

'Before God and on His Holy Gospels, I promise and swear allegiance to the Italian State, in such a manner as is proper to a Bishop. I promise and swear to respect, and to cause to be respected by my clergy, the King of Italy and the Italian Government, as constituted by the laws of the State. I further promise and swear that I shall enter into no agreement, nor attend any council, which may be prejudicial to the interests of the Italian State or to public order, and that I shall lay a similar prohibition on my clergy. Being zealous for the good and the advantage of the Italian State, 1 shall do my utmost to prevent any evil which might threaten it.'[124]

As the Jews were going back to their city-state of Jerusalem in the Old Testament and as the Holy See was signing the Lateran Treaty, an ecumenical movement was underway in both instances. In the Old Testament, the Samaritans wanted to worship with the Jews in the rebuilt Temple. The Samaritans were the remnants of the former ten northern tribes that went into apostasy way back during the revolt of Jeroboam. In Church history, the beginning stages of the ecumenical movement were underway in the early 1900s. Protestants and other schismatic sects recognized the increasing secularization of the world, and joined together to promote "christian" religion, inviting the Catholic Church to join them. Let's look at those parallels now.

Born In Babylon

King Cyrus appointed a Jewish man named Zorobabel as that region's governor to oversee the Temple's rebuilding. The name *Zoro-babel* means *planted in Babylon*, indicating that Zorobabel was born in Babylon. This is a poetic and subtle way of highlighting a tension and an area of concern for the Jewish people, who have been in exile in a pagan land for seventy years. After that long time, practically all Jews returning to Jerusalem had been born in Babylon. As the Jews traveled back to Jerusalem to rebuild, how much of the Babylonian worldview had they unintentionally absorbed?

This tension is highlighted yet again, though this time it is not so subtle, in a situation that arises once the Jews start to rebuild their Temple. They are approached by Samaritans who offer to help. We are given a strong clue that they are Samaritans because 1 Esdras 4:2 says that they were brought to this land by the Assyrian king. The Samaritans had been living in the land around Jerusalem when the Jews were in exile in Babylon.

The Jews, who were returning to Jerusalem for the specific purposes of rebuilding their Temple, to live by God's laws and to reestablish a strong Jewish identity, were all the more repulsed by the Samaritans. The Jews most certainly were cognizant of Babylonian contamination in their lives and wanted to reestablish, in Jerusalem, a purity of life consistent with the laws of God. The Samaritans represented the antithesis to this desire.

Asked to Join a Melting Pot of Religions
THE SAMARITANS WANT TO HELP REBUILD THE TEMPLE AND THE ECUMENICAL MOVEMENT OF THE EARLY 1900s

The Samaritans were a mixed race descended from the ten northern tribes. You might remember the parallels between the ten northern tribes and the Protestant Revolt (see Period 5 for a refresher). The ten northern tribes were taken into captivity by the Assyrians and scattered among the pagan peoples of that empire. The Samaritans maintained a distorted belief in the God of Israel. Amazingly, they only held the first five books of the Old Testament, the Pentateuch, as their authoritative scripture. There are over six thousand textual differences between the Samaritan version of the Pentateuch and the Jewish version[126].[g]

Thus, the Samaritans in the book of Esdras mirror the theological descendants of the Protestant Revolt. Just as the ten northern tribes were mixed with pagans and scattered, eventually morphing into the Samaritans, so too did the Protestants in the centuries following Martin Luther experience so many different theological breakups and absorbed so many secular ideas that by the early 1900s, they resembled a theological version of the Samaritans.

Old Testament: The Samaritans approached the Jews and offered to help build the Temple, stating that they also believed in the God of Israel. However, the Jews, led by Zorobabel, rejected the help of the Samaritans. The Jews had just come out of Babylon, and they wanted to keep their holy religion and their Temple pure. This desire for religious and ethnic purity is a significant theme in the books of 1 and 2 Esdras, as we will see.

> "Now the enemies of Juda and Benjamin heard that the children of the captivity were building a Temple to the Lord the God of Israel. And they came to Zorobabel and the chief of the fathers and said to them: Let us build with you, for we seek your God as ye do: behold we have sacrificed to him, since the days of Asor Haddan king of Assyria, who brought us hither. But Zorobabel and Josue and the rest of the chief of the fathers of Israel said to them: You have nothing to do with us to build a house to our God, but we ourselves alone

---

g   It is amazing how much the Samaritans and the modern-day Protestants have in common. The Samaritans only accepted the Pentateuch as authoritative scripture and rejected the rest of the Old Testament books, including the prophets. This is similar to how the Protestants deny the Catholic saints, the apparitions of Our Lady and Our Lord, and other significant events in Catholic history, which we have seen are parallels with the prophets of the Old Testament. Moreover, the Samaritan Pentateuch has over six thousand textual variances when compared to the Jewish Pentateuch, which indicates that the Samaritans altered the scripture, maybe to suit their purposes. This echoes the thousands of changes that Protestants have made to their "bibles".

will build to the Lord our God, as Cyrus king of the Persians hath commanded us. Then the people of the land hindered the hands of the people of Juda and troubled them in building."

- 1 Esdras 4: 1-4

Church History: At the beginning of the twentieth century, the secularization of Europe was far advanced. The Protestant and schismatic Eastern denominations (historically in opposition to each other over religious differences) were beginning to see each other as allies. The idea of a large-scale cooperation began to grow. A movement in the 1920s called the *Life and Work Movement* culminated in a *World Conference of Life and Work* held in Sweden in 1925.[127] All the major "christian" denominations, except the Catholic Church, were represented at this conference. The conference aimed to gather and discuss social cooperation among the denominations. This was the beginning of the ecumenical movement.

In 1928, the Catholic Church addressed the growing ecumenical movement in Pope Pius XI's encyclical *Mortalium Animos*. In this encyclical, Pope Pius XI condemned the premise that all "christian" religions are good and praiseworthy and insisted that Catholics could not participate in their assemblies. Instead, Pope Pius XI said that "the union of Christians can only be promoted" by these denominations rejecting their errors, and to "return to the one true Church of Christ".[128]

Upon Pope Pius XI's rejection, the leaders of the ecumenical movement turned away from their posture of friendship. Many Protestant and schismatic sects were threatened by the idea of the Lateran Treaty, which re-positioned the Catholic Church with a new status of influence and recognition in the world, much more so than any Protestant denomination enjoyed. There was no Protestant equivalent of Vatican City, which, because of the Lateran Treaty, was now its own sovereign country.

The Parallels Between The Two

Old Testament: The Samaritans approached the Jews who were returning from exile and asked if they could help rebuild the Temple. The Samaritans claimed they worshiped the same God as the Jews. The Samaritans truly did not see why they would not be able to work alongside the Jews to help build the Temple. They did not recognize the importance of the religious differences between themselves and the Jews.

Zorobabel rejected the Samaritans. At that point, the Samaritans turned on the Jews and became their enemies.[h] In later verses, the Samaritans actively opposed the Jews in their rebuilding[i] because they were threatened by the prominent position the Jews would enjoy once they had a temple, a city, and strong walls.

Church History: In the early 1900s, the *Life and Work Movement* aimed for religious cooperation. Around the same time, the Church was about to sign the Lateran Treaty, which would make the Holy See a sovereign state and give it official recognition on the world stage. Pope Pius XI flatly rejected the ecumenical movement. Pope Pius XI said essentially the same thing to the ecumenical movement that Zorobabel told the Samaritans:[j]

> "You have nothing to do with us to build a house to our God,
> but we ourselves alone will build to the Lord our God."

Now, let's move on to the next set of parallels: the revival and renewal of Jewish religion and culture under Esdras in the new city-state of Jerusalem and the revival of Catholicism in the public sphere in Rome as a result of the Lateran Treaty.

Religious Laws and Compulsory Religious Ed.
CYRUS MANDATES JEWISH EDUCATION AND THE LATERAN TREATY MAKES CATHOLIC EDUCATION COMPULSORY IN PUBLIC SCHOOLS THROUGHOUT ITALY

Old Testament: The books of 1 Esdras and 2 Esdras can be broken up into three basic movements:

---

h   1 Esdras 4: 4-5
i   2 Esdras 4: 1-23
j   Pope Pius XI did invite them to join the Catholic Church.

- Rebuilding of the Temple
- Religious education
- Reconstruction of the walls of Jerusalem

These three movements were all funded and officially sponsored by the Persian kings. King Cyrus funded the first movement for the Jews to leave their exile, return to Jerusalem, and build the Temple. King Artaxerxes funded the second movement. A priest and scribe named Esdras petitioned the king that he might go back to Jerusalem and teach the Law of Moses to the Jews in Jerusalem. The king gave Esdras money, supplies, and authority to teach the Jewish religion. Thus, by royal Persian decree, the Jewish religion became the official religion in Jerusalem. The king's decree even carried penalties for breaking the Jewish law, which is very striking since the Persian king was not Jewish.

In the following verses, we see that Esdras was a scribe ready to teach.

> "This Esdras went up from Babylon, and he was a ready scribe in the Law of Moses, which the Lord God had given to Israel: and the king granted him all his request, according to the hand of the Lord his God upon him. For Esdras had prepared his heart to seek the law of the Lord, and to do and to teach in Israel the commandments and judgment."
>
> - 1 Esdras 7: 6, 10

The following verses show the Persian king's sponsorship of Jewish religious education:

> "And thou Esdras according to the wisdom of thy God, which is in thy hand, appoint judges and magistrates, that may judge all the people, that is beyond the river, that is, for them who know the law of thy God, yea and the ignorant teach ye freely. And whosoever will not do the law of thy God, and the law of the king diligently, judgment shall be executed upon him, either unto death, or unto banishment, or to the confiscation of goods, or at least to prison."
>
> - 1 Esdras 7: 25-26

Church History: The period following the Lateran Treaty in Italy is also comprised of three basic movements that parallel the movements in the books of 1 & 2 Esdras. These three can roughly be categorized as follows:

- Re-establishment of the Holy See as a sovereign state *(rebuilt the Temple)*
- Legal affirmation of Catholicism as the official religion of the people of Italy *(religious education)*
- Containment of Communism in Italy following World War II *(reconstruction of the walls)*

The three movements all had official funding and backing from non-Catholic governments. The first two were backed by Mussolini's fascist government (and are incorporated into the body of the Lateran Treaty). The American government funded the third movement primarily through the intermediaries of the Vatican Bank and the Christian Democratic Party of Italy. In a larger sense, the American government rebuilt Europe through the Marshall Plan, in part, to protect Europe from the spread of Communism. This topic will be addressed shortly.

In the third section of the Lateran Treaty, the Concordat, Catholicism was made the official and state-sponsored religion of Italy. Article 11 of the Concordat officially recognized Catholic holy days.

Article 11 - Concordat

The State recognizes the Feast-days established by the Church, which are the following:

- All Sundays
- The first day of the year
- The Epiphany (January 6)
- The Feast of S. Joseph (March 19)
- The Ascension
- The Feast of Corpus Domini
- The Feast of SS. Peter and Paul (June 29)

- All Saints' Day (November 1)
- The Feast of the Immaculate Conception (December 8)
- Christmas Day (December 25) [124]

Italian State Adopts Canon Law As Its Law for Marriage

Article 34 –Concordat

Being desirous of restoring to the institution of marriage, which is the basis of the family, that dignity is in keeping with the Catholic traditions of the Italian people. The Italian State recognises the sacrament of marriage as legal for civil purposes, when administered according to Canon Law.[124]

Italian State Adopts Mandatory Catholic Education In All Public Schools, Both Primary And Secondary

Article 36 - Concordat

The teaching of Christian doctrine, in the form admitted by Catholic tradition is considered by Italy to be the basis and the apex of public education. For this reason, Italy agrees that religious education, which is now given in the public elementary schools, be in future extended to and developed in secondary schools, according to a program to be settled between the Holy See and the State.[124]

In addition to this official sponsorship of Catholicism by the Italian State, there are also a number of unofficial ways in which the fascist government of Mussolini aided the Catholic Church in Italy. A book was published on January 28, 2014, entitled *The Pope and Mussolini*, authored by David Kertzer, which reveals several of these unofficial state sponsorships of Catholicism.

The author conducted research in the Italian government archives and also in the recently opened Vatican secret archives (opened in 2006 for the years before/during/after WW II). David Kertzer reports in his book that the pope and Mussolini had a secret liaison, Fr. Pietro Tacchi Venturi, who would communicate between the two. Through Fr. Pietro Tacchi Venturi, the

213

pope would request things of Mussolini, like the suppression of immodest fashion or the suppression of Protestantism in Italy. If these claims are valid, this is just another example of how the Italian State threw its weight and authority behind Catholicism in Italy.

Espousal with the Impure, Unclean, and Illicit

Esdras Stops Jews From Marrying Pagan Wives and Pope Pius XII Issues Decree Against Communism

In the Old Testament, Esdras was dealing with a big problem in his attempts to reeducate the Jews in their religion. Men were breaking the Law of Moses by marrying pagan women. A sea of pagan peoples surrounded the little city-state island of Jerusalem, excreting powerful influence. The Jews had to keep themselves held up in their city to stay free from this influence and pressure. They needed the protection of the walls around Jerusalem, as we will see shortly.

The struggle for Esdras to keep his people pure has remarkable parallels with the struggle of Pope Pius XII in his fight against Communism after World War II.

Old Testament: Esdras returned to Jerusalem with a heart on fire for the Law of God. As the king commanded, Esdras set up judges and administrators over the Jews and taught freely those ignorant of the Law. Thus, we can see why it was so devastating for Esdras to discover that a considerably large group of Jewish men had married foreign women, and even the priests took foreign wives. The priests, much more than the people, should have known better.

> "And after these things were accomplished, the princes came to me, saying: The people of Israel, and the priests and Levites have not separated themselves from the people of the lands, and from their abominations, namely, of the Chanaanites, and the Hethites, and the Pherezites, and the Jebusites, and the Ammonites, and the Moabites, and the Egyptians, and the Amorrhites. For they have taken of their

daughters for themselves and for their sons, and they have mingled the holy seed with the people of the lands. And the hand of the princes and magistrates hath been first in this transgression. And when I had heard this word, I rent my mantle and my coat and plucked off the hairs of my head and my beard, and I sat down mourning."

- Esdras 9: 1-3

"And there were found among the sons of the priests that had taken strange wives....."

- 1 Esdras 10: 18

Church History: One of the main aspects of the Lateran Treaty of 1929 was the official promotion of the Catholic Faith as the state religion of Italy. The Italian government officially recognized the holy days of obligation of the Church; the canon law of the Church governed the Italian marriage laws; and all public school children in Italy received mandatory education in the Catholic Faith all the way through secondary school.

Mussolini was a fierce opponent of Communism, and during Fascist rule (from 1922 to 1943), the Italian Communist leadership was exiled, with rank and file members having to go underground.[k] Pope Pius XII was also ardently, unabashedly, and outwardly anti-Communist. This was a significant aspect of his papacy. Therefore, it was incredibly disheartening for him to see the immediate resurgence of Communism in Italy after the fall of the Fascist regime in 1943. After fourteen years of Catholic education and Catholic laws in Italy, how could so many Italians espouse the Communist ideology, which was clearly opposed to the Catholic Faith?[129]

Private Appeal Made Public

Old Testament: Esdras, who was bitterly surprised that the Jewish men were marrying foreign wives, lamented and wept for the Jewish people as he laid before the Temple of God. During his private (yet publicly visible) lament, a large crowd of Jews gathered to him and started to weep with him.

---

k   https://www.treccani.it/enciclopedia/partito-comunista-italiano/

They resolved to put away their foreign wives and to make a new covenant with God according to the Law.

> "Now when Esdras was thus praying, and beseeching, and weeping, and lying before the Temple of God, there was gathered to him of Israel an exceeding great assembly of men and women and children, and the people wept with much lamentation. Let us make a covenant with the Lord our God, to put away all the wives, and such as are born of them, according to the will of the Lord, and of them that fear the commandment of the Lord our God: let it be done according to the law."
>
> - 1 Esdras 10: 1, 3

Church History: After World War II, Pope Pius XII was bitterly surprised to see how many Catholics espoused Communist ideology in Italy. After a decade and a half of public Catholic education and the Fascist suppression of Communism for over twenty years, the Communists were still on track to win the pivotal Italian national elections of 1948, which would have turned over Italy to Communism.[130]

To combat Communism, Pope Pius XII issued *The Decree Against Communism* in 1949. This decree barred those from the Sacraments who voted for Communists and excommunicated those who believed in Communist ideology. The document was first leaked to the Italian people without the Vatican's knowledge. Despite no explanation or instruction accompanying the leaked document,[131] support for the *Decree Against Communism* was surprisingly strong.[132] This seems to parallel the private lament of Esdras, who did not intend it to be public, but the Jews gathered around him nonetheless.

The Great Proclamation

Old Testament: Esdras, with the support of many Jews, proclaimed that all should assemble together in Jerusalem and that the men should put away their foreign wives. If any one of the Jews did not come after three days, he would be cut off from his people and no longer be a part of the Jewish community.

"And proclamation was made in Juda and Jerusalem to all the children of the captivity that they should assemble together into Jerusalem. And that whosoever would not come within three days, according to the counsel of the princes and the ancients, all his substance should be taken away, and he should be cast out of the company of them that were returned from captivity."

- 1 Esdras 10: 7-8

Church History: The papal "Decree Against Communism" of 1949 excommunicated those who espoused Communist ideology and barred from the Sacraments those who voted for or otherwise aided the Communist cause. Excommunication is the "cutting off" of Catholics from the Catholic Church.

God's People Do What Is Right At Great Cost To Their Families

Old Testament: The Jews responded to the proclamation of Esdras and agreed to put away their foreign wives and children, casting them out from among the Jewish people. It undoubtedly would have been a complicated and emotional ordeal to separate themselves from their own wives and children. To organize such a large-scale effort, representatives of Esdras and Jewish elders were sent out to all the Jewish people. Thus, the job was thoroughly accomplished, and the Jewish people were cleansed.

"And Esdras the priest stood up and said to them: You have transgressed, and taken strange wives, to add to the sins of Israel. And now make confession to the Lord the God of your fathers, and do his pleasure, and separate yourselves from the people of the land, and from your strange wives. And all the multitude answered and said with a loud voice: According to thy word unto us, so be it done. Let rulers be appointed in all the multitude: and in all our cities, let them that have taken strange wives come at the times appointed, and with them the ancients and the judges of every city until the wrath of our God be turned away from us for this sin."

- 1 Esdras 10: 10-12, 14

Church History: The Italian Communist Party (PCI) was poised to win the pivotal 1948, post-World War II elections. The pope responded to this threat by organizing an outreach effort to the Italian people with messages against Communism. Election committees were created and worked intimately with the Church. The Church sent people to small towns and villages to show anti-Communist films. Before the run-up to the 1948 election in Italy, the Communist movement was surprisingly strong and, therefore, had penetrated deep into Italian society.[130]

Thus, for the Italian people to turn around, it would have caused a high level of turmoil inside Italian families. Families were ripped apart, for many Italians refused to reject Communism, and accepted excommunication from the Church. Italian historian Gianni Corbi said the 1948 election was the most fervent, pivotal, contentious, and unpredictable electoral campaign in Italian history.[133]

Cut Off And Cast Away

Old Testament: At the end of the story, the Jewish men responded to Esdras and actually went through with the tough task of sending away their foreign wives and children, who were now excluded from the Jewish people and from Jerusalem.

> "And the children of the captivity did so. And Esdras the priest, and the men heads of the families in the houses of their fathers, and all by their names, went and sat down in the first day of the tenth month to examine the matter. And they made an end with all the men that had taken strange wives by the first day of the first month. And they gave their hands to put away their wives, and to offer for their offense a ram of the flock."

> - 1 Esdras 10: 16-17, 19

Church History: The 1948 elections in Italy resulted in a resounding victory against Communism. The Catholic Church's efforts were successful. The Communists were part of the Italian government from 1944 until 1947, but after the election of 1948, they have been excluded from every national government since.

Purifying the people both in the Old Testament and in Church history was good and necessary, but it was not in itself sufficient. Practical measures were also adopted to stop the influence from reinfecting the people. Thus, let us explore the parallels between the wall of Nehemias and the Marshall Plan. The wall of Nehemias surrounded the city of Jerusalem. It protected its inhabitants from danger and also kept them secure in their Jewish identity, culture, and religious purity. The latter was a psychological effect of the wall, but nonetheless effective. Likewise, the Marshall Plan was the American government's effort to rebuild Europe. This had the goal and the effect of stopping the spread of Communism in Western Europe.

Destroyed and in Danger, Build a Wall

NEHEMIAS REBUILDS THE WALL IN 52 DAYS AND MARSHALL PLAN REBUILDS EUROPE IN 52 MONTHS

Old Testament: The Jews left their exile for the first time under the leadership of Zorobabel and built the Temple. Later, the scribe/priest Esdras came to Jerusalem to teach the Law of Moses. The third and final movement in the books of 1 and 2 Esdras was spear-headed by Nehemias, who came to rebuild the ruined walls of the city. Because the walls were destroyed, the Jews lived in great fear of their enemies.

> "That Hanani one of my brethren came, he and some men of Juda; and I asked them concerning the Jews, that remained and were left of the captivity, and concerning Jerusalem. And they said to me: They that have remained, and are left of the captivity there in the province, are in great affliction, and reproach: and the wall of Jerusalem is broken down, and the gates thereof are burnt with fire."
>
> - 2 Esdras 1: 2-3

Church History: Following World War II, European cities lay in ruins. The conflict left infrastructure—factories, roads, bridges, and hospitals—in shambles. The economic aftermath was equally dire, as many European nations were grappling with severe financial crises. In this desperate climate, Communism found fertile ground to take root. The Soviet Union actively propagated its ideology across Europe, causing concern among European and American leaders. Desperate Europeans, having lost everything, became susceptible to Communist appeals. The hope was that by rebuilding European economies, people would reject Communist propaganda.[134]

How Long And What Is Needed?

Old Testament: Nehemias was the cup-bearer to the king, signifying that he was well trusted. He requested of the king that he could return to Jerusalem to rebuild. The king permitted Nehemias but wanted to know how long it would take. Additionally, the king gave him the resources he needed to carry out his task.

> "Then the king said to me: For what dost thou make request? And I prayed to the God of heaven, And I said to the king: If it seem good to the king, and if thy servant hath found favour in thy sight, that thou wouldst send me into Judea to the city of the sepulchre of my father, and I will build it. And the king said to me, and the queen that sat by him: For how long shall thy journey be, and when wilt thou return? And it pleased the king, and he sent me: and I fixed him a time. And a letter to Asaph, the keeper of the king's forest, to give me timber that I may cover the gates of the tower of the house, and the walls of the city, and the house that I shall enter into. And the king gave me according to the good hand of my God with me."
>
> - 2 Esdras 2: 4-6, 8

Church History: General George Marshall was a highly trusted advisor to President Harry Truman and was appointed secretary of state by Truman in 1947. On June 5, 1947, after his appointment, George Marshall gave a speech in which he presented an idea for the rebuilding of Europe.[1] His idea was supported by the Truman Administration and the US Congress. The US Congress deliberated the issue until it was passed in April 1948. Congress wanted to know how long it would take and how much it would cost. In the end, Congress approved $13 billion for the reconstruction of Europe.

---

1   https://www.marshallfoundation.org/the-marshall-plan/speech/

Enemies Do Not Like The Plan To Rebuild

Old Testament: Upon hearing that Nehemias had come to rebuild the walls of Jerusalem, the enemies of the Jews were upset. It was to their advantage that the Jews stay in a weakened and defenseless state.

> "And I came to the governors of the country beyond the river and gave them the king's letters. And the king had sent with me captains of soldiers and horsemen. And Sanaballat the Horonite, and Tobias the servant, the Ammonite, heard it, and it grieved them exceedingly, that a man was come, who sought the prosperity of the children of Israel."
>
> - 2 Esdras 2: 9-10

Church History: The Soviet Union was upset about the Marshall Plan. The end of World War II marked the beginning of the Cold War between the United States and the Soviet Union. The Soviet Union took over Eastern Europe more or less by force, but in Western Europe, Communism was spreading by exploiting the poverty of the people. Thus, the announcement of the Marshall Plan grieved the Soviet Union exceedingly since they wanted Europe to remain in a weakened state.[m]

Surveyed Damage In Secret

Old Testament: Nehemias arrived in Jerusalem and kept his intention of restoring the walls a secret. He did not share his plan with anyone, and only inspected the walls at night when nobody could see him. He wanted to see for himself the extent of the damage. He devised his rebuilding plan first, then revealed it to the Jews.

> "And I arose in the night, I and some few men with me, and I told not any man what God had put in my heart to do in Jerusalem, and there was no beast with me, but the beast that I rode upon. And I went out by night by the gate of the valley, and before the dragon fountain, and to the dung gate, and I viewed the wall of Jerusalem which was broken down

---

m   Jones, Steve. "The Truman Doctrine." ThoughtCo, Apr. 5, 2023, thoughtco.com/the-truman-doctrine-3310122. (Be careful with immodest advertising on this weblink)

and the gates thereof which were consumed with fire. But the magistrates knew not whither I went or what I did: neither had I as yet told anything to the Jews, or to the priests, or to the nobles, or to the magistrates, or to the rest that did the work."

- 2 Esdras 2: 12-13, 16

Church History: Immediately after World War II, the American army was still stationed in Europe. The American army witnessed the destruction of European cities and could assess the damage without interference. George C. Marshall, who later became secretary of state, was a five-star general in the United States Army. It is possible that George Marshall's plan for rebuilding Europe was informed by intelligence reports from officers who saw the state of European cities across the continent first hand. Thus, like Nehemias, there could have been a discrete assessment of damage before the official plan to rebuild was announced.

Finished Fast, In Only Fifty-Two Days (Months)

Old Testament: Once the Jews started building Jerusalem's walls, they had to proceed very quickly. As soon as their enemies noticed that the walls were being built, they intensified their attacks on the Jews to stop the wall-building process. Once the walls were built, the Jews would be safe from their enemies. Amazingly, the walls were completed in only fifty-two days.

> "But the wall was finished the five and twentieth day of the month of Elul, in two and fifty days."
>
> - 2 Esdras 6: 15

Church History: After World War II, and because of the Marshall Plan, Europe was rebuilt in an incredibly short period of time. The Marshall Plan officially commenced on April 3, 1948. According to the *George C. Marshall Foundation* website, the Marshall Plan ended its official funding on June 30, 1952.[n] If you count the months of the Marshall Plan, it was in effect for fifty-one months but only one day shy of running into the fifty-second month!

---

n   https://www.marshallfoundation.org/the-marshall-plan/history/

Let's move on to what happens after the walls are built in the Old Testament and after Europe is rebuilt in Church history. In Jerusalem, large crowds came out to hear Esdras as he inspired the Jews to love and practice their religion with zeal and devotion. Likewise, Pope Pius XII drew large crowds who came out to see and hear him after World War II.

Danger Is Over, Great Crowds Come to Listen

ESDRAS DRAWS GREAT CROWDS IN THE REBUILT JERUSALEM AND POPE PIUS XII DRAWS LARGE CROWDS AFTER WORLD WAR II

Out Of Danger, Gather To Listen To God's Laws

Old Testament: With the completion of the wall around Jerusalem, the Jews finally found security and were no longer threatened by their enemies. After the wall was built, the Jews could finally let down their guard and focus on following the laws of God. All the people in Jerusalem came together to listen to Esdras, the scribe/priest, as he read the Law of Moses and expounded it for the people. Esdras stood on a "step of wood" so he would be elevated above the people.

> "And the seventh month came: and the children of Israel were in their cities. And all the people were gathered together as one man to the street which is before the water gate... Then Esdras the priest brought the law before the multitude of men and women, and all those that could understand, on the first day of the seventh month. And he read it plainly in the street that was before the water gate, from the morning until midday, before the men, and the women, and all those that could understand: and the ears of all the people were attentive to the book. And Esdras the scribe stood upon a step of wood, which he had made to speak upon..."

- 2 Esdras 8: 1, 2-4

Church History: The Communist threat that hovered over Italy and Western Europe after World War II was neutralized by 1952. In Italy, the critical election of 1948 (in which the Communists were soundly defeated) and the *Decree Against Communism* by Pope Pius XII in 1949 both served as a firewall. In Europe as a whole, the Marshall Plan effectively dried up any support for Communism that had previously existed.

Western Europeans had endured the harrowing years of World War II but were now resting peacefully, with economic growth, and renewed security. Catholics were returning to their Faith, and Pope Pius XII was ready to lead them. Pope Pius XII spoke to large crowds from his papal balcony (as compared to the "step of wood" of Esdras).[135]°

Priest, Lawyer, And Writer

Old Testament: Esdras was a scribe and priest but was also the leading religious figure in Jerusalem at the time. A scribe is someone who is an expert in the law but is also a writer.

Church History: Pope Pius XII was an avid writer, as he wrote forty-one papal encyclicals. Only Pope Leo XIII wrote more than him. Pope Pius XII had a doctorate in canon law and was a leading contributor to the first-ever published *Code of Canon Law* in 1917.

God's People Once Again Refuse To Obey

Old Testament: At the end of the book of 2 Esdras, Nehemias was disappointed that the Jews were once again neglecting the Law of Moses and turning their hearts away from God. Nehemias was saddened by this and asked God to remember him for his efforts.

> "In those days, I saw in Juda some treading the presses on the Sabbath, and carrying sheaves, and lading asses with wine, and grapes, and figs, and all manner of burthens, and bringing them into Jerusalem on the Sabbath day. And I charged them that they should sell on a day on which it was

o   For six decades, from 1870 to 1929, the popes stayed inside the Vatican and refused to appear on the balcony of St. Peter's Basilica that faced the square. They protested their loss of temporal power by becoming "prisoners in the Vatican". When Pope Pius XII came out on the balcony, he attracted huge crowds to his audience in the 1950s. His popularity after World War II and the post-war mood of joy and relief also contributed to this phenomenon.

lawful to sell. Some Tyrians also dwelt there, who brought fish and all manner of wares, and they sold them on the Sabbaths to the children of Juda in Jerusalem. And I rebuked the chief men of Juda and said to them: What is this evil thing that you are doing, profaning the Sabbath day? In those days, also I saw Jews that married wives, women of Azotus, and of Ammon, and of Moab."

- 2 Esdras 13: 15-17, 23

And here is Nehemias asking God to remember him for his efforts:

"Remember me, O my God, for this thing, and wipe not out my kindnesses, which I have done relating to the house of my God and his ceremonies. And for the offering of wood at times appointed, and for the first fruits: remember me, O my God, unto good. Amen."

- 2 Esdras 13: 14, 31

Church History: At the end of his papacy, Pope Pius XII is said to have noticeably withdrawn into himself. This could have been due to his illness, which he had for the last four years of his life. However, looking at Europe in the mid-1950s, it was once again prosperous. How quickly men forget the love of God and the fervent practice of their Faith when dangers are withdrawn from their lives. Some think that the pope lamented how Catholics put God back on a shelf and once again focused their lives on material goods, man-made ideologies, and popular culture. Perhaps also, Pope Pius XII could see the dark clouds on the horizon, those waiting for his death in order to overtake the Vatican.

It is heartbreaking to witness fervor grow cold. In prosperity, God's people forget the divine chastisements of the past that were given for their amendment. We will see in the Old Testament that God permits the greatest evil in their history to befall His chosen people, as Antiochus takes over the Temple in the books of the Machabees. In Church history, we will see God allowing the Second Vatican Council. Those events start the last period, that of the "Temple Takeover". But before we get there, I would like to share the stories of Queen Esther and of Pope Pius XII and the Nazis, because those parallels are so impressive.

Espionage, High Stakes, and Court Drama
QUEEN ESTHER, PERSIAN KING, AND AMAN AS A TYPE OF POPE PIUS XII, THE ALLIES, AND THE NAZIS

In the Old Testament, the story of Queen Esther occurred at the same time as the events described in the books of Esdras. The story of Queen Esther took place in Susan, the Persian Empire's capital city. By contrast, the story of Esdras and Nehemias took place in Jerusalem. Esther was one of the Jews who decided to remain in the Persian Empire and not return to Jerusalem.

Because the two story lines occur independently of each other, it will be much less confusing if we choose one story line to examine, and after we finish, we will then go back and start the second. Thus, we will be looking at the same period of time twice. We just examined the parallels between the times of Esdras and Pope Pius XI and Pope Pius XII, but now we are going to look at that same time period again, but this time, see parallels between the book of Esther and Pope Pius XII.

Short Summary Of The Book Of Esther

The book of Esther is about the king of Persia, Jews who chose to stay behind in Persia, and an ambitious and evil prince named Aman. He gained the king's confidence and made a plan to kill all the Jews in the Persian Empire. During this time, the king had just chosen Esther as his new queen. Esther was a Jew, but she kept her ethnicity a secret at the request of her adopted father, Mardochai, who was also a Jew. When Mardochai found out about Aman's plan to kill all the Jews, he convinced Esther to risk her life by approaching the king and exposing the evil doings of Aman. It's a dramatic story, with clandestine communications, huge plot swings, life and death decisions, and role reversals of the highest magnitude.

Author's Note: I expect some disagreement with how I portray Hitler, as he is one of the subjects of these parallels. I am aware that in recent decades, new narratives have emerged concerning Hitler. I have not substantially looked into these emergent theories concerning Hitler's and Pope Pius XII's actions and intentions during World War II. I think it is extremely difficult to determine true intentions, because of the complex political situation in Europe at the time, and the high risks involved. Pope Pius XII had to act and speak diplomatically, hiding his true intentions from both the Allies and the Nazis due to the Vatican's weak political position. The Vatican had soft power but no hard power. Likewise, Hitler had to be cautious with the Vatican because it had the support of Italy and the Allied Nations.

This is like the relationship between the Persian king, Queen Esther, and Aman in the book of Esther. The Queen had to be very discreet about her intentions and not reveal them to Aman or the king until the right time, as we will see in the parallels to be presented.

Old Testament – Book of Esther	New Testament
The king's feast	The Roaring Twenties
Crowning of Queen Esther	Coronation of Pope Pius XII
Aman given power, mandatory bow in his presence	Enabling Act of 1933, mandatory Nazi salute
Esther and Mardochai's secret plans, sackcloth and ashes	Nazi war camps and secret Vatican liaison with German resistance
Esther approached the king	Pope Pius XII approached the Allies
Esther accused Aman, he lunged onto her bed	Nazis occupied Rome; Allied Forces advanced in Italy
Institution of the Feast of Purim, Aman, and ten sons are hung	Institution of VE Day, Hitler died, and ten Nazi officers are hung after the Nuremberg Trials

Mardochai was raised high in the kingdom	German resistance is made part of the German government after World War II
Racial purity and the Aryan race of Persia	Hitler's idea of racial purity and his idea of the Aryan race

In 1929, the Catholic Church signed the Lateran Treaty with Benito Mussolini, prime minister of the Kingdom of Italy. Later, Mussolini would break free from the Kingdom of Italy and establish a dictatorship. However, the Lateran Treaty was Mussolini's project. He gained favor in the eyes of Italian Catholics for giving the Holy See back Her sovereignty after being without land since 1870. For the Church's part, She gained international recognition as a sovereign nation, a great deal of money from the Italian government, an annual income, and a considerable amount of religious consideration, as Catholicism was made the state religion of Italy.

In exchange for these benefits, the Holy See agreed to stay out of international politics, and bishops had to swear an oath of allegiance to the Kingdom of Italy. The Holy See was at the mercy of the Italian government since it no longer had any military power, no Catholic countries to which it could call for support, and no substantial source of income apart from the Italian government.

Remarkably, in many ways, the relationship of the Vatican to the Italian government after the signing of the Lateran Treaty of 1929 could be thought of as a traditional relationship of a wife to a husband. All the major elements are present in that analogy. Thus, in these parallels from the book of Esther, it is even more remarkable that Pope Pius XI and Pope Pius XII are both prefigured in the Old Testament by the two queens of the Persian king. Pope Pius XI parallels with Queen Vasthi, as we will see below, and Queen Esther parallels Pope Pius XII.

A Long Lasting Opulent Feast
THE GREAT FEAST OF THE KING AND THE ROARING TWENTIES

Old Testament: At the beginning of the book of Esther, we are introduced to a large, opulent, and long-lasting feast that was given to all the princes and nobles of the Persian king. The feast lasted over one hundred days. After the feast was over, the king hosted another feast and invited all the people of his city, from the greatest to the least. This feast lasted for seven days, and all the men of the city could come and eat and drink as much as they liked.

> "Now in the third year of his reign, he made a great feast for all the princes, and for his servants, for the most mighty of the Persians, and the nobles of the Medes, and the governors of the provinces in his sight, That he might shew the riches of the glory of his Kingdom, and the greatness, and boasting of his power, for a long time, to wit, for a hundred and fourscore days. And when the days of the feast were expired, he invited all the people that were found in Susan, from the greatest to the least: and commanded a feast to be made seven days in the court of the garden, and of the wood, which was planted by the care and the hand of the king."
>
> - Esther 1: 3-5

Church History: Following World War I, western economies began a period of expansion. This was the start of the *Roaring Twenties*, and all of the western nations experienced it. This was the time of partying, drinking, and dancing. In France, they called it the *Crazy Years*. In Germany, it was called the *Golden Twenties*, but no matter what the name, it was experienced the same way.

Heavy Amount Of Alcohol Is Consumed

Old Testament: There was wine in abundance during the great feast, and everyone who wanted to drink was able to drink their fill.

> "...Wine also in abundance and of the best was presented, as was worthy of a king's magnificence. Neither was there

anyone to compel them to drink that were not willing, but as the king had appointed, who set over every table one of his nobles, which every man might take what he would."

- Esther 1: 7-8

In the book of Esther, along with the flowing wine, there is a subtle theme of the objectification of women. After drinking too much wine, the king calls Queen Vasthi so that he might show off her beauty to his inebriated nobles. Later he quickly and easily got rid of Queen Vasthi and searched out young beautiful women from which to select a new wife. Clearly the king had a superficial view of women.

> "Now on the seventh day, when the king was merry, and after very much drinking was well warmed with wine, he commanded Mauman, and Bazatha, and Harbona, and Bagatha, and Abgatha, and Zethar, and Charcas, the seven eunuchs that served in his presence, to bring in queen Vasthi before the king, with the crown set upon her head, to shew her beauty to all the people and the princes: for she was exceeding beautiful."
>
> -Esther 1: 10-11

Church History: The Roaring Twenties were characterized by a lot of social drinking. If any decade is associated with high levels of alcohol consumption in the history of western society, the Roaring Twenties would have to be high on the list. Another startling characteristic of this time was women's immodest dance and dress. Young women engaged in provocative and de-basing dance (which seems uncharacteristic compared to other decades of early twentieth century history). The Roaring Twenties were a time in which women were highly objectified.

There are various symptoms and causes of women's behavior during the Roaring Twenties. The *flapper movement* encouraged women to smoke, drink, dance, and date freely. The birth control movement was in its early stages and women had just won the right to vote in 1920.[136]

The Queen Holds A Separate Feast

Old Testament: The queen was not present at the great feast with the king but held a separate feast for the women. Queen Vasthi refused to come when the king called for her. It can be inferred, even though her reasons for refusing are not stated, that Queen Vasthi had a strong sense of dignity.

> "Also Vasthi the queen made a feast for the women in the palace, where king Assuerus was used to dwell. But she refused, and would not come at the king's commandment, which he had signified to her by the eunuchs. Whereupon the king, being angry and inflamed with a very great fury..."
>
> - Esther 1: 9, 12

Church History: During the Roaring Twenties, hedonistic consumption and consumerism were on the rise, with societies caught up in abundance and the "good life". However, there was one very prominent organization in the western world that refused to join in the great feast. Amid the "great party" that was the Roaring Twenties, Pope Pius XI condemned unrestrained capitalism. He wrote the encyclical *Quadragesimo anno* in 1931, denouncing unbridled capitalism. Instead if a person has extra income that is beyond what is needed to sustain a dignified life, then that income "is not left wholly to his own free determination". Rather the rich are required to "practice almsgiving, beneficence, and munificence".[137]

Further, Pope Pius XI wrote about the authority of the Church vis a vis the secular rulers of the world. He wrote three papal encyclicals challenging totalitarian state ideology. Fascism claimed total authority over all aspects of society, implying authority also over the Catholic Church. To uphold the authority of Christ and His Church, Pope Pius XI wrote *Quas Primas* in 1925. He also instituted the new feast day of Christ the King. He proclaimed that Christ is King and has "supreme and absolute dominion over all things created".[138] By extension, Christ's Church shares in that authority.

Thus, just as Queen Vasthi had a separate feast, so too did the Catholic Church institute the Feast of Christ the King.

In his personal life, Pope Pius XI was known to possess a strong sense of dignity for the office of the papacy. He insisted on eating alone. When he met with world leaders, he would always greet them seated as a sign of papal supremacy. He was blunt-spoken and authoritative, and when his siblings wanted to see him, he made them refer to him as "His Holiness".[139]

Queen Deposed, The King Looks For Another Queen

Old Testament: Queen Vasthi refused to obey, so the king had her removed. The nobles advised the king that if women in the empire learned about Queen Vasthi's refusal to obey the king, then all wives might rebel likewise from their husbands. Therefore, the king published a letter to all his provinces in the vast Persian Empire, stating that wives should submit to their husbands.

> "What sentence ought to pass upon Vasthi the queen, who had refused to obey the commandment of King Assuerus, which he had sent to her by the eunuchs? And Mamuchan answered, in the hearing of the king and the princes: Queen Vasthi hath not only injured the king, but also all the people and princes that are in all the provinces of king Assuerus. For this deed of the queen will go abroad to all women, so that they will despise their husbands, and will say: King Assuerus commanded that queen Vasthi should come into him, and she would not. And by this example, all the wives of the princes of the Persians and the Medes will slight the commandments of their husbands: wherefore the king's indignation is just. If it please thee, let an edict go out from thy presence, and let it be written according to the law of the Persians and of the Medes, which must not be altered, that Vasthi come in no more to the king, but another, that is better than her, be made queen in her place. And he sent letters to all the provinces of his Kingdom, as every nation could hear and read, in divers languages and characters, that the husbands should be rulers and masters in their houses: and that this should be published to every people."

- Esther 1: 15-19, 22

Church History: On December 31, 1930, Pope Pius XI published his encyclical *Casti Connubii* on the subject of Christian marriage. A substantial portion of the document details the relationship of husband and wife. It declares that the wife is to be subject to her husband, not as a slave or a servant, but as an honored companion. Pope Pius XI states that a wife does not have to obey every request of her husband if those requests are "not in harmony with right reason or with the dignity due to wife…".[140]

Amazingly in the Old Testament, Queen Vasthi refused to obey her husband most likely because his demand was "**not in harmony with right reason or with the dignity due to wife**". And, to add another corollary, the Persian King was writing a letter to his whole kingdom that wives should obey their husbands just as Pope Pius XI was writing a letter to his whole "kingdom" that wives should obey their husbands.

However, in the mind of Mussolini, did it seem that Pope Pius XI was obeying his dictates?

Pope Pius XI died on February 10, 1939. It has been proposed that he was murdered. Pope Pius XI's personal physician, Dr. Francesco Petacci, was the father of Mussolini's mistress, Claretta Petacci. Cardinal Eugene Tisserant wrote in his diary that the pope had been murdered.[141][p] The implication was that Mussolini was dissatisfied with some aspect of Pope Pius XI's strong character. In the late 1930s and the early 1940s, Fascism was trending across Europe. Mussolini was the founder of Fascism in Europe, spreading it outward from Italy. Dissenting voices were not tolerated and were seen as a threat to Fascist authority.

A Diplomatic Choice
QUEEN ESTHER IS CROWNED; CORONATION OF POPE PIUS XII

Now, we can move on to the crowning of Esther, the new queen. In Church history, Pope Pius XII was the first pope to receive a public coronation in almost one hundred years. This is because the popes from 1870

---

p   This citation is from the online magazine, the Huffpost. If you intend to look up this citation, please be advised of very immodest images and advertisements in the article.

to 1929 were *prisoners in the Vatican*. Pope Pius XII was the first pope to be publicly crowned after the Lateran Treaty of 1929.

Call For Candidates, One Of Seven

Old Testament: Upon the death of Queen Vasthi, the king sent for beautiful young virgins from all over his kingdom. The king narrowed his choice of the young candidates to the seven he thought were the most desirable. These seven maidens received special clothes and attention. Esther was one of these seven final candidates.

> "And let some persons be sent through all the provinces to look for beautiful maidens and virgins: and let them bring them to the city of Susan, and put them into the house of the women under the hand of Egeus the eunuch, who is the overseer and keeper of the king's women: and let them receive women's ornaments, and other things necessary for their use. And whosoever among them all shall please the king's eyes, let her be queen instead of Vasthi. The word pleased the king, and he commanded it should be done as they had suggested. And she (Esther) pleased him and found favour in his sight. And he (king) commanded the eunuch to hasten the women's ornaments, and to deliver to her part, and seven of the most beautiful maidens of the king's house, and to adorn and deck out both her and her waiting maids."
>
> - Esther 2: 3-4, 9

Church History: Upon the death of Pope Pius XI, sixty-two cardinals from around the world were called to Rome to elect a new pope. Time magazine reported that there were seven likely contenders for the papacy. Among those seven favorites was Eugenio Pacelli, who would be elected as Pope Pius XII. Here are the seven favored contenders.[q]

- August Hlond of Gniezno-Poznań
- Karl Joseph Schulte of Cologne
- Eugène-Gabriel-Gervais-Laurent Tisserant

---

q   "Death of a Pope,"*Time,* 20 February 1939.

- Ildefonso Schuster of Milan
- Adeodato Giovanni Piazza of Venice
- Maurilio Fossati of Turin
- Eugenio Pacelli (the future Pope Pius XII)

Adopted Relationship

Old Testament: Esther was a Jewess who lost her father and mother when she was a young girl. She was raised by another Jew named Mardochai. He instructed her to keep her ethnicity a secret. Esther stayed close to Mardochai throughout the story, even when she became the queen.

> "There was a man in the city of Susan, a Jew named Mardochai, the son of Jair, the son of Semei, the son of Cis, of the race of Jemini, Who had been carried away from Jerusalem at the time that Nabuchodonosor king of Babylon carried away Jechonias king of Juda, And he had brought up his brother's daughter Edissa, who by another name was called Esther: now she had lost both her parents: and was exceeding fair and beautiful. And her father and mother being dead, Mardochai adopted her for his daughter."

> "And she would not tell him her people nor her country. For Mardochai had charged her to say nothing at all of that..."

> - Esther 2: 5-7, 10

Church History: Before Eugenio Pacelli (Pope Pius XII) was made a cardinal, he spent thirteen years as the papal nuncio to Germany.[r] At that time, he became familiar with the political landscape in Germany, as well as with pockets of resistance to the growing power of the Nazi Party.

The beginning of the war was looming during the papal election of 1939. Pope Pius XII quietly retained his contacts within the German resistance, especially his close ties to a devout Catholic man, Joseph Muller. Joseph Muller would later act as the representative of the German resistance to the Vatican. During his time in Germany, Bishop Eugenio Pacelli and Joseph

---

r   Apostolic Nuncio to Bavaria 1917 – 1925, Apostolic Nuncio to Germany 1920 – 1930

Muller formed a close friendship,[142][s] and they stayed in contact even when Bishop Eugenio Pacelli was called back to Rome in 1930 to be made a cardinal.

The Self-Restrained Candidate

Old Testament: Esther was favored by the king to be among the final seven choices. Those seven women were granted any gifts, jewelry, and clothes they desired so they could make themselves more beautiful. Esther did not take advantage of this chance to aggrandize herself but instead displayed temperance and prudence. She let the king's servant choose her adornments instead.

> "And when they were going into the king, whatsoever they asked to adorn themselves they received: and being decked out, as it pleased them, they passed from the chamber of the women to the king's chamber."

> "And as the time came orderly about, the day was at hand, when Esther, the daughter of Abihail the brother of Mardochai, whom he had adopted for his daughter, was to go into the king. But she sought not women's ornaments, but whatsoever Egeus the eunuch the keeper of the virgins had a mind, he gave her to adorn her. For she was exceeding fair, and her incredible beauty made her appear agreeable and amiable in the eyes of all."

> - Esther 2: 13, 15

Church History: The conclave of 1939 was thought to be a decision between a spiritual and a diplomatic pope.[143] Because tension in Europe was very high, and World War II was about to start, the cardinals decided they wanted to elect someone with a strong diplomatic background, Eugenio Pacelli. He was even-tempered, extremely modest in speech, and cautious in expressing himself publicly. These qualities served him well in his diplomatic role as Cardinal Secretary of State from 1930 to 1939.[144]

---

s   Mark Riebling, pg 45

Chosen To Be Crowned

Old Testament: Of the seven final candidates, the king chose Esther to be his new queen.

> "And the king loved her (Esther) more than all the women, and she had favour and kindness before him above all the women, and he set the royal crown on her head, and made her queen instead of Vasthi."
>
> - Esther 2: 17

Church History: Of course, among the seven favored candidates, Eugenio Pacelli was chosen and crowned as the pope on March 2, 1939.

Chosen A Second Time

Old Testament: Strangely, the virgins returned to the king even after Esther was chosen to be queen. These were the same virgins that were called the first time. When Esther was brought into the inner chambers, among the virgins to be chosen, her adopted father Mardochai took up a position at the king's gate so he could stay informed about what was happening concerning the choice of the new queen.

> "And when the virgins were sought the second time, and gathered together, Mardochai stayed at the king's gate,"
>
> - Esther 2: 19

Church History: After the ballot was cast to elect Pope Pius XII, he was the officially chosen candidate and would indeed be crowned as the new pope. However, in an extra display of caution and prudence, he asked if they would cast the ballots another time to make sure it was God's will that he be chosen for the papacy.[145]t

---

t   In 1621, the Papal Bull *Aeterni Patris Filius* established the requirement that a pope must receive a two-thirds majority vote for election. Cardinal Eugenio Pacelli (later Pope Pius XII) achieved the necessary majority on the second ballot. His subsequent request for another vote was unusual.

During this time, the German resistance to Hitler was paying close attention to the results of the papal conclave, especially to find out if their old friend, Cardinal Eugenio Pacelli, would be chosen as the next pope.

Overheard The Secret Plot

Old Testament: When Mardochai was taking up his position at the king's gate, he accidentally overheard a plot to kill the king. After Esther was chosen as queen, Mardochai related the news to Esther, and she informed the king of this plot in Mardochai's name. The king investigated and found out that the plot was real. The plot was stopped because of Mardochai and Esther.

> "At that time, therefore, when Mardochai abode at the king's gate, Bagathan, and Thares, two of the king's eunuchs, who were porters, and presided in the first entry of the palace, were angry: and they designed to rise up against the king, and to kill him. And Mardochai had notice of it, and immediately he told it to Queen Esther: and she to the king in Mardochai's name, who had reported the thing unto her."
>
> - Esther 2: 21-22

Church History: The German resistance to Hitler was concentrated in the Abwehr, the German Military Intelligence Agency.[142][u] The Abwehr would "sit at the gate of information," so to speak, similar to how Mardochai would sit at the king's gate. Because Mardochai was at the king's gate, he was in the best possible position to hear the news since everyone and everything had to pass through that gate to get to the king.

The Abwehr was the gatekeeper of military intelligence, and as such, they discovered Hitler's secret plan to invade the Low Countries of Europe in 1940. The Abwehr, through Joseph Muller, passed this information along to Pope Pius XII, who then notified the Allies, making sure to tell them that the information came from the German resistance.[142][v]

---

u   Mark Riebling, pg 47

v   Mark Riebling, pg 99

Now, let's move on from the coronation of Queen Esther and Pope Pius XII. In the Old Testament, Aman gained the trust and the signet ring of the king, giving him carte blanche ability to make laws. Likewise, the German parliament passed the Enabling Act, which made Hitler a dictator in Germany. Aman demanded that all kneel in his presence, and Hitler demanded that all give him the "Hitler salute".

Law That Forces Salute/Bow

Old Testament: A law was made that whenever Aman passed by, the servants of the king were required to bend their knees and worship him. Everyone obeyed this law except for Mardochai.

> "And all the king's servants, that were at the doors of the palace, bent their knees, and worshiped Aman: for so the emperor had commanded them, only Mardochai did not bend his knee, nor worship him."

- Esther 3: 2

Church History: On July 13, 1933, a decree was made by the Reich Minister of the Interior, Wilhelm Frick, for all public employees in Germany, requiring them to give the Hitler salute. By 1934, the salute was mandatory for all civilians in Germany, and special courts were set up to punish those who refused to use the Hitler salute. It was used in schools and even by civilians in their interactions with each other. The salute was always required in the presence of Hitler.[146]

The one group of Germans that refused to use the Hitler salute was the German army, which retained the traditional military salute in most situations. It was in the German army that the German resistance was nested. Particular individuals also refused to use the Hitler salute such as Paul Schneider, who faced the possibility of a concentration camp for his defiance.

Joseph Muller was another man of great conviction. Muller was a Catholic from Bavaria and became a vitally important member of the German resistance to Hitler. At one point in 1934, Muller was arrested by the SS Nazi police and was interrogated by Heinrich Himmler, the head of the SS, for suspicion of treason. Muller defied Himmler to his face. Himmler was impressed by Muller's bravery and offered for Muller to join the SS. Muller refused on the grounds that he was a devout Catholic. Himmler was so impressed with Muller's courage and conviction that he released him.[142][w]

Refuse To Salute / Bow

Old Testament: When Aman learned that Mardochai would not bend his knee to him, he was exceedingly angry. Aman knew that Mardochai was a Jew, and because of this, he decided that it was not enough to just kill Mardochai. He decided that he wanted to kill all the Jews. Aman realized that it was the religious beliefs of the Jews that kept Mardochai from bending his knee to him.

> "Now when Aman had heard this and had proved by experience that Mardochai did not bend his knee to him, nor worship him, he was exceeding angry. And he counted it nothing to lay his hands upon Mardochai alone: for he had heard that he was of the nation of the Jews, and he chose rather to destroy all the nation of the Jews that were in the Kingdom of Assuerus."
>
> - Esther 3: 5-6

Church History: Hitler and the Nazis were enraged whenever they found a person or group that refused to submit to their will. The German resistance, which operated inside the German army, was a group of high-ranking German military personnel who retained a sense of Christian morality.[142][x] To end Hitler's tyranny, they secretly planned for his assassination.[142][y]

Hitler realized the power of the Catholic Church, and also Protestant groups, to resist the authority of the Nazis. The problem of submission would not be solved on a case-by-case basis. Hitler knew that his authority would be undermined unless he eliminated the political power of the Catholic Church in Nazi lands. This is why he planned to kill or imprison thousands of Catholic clergy in Poland.[142][z]

---

w Mark Riebling, pg 39
x Mark Riebling, pg 25-29
y Mark Riebling, pg 62
z Mark Riebling, pg 30

Plan To Kill Those Who Will Not Assimilate

Old Testament: Aman was determined to kill all the Jews in the Persian Empire because he thought that they would never truly assimilate. He knew that the Jews had religious laws that were absolutely unbending. Therefore, Aman approached the king, saying that there were a people in the king's empire that followed their own laws, and despised the laws of the Persians. Aman warned that these people would be harmful to the empire if they were not dealt with.

> "And Aman said to king Assuerus: There is a people scattered through all the provinces of thy kingdom, and separated one from another, that use new laws and ceremonies, and moreover despise the king's ordinances: and thou knowest very well that it is not expedient for thy kingdom that they should grow insolent by impunity. "
>
> - Esther 3: 8

Church History: In the 1930s, a robust Catholic political movement challenged the growing influence of the Nazis. Known as the *Catholic Center Party*, this group, along with many bishops, actively resisted the Nazi regime. They employed newspapers, parish sermons, and other means against the Nazis.[142][aa]

Recognizing the threat posed by "political Catholicism," Hitler aimed to weaken the Catholic Church's influence. Consequently, when he revealed his plans to invade Poland to his top generals in 1939, they were shocked to learn that Hitler intended to eliminate almost all Catholic clergy.[142][ab] The persecution of the Catholic Church in Poland during this period was particularly severe.[ac]

---

aa   Mark Riebling, pg 39

ab   Mark Riebling, pg 30

ac   *Poles, Victims of the Nazi Era*, United States Holocaust Memorial Museum, https://www. ushmm. org/ m/pdfs/2000926-Poles.pdf

Prince Advanced Over All Others In The Realm

Old Testament: The king advanced Aman in the kingdom and set Aman above all the other princes in the Persian Empire.

> "After these things, king Assuerus advanced Aman, the son of Amadathi, who was of the race of Agag: and he set his throne above all the princes that were with him."
>
> - Esther 3: 1

Church History: In the run-up to World War II, Hitler's popularity soared in Germany before the Nazis invaded Poland. Hitler was made the leader of the National Socialist Party (the Nazi Party). Between 1931 and 1933, the Nazis gained more and more seats in the German parliament, becoming the majority party by 1933. Hitler was appointed the head of the German government on January 30, 1933, when he was appointed as the chancellor by the German head of state, Paul von Hindenburg.

In addition to his public approval in Germany, Hitler's popularity was also remarkably on the rise in some elite circles of American society. In the 1930s, the American elites were formulating justification, creating government policy, and carrying out measures to reduce the size of certain population segments. This was known as the *American Eugenics Movement* and was backed by the wealthiest people and groups in America, such as the Carnegie Institution, Rockefeller Foundation, the Harriman railroad fortune, and J.H. Kellogg. The American Eugenics Movement, run by the American elites, admired Hitler for his eugenics policies in Germany.[147] Hitler appeared as Time magazine's "Man of the Year" in 1938.

Prince Says He Has A Solution, Told To Keep The Money

Old Testament: When Aman approached the king, he convinced him that his kingdom was in danger. Aman also claimed to have the solution to the problem, which was the annihilation of the Jews. Aman agreed to give the king a large sum of money, but the king told Aman to keep the money.

> "And Aman said to king Assuerus: There is a people scattered through all the provinces of thy kingdom and

separated one from another, that use new laws and ceremonies, and moreover despise the king's ordinances: and thou knowest very well that it is not expedient for thy kingdom that they should grow insolent by impunity. If it please thee, decree that they may be destroyed, and I will pay ten thousand talents to thy treasurers."

"And he said to him: As to the money which thou promisest, keep it for thyself."

- Esther 3: 8-9, 11

Church History: With Hitler's popularity soaring in Germany and even to a large extent in the United States, Hitler convinced the German people that he had the answer to Germany's problems. His aggression increased, and his idea of the Aryan race was propagandized throughout Germany. Hitler persuaded the German people that by eliminating certain groups of people, he could secure the future of Germany.[148]

During these same years, in the early 1930s, Germany was absolved of its war debts from World War I. The Lausanne Conference of 1932 was a meeting of Germany, France, and the United Kingdom, at which an agreement was made that Germany's payments in reparation for the damage it caused in World War I were no longer required to the Allied Forces. From that point forward, Germany was no longer required to pay money into the Allies' national treasuries.

Power Given to the Tyrant

AMAN GETS THE KING'S SIGNET RING AND THE ENABLING ACT OF 1933, HITLER BECOMES A DICTATOR

Made Into A Legal, De Facto Dictator

Old Testament: Aman managed to convince the king that his kingdom was in jeopardy. However, the king did not want to look into the problem himself but instead gave Aman his signet ring, which symbolized the power to make laws and decrees. In giving Aman this ring, he gave Aman full power and placed his blind trust in Aman's judgment.

> "And the king took the ring that he used, from his own hand, and gave it to Aman, the son of Amadathi of the race of Agag, the enemy of the Jews, and as to the people, do with them as seemeth good to thee."
>
> - Esther 3: 10-11

Church History: The single event that made Hitler a dictator was the Enabling Act of 1933, passed in the German parliament on March 24. Hitler was granted plenary powers by the passage of this act. The Enabling Act of 1933 gave Hitler the full power to enact any law without restrictions. Soon after, all political parties were outlawed, and the Nazis seized complete control of all government institutions.[149]

Secret Plans Are Made
MARDOCHAI AND QUEEN ESTHER MAKE SECRET PLANS AND THE GERMAN RESISTANCE APPROACHES POPE PIUS XII

Sackcloth And Ashes

Old Testament: When Mardochai heard Aman's plans to kill all the Jews in the Persian Empire, he tore his garments, put ashes on his head, and vested in sackcloth, being filled with great anguish. Mardochai sat by the palace gate, but because of his sackcloth and ashes, he was not permitted through. In all the provinces in which Aman's decree was heard, the Jews all put on sackcloth and ashes, weeping and fasting. They even used ash strewn sackcloth for their bedding, so profound was their sorrow.

> "Now when Mardochai had heard these things, he rent his garments, and put on sackcloth, strewing ashes on his head: and he cried with a loud voice in the street in the midst of the city, shewing the anguish of his mind. And he came lamenting in this manner even to the gate of the palace: for no one clothed with sackcloth might enter the king's court. And in all provinces, towns, and places, to which the king's

cruel edict was come, there was great mourning among the Jews, with fasting, wailing, and weeping, many using sackcloth and ashes for their bed."

- Esther 4: 1-3

Church History: When Hitler and the Nazis invaded Poland, they had decided beforehand to annihilate the Catholic Church hierarchy. Churches were systematically closed, and most of the priests were either killed, sent to concentration camps, or forced to flee. An estimated 3,000 Catholic clergy were killed during the Nazi occupation of Poland.[150] In the concentration camps, particularly near the end of the war, the clothing of the prisoners was made of sackcloth since it was cheaper than regular clothing fabric.

When the Nazis invaded Poland in 1939, they alarmed the world. Hitler and the Nazis committed horrible atrocities in Poland and practically liquidated the Polish Catholic Church. Seeing the renewed urgency, the German resistance decided it was time to act. They decided to approach the Allies with a plan to assassinate Hitler and commandeer the German government. However, they lacked credibility in the eyes of the Allies, being as they were, members of the German Army. They needed someone with a high profile to represent them to the Allies, someone with credibility and sufficient detachment. They decided to approach Pope Pius XII.[142][ad]

The German resistance recruited a devout Catholic German named Joseph Muller, an old friend of Pope Pius XII. Through Joseph Muller and Pope Pius XII's aide, Fr. Leiber, they communicated back and forth. After sufficient information, Pope Pius XII agreed to approach the Allies on behalf of the German resistance with a plan to overthrow Hitler. If Hitler could be removed, the carnage that was taking place in Poland could be avoided for the rest of Europe.

Queen's Servant Is A Liaison

Old Testament: When Mardochai discovered the plot of Aman to kill all the Jews in the Persian Empire, he put on sackcloth and ashes and went out into the streets, wailing in anguish. Queen Esther learned of Mardochai's

---

ad   Mark Riebling, pg 60 – 63

behavior and was greatly disturbed. She sent her personal servant, a eunuch, to Mardochai to find out why he was wearing sackcloth.

> "Then Esther's maids and her eunuchs went in and told her. And when she heard it, she was in a consternation: and she sent a garment, to clothe him, and to take away the sackcloth: but he would not receive it. And she called for Athach the eunuch, whom the king had appointed to attend upon her, and she commanded him to go to Mardochai, and learn of him why he did this."
>
> - Esther 4: 4-5

Church History: In 1939, at the time of the invasion of Poland by the Nazis, Joseph Muller initiated a series of secret communications with the Vatican. He was not able to meet directly with Pope Pius XII, for it would not have been proper for the pope to meet in secret. So the pope sent his most trusted aid, Fr. Leiber. Fr. Leiber was described as intensely loyal to Pope Pius XII and took care of anything the pope requested of him. He would meet with Joseph Muller many times from 1939 to 1940, acting as liaison between him and the pope.[142][ae]

It was in September-October of 1939 that reports of the persecution of the Polish Catholic Church and the concentration camps began to filter into the Vatican. These reports were said to have deeply disturbed the pope, who felt powerless to stop the unfolding tragedy.

Relating Secret Information

Old Testament: Mardochai informed Esther's eunuch of the whole plot and how Aman had offered to fill the king's coffers with money in exchange for the annihilation of the Jews. This raises a curious question: how did Mardochai learn what was spoken in a secret meeting between Aman and the king? It appears that Mardochai was very clever and perhaps even had spies of his own.

---

ae   Mark Riebling, pg 10-11, 72-74

"And Athach (the eunuch) going out went to Mardochai, who was standing in the street of the city, before the palace gate: And Mardochai told him all that had happened, how Aman had promised to pay money into the king's treasures, to have the Jews destroyed. He gave him also a copy of the edict which was hanging up in Susan, that he should shew it to the queen, and admonish her to go into the king, and to entreat him for her people. And Athach (the eunuch) went back and told Esther all that Mardochai had said."

- Esther 4: 6-9

Church History: Joseph Muller possessed confidential information about the Nazi regime, things that only espionage could have revealed to him. The information that Joseph Muller shared with the Vatican came from his sources in the Abwehr (German Intelligence Agency). Joseph Muller communicated to the pope the Nazis' intentions to attack the Low Countries (Belgium, Luxembourg, and the Netherlands). The pope passed on this information to the Allied Nations as a gesture of good faith from the German resistance.

The Queen Herself Will Intercede

Old Testament: Esther's eunuch served as a messenger between Mardochai and Esther, carrying their words back and forth. After the eunuch brought Mardochai's words to Queen Esther, she sent him back to Mardochai with her own reply. She told Mardochai that she had no power to save her people, the Jews. She said that she could not go to the king because there was a law in the Persian Empire that forbade anyone to go to the king unless summoned; otherwise, that person could be put to death by the king, unless the king showed mercy.

"She answered him and bade him say to Mardochai: All the king's servants, and all the provinces that are under his dominion, know that whosoever, whether man or woman, cometh into the king's inner court, who is not called for, is immediately to be put to death without any delay: except the king shall hold out the golden sceptre to him, in token of clemency, that so he may live. How then can I go in to the

247

king, who for these thirty days now have not been called unto him?"

- Esther 4: 10-11

Church History: The pope was initially reluctant to get involved in helping the German resistance, even though he saw a great need, especially in light of the reports coming out of Poland.

Perhaps the greatest reason for the pope's reluctance was because of the terms of the Lateran Treaty. The Lateran Treaty was signed in 1929 with Mussolini, an ally of Hitler. The Lateran Treaty forbade the Vatican from wading into international politics unless the involved parties requested the Vatican's assistance.[142][124][afag] This is just like the law that the king could not be approached unless summoned by him.

If Pope Pius XII approached the Allies on behalf of the German resistance, and if for any reason the Allies chose to make this known to Mussolini, the Italians could have revoked the Lateran Treaty, ended Vatican City as a sovereign state, and stopped annual payment to the Vatican.

If You Will Not Speak Out

Old Testament: When Mardochai heard the complaint of Queen Esther and her reluctance to approach the king for fear of death, Mardochai chastised her through the eunuch. He told Esther that if she were reluctant to speak up in defense of the Jews, then the Jews would still be delivered by some other means, but Esther and her house would perish.

> "And when Mardochai had heard this, He sent word to Esther again, saying: Think not that thou mayst save thy life only, because thou art in the king's house, more than all the Jews: For if thou wilt now hold thy peace, the Jews shall be delivered by some other occasion: and thou and thy father's house shall perish. And who knoweth whether thou art not,

---

af   Mark Riebling, pg 175

ag   Article 24 of the Conciliation Treaty

therefore, come to the kingdom, that thou mightest be ready in such a time as this?"

- Esther 4: 12-14

Church History: I think it is fascinating to note that Pope Pius XII is criticized for not speaking out against the execution of Jews during World War II.[ah] If you re-read the previous section from the Old Testament, instead of thinking of Mardochai addressing Esther with this admonishment, think of those words being spoken to Pope Pius XII instead. I do not know what it means, but the connection is remarkable.

Speaking Out Is Dangerous

Old Testament: Upon hearing the message from Mardochai, Esther was moved. She told Mardochai to have the Jews pray and fast for her because she was going to risk her life and go before the king even though he did not call for her. Remember, Persian law stated that anyone who went before the king without being summoned could be put to death.

> "And again Esther sent to Mardochai in these words: Go and gather together all the Jews whom thou shalt find in Susan, and pray ye for me. Neither eat nor drink for three days and three nights: and I with my handmaids will fast in like manner, and then I will go in to the king, against the law, not being called, and expose myself to death and to danger. So Mardochai went, and did all that Esther had commanded him."

Esther 4: 15-17

Church History: Pope Pius XII eventually agreed to approach the Allies on behalf of the German resistance,[142][151][ai] even though it could have meant disaster for the Vatican. Indeed, if Hitler had found out that the Vatican was

---

ah By this statement I take no position on the Jewish plight under the Nazis. I am just making an objective statement that Pope Pius XII has been criticized in this way.

ai Mark Riebling, pg 62-63

secretly working with the German resistance to have him assassinated, he would have retaliated against the Vatican severely.[144][aj]

Goes to the King Despite the Risk
QUEEN ESTHER APPROACHES THE KING AND POPE PIUS XII APPROACHES THE ALLIES

Bravely Approaching The King Despite The Law

Old Testament: Mardochai urged Queen Esther to go to the king and ask him to spare her own people, the Jews. Fortified by prayer and fasting, Queen Esther faced this risk and went before the king. The king was pleased to see her, not because she was the queen, but because he had a personal affection for her. He agreed to hear her plea. Remember that the king had no problem getting rid of Queen Vasthi. It was Esther's personal qualities that pleased the king.

> "And on the third day, Esther put on her royal apparel, and stood in the inner court of the king's house, over against the king's hall: now he sat upon his throne in the hall of the palace, over against the door of the house. And when he saw Esther the queen standing, she pleased his eyes, and he held out toward her the golden sceptre, which he held in his hand: and she drew near, and kissed the top of his sceptre. And the king said to her: What wilt thou, Queen Esther? What is thy request? if thou shouldst even ask one half of the kingdom, it shall be given to thee."
>
> - Esther 5: 1-3

Church History: In 1939, the German resistance approached Pope Pius XII through their agent Joseph Muller. After prayer and reflection, the pope agreed to approach the Allies on behalf of the German resistance.

If the Allied Forces reacted the wrong way to the Vatican's interjection into the political affairs between Germany, Italy, and the United Kingdom, it

---

aj   Mark Riebling, pg 203-205

was possible that the Lateran Treaty could have been revoked. This would have been disastrous for the Vatican, and possibly could have meant the abolishing of Vatican City.

In January of 1940, the pope reached out to the British envoy to the Holy See, the British diplomat D'Arcy Osborne.[142][ak] The British had no allegiance to the pope since they were Anglicans and were not inclined to believe or trust the pope simply because of his office and position. Pope Pius XII's diplomatic ability was accommodating to the British as opposed to a blunt, strong spoken interlocutor. Just as the king was not moved by Esther's position as queen but instead by her personal qualities, so too does it seem that the British were not necessarily willing to listen to Pope Pius XII because of his office.

It All Comes to a Head

AMAN DISCOVERS ESTHER'S SUBTERFUGE AND HITLER DISCOVERS THE POPE'S INVOLVEMENT WITH THE GERMAN RESISTANCE

Gathered Together In One Place

Old Testament: Queen Esther asked that Aman and the king come to a banquet that she would prepare. At that banquet, she told the king she would make known what was on her mind. By the end of the banquet, Esther still had not made her thoughts known and invited them back the next day for another banquet.

On his way home from the first banquet, Aman saw Mardochai again, who again refused to kneel down to him. Aman was so outraged that he built a gibbet fifty cubits high on which to hang Mardochai.

> "But she answered: If it please the king, I beseech thee to come to me this day, and Aman with thee to the banquet which I have prepared."

---

ak   Mark Riebling, pg 86

"So Aman went out that day joyful and merry. And when he saw Mardochai sitting before the gate of the palace, and that he not only did not rise up to honour him but did not so much as move from the place where he sat, he was exceedingly angry:"

"...Order a great beam to be prepared, fifty cubits high, and in the morning speak to the king, that Mardochai may be hanged upon it, and so thou shalt go full of joy with the king to the banquet. The counsel pleased him, and he commanded a high gibbet to be prepared."

- Esther 5: 4,9,14

Church History: Just as Aman, Esther, and the king were all gathered in one place during the banquet hosted by Queen Esther (presumably in her section of the palace), so also did the Nazis, the Italian monarch, and Pope Pius XII all come together as well in September of 1943, when the Nazis occupied Rome. We will come back to the Nazi occupation of Rome in upcoming pages.

It was around this same time, in July-August of 1943, that the Nazis uncovered the plans of the German resistance. Upon discovering just how widespread and extensive was the network of the resistance, Hitler is said to have devolved into a raging mania. He was determined to execute all the officers who were secretly planning his assassination.[142][al]

One of the men whom the Nazis uncovered and arrested was Joseph Muller. Muller was placed in various prisons and camps. Near the end of the war, Muller was scheduled for execution by hanging. The Nazis brought him out to the gallows, where Muller waited hours for the Nazi officers to receive the order to execute him, but it never came.[142][am] It was decided that Muller might be more useful to the Nazis in negotiating a surrender since Muller had contacts in the Vatican. Thus, like Mardochai, Muller also escaped hanging at the last moment.

---

al   Mark Riebling, pg 203-205
am   Mark Riebling, pg 230-231

Aman In Esther's Space, The King Leaves

Old Testament: Queen Esther invited the king and Aman back to a second banquet where she promised to make her mind known to the king. She started by pleading with the king for her life and the lives of her people.

> "So the king and Aman went in to drink with the queen. And the king said to her again the second day, after he was warm with wine: What is thy petition, Esther, that it may be granted thee? and what wilt thou have done: although thou ask the half of my kingdom, thou shalt have it. Then she answered: If I have found favour in thy sight, O king, and if it please thee, give me my life for which I ask, and my people for which I request. For we are given up, I and my people, to be destroyed, to be slain, and to perish. And would God we were sold for bondmen and bondwomen: the evil might be borne with, and I would have mourned in silence: but now we have an enemy, whose cruelty redoundeth upon the king."

> - Esther 7: 1-4

Church History: In September of 1943, the Kingdom of Italy, under King Victor Emmanuel III, signed an armistice (a peace treaty) with the United States. The United States military landed in Sicily in July of 1943 and advanced northwards. Immediately after the armistice was signed in September of 1943, the Nazis invaded Rome.

In August of 1943, during the Nazi occupation of Rome, the Nazis painted a wide white line to signify the border with Vatican City. Whatever their purpose, it communicated an aggressive posture towards the Vatican. That same month, Pope Pius XII wrote a letter to US President, Franklin Roosevelt. In that letter, the pope pleaded with President Roosevelt to spare the city of Rome from the ravages of war as Allied Forces made their way towards Rome from southern Italy. He said that in Rome, "every street has its irreplaceable monuments of faith or art and Christian culture" and would be easily destroyed if Rome were subject to armed conflict.[152]

In summary, Queen Esther invited the king and Aman to a banquet. At that banquet, the queen pleaded for her life to the king. Similarly, the Vatican had to endure the company of the Nazis, who invaded Rome in September 1943. The pope wrote a letter to the US President, Franklin Roosevelt, pleading for him to spare Rome/Italy from the ravages of war.

Aman Is Astonished, And Fearfully Surprised

Old Testament: Esther proceeded to accuse Aman and to reveal herself as a Jew. He was astonished and fearful to learn that Queen Esther was a Jew; no longer able to bear the countenance of the king and queen. The king was in a state of rage and consternation at this development. He rose up and went into his garden. Aman took this opportunity to fall upon the bed of the queen in a desperate last attempt to save his life. But when the king came back from the garden, he saw Aman on the queen's bed and presumed that Aman was going to attack the queen, even in the king's own presence. Aman was immediately removed from the king's presence and was sentenced to death.

> "And Esther said: It is this Aman that is our adversary and most wicked enemy. Aman, hearing this, was forthwith astonished, not being able to bear the countenance of the king and of the queen. But the king, being angry, rose up and went from the place of the banquet into the garden set with trees. Aman also rose up to entreat Esther, the queen, for his life, for he understood that evil was prepared for him by the king. And when the king came back out of the garden set with trees and entered into the place of the banquet, he found Aman was fallen upon the bed on which Esther lay, and he said: He will force the queen also in my presence, in my own house. The word was not yet gone out of the king's mouth, and immediately they covered his face."

> - Esther 7: 6-8

Church History: The Nazi march on Rome in September 1943 caused the king of Italy, Victor Emmanuel III, to flee south to the city of Brindisi.[142][an]

---

an   Mark Riebling, pg 176

Meanwhile, back in Germany, in that same month, the Nazis uncovered secret documents of the German resistance. In those documents, they found a letter written on Vatican letterhead, which directly and unmistakably revealed that Pope Pius XII was personally and purposefully involved in a plot to have Hitler assassinated. Upon learning this, Hitler was utterly astonished and was bedridden for days.[142][ao]

Hitler was shocked to discover the extent of the plot against him, but most of all, that the plot went all the way to the top of the Vatican. At the end of the war, during the Nuremberg Trials, it was revealed that Hitler and his top generals devised a plan to kidnap the pope. However, the Nazi officer, Karl Wolf, who was one of the sources of the alleged kidnapping plot, was known to fabricate stories in his effort to save himself.[153]

In June 1944, the Allied Forces marched into Rome and expelled the Nazis. The involvement of the Americans in World War II marked the beginning of the end for the Nazis. In the spring of 1945, Berlin was surrounded.

In summary, Queen Esther revealed herself as a Jew and accused Aman of his evil plot. Aman was astonished and distraught to learn this about the queen. Upon hearing this, the king got up and left for his private garden. When the king came back, he saw that Aman had flung himself on the queen's bed in a last effort to save his life. The king presumed that Aman was going to attack the queen. Aman was immediately removed from their presence and sentenced to death.

In September of 1943, at the same time the Nazis were invading Rome, Hitler discovered that the pope was involved in a plot to have him killed. Hitler went into a depression and was bedridden for days. Near the same time, the king of Italy fled from Rome to Brindisi,[ap] to a private hideaway in southern Italy. During the king's absence, the Nazis allegedly developed a

---

ao   Mark Riebling, pg 203-205

ap   King Victor Emmanuel III fled on Sept. 9 to avoid capture during the Nazi occupation of northern Italy (see Mark Riebling, page 176.) On Sept. 22, Hitler discovered the Vatican's involvement in a plot to assassinate him. (see Mark Riebling, page 203.)

plot to kidnap the pope. The Americans marched into Rome and expelled the Nazis in June of 1944.

FINAL NOTE

It's intriguing to observe that Aman thrust himself onto Esther's bed in a desperate plea for his life. The queen's bed was undeniably her private space, which made it profoundly shocking for the king to witness Aman's presence there. Similarly, the border of Vatican City delineated the official territory of the Vatican. The revelation that the Nazis had devised a plan to violate Vatican City's sovereignty and potentially kidnap the pope mirrored Aman's audacious intrusion into Esther's personal space on her bed. Just as the king feared Aman's intentions toward the queen, there was genuine concern that the Nazis might launch an attack or abduct the pope.

A New Feast and Hanging of the Ten Sons

Feast of Purim and Aman's Ten Sons Are Hung; Victory Europe Day and Ten Nazi Officers Are Hung

When the thirteenth day of Adar arrived, the day that Aman had appointed for the destruction of the Jews, the Jewish people were ready to defend themselves. They gained the upper hand against their enemies and slew them. Esther requested that a second day of revenge be given to the Jews in Susan, to be accomplished on the fourteenth of Adar. The Jews took the ten sons of Aman and hanged them on gibbets. Then, Esther and Mardochai wrote to all the Jews in the Persian Empire and established a new feast day for the Jews to be celebrated every year. This is the Feast of Purim and is to be celebrated on the fourteenth of Adar. However, Jews who live in walled-in cities celebrate Purim on the fifteenth of Adar, a day later. This fact will be important later. The first celebration of Purim was one of great joy for the Jews because they escaped destruction at the hands of Aman.

Encouraged By Communication Instructing To Fight Back

Old Testament: In the book of Esther, chapter 3, Aman used the king's ring to issue a decree throughout the Persian Empire stating that the Jews were to be killed on the thirteenth of Adar. However, after Queen Esther's victory over Aman, the king gave his ring to Mardochai. Esther and Mardochai issued a decree that on the thirteenth of Adar, the Jews were to fight back against their enemies.

> "So on the thirteenth day of the twelfth month, which as we have said above is called Adar, when all the Jews were designed to be massacred, and their enemies were greedy after their blood, the case being altered, the Jews began to have the upper hand, and to revenge themselves of their adversaries. And they gathered themselves together in every city, and town, and place, to lay their hands on their enemies, and their persecutors. And no one durst withstand them, for the fear of their power had gone through every people."
>
> - Esther 9: 1-2

Church History: On May 10, 1940, the Nazis invaded France, completely occupying it by November of 1942. The French were demoralized, imagining what would become of their culture and country. However the tide began to turn when Italy changed sides and joined the Allies in 1943. Communication was sent from the Americans to the French underground resistance. Organized plans were made to fight back against the Nazis in anticipation of the American forces landing in Normandy.[aq] The French resistance had much success in their efforts to disrupt Nazi infrastructure in advance of the Allied Forces' arrival on June 6, 1944.[154]

Two Different Days To Celebrate, Different For Walled Cities

Old Testament: The Jews all across the Persian Empire defeated their enemies and saved their own lives on the thirteenth of Adar. Queen Esther approached the king and asked if the Jews in Susan (the capital city) could have another day to take revenge on their enemies. Following the fourteenth of Adar, Mardochai and Esther proclaimed a new feast day to all the Jews in Persia. This new feast day is called *Purim* and was to be celebrated on the fourteenth of Adar, the day after their victory on the thirteenth of Adar.

---

aq   https://www.dday-overlord.com/en/battle-of-normandy/resistance

Curiously, cities that were behind walls celebrated it on the fifteenth of Adar to express the extra day of revenge the Jews were given in Susan.

> "And he said to the queen: The Jews have killed five hundred men in the city of Susan, besides the ten sons of Aman: how many dost thou think they have slain in all the provinces? What askest thou more, and what wilt thou have me to command to be done? And she answered: If it please the king, let it be granted to the Jews, to do tomorrow in Susan as they have done today. "

> "But they that were killing in the city of Susan were employed in the slaughter on the thirteenth and fourteenth day of the same month, and on the fifteenth day, they rested. And therefore, they appointed that day to be a holy day of feasting and gladness. But those Jews that dwelt in towns not walled and in villages appointed the fourteenth day of the month Adar for banquets and gladness, so as to rejoice on that day, and send one another portions of their banquets and meats."

> "That they should receive the fourteenth and fifteenth day of the month Adar for holy days, and always at the return of the year should celebrate them with solemn honour."

> Esther 9: 12-13, 18-19, 21

Church History: With the entry of the Americans, the Allied Forces were able to take back Nazi-occupied lands and advance towards Berlin. The war was soon won, and the official day of surrender was scheduled for May 7, 1945, in Rheims, France. The surrender was to take effect the next day, on May 8, 1945. However, the Soviets (who were also part of the Allied Forces) did not have official representation at the surrender ceremony, so the Soviets organized another surrender ceremony for May 8, 1945, which took place in Berlin. To commemorate the war's end, a new holiday was established called *VE Day* (Victory Europe Day). This holiday is celebrated in every single European country to this day. All the Western European countries celebrate this day on May 8 due to the surrender made in Rheims on May 7. However, the Soviet countries (behind the Iron Curtain) celebrate this day on May 9 because of the surrender made in Berlin on May 8.[155][156]

Thus, astonishingly, just like how the Jews celebrated Purim on two separate days, the Europeans also celebrate VE Day on two separate days. And, even more astonishingly, it was the walled-in cities that celebrated Purim one day later, on the fifteenth of Adar, and it was the Soviet European countries (behind the Iron Curtain) that celebrate VE Day on May 9, which was also one day later.

Great Joy, Dancing In The Streets

Old Testament: The Feast of Purim commemorates the deliverance of the Jewish people from the evil plot of Aman. The Jews were overjoyed and relieved when they learned that they had been spared from certain death. To this day, they celebrate Purim with joy and gratitude, mocking Aman's name with various games, enjoying festive meals, dancing, and holding public parades and events.

Church History: The first VE Day was a tremendous celebration with dancing in the streets erupting throughout Europe. Pictures of VE Day, 1945, show how jubilant and excited Europe was after the war was over. Hitler's name is still notorious in Western society as a name of infamy, just like the name of Aman is for the Jews.

Ten Sons Of Aman Are Hung

Old Testament: During the time in which the Jews were defending themselves and taking revenge on their enemies, Queen Esther made a special petition to the king that the ten sons of Aman might be hanged. Additionally, it is said in Jewish literature that Aman also had a daughter who committed suicide. This is not Biblical but comes from Jewish sources after the time of Christ.[ar]

> "And he said to the queen: The Jews have killed five hundred men in the city of Susan, besides the ten sons of Aman: how many dost thou think they have slain in all the

---

ar *Talmud*, Megillah tractate, 16a

provinces? What askest thou more, and what wilt thou have me to command to be done? 13 And she answered: If it please the king, let it be granted to the Jews, to do tomorrow in Susan as they have done today, and that the ten sons of Aman may be hanged upon gibbets."

- Esther 9: 12-13

Church History: After the end of the war, the Allies held the Nuremberg Trials, which started in November 1945. Top Nazi officials were put on trial for breaking the international laws of war during World War II. Of the twenty-four accused Nazi officials, twelve of them were condemned to death. However, the Allies did not realize that one of them, Martin Bormann, had been killed during the siege of Berlin in May of 1945. Of the eleven remaining Nazi officials present at the trial and were condemned to die, only ten of them were actually executed. Hermann Göring committed suicide the night before his execution.[157] These ten Nazi officials were executed on October 16, 1946, by hanging:

•Hans Frank

•Alfred Jodl

•Wilhelm Keitel

•Alfred Rosenberg

•Arthur Seyss-Inquart

•Wilhelm Frick

•Ernst Kaltenbrunner

•Joachim von Ribbentrop

•Fritz Sauckel

•Julius Streicher

Rewarded With a High Place

MARDOCHAI IS GIVEN A HIGH PLACE IN THE KINGDOM AND THE GERMAN RESISTANCE IS GIVEN A HIGH PLACE IN POST-WORLD WAR II GERMANY

Mardochai Is Given A High Place In The Kingdom

Old Testament: After the Jews were saved from destruction and Aman was killed, the king exhibited renewed favor toward Queen Esther, who introduced her cousin Mardochai to the king. The king gave Mardochai his signet ring, previously in Aman's possession. Mardochai was raised up to be the first man under the king. Mardochai lived out his days in his new position, using it to help the Jews for the rest of his life.

> "And king Assuerus made all the land and all the islands of the sea tributary. And his strength and his empire, and the dignity and greatness wherewith he exalted Mardochai, are written in the books of the Medes, and of the Persians: And how Mardochai of the race of the Jews, was next after king Assuerus: and great among the Jews, and acceptable to the people of his brethren, seeking the good of his people, and speaking those things which were for the welfare of his seed."
>
> - Esther 10: 1-3

Church History: After World War II, Joseph Muller co-founded a political party in Germany called the *Christian Social Union* or CSU. He served in government in an official capacity until 1952. He maintained a high profile in Germany and was even considered a possible successor to Bavarian Prime Minister Fritz. He was the leading advocate for the European Common Market, which earned him the nickname *godfather of the Euro*. Most interesting is the assertion that Joseph Muller worked as a CIA spy after World War II. The CIA wanted Europe to sway towards *Christian democracy* and away from Communism. Joseph Muller's high profile and service record during World War II made him an influential person in advancing American interests in Europe. His CIA code name was ROBOT.[142][as]

This concludes the story of Queen Esther and also to the end of World War II. However, there are a couple miscellaneous parallels to cover before moving on to the final time period in Old Testament and Church history.

Ironically, Aman Was Not Part Of The Aryan Race

Old Testament: The Persians were an ethnic branch of the ancient Iranian peoples. The word *Iranian* is derived from the word *Aryan*, which has its origins in the sixth century BC. The first-ever discovered record of the word *Aryan* was contained in the *Behistun inscription*, an inscription on a rock relief

---

as   Mark Riebling, pg 247-250

on a cliff at Mount Behistun in the Kermanshah Province of Iran sometime in the 500s BC.

This inscription was made during the height of the Persian Empire and was the first self-identification of the Persians as Aryan. Later, Persian kings Darius and Artaxerxes would claim to be Aryan on their official inscriptions. [158] King Artaxerxes was the king in the story of Queen Esther. At the end of the book of Esther, after Aman had been killed and the Jews had been vindicated, the king made a public pronouncement concerning Aman. The king pronounced that Aman was not a genuine Aryan and was devoid of Persian blood.

> "Now that you may more plainly understand what we say, Aman the son of Amadathi, a Macedonian both in mind and country, and having nothing of the Persian blood, but with his cruelty staining our goodness, was received being a stranger by us:"
>
> - Esther 16: 10

Church History: Hitler was intent on forming a master race. In his mind, the master race was the Aryan race. In the Nazis' view, the Europeans were descendants of the Iranian peoples of Persia. These people in Persia, who identified as Aryans, were some of the same people in the story of Queen Esther.

Ironically, Aman was passing himself off as a prince of Persia and wanted to rid the empire of all Jews. However, after his death, the king pronounced that Aman had no Persian blood in him. Hitler, who was obsessed with cleansing Germany of unwanted races, was trying to build the master race of Aryans.

First Use of Mass Communication

LETTER WRITING IN THE BOOK OF ESTHER; RADIO TECHNOLOGY
DURING WORLD WAR II

Old Testament: Throughout the book of Esther, many letters were sent from Susan, the capital city. Each time a letter was sent, it was always a uniform message sent to all the provinces in the Persian Empire. Here are some examples:

Esther 1:22 - THE KING SENDS LETTERS

"And he sent LETTERS to all the provinces of his kingdom, as every nation could hear and read, in divers languages and characters, that the husbands should be rulers and masters in their houses: and that this should be published to every people."

Esther 3:12-13 - Aman SENDS LETTERS

"The LETTERS, sealed with his ring, were sent by the king's messengers to all provinces to kill and destroy all the Jews"

Esther 9:20 - Mardochai SENDS LETTERS IN THE KING'S NAME

"And Mardochai wrote all these things and sent them comprised in LETTERS to the Jews that abode in all the king's provinces, both those that lay near and those afar off"

Church History: The invention of the radio occurred gradually, starting in the late 1800s, but it was not until 1896 that Guglielmo Marconi developed commercial radio. The radio was used for military purposes in World War I (1914-1918). The 1920s were the "Golden Age of Radio," as the radio became available to the general public. It took only a short time before world leaders realized the unprecedented potential to reach the masses with their messages.

For the first time in history, a leader (such as Hitler, the pope, etc.) could speak once in front of a microphone, and that one message could be carried far and wide and heard by all. Pope Pius XI saw this potential and founded

Radio Vaticana in 1931. During World War II, Hitler and the Nazis made extensive use of radio to reach the masses with their messages and propaganda.

Pope Pius XII also extensively used radio to reach people throughout Europe. During his pontificate, Pope Pius XII made approximately 1,000 radio addresses. Remarkably, the advent of radio technology for mass communication is prefigured in the book of Esther, with the Biblical introduction of empire-wide letters. The use of letters in this fashion appears in the Bible for the first time in the book of Esther.

Now we are finally done with time Period 7. Let's move on to the last time period, "Temple Takeover".

Period 8

Temple Takeover

Many of God's people acquiesce to worldly influence. The Temple is taken and the holy religion is changed. A small remnant flees to the hills, preserves tradition, and fights back.

OLD TESTAMENT: Books of the Machabees

The Greek king, Alexander the Great, conquered the Persian Empire. Upon his sudden death, his kingdom was divided into four parts. The Greek Seleucid Kingdom ruled over the partition of Syria and Anatolia. The Seleucids invaded Jerusalem, outlawed the Jewish Temple sacrifice, and mandated a new, pagan sacrifice, the *abomination of desolation*. The Seleucid king, Antiochus, built a new altar over and against the true altar of God in the Temple. He stripped the Temple of its ornaments and brought in new, pagan practices. An old priest, Mathathias, fled to the hills to preserve Jewish tradition. The Jews would eventually fragment, disagreeing about how to respond to this crisis.

CHURCH HISTORY: 1950[AD] to the Present Day

The Allied Nations, led by Franklin D. Roosevelt, conquered the Nazis in World War II. After Roosevelt's sudden death, Germany was divided into four occupation zones. It is thought that Communism infiltrated Church institutions, as testified by Bella Dodd. In 1962, John XXIII called the Second Vatican Council. Through the council's initiative, the Vatican outlawed the Tridentine Mass and mandated the Novus Ordo Rite. A second "altar" was placed in every Catholic church. Statues and ornaments were removed, and churches were renovated in banal, modern design. Archbishop Marcel Lefebvre founded a seminary in the Alps to preserve Catholic tradition and liturgy. The Traditional Catholic world fragmented as it strove to contend with this crisis in the Church.

265

Old Testament	New Testament
Alexander the Great formed the Hellenic League, conquered the Persians, and died suddenly; his empire was divided into four parts.	Roosevelt formed Allied Nations, defeated the Nazis, died suddenly after World War II, and Germany was divided into four parts.
Age of Hellenization and Hellenistic Age Trade	Americanization and Globalization
Ptolemaic and Seleucid Greeks	NATO and the Soviet Union
Faithful Old Eleazar	The Cardinal Mindszenty Affair
Mother and her seven sons	Eastern Catholic Churches
Invasion of the Jewish Temple	Events surrounding the Second Vatican Council
The Machabees fled to the hills, and fought back.	Traditional Catholics "fled" to Econe in the Alps, and fought back.

This period starts with the Persian Empire being conquered by the Greek city-states. The Greek city-states were loosely aligned states, sometimes fighting with each other and sometimes getting along. However, before the Greeks defeated the Persians, they were first invaded by them. The Greeks realized that they must band together against their common enemy, Persia.

The Persians retreated after the Greeks repelled the Persian offensive at the Battle of Marathon in 490 BC. The Persian king, Darius vowed revenge on the Athenians for his humiliation at Marathon; however, he died in 486 BC before regrouping and returning for revenge. Thus, the task of revenge fell upon the next Persian king, Xerxes.

Xerxes launched a second invasion force into Greece in 480 BC. By the time of the second Persian invasion, the Greeks had already allied together. This alliance is termed the *Hellenic League* and explicitly aimed to defend the Greeks from the Persian Empire. Over seventy city-states joined the league, but the two leading and most powerful city-states were Athens and Sparta, providing the backbone for the league's formation.

Great Leader and League of Allies
ALEXANDER THE GREAT AND THE HELLENIC LEAGUE; FRANKLIN ROOSEVELT AND THE ALLIED NATIONS

A League Of Independent Governments

Old Testament: Even though the first Persian invasion of Greece in 490 BC was repelled, the Greeks knew that the Persian Empire would come back. In the fall of 481 BC, a congress of Greek city-state representatives met in Corinth (a leading Greek city-state) and formed a confederation. This confederation was called the *Hellenic League* and was invested with official powers to request military assistance and dispatch soldiers from member states for defensive purposes.

The explicit reason for forming such a league was to protect member states from the Persian Empire. Later, in 337 BC, this idea would be taken to a higher level when Philip II of Macedon formed the *League of Corinth*, also called the *Hellenic League*. Philip II's league was deliberately modeled after the original league formed in 481 BC. Philip II's goal for forming this league was not just the mere protection of the member states, but the complete destruction of the Persian Empire.[159] Philip II of Macedon was the father of Alexander the Great.[160]

Church History: The Soviet Union was able to repel the Nazi attack on Moscow in the fall of 1941. The cold Russian winter and a rally of Russian forces were able to push the Nazis back and eliminate a substantial portion of the Nazi forces. However, Hitler planned to launch another powerful assault in the summer of 1942.[161] It was in between those two Nazi offensives, in the winter of 1941, that the first meeting took place to establish a confederated group of allied nations. On December 29, 1941, American President Franklin Roosevelt met with British Prime Minister Winston Churchill and drafted the *Declaration of the United Nations*. Russian suggestions were incorporated into the document as well.

Only days later, on January 1, 1942, President Roosevelt, Prime Minister Churchill, Russian representative Maxim Litvinov, and T. V. Soong of China signed the document. The next day, twenty-two other countries added their signatures. The United Nations contained many members, but it was essentially the initiative of the United States and Britain, the two leading powers in the confederation. This is similar to Athens and Sparta providing the gravity for the coalescence of the Hellenic League in 481 BC. Here is selected text from the Atlantic Charter, which is a precursor document for the founding of the United Nations. Note the stated purpose of complete victory over Hitler. This is similar to Phillip II's goal of total victory over the Persians.

> "The Governments signatory hereto, Having subscribed to a common program of purposes and principles embodied in the Joint Declaration of the President of the United States of America and the Prime Minister of the United Kingdom of Great Britain and Northern Ireland dated August 14, 1941, known as the Atlantic Charter, Being convinced that complete victory over their enemies is essential to defend life, liberty, independence, and religious freedom, and to preserve human rights and justice in their lands as well as in other lands and that they are now engaged in a common struggle against savage and brutal forces seeking to subjugate the world, Declare: (1) Each Government pledges itself to employ its full resources, military or economic, against those members of the Tripartite Pact and its adherents with which such government is at war. (2) Each Government pledges itself to cooperate with the Governments signatory hereto and not to make a separate armistice or peace with the enemies. The foregoing declaration may be adhered to by other nations which are, or which may be, rendering material assistance and contributions in the struggle for victory over Hitlerism."[162]

The League Works To Defeat The Common Enemy

Old Testament: Philip II, after creating the League of Corinth, was assassinated in 336 BC. Control of the league was passed to his son, Alexander the Great. Alexander the Great led Greek forces into Persia, completely destroying the Persian Empire in 330 BC. However, Alexander the Great did not stop with the Persian Empire but went on to conquer Egypt, and even continued to India. He conquered virtually the entire known ancient world.

Church History: The United Nations (Allied Nations) invaded the Nazi Empire from the west and the east. A coordinated attack from thirteen allied nations landed in France on D-Day, June 6, 1944. In 1943, the Russians, also members of the Allied Nations, started their advance westwards towards Berlin. In 1945, the Nazis surrendered to the Allied Forces. After World War II, the British forces gained control over the Middle East, the United States came to dominate Japan, and the Soviet Union came to dominate Eastern Europe. Just as Alexander the Great and his league came to dominate the whole ancient world after the defeat of the Persian Empire, so too did the Allied Nations come to dominate virtually the entire world after World War II.

Conqueror Rules For Twelve Years

Old Testament: Alexander the Great reigned as king of Macedon, and all of Greece, after his father's assassination in 336 BC. Alexander himself died only a short time later, in 323 BC. During that time, Alexander the Great conquered almost the entire ancient world. The book of 1 Machabees disagrees with the time of his reign or counts it slightly differently. The book of 1 Machabees states that Alexander the Great reigned for twelve years.

> "Now it came to pass, after that Alexander the son of Philip the Macedonian, who first reigned in Greece, coming out of the land of Cethim, had overthrown Darius king of the Persians and Medes: He fought many battles, and took the strong holds of all, and slew the kings of the earth: And he went through even to the ends of the earth, and took the spoils of many nations: and the earth was quiet before him."

> "And Alexander reigned twelve years, and he died."

> - 1 Machabees 1:1-3, 8

Church History: Franklin Roosevelt was the only president to serve for twelve consecutive years, from March 1933 to April 1945. Because of the Great Depression and the widespread popularity of Roosevelt, the traditional two-term limit for American presidents was overlooked, and Roosevelt served into his fourth term. He died in the middle of his fourth term, thus ending his twelve-year reign as president.

The League Dominates

Old Testament: Alexander the Great was a brilliant military leader. His army also had tactical advantages over the Persians. The Greeks developed a long pike called the *sarissa*, changing the nature of ancient combat. Alexander the Great's army swept through Persian lands, never losing a battle. The Greeks conquered Asia Minor, Egypt, Syria, Palestine, Persia, and even parts of India.

> "And he went through even to the ends of the earth, and took the spoils of many nations: and the earth was quiet before him. And he gathered a power and a very strong army: and his heart was exalted and lifted up. And he subdued countries of nations, and princes: and they became tributaries to him."
>
> - 1 Machabees 1:3-5

Church History: The Allied Forces of World War II defeated the Nazis swiftly. Once the Allied Forces landed in Normandy, it was a steady push eastward to Berlin. After World War II, the Allied Nations dominated vast regions, from Japan to the Middle East to North Africa to Eastern Europe. Sometimes this took the form of economic domination; sometimes it was military. However, the world was in the shadow of the United Nations after World War II.

Died Suddenly After The Conquest

Old Testament: After conquering the ancient world, Alexander was poised to rule over the largest empire in history. He was famous everywhere and ruled with clemency to those who submitted to him. However, Alexander died very suddenly. The reason for his death is not known, but his death was so sudden and unexpected that when reports of his death reached Greece, they were dismissed.[163]

Church History: Franklin Roosevelt surprised the world with his sudden death. Roosevelt hid his illness from the general public. Newspaper headlines from the time bear the title "President Roosevelt Dies Suddenly".

Forefather Only Has One Eye

Old Testament: Alexander the Great's father was Philip II. Philip was king of Macedon, which became Alexander's title. Interestingly, Philip only had one eye, having lost one in combat.

Church History: Franklin Roosevelt was not the only Roosevelt who was president of the United States. His fifth cousin, Theodore Roosevelt, became president in 1901. Franklin's father had died in 1900, so the young Roosevelt came to look up to his cousin Theodore as a role model. When Franklin Roosevelt grew up, he occupied the same office as his role model and relative. Theodore Roosevelt was blind in one eye. He was hit so hard in a boxing match that it detached the retina nerve.

From "Greek" Origins

Old Testament: As stated above, Alexander the Great was from Macedon. Macedon is the region just north of Greece proper, and it is hotly contested as to whether Macedon should be considered part of Greece or not. However, Macedon did have Greek culture, and all the Greeks accepted Alexander's rule over them. For all intents and purposes, Alexander was Greek.

Church History: Franklin Roosevelt came from the eastern region of New York state. This part of the state has an excessive amount of cities and towns with Greek names. Here are a few: Utica, Syracuse, Troy, Ithaca, Athens, Sparta, Ulysses, Virgil, Ilion, Macedon, and Greece. I do not know of any region in the United States with as many Greek-named towns and cities as eastern New York.

Sudden Death and Division Into Four Parts

ALEXANDER DIES SUDDENLY, EMPIRE IS DIVIDED INTO FOUR PARTS
AND ROOSEVELT DIES SUDDENLY, GERMANY IS DIVIDED INTO FOUR
OCCUPATION ZONES

After A Sudden Death, A Fight For The Territory

Old Testament: After the death of Alexander the Great, there was no provision given for a successor to his vast empire. When asked who should inherit the empire, Alexander said, "It should go to the strongest". Therefore, following his sudden death, there was a series of intrigues and conflicts as Alexander's generals scrambled to secure territory. This is alluded to in 1 Machabees:

> "And Alexander reigned twelve years, and he died. And his servants made themselves kings, every one in his place: And they all put crowns upon themselves after his death, and their sons after them many years, and evils were multiplied in the earth."
>
> - 1 Machabees 1: 8-10

Church History: After the death of Franklin Roosevelt in April of 1945, there was no finalized agreement for the governance of conquered Germany. At the Potsdam Conference in July of 1945, the leaders of the Allied Forces got together to determine how conquered Germany would be partitioned and how the future of other Eastern European states would be handled.[164]

However, the relationship between the heads of state for the Allied Forces was markedly different after the death of Franklin Roosevelt. Franklin Roosevelt was criticized for having blind trust in Joseph Stalin. Upon the death of Roosevelt, Harry Truman became president. Truman was suspicious of Stalin, seeing in him a desire for aggressive expansion. Winston Churchill was also critical of Stalin.

The Potsdam Conference was held in the home of Crown Prince Wilhelm of Germany. Each of the three heads of state (Truman, Churchill, and Stalin) were given a private wing of the mansion for his residence. They would meet each day in the main lobby. It has been speculated that Stalin had listening devices placed strategically in the mansion to overhear the private discussions between Churchill and Truman, who both wanted to contain the power of the growing Soviet Union. Stalin came out of the Potsdam Conference with favorable agreements concerning the Soviet Union's expansion into Eastern Europe. It was as if he knew the discussion strategies of the Americans and British, probably because he was eavesdropping on them.

Another tension that occurred at the Potsdam Conference was the indication by Truman to Stalin that the Americans had developed an atomic bomb. Truman mentioned this to Stalin in a clear attempt to intimidate him and thus gain a more favorable position for America during the negotiations. The Americans would find out much later that Stalin was already aware of the atomic bomb since Russian spies had infiltrated the Manhattan Project.

In addition, a conflict occurred between the United States and France. At the Yalta Conference, some months before, it was agreed that France would be involved in the partition of Germany. However, Truman insisted that the French not be invited to the Potsdam Conference. The French took this diplomatic slight very hard, and they did not forget it.

All these occurrences are meant to show the almost immediate distrust and competition between members of the Allied Forces after the death of Roosevelt and the end of World War II. In like fashion, after Alexander's death, his previously united generals began to fight for power and territory among themselves.

The Two Major Parties From The Four-Part Division

Old Testament: Two of the four parties to the division of Alexander's empire became bitter enemies. Those two parties were the Ptolemaic and Seleucid kingdoms.

The Ptolemaic Kingdom developed into a booming economy after Alexander's conquest, due in large part to the new city of Alexandria.[165][a] Alexandria was known as a melting pot and a land of opportunity.[166] By comparison, the Seleucids developed a policy of forced ethnic unity.[167] This policy imposed Greek culture and belief on the people of their vast kingdom, including, eventually, worshiping the Greek king as a god. This will be shown later, particularly with King Antiochus IV Epiphanes in the books of the Machabees.

Church History: Two of the four countries who ruled over occupied Germany became bitter enemies. Those two are the United States and the Soviet Union, the two superpowers of the world after World War II.

The United States of America had a growing and thriving economy. America was the land of opportunity, as many people worldwide came to find jobs and a better standard of living. America became the center of modern culture, as American cuisine, movies, fashion, and ideas were spread worldwide during this time.

The Soviet Union had a vast territory that spanned the majority of Asia. Under Stalin, the Soviet Union was highly oppressive, requiring all people to accept Communist propaganda.[168] The Soviets shut out influences from the Western World to create a unified people.

Stalin's image was everywhere in the Soviet Union. It was almost like he wanted himself to be worshiped as a god.[168] The next leader of the Soviet Union, Nikita Khrushchev, would come to criticize Stalin for building such a cult around his image and person.[b]

---

a   During the Ptolemaic period, Egypt emerged as a significant economic force in the ancient world. Its prosperity was due to the abundant fertility of the Nile, which transformed it into the breadbasket of the ancient world. Ptolemaic Egypt grew wealthy also because of the introduction of official coinage, new crops, and the expansion of international trade.

b   In the iconic "Secret Speech" to the Twentieth Party Congress in 1956, Khrushchev openly criticized Stalin for fostering a leadership cult centered on his image and persona.

Conqueror's Economic and Cultural Dominance
THE AGE OF HELLENIZATION AND THE AGE OF AMERICANIZATION

Massive Spread Of Conqueror's Culture And Language

Old Testament: Alexander conquered virtually the entire ancient world. During his conquest, Alexander the Great founded dozens of Greek cities around the ancient world, which served as centers of Greek culture. Furthermore, the division of Alexander's empire after his death ultimately led to the creation of new Greek kingdoms. The local native populations in these kingdoms were ruled over by an elite Greek ruling class, facilitating the diffusion of Greek culture and language across the ancient world.[169] For locals to advance socially, they needed to embrace Greek language and culture, or in some other way obtain the favor of the "aristoi," the Greek ruling class. Since all the cultures in the ancient world were exposed to Greek, it became the universal language in which different cultures and societies could communicate.

Church History: After the destruction of Europe in World War II, the Americans funded the rebuilding of Western Europe through the Marshall Plan. This plan gave the Europeans over $13 billion to rebuild. Much of that money was used to purchase goods from the United States. This was the start of the age of *Americanization*, in which American products and culture were exported en masse throughout much of the world. At this same time, "English as a second language" became a reality for nations around the world. English speakers had enhanced advancement possibilities.

Advanced Civilization Rules The World

Old Testament: The hegemony of the Greeks enabled their language and culture to flourish throughout the ancient world, from the Balkans in the west to India in the east and as far south as Egypt.

Greek culture was the most advanced culture of the ancient world, excelling in logic, mathematics, art, natural sciences, political organization, philosophy, and economics. The result was that the people of the ancient world were enticed to make themselves part of this international Greek society by learning to speak Greek and adopting Greek practices. The adopting of Greek culture was called "Hellenization" and it gave native populations a much better chance of success.

Church History After World War II, the founding countries in the Allied Forces found themselves ruling over or exerting powerful influence throughout most regions of the world. The United States was paying to rebuild Europe, which gave it considerable influence there. In a short time, American products, ideas, the English language, business practices, etc., were exported to the four corners of the world, especially as technology improved over the decades following the war's end.

The American economy, business and industrial practices, technology, and political system were more advanced than most of the world. The result was the Americanization of much of the world.[170] Learning "English as a second language" and being familiar with American culture gave people worldwide a better chance for success in the emerging international community.

Standardized Language And Culture For Trade

Old Testament: Because the Greek language and culture became so widespread across the ancient world, it facilitated a much easier transfer of people and ideas from one part of the Greek Empire to the next. Before the Greeks ruled the ancient world, one would have to learn the language and culture of a specific location if you wished to live and work there. After Alexander's conquest, one could live and work in virtually any city of the ancient world if one knew Greek. This international mobility was an impetus for the flourishing of trade and the sharing of ideas.

Church History: The Americanization of the modern world, especially the international adoption of "English as a second language", played a large role in globalization. Globalization can be defined in many ways, but it generally refers to the integration of world economies. American companies established operations worldwide, and those who could communicate in the desired American cultural context enjoyed advantages for advancement and promotion.

Production was increasingly outsourced to developing countries. In America, a much greater proportion of the workforce was "white collar". This is paralleled by the Greeks, who retained their positions in the upper class.

Standardized Trade Currency Facilitates Trade

Old Testament: The ancient world adopted a common currency thanks to Greek dominance. Greek coins were widely accepted across different regions and cultures. This boosted trade and innovation in this era. Like language and culture, having a uniform monetary system made it easier to do business in the ancient world.[171]

Church History: After World War II, during the age of globalization, the American dollar emerged as the dominant global reserve currency. Foreign companies recognized that future transactions were likely to involve American dollars, so they strategically held monetary reserves in dollars. By doing so, they avoided the need for frequent currency exchanges. The widespread acceptance of the American dollar facilitated seamless international business transactions.

Government Tax And Economic Policies Favored Trade

Old Testament: Governmental policies implemented by Greek kingdoms during the Hellenistic Age played a pivotal role in promoting and facilitating trade. These policies created an environment favorable to commerce, contributing significantly to the flourishing trade networks of the time. The Greek Ptolemaic Kingdom is the best example, as it came to understand that it could generate wealth for the kingdom not just by imposing taxes on its people but also by stimulating trade into its ports and cities. More trade meant more wealth for the kingdom, including more tariffs, taxes, and political power.[172]

Church History: International trade grows in an environment of deregulation.[c] The American government realized that by facilitating

---

c   This is my opinion, which if not shared by the reader, no amount of citations will persuade
      to the contrary.

business activities, it could increase its revenue and economic growth. The American government, thus, adopted foreign policies benefiting American firms in the global markets. The age of globalization was marked by the awareness (or perhaps the propaganda) that increased trade meant increased wealth.

The Old Priest Refused to Give Scandal

ELEAZAR REFUSES TO PRETEND TO EAT PORK AND CARDINAL MINDSZENTY REFUSES TO BEND TO COMMUNISM

A Focus On God's People And The Temple

The Seleucid Kingdom, particularly King Antiochus IV, was responsible for the great persecution of the Jews that took place in the books of the Machabees. If you recall, Alexander the Great's empire was divided upon his death. The regions of Juda and Jerusalem were initially part of the Ptolemaic Kingdom. Under Ptolemy, the Jews were free to practice their religion in peace.[173][d] The Seleucids took control of Jerusalem from the Ptolemaic Kingdom in 200 BC. It was shortly after, in 167 BC, that the Seleucid King Antiochus IV raided Jerusalem and the Temple and imposed the Hellenization of the Jewish religion as documented in the books of the Machabees. This brings us to the iconic story of Eleazar. In Church history, this brings us to the saga of Cardinal Mindszenty.

Eleazar refused to submit to the mandates of the evil Seleucid King Antiochus. Cardinal Mindszenty refused to accommodate the Communists and was tortured and imprisoned, only later to be betrayed by Paul VI upon his release.

Old Testament: Eleazar was commanded to eat pork, against the Law of Moses. Eleazar refused and was manfully walking to receive his torture and death when some of his fellow Jews, who were aiding the Seleucids in the persecution, offered to save his life if he just pretended to eat pork. That way, he would not have to break Jewish religious law and also could avoid torture

---

d   At the bottom of paragraph 4 in his work *Against Apion*, Josephus praises the policies of the Ptolemaic Kingdom towards the Jews. See the bibliographical citation.

and death. But Eleazar responded that it would not become his old age and distinction to perform such a cowardly act. Such an act would scandalize those who believed he surrendered and violated God's laws. Eleazar was tortured and killed while providing a heroic and manly example for others to follow.

"Eleazar, one of the chief of the scribes, a man advanced in years and of a comely countenance, was pressed to open his mouth to eat swine's flesh. But he, choosing rather a most glorious death than a hateful life, went forward voluntarily to the torment. And considering in what manner he was come to it, patiently bearing, he determined not to do any unlawful things for the love of life. But they that stood by, being moved with wicked pity, for the old friendship they had with the man, taking him aside, desired that flesh might be brought, which it was lawful for him to eat, that he might make as if he had eaten, as the king had commanded of the flesh of the sacrifice: That by so doing he might be delivered from death: and for the sake of their old friendship with the man they did him this courtesy. But he began to consider the dignity of his age and his ancient years, and the inbred honour of his grey head, and his good life and conversation from a child: and he answered without delay, according to the ordinances of the holy law made by God, saying, that he would rather be sent into the other world. For it doth not become our age, said he, to dissemble: whereby many young persons might think that Eleazar, at the age of fourscore and ten years, was gone over to the life of the heathens: And so they, through my dissimulation, and for a little time of a corruptible life, should be deceived, and hereby I should bring a stain and a curse upon my old age. For though, for the present time, I should be delivered from the punishments of men, yet should I not escape the hand of the Almighty neither alive nor dead. Wherefore by departing manfully out of this life, I shall shew myself worthy of my old age: And I shall leave an example of fortitude to young men, if with a ready mind and constancy I suffer an honourable death, for the most venerable and most holy

279

laws. And having spoken thus, he was forthwith carried to execution. And they that led him, and had been a little before more mild, were changed to wrath for the words he had spoken, which they thought were uttered out of arrogance. But when he was now ready to die with the stripes, he groaned, and said: O Lord, who hast the holy knowledge, thou knowest manifestly that whereas I might be delivered from death, I suffer grievous pains in body: but in soul am well content to suffer these things because I fear thee. Thus did this man die, leaving not only to young men but also to the whole nation, the memory of his death for an example of virtue and fortitude."

- 2 Machabees 6: 18-31

Summary Of 2 Machabees 6: 18-31

1. Eleazar was an honored elder of Israel.

2. Eleazar would rather die than break the law of God.

3. His persecutors were fellow Jews who wanted to accommodate the Greeks in their persecution of their people.

4. Eleazar was given a chance to save his life by pretending to go along with the king's evil demands. However, Eleazar did not want to lead other Jews into scandal. He died with great honor and great virtue because he never submitted to the evil demands of the king despite torture and death.

Church History: Hungarian József Cardinal Mindszenty was a staunch and vocal opponent of Communism following World War II. Pope Pius XII raised him to the position of Primate of Hungary.

Cardinal Mindszenty toured the country urging his fellow Hungarians to resist the Communists, making public speeches against the Communist regime in Hungary. In 1946, Pope Pius XII made him a cardinal, presumably for his heroic public stance against Communism. By December 1948, the Communist regime in Hungary finally arrested Cardinal Mindszenty for treason.[174]

He was taken to prison and tortured horribly for forty days and nights, deprived of sleep, and beaten.[e] He was given mind-altering drugs in his food to break his mind and will. Finally, on February 3, 1949, he was brought out of jail for a televised Communist show trial. After days of torture and mind-altering drugs, Cardinal Mindszenty admitted to a list of the most ridiculous charges. The world was watching the trial and could see the bruises on the cardinal's face; they knew the trial was a farce, and the confession was coerced. Prior to his initial arrest and anticipating the torture he would receive, he wrote a message indicating that any confessions that he might make in the future would be false and coerced.[174] The verdict of the trial was life imprisonment.

Cardinal Mindszenty came to be seen as the symbol of the Catholic Church's opposition to Communism. He would not relent in his opposition to the Communists. In 1956, when the Hungarians managed to throw out the Communist Party for a very brief period of time, Cardinal Mindszenty was freed from his Communist prison and fled to the American embassy in Hungary, where he lived under American protection for the next fifteen years. He refused to leave Hungary. When the Communists took back control of Hungary, even they volunteered to escort him out of the country. However, the good cardinal wanted to be close to his flock, who were suffering from a harsh persecution. It was not until 1971 that Paul VI persuaded Cardinal Mindszenty to leave Hungary. The cardinal opposed the idea, but ultimately agreed to leave under obedience.

With its policy of *Ostpolitik*, the Vatican seemed to yield to the Hungarian Communist regime; not opposing them. This policy made Cardinal Mindszenty a hindrance to the Vatican's ties with the Hungarian Communists. Therefore, Paul VI persuaded Cardinal Mindszenty to depart from Hungary, as the cardinal represented Catholic opposition; an embarrassment to the Vatican.[175]

The trials and sufferings for Cardinal Mindszenty did not end when he left Hungary. Now that he was free from the hands of the Communists, he hoped he could help his people by going public with his story. As he was

---

e   See *Acerrimo Moerore* (January 2, 1949), a letter of Pope Pius XII to the Hungarian Episcopate after the jailing and torturing of Cardinal Joseph Mindszenty.

preparing his memoirs during his exile in Vienna, he was requested by the Vatican to resign from his position as Primate of Hungary. When Cardinal Mindszenty refused to resign, the Vatican declared publicly that his seat was now vacant. The Vatican forcibly removed him from his position.

Following the Vatican's forced removal of Cardinal Mindszenty, presumably because he was about to publish his memoirs, the impression was given to the public that he resigned of his own free will. Therefor, the cardinal's office issued a statement that made several points very clear, including his forced resignation.[174][f] Cardinal Mindszenty spent the rest of his days ministering in his priestly capacity and finally died in 1975. He declared until his dying day that he had never resigned but had been forcibly removed by the Vatican. He did not want anyone to think he gave up, but instead, he opposed the Communists to the end of his life.

The Parallels Between Eleazar And Cardinal Mindszenty

1.Eleazar and Cardinal Mindszenty refused to submit to the evil persecutors until their dying day. They were both aware of their public image and wanted to give a solid example of courage and virtue in the face of great evil.

2.They both were given an easy way out of their persecution, but both chose not to accept the easy way out. They were motivated by the love of God's people, and a desire to be a good example.

3.Both Eleazar and Cardinal Mindszenty were betrayed by their own people.

4.The Jews asked Eleazar to pretend to eat pork in order to save his life. He refused to do so. Similarly, Cardinal Mindszenty was tortured and forced to pretend that he committed all the ridiculous "crimes" to which he "confessed" at his show trial.

---

f   On page 246 of the accompanying bibliographical citation, where Cardinal Mindszenty shares the press release published by his office, he emphatically declares that he did not abdicate his office as the Primate of Hungary.

Encouraging Faithful Martyr Sons in their Death

MOTHER AND HER SEVEN SONS AND POPE PIUS XII AND EASTERN
CATHOLIC CHURCHES BEHIND THE IRON CURTAIN

The Catholic Faith is expressed in various ancient liturgies. Most of us are familiar with the Latin Rite, but throughout the history of the Church, other rites have organically developed that have always been recognized as not only valid but rich in history and expression. These rites are usually termed the *Eastern Catholic Rites*. Almost all of these rites went into schism by rejecting papal authority. These schisms occurred in the early years of Church history, alongside the heresies of Nestorianism (fifth century), Monophysitism (fifth century), and the Great Schism of 1054 when the Byzantine Empire was excommunicated.

In the seventeenth, eighteenth and nineteenth centuries, portions of the clergy and laity in many Eastern Rites chose to return to the Catholic Church. These returns reestablished these ancient and valid rites in the Catholic Church. These new "sons of the Church" faced many obstacles after centuries of schism and were cared for by various acts and decrees of the popes throughout the eighteenth and nineteenth centuries. Many of these Eastern Rites were given special privileges because of their unique character and to preserve their historical identity and beauty.[g]

After World War II, the Soviet Union occupied Eastern European countries. The Communists were especially interested in breaking Eastern Catholic Churches of their allegiance to the pope. Unfortunately these Eastern Rite Catholic Churches were faced with the most terrible tortures at the hands of the Soviet Communists. However, the Eastern Rite Catholic Churches refused to deny their allegiance to the pope, which was explicitly demanded of them by the Communists.

Finally, a brief word about the Old Testament story of the *mother and her seven sons* might also be helpful. The story evokes feelings of fear and horror

---

g   See: (**Orientalium Dignitas** *On the Churches of the East,* Pope Leo XIII – 1894) and (**Demandatam Coelitus Humilitati Nostrae**, an apostolic constitution promulgated by Pope Benedict XIV on December 24, 1743.)

but also inspires deep feelings of religious zeal. It demonstrates the glory of holy martyrdom. In this story, the Greek Seleucid King, Antiochus IV, demanded that each of the seven sons reject the Law of Moses and submit to Greek ways. Each of the seven sons bravely refused the evil king and virtuously and fearlessly proclaimed belief in the God of Israel and obedience to His laws. As a consequence, each of the seven sons was tortured and martyred in cruel ways. The mother witnessed this whole ordeal and encouraged them to die with manly courage for the laws of God.

The Mothering Of The Children

Old Testament: In the story of the *mother and her seven sons*, the mother described how she bore and raised her children, then encouraging them to receive death instead of denying God.[h]

> "So bending herself towards him, mocking the cruel tyrant, she said in her own language: My son, have pity upon me, that bore thee nine months in my womb, and gave thee suck three years, and nourished thee, and brought thee up unto this age. I beseech thee, my son, look upon heaven and earth, and all that is in them: and consider that God made them out of nothing, and mankind also: So thou shalt not fear this tormentor but being made a worthy partner with thy brethren receive death, that in that mercy I may receive thee again with thy brethren."
>
> - 2 Machabees 7: 27-29

Church History: The Eastern Rite Catholic Churches were given special privileges, cared for, and "raised up" by various popes throughout the centuries to ensure they were not absorbed into the Latin Rite. The Holy Father did not want each of these individual Eastern Rites to lose their unique identity, deeply rooted in history.

---

h   We have just portrayed the parallels between Cardinal Mindszenty and Eleazar, whose narrative appears in the Books of the Maccabees along side of the Mother and Her Seven Sons. It is amazing to note that Cardinal Mindszenty's famous work entitled *The Mother*, extols the importance of motherhood.

Here are some examples of Eastern Rite Churches and when they reunited with the pope:

•Albanian Greek Catholic Church: Reunited in 1628
•Armenian Catholic Church: Reunited in 1742
•Greek Catholic Church of Croatia and Serbia: Reunited in 1611
•Ruthenian Byzantine Catholic Church: Reunited in 1646
•Ukrainian Greek Catholic Church: Reunited in 1595

Each of these Churches was given special attention. Pope Pius XII issued several encyclicals just for the Eastern Rites. Also, he reformed Eastern Rite canon law, which gave them special privileges that the Latin Rite did not enjoy.

The Sons Choose Death Rather Than Deny God's Laws

Old Testament: Each of the seven sons chose to die for their religion instead of denying God's laws. They gave manly speeches with full knowledge of the torture they would soon endure.

> "But one of them, who was the eldest, said thus: What wouldst thou ask, or learn of us? We are ready to die rather than to transgress the laws of God, received from our fathers. Then the king being angry commanded frying pans, and brazen caldrons to be made hot: which forthwith being heated, He commanded to cut out the tongue of him that had spoken first: and the skin of his head being drawn off, to chop off also the extremities of his hands and feet, the rest of his brethren, and his mother, looking on. And when he was now maimed in all parts, he commanded him, being yet alive, to be brought to the fire, and to be fried in the fryingpan: and while he was suffering therein long torments, the rest, together with the mother, exhorted one another to die manfully,"
>
> - 2 Machabees 7: 2-5

Church History: Perhaps the Eastern Rite that was the most horribly persecuted was the Ukrainian Catholic Church. The Soviets unleashed a satanic persecution on the Ukrainian people, particularly against the Catholics. So many priests and religious were brutally tortured and killed because they would not reject their Catholic Faith. In the Ukrainian region of Lemko, in 1945, over five hundred Catholic priests were deported and sent into the dreaded gulags (Soviet torture prisons). Throughout Ukraine, Church properties were confiscated, looted, and closed.

The Communist regime demanded that the hierarchy of the Ukrainian Catholic Church renounce their loyalty to the pope and submit to Communist authority. If they complied, their Churches could remain open. However, the brave bishops of the Ukrainian Catholic Church all rejected the Communist demands, and one after another, they were tortured in the cruelest ways and sent off to the gulags. Some would come back only to be sent off again. Here is a list of Ukrainian Catholic Bishops who refused to submit to Communist demands and were tortured and martyred. Some of them did not die immediately but died in later years as a consequence of the treatment they received while in captivity.

Between the years 1945 and 1964, seven Ukrainian Catholic Bishops were tortured and martyred. Two additional bishops died in 1973, thus bringing the total to nine.

- Bishop and Martyr, Gregory Khomyshyn: died in 1945
- Bishop and Martyr, Theodore Romzha: died in 1947
- Bishop and Martyr, Josaphat Kotsylovskyi: died 1947
- Bishop and Martyr, Nykyta Budka: died in 1949
- Bishop and Martyr, Gregory Lakota: died in 1950
- Bishop and Martyr Nicholas Charnetskyi: died in 1959
- Bishop and Martyr, Simeon Lukach: died in 1964

The laity in Ukraine also were treated brutally by the Communists. The regime starved millions of Ukrainians intentionally.

Mother Is Powerless To Stop Sons' Deaths, She Encourages Them

Old Testament: The mother was powerless to help her sons. She encouraged them to persevere to the end. She also gave them hope that God would raise them up again because of their faithfulness.

> "I beseech thee, my son, look upon heaven and earth, and all that is in them: and consider that God made them out of nothing, and mankind also: So thou shalt not fear this tormentor but being made a worthy partner with thy brethren receive death, that in that mercy I may receive thee again with thy brethren."
>
> - 2 Machabees 7: 28-29

Church History: During the persecution of the Ukrainian Catholic Church by the Communists, Pope Pius XII was aware of what was happening but was utterly powerless to stop it. He had written encyclicals for the Eastern Rite Catholic Churches, including *Orientales Omnes Ecclesias* and *Orientales Ecclesias*.

In his encyclical *Orientales Omnes Ecclesias*, written in 1945, Pope Pius XII called to mind all of the special attention that the Holy See had given to the Ukrainian Catholic Church. He also encouraged the Ukrainian Catholics to remain strong in their Faith and not to deny their "sacred and religious allegiance". Pope Pius XII urged his "beloved **sons**, to be terrified by no menaces or injuries" that could befall them at the hands of the Communists. He finally urged them to retain their faith and "fidelity to **Mother** Church". [176]

First Time Ever: Greek Games in the Holy City

JASON BRINGS THE GREEK GAMES TO JERUSALEM AND JOHN XXIII
BLESSES THE OLYMPICS IN ROME

The Olympics Come To The Holy City

The Olympic Games can be traced back to 776 BC in ancient Greece. They were initially held to honor the false god Zeus. They kept their overt religious significance throughout ancient times. After the Romans conquered the ancient Greek world, they still observed the Olympic Games. The Romans were pragmatic and adopted many Greek ideas, including Greek gods, to whom they gave Roman names.

The Olympics remained popular throughout Roman times until the Christianization of the Roman Empire in the fourth century. In 393, Emperor Theodosius banned the Olympics in the Roman Empire, as he was making Christianity the state religion of the Roman Empire; the Olympics were pagan ceremonies. Throughout the history of Christendom, the Olympics remained banned and were left in the dustbin of history.

With the dismantling of the remnants of Christendom by the French Revolution in 1789 and the subsequent secular Napoleonic Empire, the "shackles" of Christianity were removed from Western Civilization. In Athens in 1896, the Olympics were once again conducted on European soil, after being banned by the Christian Roman Emperor Theodosius and remaining thus for 1503 years.

Two Groups, One Wants To Apostatize

Old Testament: In Jerusalem, at the beginning of the books of the Machabees, there were many upper-class Jews who wanted to *hellenize* Jerusalem. Most of the ancient world had accepted Greek religion, customs, and practices to some degree or another. Up until that point, the Jewish people as a whole had remained steadfastly opposed to adopting Greek ways. However, the forces and numbers of Hellenizing Jews grew to such a point that a confrontation was imminent between the traditionally minded Jews and their modern, apostate, Hellenizing Jewish counterparts.

"In those days, there went out of Israel wicked men, and they persuaded many, saying: Let us go, and make a covenant with the heathens that are round about us: for since we departed from them, many evils have befallen us. And the word seemed good in their eyes. And some of the people determined to do this and went to the king: and he gave them license to do after the ordinances of the heathens."

- 1 Machabees 1: 12-14

Church History: Back in the early 1900s, Pope St. Pius X warned Catholics about the forces of Modernism that were alive and active inside the walls of the Church. Modernists wanted to change Catholic rites, beliefs, and practices to align with the modern world. Pope St. Pius X conducted a fierce campaign against Modernism inside the Church. He employed a secret spy force to detect hidden Modernists. He issued encyclicals in which he identified modernist tactics and ways to overcome them, and he even initiated an Oath Against Modernism. Like the Hellenizing Jews who were opposed by the Traditionally minded Jews, so too were the Modernists in the Church opposed by Traditionally minded Catholics.

However, upon the death of Pope St. Pius X, the Church relaxed its vigilance against Modernism. The Modernists, driven underground by Pope St. Pius X, slowly resurfaced throughout the mid-1900s. The term *Modernism* fell out of mainstream use by the 1960s. The Oath Against Modernism, established by Pope St. Pius X, was also abolished.

Usurper High Priest Oversees Olympic Games In The Holy City

Old Testament: The first official promoter of Hellenization in Jerusalem came from the usurper, Jason. He obtained the office of high priest through dishonesty and bribery. The name *Jason* is a Greek name, signifying that he intentionally chose to identify himself with the Greeks and not with the Jews. Jason was responsible for bringing the Greek games to Jerusalem, which were abhorrent to traditional Jews. The Greek games involved nudity and participation in the Greek religion. Jason was an **"impious wretch and no priest"**.[i]

---

i   2 Machabees 4: 13

289

"But after the death of Seleucus, when Antiochus, who was called the Illustrious, had taken possession of the kingdom, Jason the brother of Onias ambitiously sought the high priesthood: And went to the king, promising him three hundred and sixty talents of silver, and out of other revenues fourscore talents. Besides this, he also promised a hundred and fifty more if he might have a license to set him up a place for exercise, and a place for youth, and to entitle them, that were at Jerusalem, Antiochians. Which when the king had granted, and he had gotten the rule into his hands, forthwith he began to bring over his countrymen to the fashion of the heathens."

"For he had the boldness to set up, under the very castle, a place of exercise, and to put all the choicest youths in brothel houses. Now this was not the beginning, but an increase, and progress of heathenish and foreign manners, through the abominable and unheard of wickedness of Jason, that impious wretch, and **no priest**."

- 2 Machabees 4: 7-10, 12-13

Church History: Following the death of Pope Pius XII in 1958, a conclave was called to elect his successor. There was confusion during the conclave when white smoke came out of the chimney on two separate occasions on October 26, 1958. On the second occurrence, the chimney emitted white smoke for five minutes. Because of the white smoke, Vatican Radio said, "The smoke is white... There is absolutely no doubt. A pope has been elected".[177]

The 200,000 faithful present in St. Peter's Square were cheering and waiting for their new pope to appear on the papal balcony that night of October 26, 1958. Later that evening, Vatican Radio announced that there had been a mistake and that no pope had been elected. Two days later, on October 28, 1958, white smoke plumed again from the chimney. This time, Angelo Roncalli emerged onto the papal balcony, taking the name "John XXIII".

Because of these strange occurrences of white smoke two days before the election of John XXIII, there persists a theory that perhaps another pope was elected, but his election was somehow suppressed. Considering later actions of John XXIII, it is not unreasonable to conjecture that Angelo Roncalli rose through dishonest means, just as Jason usurped his position as high priest.

In 1925, at the age of forty-four, Fr. Angelo Roncalli (John XXIII) was removed from his teaching position mid-semester for teaching the modernist ideas of Rudolf Steiner. Rudolf Steiner was an Austrian philosopher and esotericist who spread non-Catholic, secular, "spiritual" ideas. Fr. Angelo Roncalli was called before his superiors and ordered to stop teaching Modernism.[178] He was then sent to Bulgaria on a diplomatic mission.

Fr. Angelo Roncalli also kept close acquaintances with well-known and excommunicated Modernists, including Ernesto Buonaiuti, excommunicated for heresy in 1926.[179]

When Fr. Roncalli was made a cardinal, he chose to have his red hat placed on his head by the atheistic and anti-clerical president of France, Vincent Auriol.[j]

Condoning The Once Forbidden Games

Old Testament: As we can see from the previous Scripture passages, Jason brought the Greek games into Jerusalem.

Church History: Just as Jason brought the Greek games into Jerusalem, so did John XXIII witness the Olympics in Rome in 1960. He came out into St. Peter's Square in 1960 and blessed all the Olympic athletes present and the Olympic crowds. There is no evidence to suggest that he had anything to do with bringing the Olympics to Rome, but it does not appear to be a coincidence that the Olympics, which the Church had banned for over 1500 years, made their first ever appearance in Rome under the reign of John XXIII.

---

j   There are extant images of this event readily accessible online.

Appeasement To The Evil Persecutors

Old Testament: Jason was a sympathizer with the Greek Seleucids. He wanted to be on good terms with them.

Church History: The Second Vatican Council, guided by John XXIII, was known for its absolute silence concerning Communism. The Vatican's position towards Communism following the Second Vatican Council can be seen in the Vatican's policy of *Ostpolitik*, which tried to appease the Communists instead of confronting them.[180]

Furthermore, at social functions in Paris, the then Fr. Angelo Roncalli would socialize with the Soviet ambassador, M. Bogomolov[181], despite the Soviet Union's brutal extermination policy of Catholics at the time. Indeed, there is a stark difference between the courageous and outspoken opposition to Communism by Pius XII and the stance of John XXIII. Thus, just as Jason was a sympathizer with the Seleucids, it also appears that John XXIII sympathized with the Communists.

Look at this quote from the books of the Machabees regarding the relationship between the Hellenizing Jews and the Seleucid Greeks. Remember the murder of Catholics by Communists throughout Eastern Europe and the Soviet Union, and keep in mind the parallels between the Communists and the Seleucids.

> "And setting nought by the honours of their fathers, they (the Hellenizing Jews) esteemed the Grecian glories for the best: For the sake of which they incurred a dangerous contention, and followed earnestly their ordinances, and in all things they coveted to be like them, who were their enemies and murderers."
>
> - 2 Machabees 4: 15-16

God's Holy House Is Stripped of Ornaments

ANTIOCHUS STRIPS THE TEMPLE OF BEAUTY AND TRADITION, AND CATHOLIC CHURCHES ARE STRIPPED OF HOLY PICTURES AND STATUES

Old Testament: Following the Hellenizing efforts of the high priest Jason, King Antiochus IV (the Seleucid king) came to the Temple in Jerusalem and stripped it of all its ornaments and sacred vessels. Then, he broke all the ornaments and vessels into pieces.

> "And after Antiochus had ravaged Egypt in the hundred and forty-third year, he returned and went up against Israel. And he went up to Jerusalem with a great multitude. And he proudly entered into the sanctuary, and took away the golden altar, and the candlestick of light, and all the vessels thereof, and the table of proposition, and the pouring vessels, and the vials, and the little mortars of gold, and the veil, and the crowns, and the golden ornament that was before the Temple: and he broke them all in pieces. And he took the silver and gold, and the precious vessels: and he took the hidden treasures which he found: and when he had taken all away he departed into his own country."
>
> - 1 Machabees 1: 21-24

Church History: In the years following the Second Vatican Council (which was called and overseen by John XXIII and Paul VI) many changes occurred in Catholic churches worldwide. One of the most notable changes was to the interior of church buildings. To varying degrees, depending on the diocese or country:

- Statues were removed
- Tabernacles were moved off to the side or into adjoining rooms
- Altar rails were removed
- Ornate traditional altars were removed
- In many churches, kneelers were removed
- Classical religious art was removed and replaced with modern art

- Sacred vessels made of precious metal were replaced with profane vessels made of ceramic, wood, or glass
- Floor plans were re-arranged

There are many other examples of this radical and sudden stripping of the traditional Catholic ornamentation in churches across the world. The destruction of churches after the Second Vatican Council was given a name: *wreckovation*. This word captures the horror of the changes that were made to sacred places. Some statues were intentionally smashed by those who wanted to erase the past, just as Antiochus did in 1 Machabees 1: 21-24.

Women Thrust Themselves into the Sanctuary

Women Inserted Themselves into the Temple Holy Places, and Women Insisted on New Roles

Old Testament: During the time of the desecration of the Temple by Antiochus, Sacred Scripture says that women "thrust themselves" into the holy places of the Temple.

> "And women thrust themselves of their own accord into the holy places, and brought in things that were not lawful. The altar also was filled with unlawful things, which were forbidden by the laws."
>
> - 2 Machabees 6: 4-5

Church History: After the Second Vatican Council and the new rite of Paul VI, women started to perform tasks in the sanctuary. In most mainstream parishes, these new roles were usually the positions of lector, extraordinary minister, or, later on in the 1990s, the altar girl. More rarely seen, but not uncommon, was the new role of the liturgical dancer.

Growing up attending the rite of Paul VI, I invariably overheard or was party to conversations concerning the liturgy, especially the older and more involved I became in my parish. I remember the extensive discussions about altar girls. The parents who advocated for their daughters to become altar girls were very forceful and persistent. They wanted to challenge the old rule that excluded girls. In these ways, women thrust themselves into the holy places.

Sacred Vessels Are Given Away

MENELAUS SELLS OR GIVES AWAY SACRED VESSELS, AND PAUL VI GIVES AWAY THE PAPAL TIARA AND PAPAL RING

Old Testament: After Jason obtained the high priesthood by paying money to the Greek Seleucid King Antiochus IV, he introduced Greek religion and practices into Jerusalem. But what can be bought by one can also be bought by another. Just as Jason obtained the position of high priest through bribery, it was likewise taken away from him. Another Jew, named Menelaus, offered to pay more than Jason, and Antiochus IV granted him the office of high priest instead.

In doing so, Menelaus implicitly admitted the power and authority (albeit false authority) of King Antiochus IV over himself and the Temple. Menelaus took sacred vessels from the Temple and sold them.

> "But he [Menelaus] being recommended to the king, when he had magnified the appearance of his power, got the high priesthood for himself, by offering more than Jason by three hundred talents of silver. So having received the king's mandate, he returned bringing nothing worthy of the high priesthood: but having the mind of a cruel tyrant, and the rage of a savage beast."
>
> - 2 Machabees 4: 24-25

> "Then Menelaus, supposing that he had found a convenient time, having stolen certain vessels of gold out of the Temple, gave them to Andronicus and others he had sold at Tyre and in the neighboring cities."
>
> - 2 Machabees 4: 32

Church History: Following the death of John XXIII in June of 1963, Giovanni Battista Montini was elected, taking the name Paul VI. At the end of the second session of the Second Vatican Council in 1964, Paul VI formally relinquished the papal tiara. Just as Menelaus took sacred vessels and sold them, so did Paul VI sell the papal tiara. He announced in 1964 that the papal tiara would be sold and the proceeds given to the poor. Cardinal Spellman and American Catholics purchased the tiara. Since the selling of the papal tiara, it has never been worn again.

Furthermore, in October of 1964, Paul VI gave away his papal cross and papal ring to the United Nations as a sign of tribute and deference to their authority. He gave a speech in front of the United Nations General Assembly in which he praised the United Nations and even asked their permission to carry out his work at the Vatican.

Paul VI first conveyed to the United Nations that the papacy was not in competition with any sovereign nation and that he disavowed any desire for temporal power for the Church. Then Paul VI went on to say that he has nothing to ask of the United Nations other than "being allowed to serve" them.[182]

Further in the speech, Paul VI praised the United Nations as the "last hope for peace and harmony in the world". He then offered his "tribute of honor and hope" to the United Nations.[182]

Summary

The papacy was established by Our Lord Jesus Christ to be His direct representative on Earth and to be the head of His Mystical Body, the Catholic Church. No power on Earth or under the Earth has greater authority than the papacy.

Thus, just as Menelaus deferred to the authority of the pagan Greek king Antiochus, so too did Paul VI when he handed over the papal tiara, his papal cross, and papal ring. He gave his cross and ring to the United Nations, praising them as the last hope for peace on Earth.

Profane "Sacrifice" Is Mandated

THE ABOMINATION OF DESOLATION AND THE NOVUS ORDO RITE

These parallels demonstrate the omnipotence and glory of God. They also give us a deeper understanding of recent Church history. Those who love the Church and are confused with the current circumstances can draw some answers from these parallels, objectively understood. If Church history really is prefigured by the Old Testament, in the same chronological order, then it is certain that God has allowed or caused this. If God has done this, then please carefully consider this next topic about the *abomination of desolation*.

Some Background Info

The reign of Antiochus IV was the worst persecution that the Jews had ever endured. The Jews had their Temple destroyed by King Nabuchodonosor and were carried into exile in Babylon, but they probably never imagined that God would have allowed a pagan Greek king to enter their Temple and take it over from the inside. It's one thing to destroy the Temple, but it's another to turn the Temple into the center of pagan Greek worship.

In summary, King Antiochus IV stripped the Temple of its ornaments and beauty. Then, he erected a new, second altar, over and against God's altar in the Temple's very heart. On this new, second altar, he performed an unholy sacrifice. Then, he outlawed the traditional Jewish religion and mandated that everyone perform his new sacrifice. Anyone who remained in Jerusalem had to either capitulate to the Greek king or die.

Old Testament: After having stripped the Temple, Antiochus IV went even further in his profanation of God's holy religion. On the fifteenth day of the month of Kislev (Casleu), King Antiochus IV erected a new, second altar right on top of the traditional altar. On this new and second altar, he performed a pagan sacrifice that was profane to the Jews. He placed an idol there as well. We will get to that idol in upcoming pages.

The new sacrifice on the second altar, along with the idol, is called the *abomination of desolation* in the text. Of course, the abomination of desolation has immense significance.

> "And on the fifteenth day of the month Casleu, in the hundred and forty-fifth year, king Antiochus set up the abominable idol of desolation upon the altar of God, and they built altars throughout all the cities of Juda round about:"

> "And on the twenty-fifth day of the month they sacrificed upon the altar of the idol that was over against the altar of God."

> - 1 Machabees 1: 57, 62

In verse 57, it mentions the idol placed on the altar of God, but in verse 62, it says that there was a new and second altar for the idol, and it was on that new and second altar that the profane sacrifice was performed.

Church History: Sometime after "the changes" following the Second Vatican Council (changes such as statues being removed, tabernacles moved to the side, modern art, etc.), Paul VI announced a new rite to be used in Latin Rite Catholic churches.

In addition to the new rite, a new and second "altar" was erected in virtually every Catholic church worldwide. The Catholic churches constructed before the Second Vatican Council all had the traditional Catholic altar, almost always against the back wall. The priest would say the Holy Mass facing the altar, leading the faithful behind him. Sometime after the council, a new and second altar was constructed in these churches. In some cases, the back altar was taken out, while in other cases, the back altar remained. We will examine the churches built after the Second Vatican Council because they share in specific Old Testament parallels as well.

The new rite of Paul VI is only performed on the new, second altar, not the traditional Catholic altar.

At the time of the promulgation of this new rite, there was a great deal of concern about it. Cardinal Alfredo Ottaviani issued a letter on September 25, 1969, signed by many concerned clerics. This document was called *The Ottaviani Intervention* and was addressed to Paul VI. It communicated grave concerns with the new rite.

1. The Novus Ordo Rite is a significant departure from Session 22 of the Council of Trent.[183]

2. The Novus Ordo Rite does not mention a word about the priest as the one offering a sacrifice. Instead, the impression is given that the priest is like a Protestant minister.[183]

3. Changing a liturgical tradition that united Catholics for 400 years with a new one that allows many deviations and errors is a huge mistake.[183][k]

Cardinal Ottaviani resigned from his position in the Roman Curia on January 8, 1968.

The Ottaviani Intervention referenced the Council of Trent. In the mid-1500s, the Council of Trent codified the Catholic Mass. Pope St. Pius V reached back as far into Catholic history as possible and retrieved the Catholic Mass from ancient days. He then codified the Catholic Mass, giving it specific rubrics and prayers that now applied universally to the Catholic Church. This was possible because of the new invention of the printing press. The Catholic Mass remained in this state from the Council of Trent until modern times.

The Fifteenth Of Kislev

Another striking parallel is the date this new rite was finally and universally mandated. Paul VI first signed and officially promulgated this new rite on April 3, 1969. However, the Tridentine Catholic Mass was not formally outlawed as of 1969. The Tridentine Mass was still permitted if bishops worldwide wished until translations were prepared for the new rite.

---

k   https://archive.org/details/ottavianiinterve0000otta/mode/2up

Remember, the Tridentine Rite was only in Latin, but the new rite would be in the local language, thus necessitating many different translations.

Paul VI finally and universally mandated that all dioceses use the new rite by November 28, 1971.[184] After that date, bishops were no longer allowed to have the Tridentine Rite in their diocese and were required to use the new rite.

If you convert the date of November 28, 1971, into a date on the Jewish calendar, it is remarkably close to the fifteenth of Kislev. If you recall from 1 Machabees 1:57, the fifteenth of Kislev is the date on which Antiochus IV erected the second altar. He sacrificed on that altar on the twenty-fifth of Kislev. November 28, 1971, is the closest Sunday to the fifteenth of Kislev possible, without going past the Jewish calendar date.

New Churches And New Altars

Old Testament: Once Antiochus IV set up the abomination of desolation in the Jewish Temple, he had new altars constructed around the province of Juda. The purpose of the new altars was to create designated worship sites for the newly mandated pagan sacrifices of Antiochus.

The text of Sacred Scripture does not indicate such, but given the Hellenization of the ancient world, it is likely these altars were built in the Greek style.

> "On the fifteenth day of the month Casleu, in the hundred and forty-fifth year, king Antiochus set up the abominable idol of desolation upon the altar of God, and they built altars throughout all the cities of Juda round about:"
>
> - 1 Machabees 1: 57

Church History: Following the mandated implementation of the new rite of Paul VI, new, modern churches began popping up worldwide. Many were built with Greek amphitheater seating instead of the traditional straight-lined pews from front to back. The architecture of these new churches is usually overemphasized in some way, lacking majesty and beauty.

The altar area is their most important aspect. In every single new modern church, there is one "altar," the one designated explicitly for the new rite of Paul VI. None of them possess the traditional Catholic altar. Upon reflection, these new churches are designed and constructed specifically for the new, mandated rite of Paul VI.

The Uprising Begins in the Hills with the Old Priest

MATHATHIAS FLEES TO THE HILLS OF JUDA; ARCHBISHOP MARCEL LEFEBVRE FLEES TO THE ALPS

Faithful Flee To The Hills

Old Testament: Antiochus IV had placed the abomination of desolation and then sacrificed on the new, second altar in the Temple. This sacrilege, along with the forced apostasy of the Jews, caused faithful Jews to flee to the hills west of the city. It was from the hill town of Modin that the old priest Mathathias launched his uprising.

Church History: After the promulgation of the new rite of Paul VI, any clerics, bishops, or cardinals in Rome who opposed the reforms of Paul VI and the Second Vatican Council had to either go along with the changes or were removed. However, in 1969-1970, a group of seminarians in Rome approached a senior and experienced bishop and asked him to open a new seminary that would form priests as traditional Catholics, rejecting the novelties of the Second Vatican Council.

The name of this bishop was Marcel Lefebvre. He had previously spent decades in West Africa as a missionary, and was looking forward to retirement. However, he agreed to open a seminary to preserve Catholic teaching and the 1962 Rite of Mass. He opened this new seminary near the town of Econe, high up in the Swiss Alps.

Representatives Sent To Compel Faithful To The New Sacrifice

Old Testament: King Antiochus IV sent a representative to the town of Modin, in the hills of Juda, to compel those who had fled there to perform the new sacrifice of Antiochus. The king's representative first approached Mathathias and asked him to be the first to fulfill the king's decree.

> "And they that were sent from king Antiochus came thither, to compel them that were fled into the city of Modin, to sacrifice, and to burn incense, and to depart from the law of God. And many of the people of Israel consented and came to them: but Mathathias and his sons stood firm. And they that were sent from Antiochus, answering, said to Mathathias: Thou art a ruler, and an honourable, and great man in this city, and adorned with sons, and brethren. Therefore come thou first, and obey the king's commandment, as all nations have done, and the men of Juda, and they that remain in Jerusalem: and thou, and thy sons, shall be in the number of the king's friends, and enriched with gold, and silver, and many presents."

1 Machabees 2: 15-18

Church History: The new seminary in Econe, Switzerland grew in size and scope. In November 1970, Bishop François Charrière of Fribourg (bishop of the diocese in which Econe was located) established the International Priestly Society of St. Pius X. This new Society, which is called the SSPX (Society of St. Pius X), was an organization of priests who, for the most part, were ordained in Econe by Archbishop Lefebvre. Clerics who did not want to participate in the changes of the Second Vatican Council and the new rite of Paul VI were welcome.

In 1972, the bishops of France came together to condemn the SSPX seminary as a "rebel seminary,"[185] refusing to accept any of its seminarians. Cardinal Vilot also accused Archbishop Lefebvre of rebellion against Paul VI. In following years, the Vatican would sent various visitors to Econe to persuade the SSPX to adopt the reforms of the Second Vatican Council.

Defied The King's Decree

Old Testament: Mathathias boldly and loudly defied the king's decree to perform the profane sacrifice. He killed the king's representative and then cried out in a loud voice that if anyone wished to preserve their sacred religion, they should follow him. Together, they fled into the hills to establish their camp.

> "Then Mathathias answered and said with a loud voice: Although all nations obey king Antiochus, so as to depart every man from the service of the law of his fathers and consent to his commandments: I and my sons, and my brethren will obey the law of our fathers. God be merciful unto us: it is not profitable for us to forsake the law and the justices of God. We will not hearken to the words of King Antiochus, neither will we sacrifice and transgress the commandments of our law to go another way."

> "And Mathathias cried out in the city with a loud voice, saying: Everyone that hath zeal for the law, and maintaineth the testament, let him follow me. So he and his sons fled into the mountains and left all that they had in the city."

1 Machabees 2: 19-22, 27-28

Church History: In 1975-1976, the Vatican arranged as many as six separate visits to inspect the seminary in Econe, Switzerland. Archbishop Lefebvre reported the Vatican visitors as being liberal. They made statements in favor of married priests and other revolutionary ideas. It is also reported that they conveyed to Archbishop Lefebvre that, even though his seminary opposed the novelties of Second Vatican Council, if only he would use the Novus Ordo Missae (new rite of Paul VI) one time, then the Vatican would overlook the rest, and all would be well again.[1] Archbishop Lefebvre refused to use the Novus Ordo Missae even one time.

---

1 Recounting the summer of 1976, the Vatican visitations, and Archbishop Lefebvre's refusal to say even one "Novus Ordo". (https://sspx.org/en/hot-summer-1976-and-archbishop-lefebvre)

Brought Back Religion To The People

Old Testament: Mathathias led the rebellion against King Antiochus. Together with his followers, they reconquered many cities and towns around Jerusalem and brought the Jewish religion back to the people in defiance of the king. However, Mathathias was growing old and was about to die. He gathered his five sons together and passed on the rebellion to them. Judas Machabeus assumed leadership of the uprising. Mathathias was buried in the hill town of Modin, where the rebellion had started.

> "And Mathathias and his friends went round about, and they threw down the altars: And they circumcised all the children whom they found in the confines of Israel that were uncircumcised: and they did valiantly. And they pursued after the children of pride, and the work prospered in their hands: And they recovered the law out of the hands of the nations, and out of the hands of the kings: and they yielded not the horn to the sinner. Now the days drew near that Mathathias should die, and he said to his sons: Now hath pride and chastisement gotten strength, and the time of destruction, and the wrath of indignation: Now, therefore, O my sons, be ye zealous for the law, and give your lives for the covenant of your fathers. And call to remembrance the works of the fathers, which they have done in their generations: and you shall receive great glory, and an everlasting name. "

> "You, therefore, my sons, take courage and behave manfully in the law: for by it you shall be glorious. And behold, I know that your brother Simon is a man of counsel: give ear to him always, and he shall be a father to you. And Judas Machabeus who is valiant and strong from his youth up, let him be the leader of your army, and he shall manage the war of the people. And you shall take to you all that observe the law: and revenge ye the wrong of your people. Render to the Gentiles their reward, and take heed to the precepts of the law. And he blessed them, and was joined to his fathers. And he died in the hundred and forty-sixth year: and he was

buried by his sons in the sepulchres of his fathers in Modin, and all Israel mourned for him with great mourning."

- 1 Machabees 2: 45-51, 64-70

Church History: Years passed, and Archbishop Lefebvre and the Vatican continued to have disagreements. Paul VI suspended Archbishop Lefebvre, who continued his work in Econe.

The situation came to a head in 1988. Archbishop Lefebvre was advancing in years and facing declining health. He needed bishops for the SSPX to carry on his work after he died. If the SSPX lacked a bishop, it would be unable to ordain new priests, leading to its eventual extinction.

In defiance of Rome, on June 30, 1988, Archbishop Lefebvre personally consecrated four new bishops to carry on the work of the SSPX. John Paul II "excommunicated" him and the four new bishops for this act. Archbishop Lefebvre died three years later, in 1991, and was buried in Econe Switzerland.

In the years between 1969 and 1988, the SSPX grew in popularity. Many Catholics who were upset with the bizarre changes in Catholic parishes were delighted to know that they could attend a non-Novus Ordo Rite. The SSPX opened up chapels throughout the region and eventually throughout the whole world.

It must be noted the SSPX was not the only organization in the world that resisted the changes of the Second Vatican Council. Indeed, there are others who also share this parallel with the Old Testament Mathathias. However, it does seem to me that Archbishop Lefebvre was the most well-known and was the primary parallel with Mathathias. In upcoming parallels, however, we will see that neither the Machabees nor the SSPX retained their initial ideology. Both accept compromise with their former enemies.

SUMMARY:

- Mathathias and Archbishop Lefebvre were both old and honored priests. They were both approached by a representative of the "king" and asked to perform the new sacrifice. They both refused and started a rebellion to bring the traditional religion back to the people.

- Mathathias and Archbishop Lefebvre both established their group in the hills; Mathathias in the hills of Juda and Archbishop Lefebvre in the Alps of Switzerland.

- The word *Machabees* means *hammer* in Hebrew. Amazingly, the name *Marcel* is a French form of the Latin name *Martellus,* which also means *hammer.*

- Mathathias and Archbishop Lefebvre were both old and in declining health. They each passed on their work to their sons. Mathathias passed it on to his natural sons, and Archbishop Lefebvre consecrated four bishops from among the priests he ordained. Thus, they were his spiritual sons.

When the Jews saw the abomination of desolation in the Temple, faithful Jews fled to the mountains to join the Machabees. Thus, by parallel, when Catholics saw the new rite of Paul VI, they fled to the Alps to join up with Archbishop Lefebvre and the SSPX. This is what so many men did, who were called to the priesthood, but rejected the Novus Ordo and the changes of the Second Vatican Council.

Do Not Let Those In Jerusalem Know About The Revolt

Old Testament: This is my speculation, but I think you would agree it is likely. King Antiochus IV and the Greek Seleucids would have probably not publicized the actions of the Machabees to the Jews who remained in Jerusalem.

If you recall, any Jews who remained in Jerusalem had to comply with the new decrees of Antiochus. Thus, it would have been to Antiochus's advantage to try to keep the news of the Machabean uprising away from the Jews in Jerusalem, lest any of them be inspired to rise up and join them. The Greeks, who had one hundred percent control of Jerusalem, would have employed as much "spin" and "fake news" as possible to diminish the growing popularity of the Machabean uprising outside of Jerusalem.

Church History: I was born in the late 1970s. I went to a parochial school and a Catholic high school. I grew up attending the new rite of Paul VI, and I never knew anything different. In high school, I never once heard of Traditional Catholicism.[m] Years later, when my wife and I had a conversion at Lourdes, we became very interested in our Catholic Faith. We would devour anything we could find concerning the Catholic Faith, and yet, unbelievably, we never heard of Traditional Catholicism. It did not appear on any Novus Ordo media platform, magazine, or parish bulletin. It was as if it did not exist.

It was only many years later that I first learned about it, but even then, I was given a very poor impression and told to stay away. Therefore, you can imagine my shock when I first started seeing these parallels in the books of the Machabees. Just like how the Greeks would have downplayed the Machabees to those in Jerusalem, so too did all mainstream Novus Ordo sources omit any mention of, downplay, or denigrate Traditional Catholicism.

Taking Back The Temple

Now let's explore an interesting occurrence in which Traditional Catholics commandeered a beautiful Catholic church in downtown Paris, Saint-Nicolas-du-Chardonnet. This story shares many parallels with the Machabees taking back their Temple by force. But first, let's recap the significant events of the Temple takeover so far:

Old Testament: If you recall from previous pages:

- King Antiochus IV acted together with Hellenizing Jews to bring pagan practices to Jerusalem and to promote them among the people.

- King Antiochus IV soon came to Jerusalem and stripped the Temple of its ornaments, smashing them to pieces.

---

m   I recognize the growing divergence of agreement among Catholics as to what constitutes Traditional Catholicism. For the purpose of this book, I use this term in a general sense, to mean any Catholic group that has substantially rejected the novelties of the Second Vatican Council.

- King Antiochus IV erected a second altar over and against the altar of God, on which he placed the abomination of desolation and performed a new, pagan sacrifice on that second altar.

- King Antiochus IV outlawed traditional Jewish worship and religion, and he mandated that all Jews perform his new, pagan sacrifice.

- The king sent a representative to the Jews who had fled to the hills in the small town of Modin. He compelled them to perform the king's new sacrifice. One old priest named Mathathias openly and boldly refused. Mathathias started a rebellion to keep the Jewish religion alive and led his followers into the hills. He was old, so before he died, he passed on the rebellion to his sons, the Machabees.

- The Machabees fought a guerrilla war against the overwhelmingly large Greek forces. The Machabees fought brilliantly and succeeded in eventually taking back their Temple. They re-dedicated the Temple after its profanation by the Greeks.

Here are some selected verses from the book of Machabees to tell us about re-taking the Jewish Temple:

> "Then Judas, and his brethren said: Behold our enemies are discomfited: let us go up now to cleanse the holy places and to repair them. And all the army assembled together, and they went up into mount Sion. And they saw the sanctuary desolate, and the altar profaned, and the gates burnt, and shrubs growing up in the courts as in a forest, or on the mountains, and the chambers joining to the Temple thrown down. And they rent their garments, and made great lamentation, and put ashes on their heads: And they fell face down to the ground on their faces, and they sounded with the trumpets of alarm, and they cried towards heaven."

> "Then they took whole stones according to the law, and built a new altar according to the former: And they built up the holy places, and the things that were within the Temple: and

they sanctified the Temple, and the courts. And they made new holy vessels, and brought in the candlestick, and the altar of incense, and the table into the Temple. And they put incense upon the altar, and lighted up the lamps that were upon the candlestick, and they gave light in the Temple. And they set the loaves upon the table, and hung up the veils, and finished all the works that they had begun to make. And they arose before the morning on the five and twentieth day of the ninth month (which is the month of Casleu) in the hundred and forty-eighth year. And they offered sacrifice according to the law upon the new altar of holocausts which they had made."

1 Machabees 4: 36-40, 47-53

Church History: If you recall from previous pages:

- John XXIII called the Second Vatican Council, after which many Catholic traditions and practices were discontinued, and new modern "experiments" were ushered into parishes across the world.

- In the years following the Second Vatican Council, Catholic Church ornaments, statues, and pious paintings were smashed or otherwise removed.

- In 1969, the new rite of Paul VI was signed and officially promulgated. By November 28, 1971, every parish worldwide had to use the new rite of Paul VI, and the Tridentine Rite of Mass was effectively outlawed.

- The new rite of Paul VI was only performed on the new, second altars erected in every parish worldwide.

- Archbishop Lefebvre refused to perform even one rite of Paul VI. Resistance coalesced around him, and he started a seminary for Traditional Catholics in the Alps. He was old, and before he died, he consecrated four bishops to carry on his organization's work.

- The SSPX did not spread through the Catholic diocesan system. Their finances were limited, so they had to improvise and spread unconventionally. The Vatican made it a solemn point to ensure that no parish church building ever ended up in the hands of Traditional Catholics. So, the SSPX was forced to buy old Protestant churches or other non-conventional buildings and convert them into chapels to provide the 1962 Rite of Mass to the faithful around the world.

One exception to this, however, occurred early on during the history of the SSPX. On February 27, 1977, a Catholic priest named Fr. François Ducaud-Bourget led hundreds of lay members of the SSPX into a literal takeover of a big, beautiful Catholic church in Paris.

Fr. François Ducaud-Bourget had refused to say the Novus Ordo since its inception in 1969. He continued to say the Traditional Mass undetected by his local bishop for years at a small chapel in a local hospital. However, so many people were disenfranchised by the Novus Ordo Rite that word spread quickly about Fr. François Ducaud-Bourget. His group grew so big that he was forced to find another location. He asked Archbishop Lefebvre what to do, and he was given the reply, "Go find a church".

So, on February 27, 1977, his group of Catholics simply walked in and occupied the church of Saint-Nicolas-du-Chardonnet in Paris. They escorted the diocesan Novus Ordo priest to the door. Upon the death of Fr. François Ducaud-Bourget, the church was turned over to the SSPX, which has kept it ever since. It is the flagship church of the SSPX in Paris and a beautiful church building.

Just like the Machabees when they took over the Temple, the SSPX had to remove the second altar and make other modifications to the church building after it having been used by the Novus Ordo for the last seven years. The church building had to be re-consecrated or re-dedicated again, just like the Temple in the Old Testament.

The Changer of Times, Laws, and Seasons

ANTIOCHUS IV EPIPHANES CHANGES THE RELIGION OF THE JEWS
AND JOHN PAUL II CHANGES VIRTUALLY EVERY FACET OF
CATHOLICISM

Came From The Seleucids (Communists)

Old Testament: King Antiochus IV was a Seleucid Greek.

Church History: John Paul II rose through the ranks of the Church even when Communism was engaging in harsh anti-Catholic initiatives in Poland. During this time, the Polish Communist government had programs in place, one of which was called *Patriot Priests*, which rewarded Catholic priests who cooperated with Communist authorities.[186] Any priest who cooperated with the Communists was allowed to communicate with and travel to Rome, as well as being granted other liberties. During this time as well, the Communists were placing agents into the seminaries as spies/informants and also as long-term "plants" that would advance through the Church hierarchy and undermine the Church from within. Recall the parallels between the Communists and the Seleucids previously identified.

The King From The North

Old Testament: King Antiochus IV descended from the north. In Biblical prophecy, there is a term, *the king from the north*, and it applies to the Seleucids,[n] who came from the north and profaned Jerusalem and the Temple.

But, King Antiochus IV had the way prepared for him by Hellenizing Jews who were from the land of Juda but sympathized with Greek ideas/religion/culture. Two of the most prominent Hellenizing Jews usurped the role of high priest in the Temple: Jason and Menelaus. Again, refer to previously identified parallels.

Church History: John Paul II came from Poland, north of Rome. He was the first non-Italian to reign as king of the Vatican for over 400 years.

---

n   See the Douay-Rheims Bible, book of Daniel, Chapter 11 and explanatory footnotes.

The public actions of John Paul II would have caused a great uproar if they had been performed in the late 1950s, such as the *World Day of Prayer* in Assisi in 1986. However, just like Antiochus, who had the way prepared for him by the Hellenizing high priests Jason and Menelaus, so too did John Paul II have the way prepared for him by the Second Vatican Council and the conditioning of John XXIII and Paul VI, both of whom were Italians, just as Jason and Menelaus were Judeans. Both John XXIII and Paul VI wore the papal tiara. John Paul II never wore the papal tiara.

Apparently, both John XXIII and Paul VI were special in the eyes of John Paul II since he took both of their names into his name: John Paul.

Premature Death Of The King Before Him

Old Testament: For him to become the sole king, it is hypothesized that Antiochus IV killed the younger heir and rightful king of Seleucia. This child shared the same name: Antiochus, although due to his premature death, he was not given a number designation, such as III or IV.[187]°

Church History: Mysteriously and suddenly, John Paul I died after reigning for thirty-three days.[188] He is speculated to have been murdered because he wished to reform the Vatican Bank. I can offer no proof that he was murdered, but instead point out that if he was murdered, it mirrors the death of the infant Antiochus.

John Paul I made history by adopting two names simultaneously—a departure from the tradition unanimously followed in Church history. Typically, popes were known by a single name, such as Innocent, Clement,

---

o   The claim that the infant Antiochus was assassinated by his uncle, Antiochus IV, originates from the Babylonian astronomical diaries. Unfortunately, I could not access these diaries to verify the assertion cited by Grainger. However, there exists a work titled "New Information on Antiochus IV from Babylonian Astronomical Diaries" by M. J. Geller, published in the *Bulletin of the School of Oriental and African Studies*, University of London (Vol. 54, No. 1, 1991, pp. 1-4). It is presumed that this work by Geller contains the minute details I seek—specifically, whether Antiochus IV *could* have been responsible for the sudden and unexpected death of the infant Antiochus. Given ample historical examples of corrupt and ambitious kings, we may safely assume this possibility. Antiochus IV was known for his ruthlessness. The mysterious demise of the infant Antiochus, aligned with his interests, provide enough context for the speculation of his guilt.

or Pius. However, John Paul I broke this norm. Not only did he choose two names, but he also insisted on being called *the first*.

In all other cases (as far as I am aware), when a pope selected a new and previously unused name, he refrained from labeling himself as *the first*. For instance, the initial pope to adopt the name *Pius* did not refer to himself as "Pope Pius the First". Instead, he was simply known as "Pope Pius". It was only later, when another pope chose the same name, that the original Pope Pius received the suffix "the first," retroactively acknowledging his precedence. The fact that John Paul I insisted on being called "the first" presupposed he was anticipating another would come along after him and take that same exact, and very unusual, double name of John Paul.

It is interesting to note that the infant Antiochus was not given a number designation after his name. He reigned for just a short time before he was allegedly murdered by Antiochus IV. The infant Antiochus shared the same name as his successor, Antiochus IV. In similar fashion, John Paul I gave himself a number designation when all previous practice was not to do so. He also reigned a very short time before his alleged murder. He shared the same name as his successor, John Paul II.

Changer Of Times, Laws, And Seasons

Old Testament: King Antiochus IV took over the Temple in Jerusalem. From his seat in Jerusalem, he outlawed the religion of the Jews. He changed all the laws and practices of the Jews, including dietary laws, laws of worship, and many other religious laws. By his decrees, Antiochus IV forced the Jews to abandon their religion.

Church History: John Paul II altered virtually every aspect of the Catholic Faith during his reign. He:

- Issued a new catechism to reflect the teachings of the Second Vatican Council

- Issued a new code of canon law to reflect the teachings of the Second Vatican Council

- Added a new group of mysteries to the rosary

- Started World Youth Day

- Allowed altar girls

- "Apologized" for the "past sins" of the Church[189]

- Renegotiated the Lateran Treaty to remove the privileged place of Catholicism in Italian state-run education

- Prayed in a Mosque; received the "sign of Shiva" on his forehead by a Hindu priestess; drank a potion prepared by pagans in Papua New Guinea; "dotted the eyes of the lion," which was a pagan practice in the Solomon Islands; was "blessed" by a Native American witch doctor; and committed many more acts of apostasy from the Catholic Faith

- Universally established the new devotion of *Divine Mercy*, even after the Holy Office had placed it on the forbidden book list in 1959

- Gave a new teaching on sex/marriage called *The Theology of the Body*, based on the new teachings on Christian marriage given at the Second Vatican Council. The two ends of marriage were re-arranged. Before the council, the two ends of marriage were hierarchical. Procreation was placed over and was superior to the second end: mutual aid of the spouses. The council document, *Gaudium et Spes* placed these two ends on equal footing.

Treasury Robbed

Old Testament: During the time of Antiochus, the Jewish Temple was robbed repeatedly, and its money and other wealth were taken by the Seleucids.[p]

Church History: During the reign of John Paul II, in 1982, the Vatican Bank was involved in a great scandal that included the Italian Mafia and a leading Italian Freemasonic Lodge called P2. This was called the *P2 scandal*, in which the Vatican Bank lost the equivalent of $200 to $250 million. This is still shrouded in mystery by the murder of journalist Mino Pecorelli and banker Roberto Calvi and by the intrigues of powerful men.[190]

---

p   See 2 Machabees 5:15-21 and 1 Machabees 1:20-24 among other passages

Fought Against The Faithful Rebels

Old Testament: Antiochus IV almost successfully destroyed the Jewish religion, except for the rebellion of Mathathias and the Machabees. At first, Antiochus IV reached out to Mathathias, but after Mathathias' rigid and unwavering stance to preserve the traditions and laws of his Jewish fathers, Antiochus IV sought to kill Mathathias instead.

Church History: Under John Paul II, the Vatican discussed with Archbishop Lefebvre the possibility of providing the SSPX with a bishop for the society before the archbishop passed away. This is important because, without a bishop, the society would not be able to ordain priests and would die out. After many years of discussion, Archbishop Lefebvre was old and approaching death. It seemed that the Vatican had no interest in providing a bishop for the SSPX but was merely playing for time, waiting for him to die. Archbishop Lefebvre took the matter into his own hands and consecrated four bishops himself, thus guaranteeing the future of the society.

Immediately following this act by Archbishop Lefebvre, the Vatican quickly proclaimed him "excommunicated", forbidding Catholics from receiving Sacraments provided by the SSPX. What is unusual about this act of "excommunication" by the Vatican is the otherwise lenient reactions of the Vatican for nearly all other groups. It seems that Catholics who wanted to preserve Tradition were dealt a severe and swift retribution, but others who promoted abortion, who abused children, and taught all manner of heresy were left to continue their deeds relatively unhindered.

The Illustrious One

Old Testament: Antiochus IV is known along with the suffix *Epiphanes*, which can be translated as *The Illustrious One*.

Church History: John Paul II, almost immediately upon his death, was unofficially, but nonetheless popularly, given the suffix title *The Great*.

Puts Idol On The Altar

Old Testament: Antiochus IV put an idol on the Jewish altar.

Church History: The World Day of Prayer was organized by John Paul II in Assisi, in 1986. At this event, leaders of the world's religions were called together to offer "prayers" to their god/gods. Attending this event were Voodoos, Muslims, Hindus, Animists, Buddhists, Shinto, Jews, and many schismatic and heretical sects. At this world-historic event, John Paul II witnessed the placement of a statue of Buddha on the tabernacle of the church in Assisi in full view.[191]

Uprising Starts Good but Capitulates

THE MACHABEES START TO MAKE ALLIANCES WITH THEIR FORMER GREEK ENEMIES AND THE SOCIETY OF ST. PIUS X MAKES DEALS WITH THE VATICAN

Deal With Rome

After the death of their founder, Mathathias, the Machabees continued the fight against the Greeks. The Greek Seleucids had taken control of the city of Jerusalem, and even though the Machabees were able to win many battles and were able to bring the Jewish religion back to the Jews, still the Greeks were an overwhelming enemy with massive armies, vast resources, and an entire hellenized world that thought as they did.

The Machabees reached out to Rome and sought to ally with them. Rome promised the Machabees protection from their enemies. This treaty with Rome marked a shift in the Machabees' strategy and philosophy: away from fighting and towards that of diplomacy and political maneuvering. To achieve their aims, they started to play politics and gave up the burning, uncompromising zeal which they exhibited in the early part of their rebellion from the Greeks.

The Machabean rebellion can be broken down into distinct phases:

- Founding of the Machabean rebellion by Mathathias
- The Machabees fought vigorously against the Seleucids
- The Machabees were worn down by constant fighting
- The Machabees shifted to a more diplomatic stance

- The Romans took control of Judea/Jerusalem

Great Start To The Rebellion

Old Testament: After the death of Mathathias, the Machabean revolt was led by Judas Machabeus, who was an uncompromising and effective military leader. He defeated the Seleucid armies time and again, bringing the Jewish religion to any Jews who still wanted to practice it. At this point, the Seleucids and the Machabees were enemies.

Church History: Traditional Catholics witnessed the Modernism that had infected Rome and spread to all parishes across the world. Under effective leadership, the SSPX spread all over the world, bringing Traditional Catholicism back to Catholics. Very often, it was inconvenient for Traditional Catholics, who would have to drive long distances for Sunday Mass. Gone were the days of driving to your local parish.

During the years following the "excommunications" of 1988, the SSPX maintained a stance of opposition to the Vatican. The SSPX exhibited strong rhetoric against the Modernists in the Vatican.

Signs Of Weakening

Old Testament: After so many battles, the Machabees were showing signs that their fire was burning out. From the start of the Machabean uprising, the Machabees won battle after battle against overwhelming odds. God was with them, and He delivered them and gave them victory. But, towards the middle of the story, for the first time the Machabean fighters showed signs that "common sense" was starting to overcome their burning zeal and blind trust in God.

After the death of Antiochus, the Machabees reached out to the moderate, hellenized. apostate. usurper high priest in Jerusalem, Alcimus. The Machabees tried to establish friendly relations with the Greek general, Nicanor, through this diplomatic effort. It was not long before the friendship fell apart, and the Machabees fought and won another battle against the Seleucids, killing Nicanor. (1 Machabees 7)

The Machabees then reached out to Rome to make an alliance. The Romans agreed to come to the defense of the Machabees if they were threatened, and the Machabees agreed to support Rome if they needed assistance. This treaty with Rome never proved helpful to the Machabees. (1 Machabees 8)

At this point, the Machabees were besieged by another overwhelming Greek army. This time, however, the Machabean soldiers showed signs that they had lost some of their zealotry because, as the army approached, the Machabean warriors told Judas Machabeus that the Greek army was just too large and that they should retreat. About three-fourths of Judas' army fled, leaving Judas to stand and fight with only 800 men. Judas and his men were killed in battle. (1 Machabees 9)

Church History: After the death of John Paul II, Benedict XVI was elected. He was the new king of Vatican City and the new "high priest". Benedict XVI made many overtures to Traditional Catholics, including wearing papal garments that Paul VI, John Paul I, and John Paul II had abandoned. He projected a much more traditionally Catholic image by wearing such garments.

In July of 2007, Benedict XVI wrote a *Motu Proprio*, in which he famously permitted the Latin Rite of 1962 to be said in any diocese. On paper, this looked good. Traditional Catholics thought that they could now attend the Latin Rite of 1962 much closer to home. But, in reality, local bishops would set up many roadblocks, and very few Novus Ordo clerics even knew how to say the Latin Rite.[q]

But the SSPX saw the chance for diplomacy with Benedict XVI, who seemed like he could be a friend to them. In January 2009, after diplomatic efforts, Benedict XVI announced that he would lift the "excommunications" on the four SSPX bishops. This created a bizarre situation in which the SSPX appeared to be in canonical limbo. On the one hand, the SSPX was no longer

---

q Beyond the practical challenges, a deeper deception loomed over these Motu Masses. The crux lay in their potential invalidity, as they were administered by men ordained through the post-Second Vatican Council ordination rites.

"excommunicated", but on the other hand, voices in the Vatican were saying that they were still in an "irregular situation".

Just about the same time that Benedict XVI and the SSPX were becoming friendly, Swedish television aired a previously recorded interview of SSPX Bishop Williamson on January 21, 2009.

Bishop Williamson was on tape being asked questions about the Holocaust. He did not deny that Jews were targeted, but he did contest the asserted number of six million Jews. He referenced evidence supplied by contemporary investigations for his arguments.[192] Bishop Williamson also was vocally opposed to any deal with the Vatican. Because of Bishop Williamson's opposition to diplomacy and because he refused to retract his statement about the Holocaust, he was removed from the SSPX in 2012.

There are many parallels between Judas Machabeus and Bishop Williamson. Judas Machabeus was not afraid to face the vast numbers of Greeks, but his fellow soldiers thought there were just too many. They retreated, leaving Judas to face the vast numbers of enemy soldiers by himself. About three-fourths of the Jews retreated, leaving about one-fourth with Judas.

> "Now Judas had pitched his tents in Laisa, and **three thousand chosen men with him**: And they saw the multitude of the army that they were many, and they were seized with great fear: and many withdrew themselves out of the camp, and there remained of them no more than **eight hundred men**. And Judas saw that his army slipped away, and the battle pressed upon him, and his heart was cast down: because he had not time to gather them together, and he was discouraged. Then he said to them that remained: Let us arise, and go against our enemies, if we may be able to fight against them. But they dissuaded him, saying: We shall not be able, but let us save our lives now, and return to our brethren, and then we will fight against them: for we are but few. Then Judas said: God forbid we should do this thing,

and flee away from them: but if our time be come, let us die manfully for our brethren, and let us not stain our glory. "

- 1 Machabees 9: 5-10

Bishop Williamson was not afraid to question the high numbers of Holocaust victims. He thought that there were just too many. His fellow SSPX bishops could not take the heat that his comments were making around the world. They retreated and cut Bishop Williamson loose from the Society. There were four bishops, so by ejecting him, they retained three-fourths of their original numbers.

Accepts Title From The King

Old Testament: Upon the death of Judas Machabeus, his brother Jonathan, also the son of Mathathias, took over the leadership of the Machabees. Although Jonathan was a warrior like his brother Judas Machabeus, the strongest quality of Jonathan's leadership was his diplomacy. Jonathan took advantage of infighting among the Seleucids and was able to gain a high position inside the Seleucid Kingdom. Jonathan even received the title *friend of the king*:

> "And he commanded that Jonathan's garments should be taken off, and that he should be clothed with purple: and they did so. And the king made him sit by himself. And he said to his princes: Go out with him into the midst of the city, and make proclamation, that no man complain against him of any matter, and that no man trouble him for any manner of cause. So when his accusers saw his glory proclaimed, and him clothed with purple, they all fled away. And the king magnified him, and **enrolled him amongst his chief friends,** and made him governor and partaker of his dominion."

- 1 Machabees 10: 62-65

Thus, we have an ironic situation. If you recall, Mathathias refused to be "counted among the friends of the king" at the beginning of the story. His son

Jonathan, through his cooperation with the Seleucids, had just accepted the title "chief friend of the king".

Church History: After the expulsion of Bishop Williamson in 2012, the SSPX was free to pursue diplomatic discussions with the Vatican without the public interference and opposition of Bishop Williamson. A growing uneasiness was felt by many, uncomfortable with the new posture of the SSPX vis-a-vis the Vatican. The strong and zealous language of the SSPX from its early days was being mitigated by more measured and tempered statements regarding the Second Vatican Council and the Novus Ordo.

A Deal With Rome

Old Testament: The Greek Seleucids eventually lost their throne. Meanwhile, the Roman Empire expanded, and in 63 BC, the Romans assumed control over Judea and Jerusalem. Ironically, the treaty previously signed by the Maccabees with Rome now worked against them. Over time, Rome tightened its grip on the Jewish population in Judea. Although the Romans removed the descendants of the Maccabees from the Judean throne, they allowed them to continue serving as high priests.

Church History: In 2013, Benedict XVI resigned unexpectedly. The rumors of what occurred behind the scenes in the Vatican speculate about all kinds of political intrigue, outside pressures, financial scandals, abuse cover-ups, etc. Benedict XVI was likely forced to resign for some reason, and it is evident from the new administration that a radical change has occurred in the Vatican. Benedict XVI could have spoken up at any point before his death, but he remained silent. Only the most determined optimism will fail to see the nefarious elements likely at play behind the scenes in the Vatican. Perhaps this "regime change" symbolizes the Romans occupation of Jerusalem after having dethroned the Greeks.

Conclusion

The history of Israel in the Old Testament is a prefigurement for the history of the Catholic Church. In addition to the surface-level similarities, stories with deeper meanings in the Old Testament have transcendent, yet similar meanings in Church history. This is reflective of the "supernatural" nature of the Catholic Church in comparison with the carnal and physical nature of Old Testament. As an example, manna was food for the body but the Holy Eucharist is supernatural food.

I once heard a proverb that said "If someone can't see the sky, then don't bother trying to show it to him". Therefore, after reading this book, if you haven't come to the conclusion that the history of the Catholic Church is prefigured in chronological order by the Old Testament, then I would respectfully and kindly wish you a good day. However, if you have read this book and do conclude that the history of the Catholic is prefigured by the Old Testament, then there are many implications. St. Jerome said "Ignorance of Scripture is ignorance of Christ." If the Church is the Mystical Body of Christ, and if the Church's history is prefigured by the Scriptures, then can it likewise be said "Ignorance of the Church's history is ignorance of Christ"?

God is directly responsible for these chronological parallels, because to suggest otherwise would fly in the face of statistical probability. Even more, to think that God is not responsible for these parallels denies His omnipotence. If these chronological parallels are objectively present, then God has either directly caused them or has permitted them. I have deliberated over both possibilities and am afraid to publicly declare one over the other.

Although these parallels are clearly present, I do not assert that I have seen or understood them correctly. Of course I am completely susceptible to error and bias. I further acknowledge that there are large portions of Church history and the Old Testament that have not been included in this book. There is still so much work to do.

Afterword

Throughout the years, I have presented these parallels to many friends and acquaintances. Sometimes it was an abridged version, sometimes it was a long presentation. Very often at the end of either, the question was asked, "What happens next?"

I admit I have wondered this same thing myself. I have reasoned that since the Old Testament books of the Machabees end around 134 BC, then there is still more to this story that is not recorded in the Old Testament. Secular history fills in the gap between the end of the books of the Machabees and the beginning of the New Testament.

I have identified prominent people and events in the Roman Empire leading up to the birth of Christ and have noticed uncanny parallels with prominent people and events from recent history in the western world, particularly the United States. I plan to write about these parallels in an upcoming book. Currently throughout the world, governments and news outlets are decrying the "death of democracy", indicating the emergence of a new, non-representative form of government. Likewise, the Roman Republic transitioned from being a representative form of government (a republic) into the Roman Empire, ruled by one emperor. The very first emperor was Augustus Caesar, whose reign coincided with the birth of Christ.

Perhaps some of these parallels have piqued your interest more than others? Undoubtedly, most readers will be interested in the parallels between the Novus Ordo and the abomination of desolation. Likewise, the parallels between the Machabees and the SSPX might be intriguing. In this book, I have omitted many details concerning the Old Testament period of the Machabees and their foreshadowings. This book is an introduction and as such, I was uncertain how many details to include and which controversial topics to touch upon.

I intend to write more books, going deeper into some of these unmentioned parallels and also their tie-ins with Biblical prophecy. Of particular note is the abomination of desolation, a subject of immense significance for the end times. Traditional Catholics have fled from many abominations in holy places, leaving their Novus Ordo parishes in response to sacrilege and blasphemy. In that context alone, it is difficult to say with certainty that this blasphemy or that sacrilege was THE abomination of desolation.

However, if the entire history of the Catholic Church is prefigured by the entire history of Israel in the Old Testament, and if the abomination of desolation in the books of the Machabees is part of this seamless prefigurement, then we now have a foundation from which to build a hypothesis as to what exactly constitutes THE abomination of desolation. As it was demonstrated in this book, it is the Novus Ordo rite of Paul VI.

Having an objective identification of the abomination of desolation gives us a concrete starting place to interpret certain Biblical prophecies. The *Seventy Weeks* prophecy from the book of Daniel, chapter 9, is such an example in which the abomination of desolation is specifically mentioned. In a forthcoming book, I will give my analysis of this prophecy and other prophecies from the book of Daniel with this system of parallels as a foundation and starting point. There is so much more to write about.

I believe that all of ancient history serves as a prefigurement for the entire history of the world after the birth of Christ. Christ is the center of all history. If this is true then the very last sentence from the Gospel of St. John seems particularity relevant.

> "But there are also many other things which Jesus did; which, if they were written every one, the world itself, I think, would not be able to contain the books that should be written."
>
> - John 21: 25

Traditional Catholics will no doubt be looking for themselves in these parallels. In my contemplation and prayer, I have sought the parallels for various Traditional Catholic groups as well. I think I see many of them. During the reign of Antiochus IV, two distinct reactions emerged among devout Jews: fight or flight. The Machabees opted for resistance, engaging in a fierce struggle against the Greeks. However, over time, they found themselves making compromises with their oppressors and integrating with them. The first and second centuries before Christ were marked by significant interactions among the Greeks, Romans, and the Hasmoneans (descendants of the Maccabees). During this time, the Pharisees, Zealots, Sadducees, and Essenes all emerged as core Jewish groups, shaping the context of the Jewish world, leading up to the birth of Christ.

In contrast, another group led by a descendant of the last legitimate high priest, Onias, chose a different path. They fled to Egypt and established a Temple near present-day Cairo, which became known as the *Land of Onias*. In this sanctuary, they remained unaffected from the complexities of Greek and Roman interference in Jerusalem.

This is just the beginning of the piece of yarn dangling out from the ball. Let's begin pulling the thread and watch the whole thing unravel. Perhaps instead I should say, let's watch it be unveiled.

Future Books

- **Biblical Prophecy** – Using these parallels as a foundation, prophecies in the book of Daniel that were fulfilled in the Old Testament can be shown to have counterpart fulfillments in Church history.

- **Rome and America** – The history of the Roman Republic and the history of the American Republic parallel each other in chronological order, even up to our present day.

- **Church History and Gospel Parallels** – Not only do Old Testament and Church history parallel each other in chronological order, but the Gospels share in this phenomenon as well.

Bibliography

1: St. Louis De Montfort, Translated by Francoise De Castro Ph.D, T.O.P., *True Devotion to Mary*, Pg. 8 , 1956 , Montfort Publications

2: Barnes, T. D. Constantine, *Dynasty, Religion and Power in the Later Roman Empire*, See chapter 2, "Constantine's Career to 312", pp. 23-24 , 2011 , Chichester, West Sussex: Wiley-Blackwell , 978-1-4051-1727-2

3: Lenski, Noel, *The Cambridge Companion to the Age of Constantine. 2nd ed.*, See chapter 5, "The Reign of Maxentius", pp. 90-91 , 2012 , Cambridge: Cambridge University Press, , ISBN: 978-1-107-00271-8

4: Pope Pius IX, *Quartus Supra*, Par. 16 , Jan. 6, 1873 , Libreria Editrice Vaticana

5: Empires Besieged, *The Roman Decline*, p. 38 , 1988 , Time-Life Books Inc , ISBN 070540974

6: Wasson, Donald L, *Sack of Rome 410*, https://www.worldhistory.org/article/1449/sack-of-rome-410-ce/ , September 23, 2019 , World History Encyclopedia

7: Halsall, Guy, *Barbarian Migrations and the Roman West, 376–568*, p. 216 , 2007 , Cambridge University Press , ISBN 978-0-52143-543-7

8: Britannica, The Editors of Encyclopaedia, *Salic Law*, https://www.britannica.com/topic/Salic-Law , 11 Apr. 2018 , Encyclopedia Britannica

9: John Meyendorff, *Eastern Orthodoxy*, https://www.britannica.com/topic/Eastern-Orthodoxy , March 17, 2014 , Encyclopedia Britannica

10: Bunting, Tony, *Battle of Manzikert*, https://www.britannica.com/event/Battle-of-Manzikert , 24 Mar. 2017 , Encyclopedia Britannica

11: Norwich, John Julius, *A Short History of Byzantium*, p. 90 , 1997 , Vintage Books , ISBN 978-0-679-77269-9

12: Fortescue, A, The Catholic Encyclopedia., *Henoticon*, , 1910 , Robert Appleton Company , http://www.newadvent.org/cathen/07218b.htm

13: A. A. Vasiliev, *History of the Byzantine Empire, 324-1453. Vol. 1*, p. 255 , 1964 , University of Wisconsin Press

14: Schoenfeld, Edward J, *Battle of Poitiers". In Cowley, Robert; Parker, Geoffrey (eds.). The Reader's Companion to Military History.*, p. 366 , 2001 , Houghton Mifflin , ISBN 978-0-618-12742-9

15: Davis, Paul K., *100 Decisive Battles From Ancient Times to the Present*, pg. 104 , 1999 , ABC-CLIO , ISBN 978-1-57607-075-8

16: Einhard, Translated by S.E. Turner, *Einhard: The Life of Charlemagne*, Part 1: The Merovingian Family , 1880 , Harper & Brothers

17: Gibbon, Edward, *The Decline And Fall Of The Roman Empire*, Ch. 52 , 1776 , Strahan & Cadell, London

18: Bradbury, Jim, *The Medieval Siege*, p. 55 , 1992 , Boydell & Brewer , ISBN 978-0-85115-357-5

19: Toth W, *The Christianization of the Magyars*, Church History,1942, Vol. 11, No. 1, pp. 33-54 , July 28, 2009 , Cambridge University Press , doi:10.2307/3160418

20: Jean Richard, , 149 , 1979 , North-Holland Pub. Co. , ISBN 0444850929

21: William of Tyre, , Book 18, Chapter 3 , 12th Century

22: Torre, Ignacio de la, *The Monetary Fluctuations in Philip IV's Kingdom of France and Their Relevance to the Arrest of the Templars*, 2010 , Routledge , 9781315615349

23: Britannica, The Editors of Encyclopaedia, *Clement V*, https://www.britannica.com/biography/Clement-V , 16 Apr. 2023 , Encyclopedia Britannica

24: Burgtorf, J., Crawford, P. F., & Nicholson, H. J. (Eds.), *The Debate on the Trial of the Templars (1307–1314)*, p. 21 , 2013 , Routledge , ISBN 978-1-4094-0779-9

25: Jones, D., *The Templars: The Rise and Spectacular Fall of God's Holy Warriors*, p. 301 , 2017 , Viking , ISBN 978-0-7352-1967-0

26: Demurger, A, *The Last Templar: The Tragedy of Jacques de Molay*, p. 275 , 2009 , Profile Books , ISBN 978-1-84668-224-7

27: Allmand CT, *The Hundred Years War: England and France at War c.1300–c.1450*, p. 11-12 , 1988 , Cambridge University Press , ISBN: 978-0-521-31923-2

28: Britannica, T. Editors of Encyclopaedia, *Benedict XII. Encyclopedia Britannica.*, , 2024, January 30 , https://www.britannica.com/biography/Benedict-XII

29: Britannica, The Editors of Encyclopaedia, *Salic Law of Succession*, https://www.britannica.com/topic/Salic-Law-of-Succession , 6 Apr. 2016 , Encyclopedia Britannica

30: Allmand, Christopher, *The Hundred Years War: England and France at War c. 1300 – c. 1450.*, p. 70 , 1988 , Cambridge University Press. , ISBN 0-5212-6499-5

31: Wilde, Robert, *Effects of the Hundred Years War*, thoughtco.com/aftermath-of-the-hundred-years-war-1221904 , Apr. 5, 2023 , ThoughtCo

32: Michelet, Jules, *History of France, Vol. II*, p. 162-163 , 1882 , D. Appleton and Co.

33: Britannica, The Editors of Encyclopaedia, *Clement (VII)*, https://www.britannica.com/biography/Clement-VII-antipope , 1 Jan. 2024 , Encyclopedia Britannica

34: Christian Classics Ethereal Library, *HUSS, JOHN, HUSSITES*, paragraph 2 , 1953 , Calvin College , https://ccel.org/ccel/schaff/encyc05/htm/iii.xv.xvi.htm#iii.xv.xvi.i.ii

35: Christian History Institute, *Five Bulls of Pope Gregory XI Against Wycliffe, Christian History Issue #3*, https://christianhistoryinstitute.org/magazine/article/archives-five-bulls-of-pope-gregory-xi-against-wycliffe , 1983 , Christian History Institute

36: Christian Classics Etherael Library, *Huss, John, Hussites*, p. 3 , 2006 (last modified) , Calvin College , https://ccel.org/ccel/schaff/encyc05/htm/iii.xv.xvi.htm#iii.xv.xvi.i.ii

37: Schaff, Philip, *Huss, John, Hussites*, pp. 415–420. , 1953 , The New Schaff-Herzog Encyclopedia of Religious Knowledge

38: New World Encyclopedia, *Jan Hus*, Retrieved 01:42, February 9, 2024 , 2018, March 20 , New World Encyclopedia , https://www.newworldencyclopedia.org/p/index.php?title=Jan_Hus&oldid=1009917

39: Cartwright, M, *1453: The Fall of Constantinople*, , 2018, January 23 , World History Encyclopedia , https://www.worldhistory.org/article/1180/1453-the-fall-of-constantinople/

40: Gregorovius, *History of the City of Rome in the Middle Ages*, pp. 205-209 , , Volume 7, Part 1 ,

41: Feridun M. Emecen, *THE FINAL SIEGE AND FALL OF CONSTANTINOPLE (1453)*, History of Instanbul , https://istanbultarihi.ist/424-the-final-siege-and-fall-of-constantinople-1453

42: Nicolo Barbaro, *Diary of the Siege of Constantinople 1453*, , trans. John Melville-Jones (New York, 1969)

43: Gregersen, Erik, *9 Celestial Omens*, https://www.britannica.com/story/9-celestial-omens , 23 Jun. 2023 , Encyclopedia Britannica

44: Britannica, The Editors of Encyclopaedia, *Papal States*, https://www.britannica.com/place/Papal-States , 7 Dec. 2023 , Encyclopedia Britannica

45: Reynolds, L. D.; Wilson, Nigel, *Scribes and Scholars: A Guide to the Transmission of Greek and Latin Literature*, pp. 113 - 123 , 1974 , Clarendon Press , ISBN 978-0199686339

46: Britannica, The Editors of Encyclopaedia, *Treaty of Tordesillas*, https://www.britannica.com/event/Treaty-of-Tordesillas , 24 Nov. 2023 , Encyclopedia Britannica

47: Thurston, H., *Roman Catholic*, , 1912 , The Catholic Encyclopedia, Robert Appleton Company , http://www.newadvent.org/cathen/13121a.htm

48: Council of Trent, *25th Session, Decree 3*, , 1563

49: Löffler, Klemens, *Pope Leo X, The Catholic Encyclopedia. Vol. 9*, , 1910 , Robert Appleton Company , http://www.newadvent.org/cathen/09162a.htm

50: Britannica, The Editors of Encyclopaedia, *Wartburg*, https://www.britannica.com/topic/Wartburg , 10 Dec. 2013 , Encyclopedia Britannica

51: Bunting, Tony, *Sack of Rome*, https://www.britannica.com/event/Sack-of-Rome-1527 , 29 Apr. 2023 , Encyclopedia Britannica

52: Britannica, The Editors of Encyclopaedia, *Schmalkaldic League*, https://www.britannica.com/event/Schmalkaldic-League , 6 May. 2020, , Encyclopedia Britannica

53: Wikipedia, *Five solae*, Par. 1 , https://en.wikipedia.org/wiki/Five_solae

54: Denis Janz, *A Reformation reader: primary texts with introductions*, p. 183 , 2008 , Fortress Press , ISBN 978-0-8006-6310-0

55: Gäbler, Ulrich, *Huldrych Zwingli: His Life and Work*, pp. 148 - 150 , 1986 , Fortress Press , ISBN 0-8006-0761-9

56: Gottheil, Richard; Ryssel, Victor; Jastrow, Marcus; Levias, Caspar, *Captivity, or Exile, Babylonian". Jewish Encyclopedia. Vol. 3.*, 1906 , Funk & Wagnalls Co. ,

57: Paul W, Nancy L. Lapp, *Discoveries in the Wadi El-Daliyeh*, Chapter 3 , 1974 , American School of Oriental Research

58: Robin Gwynn, *England's 'First Refugees'*, 1985 , History Today Volume 35 Issue 5 ,

59: Britannica, The Editors of Encyclopaedia, *House of Guise*, https://www.britannica.com/topic/house-of-Guise , 3 Aug. 2023 , Encyclopedia Britannica ,

60: Women in World History: A Biographical Encyclopedia, *Margaret of Valois (1553–1615)*, https://www.encyclopedia.com /women/encyclopedias-almanacs-transcripts-and-maps/margaret-valois-1553-1615 , February 07, 2024 , Encyclopedia.com

61: Carroll, Stuart , *Martyrs and Murderers: The Guise Family and the Making of Europe*, p. 214 , 2009 , Oxford University Press.

62: Britannica, The Editors of Encyclopaedia, *Massacre of St. Bartholomew's Day*, https://www.britannica.com/event/Massacre-of-Saint-Bartholomews-Day , 18 Jan. 2024 , Encyclopedia Britannica

63: Britannica, The Editors of Encyclopaedia, *Counter-Reformation summary*, https://www.britannica.com/ summary/Counter-Reformation , 19 Aug. 2021 , Encyclopedia Britannica

64: edited by Marion Habig, ofm, *The Franciscan Book of Saints*, Section on St. Francis De Sales , 1959 , Franciscan Herald Press

65: William Doino Jr., *FIVE LESSONS FROM FRANCIS DE SALES*, April 10, 2017 , First Things , https://www.firstthings.com/web-exclusives/2017/04/five-lessons-from-francis-de-sales

66: Pope Pius IX, *Dives in misericordia Deus*, Paragraph 2 , 1877 , apostolic letter to the universal Church , proclaiming St. Francis de Sales a "Doctor of the Church"

67: Britannica, The Editors of Encyclopaedia, *Catherine of Aragon*, https://www.britannica.com/biography/Catherine-of-Aragon , 3 Jan. 2024 , Encyclopedia Britannica

68: Amanda Glover, Claire Ridgway, *Catherine of Aragon – The Case for Non-consummation*, , 2024 , The Tudor Society , https://www.tudorsociety.com/catherine-of-aragon-the-case-for-non-consummation-by-amanda-glover/

69: Şeker, Nesim, *Forced Population Movements in the Ottoman Empire and the Early Turkish Republic: An Attempt at Reassessment through Demographic Engineering*, , 2013 , European Journal of Turkish Studies (16) , doi:10.4000/ejts.4396

70: Britannica, The Editors of Encyclopaedia, *Janissary*, https://www.britannica.com/topic/Janissar , 11 Oct. 202 , Encyclopedia Britannic

71: Giovanni Botero, *The Reason of State*, pp. 223-24 , 1956 , Yale U. P.

72: Britannica, The Editors of Encyclopaedia, *Siege of Vienna*, https://www.britannica.com/event/Siege-of-Vienna-1683 , 19 Jan. 2024 , Encyclopedia Britannica

73: Harbottle, Thomas, *Dictionary of Battles*, p. 262 , 1905 , E.P. Sutton & Co ,

74: Drane, Augusta, *The Knights of st. John: with The battle of Lepanto and Siege of Vienna*, p. 136 , 1858 , Burns and Lambert

75: Tucker, Spencer, *A Global Chronology of Conflict,Vol. Two*, 2010 , Santa Barbara: ABC-CLIO LLC , ISBN 978-1851096671

76: Zubair Simonson, *"We Came, We Saw, God Conquered" — Our Lady's Victory at the Siege of Vienna*, , September 12, 2020 , National Catholic Register , https://www.ncregister.com/blog/we-came-we-saw-god-conquered-our-lady-s-victory-at-the-siege-of-vienna

77: Translated by Vincent Kerns, *The Autobiography of Saint Margaret Mary*, , 1962 , The Newman Press

78: Britannica, The Editors of Encyclopaedia, *Gregorian calendar*, https://www.britannica.com/topic/Gregorian-calendar , 26 Jan. 2024 , Encyclopedia Britannica

79: Steve Weidenkopf, *The Day the Jesuits Were Suppressed*, https://www.catholic.com/magazine/online-edition/this-day-in-church-history-the-suppression-of-the-jesuits-july-21-1773 , 7/21/2019 , Catholic Answers Magazine

80: João Capistrano de Abreu , *João Capistrano de Abreu (1998). Chapters of Brazil's Colonial History 1500–1800*, p. 155 , 1997 , Oxford University Press , ISBN 0-19-510302-5

81: Mark, H. W., *Louis XVI of France*, https://www.worldhistory.org/Louis_XVI_of_France/ , 2022, September 05 , World History Encyclopedia

82: , *The Attack on the Tuileries*, https://worldhistorycommons.org/attack-tuileries-10-august-1792 , 10 August 1792 , World History Commons , [accessed February 8, 2024]

83: 1789, Bibliothèque Nationale de France, *Demolition of the Bastille*, https://worldhistorycommons.org/demolition-bastille , Watercolor Painting and accompanying description of the demolition of the Bastille , World History Commons , [accessed February 10, 2024]

84: retreived 2/10/24, *History of the Abbey of Cluny, The Revolution and the destruction of the abbey.*.https://www.cluny-abbaye.fr/en/discover/history-of-the-abbey-of-cluny , Centre des monuments nationaux

85: Hunt, Lynn, *The Imagery of Radicalism. Politics, Culture, and Class in the French Revolution*, pp. 87–120 , 2019 , ISBN 978-0-5209-3104-6

86: Mark, H. W., *Napoleon Bonaparte*, Retrieved from https://www.worldhistory.org/Napoleon_Bonaparte/ , 2023 , World History Encyclopedia

87: Una McIlvenna, *Why Napoleon Kidnapped One Pope After Another, Pope Pius VI died in captivity, while his successor Pope Pius VII was held hostage for five years.*, https://www.history.com/news/napoleon-catholic-church-kidnap-pope-pius-vii , Aug. 15, 2019, Updated: Aug. 11, 2023 , History.com

88: , *Hanging Gardens of Babylon*, 2018, July 27 , World History Encyclopedia , https://www.worldhistory.org/Hanging_Gardens_of_Babylon/

89: Susan Taylor-Leduc, *oséphine at Malmaison: Acclimatizing Self and Other in the Garden*, https://www.journal18.org/4289. , (Fall 2019 , Journal18 Issue 8 Self/Portrait

90: Marc Madrigal, *The Isthar gate and processsional way*, https://evangelicalfocus.com/archaeological-perspectives/5120/the-isthar-gate-and-processsional-way , 19 Feb. 2020 , evangelicalfocus

91: Murray, Lorraine, *Arc de Triomphe*, https://www.britannica.com/topic/Arc-de-Triomphe , 27 Dec. 2023 , Encyclopedia Britannica

92: Garcia, B, *Ishtar Gate*, https://www.worldhistory.org/Ishtar_Gate/ , 2013, August 23 , World History Encyclopedia

93: , *Arc De Triomphe*, https://www.paris-arc-de-triomphe.fr/en/discover/the-sculpted-groups , , Centre Des Monuments Nationaux

94: Sachs, William L. and Dean, Ralph Stanley, *Anglicanism*, https://www.britannica.com/topic/Anglicanism , 3 Feb. 2024 , Encyclopedia Britannica

95: Knight, Dr Frances; Morgan-Guy, Dr John; Brown, Professor Stewart J., *Religion, Identity and Conflict in Britain: From the Restoration to the Twentieth Century: Essays in Honour of Keith Robbins*, 2013 , Ashgate Publishing, Ltd. , ISBN 978-1-4094-7222-3

96: Pat McNamara, *Newman's Road to Rome*, https://www.catholiceducation.org/en/faith-and-character/faith-and-character/newman-s-road-to-rome.html , , Catholic Education Resource Center

97: *Apparition of the Blessed Virgin on the Mountain of LaSalette on the 19th of September, 1846*, , 1879 , Shepherdess of La Salette with Imprimatur by Mgr. Bishop Zola of Lecce

98: Walsh, Michael, *Butler's Lives of the Saints*, p. 236 , 1991 , HarperCollins Publishers

99: D.D. EMMONS, *The Priestly Heart of St. John Vianney*, Par. 1-5 , , The Priest, Online Blog , https://thepriest.com/2017/08/01/the-priestly-heart-of-st-john-vianney/

100: Britannica, The Editors of Encyclopaedia, *Babylonian Captivity*, https://www.britannica.com/ event/Babylonian-Captivity , 13 Feb. 2024 , Encyclopedia Britannica

101: Pope Pius IX, *Non-Semel, Papal Allocution*, April 29, 1848 , Libreria Editrice Vaticana

102: Holt, Edgar Crawshaw, *Giuseppe Mazzini*, https://www.britannica.com/biography/Giuseppe-Mazzini , 30 Nov. 2023 , Encyclopedia Britannica

103: Laurentin, Rene, translated by John Lynch, *Bernadette Speaks*, p. 548 , 2000 , Pauline Books and Media , ISBN 0-8198-1154-8

104: Joe Tremblay, *The 100 year test* , https://www.catholicnewsagency.com/column/52453/the-100-year-test , 2013 , Catholic News Agency

105: Fr. Domenico Pechenino, V. LXIX, pp 54–60 , 1955 , Ephemerides Liturgicae

106: Timothy Nerozzi, *Restored 1896 Footage May Reveal New Details Of Pope Leo XIII, Earliest-Born Person On Film*, https://religionunplugged.com/news/2021/10/21/restoration-brings-to-life-pope-leo-xiii-in-1896-earliest-born-person-on-film , October 22, 2021 , Religion Unplugged

107: Mendl, Michael, *The Dreams of St. John Bosco*, pp. 321-348 , 2004 , Journal of Salesian Studies. Vol. 12 (2 ed.)

108: Neugebauer, Wolfgang, *Religion in History and the Present. Vol. 6]*, p. 1636 , 2003 , übingen: Mohr Siebeck

109: Meyer A, *Charles Darwin's Reception in Germany and What Followed. PLoS Biol 7(7): e1000162*, 2009 , PLOS Biology , https://doi.org/10.1371/journal.pbio.1000162

110: Brian W. Harrison, *EARLY VATICAN RESPONSES TO EVOLUTIONIST THEOLOGY*, http://www.rtforum.org/lt/lt93.html , 2001 , RTFORUM.org , No. 93

111: The Editors of Encyclopaedia, *Kulturkampf*, https://www.britannica.com/event/Kulturkampf , 25 Feb. 2013 , Encyclopedia Britannica ,

112: Freudenthal, H. W. L, *Kulturkampf*, https://www.encyclopedia.com> , 7 Feb. 2024 , New Catholic Encyclopedia. Encyclopedia.com

113: Kertzer, David I., *Prisoner of the Vatican: The Popes, the Kings, and Garibaldi's Rebels in the Struggle to Rule Modern Italy*, pp. 57-58 , 2006 , Houghton Mifflin Harcourt , ISBN 0618619194.

114: First Vatican Council, *Dei Filius*, https://www.vatican.va/archive/hist_councils/i-vatican-council/documents/vat-i_const_18700424_dei-filius_it.html , 1870 , Libreria Editrice Vaticana , Section 4 "Faith and Reason"

115: Kennedy, Emmet, *A Cultural History of the French Revolution*, p. 343 , 1989 , Yale University Press , SBN 978-0-300-04426-3

116: First Vatican Council, *Pastor Aeturnus*, https://www.vatican.va/archive/hist_councils/i-vatican-council/documents/vat-i_const_18700718_pastor-aeternus_it.html , 1870 , Libreria Editrice Vaticana , Section 4

117: Schmidlin, Josef; de Waal, Anton, *Life of His Holiness Pope Pius X*, pp. 186 , 1904 , Benziger Brothers

118: Brian Kelly, *L'Osservatore Romano Releases Stunning Unpublished Note on 1903 Conclave,* , 6 - 11- 2014 , Catholicism.org , https://catholicism.org/losservatore-romano-releases-stunning-unpublished-note-on-1903-conclave.html

119: Fr. Hieronymo Dal-Gal, Translated by Thomas F. Murray M.A., *The New Italian Life of Pope Pius X*, Pg. 186 , 1953 , M. H. Gill and Son, LTD

120: Pope St. Pius X, *The Oath Against Modernism*, https://www.papalencyclicals.net/pius10/p10moath.htm , 1910-09-01 , Papal Encyclicals ,

121: Britannica, The Editors of Encyclopaedia, *St. Pius X*, https://www.britannica.com/biography/Saint-Pius-X , 30 Jan. 2024 , Encyclopedia Britannica

122: 7 Feb 2024, *Sodalitium Pianum*, New Catholic Encyclopedia , https://www.encyclopedia.com

123: Britannica, The Editors of Encyclopaedia, *Lateran Treaty*, https://www.britannica.com/event/Lateran-Treaty , 7 Oct. 2014 , Encyclopedia Britannica ,

124: , *Lateran Pacts Lateran Treaty*, 1929 , Internet Archive / Public Domain , https://archive.org/details/TheLateranTreaty11thFebruary1929/page/n5/mode/2up?q=Financial+Convention

125: Josephus, *Antiquities of the Jews*, https://ccel.org/j/josephus/works/ant-11.htm , Christian Classics Ethereal Library , Antiquities of the Jews Book XI, chpt. 4, par. 6

126: Ingrid Hjelm, *The Samaritans and Early Judaism: A Literary Analysis*, p. 77 , 2000 , Sheffield Academic Press , ISBN 1-84127-072-5

127: , *The New American Church Monthly, Volume 20, Issue 3*, p. 252 , 1926 , Temple Publishing Corporation

128: Pope Pius XI, *Mortalium Animos*, Jan. 6, 1928 , Libreria Editrice Vaticana , Paragraph 10

129: Simona Cannalire, *GENERAL TOPICSA Brief History of Italian Communism*, https://communistcrimes.org/en/brief-history-italian-communism , 09. October 2020 , communistcrimes.org

130: Effie G. H. Pedaliu, *The 18 April 1948 Italian election: Seventy years on*, , April 18th, 2018 , LSE , https://blogs.lse.ac.uk/europpblog/2018/04/18/the-18-april-1948-italian-election-seventy-years-on/

131: Peter C. Kent, *The Lonely Cold War of Pope Pius XII: The Roman Catholic Church and the Division of Europe, 1943-1950*, 2002 , McGill-Queen's University Press , ISBN 077352326X

132: Peter C. Kent, *The Lonely Cold War of Pope Pius XII: The Roman Catholic Church and the Division of Europe, 1943-1950*, pp. 242–243 , 2002 , McGill-Queen's University Press , ISBN 077352326X

133: Robert A. Ventresca, *From Fascism to Democracy*, 4 , 2004 , University of Toronto Press , ISBN 0-8020-8768-X

134: Britannica, The Editors of Encyclopaedia, *Marshall Pla*, https://www.britannica.com/event/Marshall-Plan , 21 Dec. 2023 , Encyclopedia Britannica

135: Justin McLellan, *Pious protector: After 80 years, a pope is remembered for saving Rome*, https://www.usccb.org/news/2023/pious-protector-after-80-years-pope-remembered-saving-rome , July 14, 2023 , USCCB

136: Antonio Daniel Juan, Rubio Isabel María García Conesa"The Role of Women in the Roaring Twenties ,https://repositorio.upct.es/bitstream/handle/10317/2192/rwr.pdf

Bibliography

137: Pope Pius XI, *Quadragesimo Anno*, May 15, 1931 , Libreria Editrice Vaticana , Par. 50

138: Pope Pius XI, *Quas Primas*, Par. 7 , Dec, 11, 1925 , Libreria Editrice Vaticana

139: Author Interviews :David Kertzer, , Jan. 27, 2014 , NPR , https://www.npr.org/2014/01/27/265794658/pope-and-mussolini-tells-the-secret-history-of-fascism-and-the-church

140: Pope Pius XI, *Casti Connubii*, Dec. 31, 1930 , Libreria Editrice Vaticana , Par. 26-27

141: Peter Eisner, *Pope Pius XI's Last Crusade*, , Apr 15, 2013, Updated Jun 15, 2013 , Huffpost

142: Mark Riebling, *Church of Spies*, 2015 , Basic Books , ISBN 978-0-465-02229-8

143: Feldkamp, Michael F., *Pius XII und Deutschland*, 2000 , Vandenhoeck & Ruprecht , ISBN: 3-525-34026-5

144: John H. Dombrowski, *THE UNNEUTRAL DIPLOMACY OF THE VATICAN DURING 1939 AND 1940, Vol. XIV, No. 4*, 1988 , Faith and Reason, Journal of Christendom College , https://media.christendom.edu/1988/11/the-unneutral-diplomacy-of-the-vatican-during-1939-and-1940/

145: Walsh, Michael, *The Conclave: A Sometimes Secret and Occasionally Bloody History of Papal Elections*, p. 150 , 2003 , Sheed & Ward , ISBN 9781461601814

146: Allert, Tilman (Translated by Jefferson Chase), *The Hitler Salute: On the Meaning of a Gesture*, p 33 , 2009 , Picador , ISBN 9780312428303.

147: Stefan Kuhl, *The Nazi Connection: Eugenics, American Racism, and German National Socialism*, , 1994 , Oxford University Press

148: Hitler, Adolf, *Hitler's Secret Book*, pp. 17–18 , 1961 , Grove Press , ISBN 978-0-394-62003-9

149: Britannica, The Editors of Encyclopaedia, *Enabling Act*, https://www.britannica.com/topic/Enabling-Act , 19 Dec. 2018 , Encyclopedia Britannica

150: Thomas J. Craughwell, *The Gentile Holocaust (Excerpt from Sursum Corda!)*, (Excerpt pages 28-30, 47-49) , 1998 , Catholic Culture , https://www.catholicculture.org/culture/library/view.cfm?recnum=472

151: Martin Gilbert, *Second World War*, pp. 58-59 , 1989 , Butler & Tanner Ltd

152: Pope Pius XII, *Lettera di Sua Santità Pio XIIal Presidente degli Stati Uniti, Franklin Delano Roosevelt, in seguito al bombardamento su Roma*, July, 1943 , Libreria Editrice Vaticana

153: Kurzman, D., *A Special Mission: Hitler's Secret Plot to Seize the Vatican and Kidnap Pope Pius XII*, p. 10 - 12 , 2007 , Da Capo Press , ISBN-10 : 0306816172ISBN-13 : 978-0306816178

154: Crowdy, Terry, *French Resistance Fighter: France's Secret Army*, p. 49 , 2007 , Osprey Publishing , ISBN 978-1-84603-076-5

155: Parfitt, Tom, *Russia's Victory Day Parade marks new East-West divide*, https://www.telegraph.co.uk/news/worldnews/europe/russia/11594959/Russias-Victory-Day-Parade-marks-new-East-West-divide.html , 9 May 2015 , The Daily Telegraph

156: Earl F. Ziemke, *Washington DC, CENTER OF MILITARY HISTORY, CHAPTER XV:The Victory Sealed*, Page 258 last 2 paragraphs , 1990

157: BBC, *Guard 'gave Goering suicide pill'* http://news.bbc.co.uk/1/hi/world/americas/4247069.stm , 8 February, 2005 , BBC ,

158: Bailey, H. W., *Arya, Encyclopædia Iranica. Vol. 2*, https://iranicaonline.org/articles/arya-an-ethnic-epithet , 1987 , Iranica Foundation

159: Kinzl, Konrad H., *A Companion to the Classical Greek World*, p. 553 , 2010 , John Wiley & Sons , ISBN 1444334123.

160: Britannica, The Editors of Encyclopaedia, *League of Corinth*, https://www.britannica.com/topic/League-of-Corinth , 3 Apr. 2020 , Encyclopedia Britannica

161: Britannica, The Editors of Encyclopaedia, *The Germans' summer offensive in southern Russia, 1942*, https://www.britannica.com/place/Papal-States , Encyclopedia Britannica

162: Churchill, W., & Roosevelt, F. D., *Atlantic Charter*, (1941, August 14) , The Avalon Project

163: Roisman, Joseph; Worthington, Ian, *A Companion to Ancient Macedonia*, p. 199 , 2010 , John Wiley & Sons , ISBN 978-1-4051-7936-2

164: Britannica, The Editors of Encyclopaedia, *Potsdam Conference*, https://www.britannica.com/event/Potsdam-Conference , 12 Jan. 2024 , Encyclopedia Britannica

165: Arienne King, *The Economy of Ptolemaic Egypt*, https://www.worldhistory.org/article/1256/the-economy-of-ptolemaic-egypt/ , 2018 , World History Encyclopedia

166: Moya K. Mason, *Alexandria and the Hellenistic World*, www.moyak.com , https://www.moyak.com/papers/ancient-alexandria.html#23

167: Britannica, The Editors of Encyclopaedia, *Seleucid empire*, https://www.britannica.com/place/Seleucid-Empire , 6 Dec. 2023 , Encyclopedia Britannica

168: Smith, Gordon, *Soviet Politics: Continuity and Contradictions*, Chapter 4 , 1994 , St. Martin's Press , ISBN 978-0333535769

169: Britannica, The Editors of Encyclopaedia, *Hellenistic Age Summary*, https://www.britannica.com/summary/Hellenistic-Age , 29 Apr. 2021 , Encyclopedia Britannica

170: Dexter Fergie, *How American Culture Ate the World* , https://newrepublic.com/article/165836/american-culture-ate-world-righteous-smokescreen-globalization-review , March 24, 2022 , newrepublic.com

171: Elliott, C.P, *The Role of Money in the Economies of Ancient Greece and Rome*, https://link.springer.com/referenceworkentry/10.1007/978-981-13-0596-2_46 , 2020 , Springer, Singapore , Battilossi, S., Cassis, Y., Yago, K. (eds) Handbook of the History of Money and Currency.

172: assist.prof saad omar, *Part of the economic policy of the Ptolemaic state Foreign Trade (323-222 BC)*, Article 22, Volume 19, Issue 1, 2023, Pages 516-529 , Mosul University , DOI: 10.33899/berj.2023.178125

173: Josephus, *Flavius Josephus Against ApionBOOK II*, Bottom of Paragraph 4 , 1st Century AD , Emperor Vespasian

174: Jozsef Cardinal Mindszenty, *Memoirs*, 1974 , New York: Macmillan Publishing Co. Inc.

175: Marcelo Dufaur, *Cardinal Mindszenty, a Victim of Communism, Fully Rehabilitated in Hungary*, https://www.tfp.org/cardinal-mindszenty-a-victim-of-communism-fully-rehabilitated-in-hungary/ , April 19, 2012 , TFP

176: Pope Pius XII, *Orientales Omnes Ecclesias*, Dec. 23, 1945 , Libreria Editrice Vaticana , Par. 62

177: Williams, Paul, *The Vatican Exposed: Money, Murder, and the Mafia*, pg. 239 , 2009 , The Tablet

Bibliography

178: Michael Sean Winters, *Remembering Roncalli*, https://www.ncronline.org/blogs/distinctly-catholic/remembering-roncalli , April 24, 2014 , National Catholic Reporter

179: Hebblethwaite, Peter, *John XXIII: Pope of the Council*, 1984 , Chapman , ISBN 0-225-66419-4

180: George Weigel, *The Ostpolitik Failed. Get Over It.*, https://www.firstthings.com/web-exclusives/2016/07/the-ostpolitik-failed-get-over-it , July 20, 2016 , First Things Blog ,

181: Rev. Francis X. Murphy, C.SS.R., *John XXIII Comes To The Vatican*, p. 139 , 1959

182: Paul VI, *Address of Paul VI to the United Nations Organization*, Oct. 4, 1965 , Libreria Editrice Vaticana

183: Rev. Anthony Cekada, *The Ottaviani intervention : short critical study of the new order of Mass*, 2010 , Philothea Press , ISBN 978-0-9826867-2-0

184: Rev. Anthony Cekad, *Did Paul VI "Illegally"Promulgate the New Mass?*, 2000 , (St. Gertrude the Great Newsletter 49, February 2000 https://www.traditionalmass.org/images/articles/P6Illegally.pdf

185: Lefebvre, Marcel, *Open Letter to Confused Catholics*, Chapter 19 , 1986

186: Janusz Wrona, *The Activities of the So-Called Patriot Priests and CatholicsCollaborating with Communists in the Lublin Voivodeship duringthe Stalinist Period (1950–1956)*, 2020 , Maria Curie-Skłodowska University in Lublin , VOL. LXXV

187: Grainger, John D, *The Syrian Wars*, pp. 292–293 , 2010 , Brill , ISBN 9789004180505

188: Britannica, The Information Architects of Encyclopaedia, *John Paul I* https://www.britannica.com/facts/John-Paul-I , 16 Feb. 2024 , Encyclopedia Britannica ,

189: Holly Meyer and Peter Smith, *Church apologies: Top leaders say sorry for historical sins*, https://apnews.com/article/pope-francis-canada-religion-sexual-abuse-by-clergy-11563ae36c003eaf46ed68a928b41317 , July 24, 2022 , AP News

190: Nick Mathiason, *Who killed Calvi?* https://www.theguardian.com/business/2003/dec/07/italy.theobserver , Sat 6 Dec 2003 , The Guardian

191: John Cotter, *Assisi Revisited* , https://www.remnantnewspaper.com/Archives/2011-0315-cotter-assisi.htm , 3/14/11 Reprinted from The Remnant, 2/15/87 , The Remnant Newspaper

192: The Associated Press, *British bishop convicted of Holocaust denial*, https://www.nbcnews.com/id/wbna36595788 , April 16, 2010 , NBC News

Appendix 1

LIST OF PARALLELS

Aaron	Pope Liberius
Abner's Massacre	Massacre of the Latins
Abomination of Desolation	The Novus Ordo Rite
Abraham	St. Joseph
Absalom's Revolt	Papal Schism
Alexander the Great	Franklin D. Roosevelt
Aman	Hitler
Amnon and Thamar	100 Years War / St. Jon of Arc
Amri	John Calvin
Antiochus	John Paul II
Antiochus IV (Worship His Image)	Stalin
Arius	King Eglon
Ark (Built in Wilderness)	Theotokos
Ark is Taken	The True Cross is Taken
Assyrians	Ottoman Turks
Baasa	Huldrych Zwingli
Babylonian Conquest of Jerusalem	French Revolution
Babylonian Conquest of Jerusalem	Spoliation of the Papal States
Babylonians	19th Century Freemasons
Bathsabee	Templar Wealth
Book of Ecclesiastes	1497 Bonfire of the Vanities
Book of Proverbs	Glories of Mary
Canticle of Solomon	St. Teresa of Avila
City of Samaria	Calvin's Geneva
Daniel (Dreams)	St. John Bosco
Daniel (Interprets Writing on the Wall)	Vision of Pope Leo XIII
Daniel (Lion's Den)	Pope St. Pius X and Modernism
David (Defeats Saul's Enemies)	Magyar Defeat at Lechfeld
David (Husband of Michol)	Otto II
David (Kills Murderers of Isboseth)	Pope Innocent III
David (Young Boy)	Charles Martel
Decree of Cyrus	The Lateran Treaty
Diadochi	German 4 Part Partition
Eleazar	József Cardinal Mindszenty
Elias (Jezabel Hunts for Him)	Jesuits in Protestant England
Eliseus	St. Francis de Sales
Esau	St. John the Baptist
Esdras	Pope Pius XII
Ezechiel	St. Jean Vianney
Ezechiel (Dry Bones)	St. Philomena's Miraculous Relics
Ezechiel (Sticks Come Together)	Cardinal John Henry Newman (Branch Theory)
Ezechiel (Temple Vision)	Lourdes Basilica and Spring

Appendix 1

337

Mother and Seven Sons............................Catholic Eastern Rites Behind the Iron Curtain
Murder of Isboseth...1204 Sack of Constantinople
Nabuchodonosor...Napoleon Bonaparte
Nabuchodonosor...King Victor Emmanuel II
Nabuchodonosor (Fiery Furnace).. Kulturkampf
Nabuchodonosor (Golden Idol)..Darwin's Evolution
Nabuchodonosor (Insists Idol Must Be Worshiped)...........................Otto Von Bismarck
Nabuchodonosor (Loses Reason)...The First Vatican Council
Nehemias (Rebuilds the Wall)...The Marshall Plan
Persian King..The Allied Forces
Persian King (Great Feast)..Roaring Twenties
Pharao...Maxentius, Diocletian
Philistines..Early Muslim Threats
Ptolemaic Kingdom/Alexandria...Post World War II West
Queen Esther...Pope Pius XII
Queen Vasthi...Pope Pius XI
Ruth and Booz...Clovis and St. Clothilda
Samaritans Refused..Mortalium Animos
Samson..St. Jerome
Samuel (Anoints David)..Pope Leo III
Samuel (Rejects Saul)..Pope Gregory III
Sarah...Our Lady
Saul (Death of Descendants)...Fall of Constantinople
Saul and Jonathan (Death)...Battle of Manzikert
Seba's Revolt...Jan Hus
Seleucid (Invade Temple)..Second Vatican Council
Seleucid Kingdom..Post Word War II Soviet Union
Solomon's Reign (Beginning)...Pope Nicholas V
Solomon's Reign (Entire)..The Renaissance
Temple..St. Peter's Basilica
Tobias and Sarah..King Henry VIII and Queen Catherine
Urias the Hethite..Knights Templar/Jacques DeMolay

Appendix 2

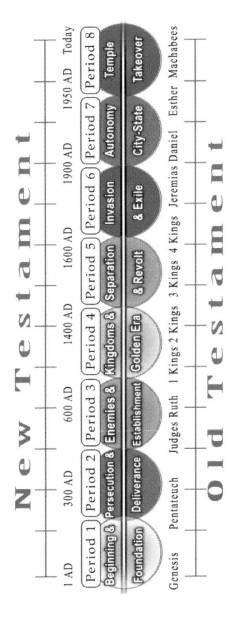

This graphic is not meant to be exact, but rather to show the general timeline of the historical periods. It also shows the Old Testament books and their corresponding dates in Church history. I think it is more meaningful and useful to present the Old Testament parallels in terms of their references in the Old Testament books, rather than using the dates from the Old Testament.

Index

Alphabetical Index

340

Index

Index

Index

Index

Index

Index

Index

Index

Made in the USA
Columbia, SC
22 April 2024

34475647R00209